Buick, Olds & Pontiac Full-size FWD Models Automotive Repair Manual

by Mike Stubblefield and John H Haynes
Member of the Guild of Motoring Writers

Models covered:
Buick, Oldsmobile and Pontiac
Full-size front-wheel drive models (C and H body types)
1985 through 1998
Does not cover diesel engine and related information, supercharger information or rear-wheel drive models

(3A13 – 19020)

(1627)

ABCDE
FGHIJ
K   2

Haynes Publishing Group
Sparkford Nr Yeovil
Somerset BA22 7JJ England

Haynes North America, Inc
861 Lawrence Drive
Newbury Park
California 91320 USA

Acknowledgements

We are grateful for the help and cooperation of General Motors Corporation for assistance with technical information, certain illustrations and vehicle photos. Technical writers who contributed to this project include Jon LaCourse and Ken Freund. Portions of materials contained herein have been reprinted with permission of General Motors Corporation, Service Technology Group.

A book in the **Haynes Automotive Repair Manual Series**

Printed in the U.S.A.

ISBN 1 56392 321 1

Library of Congress Catalog Card Number 98-85019

While every attempt is made to ensure that the information in this manual is correct, no liability can be accepted by the authors or publishers for loss, damage or injury caused by any errors in, or omissions from, the information given.

Contents

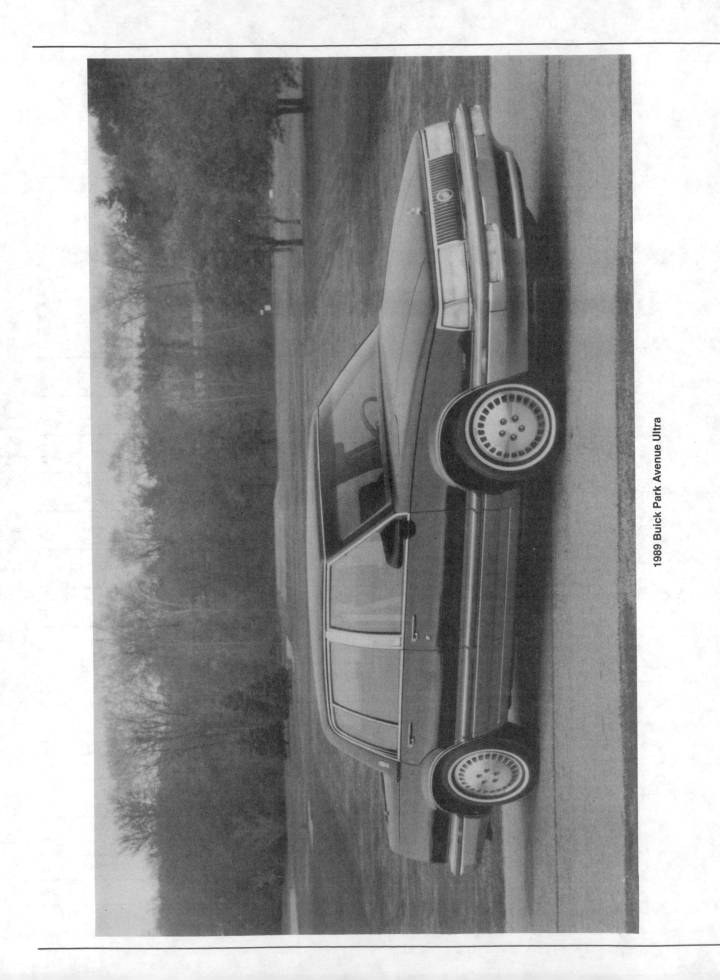

1989 Buick Park Avenue Ultra

1986 Oldsmobile Delta Eighty-eight

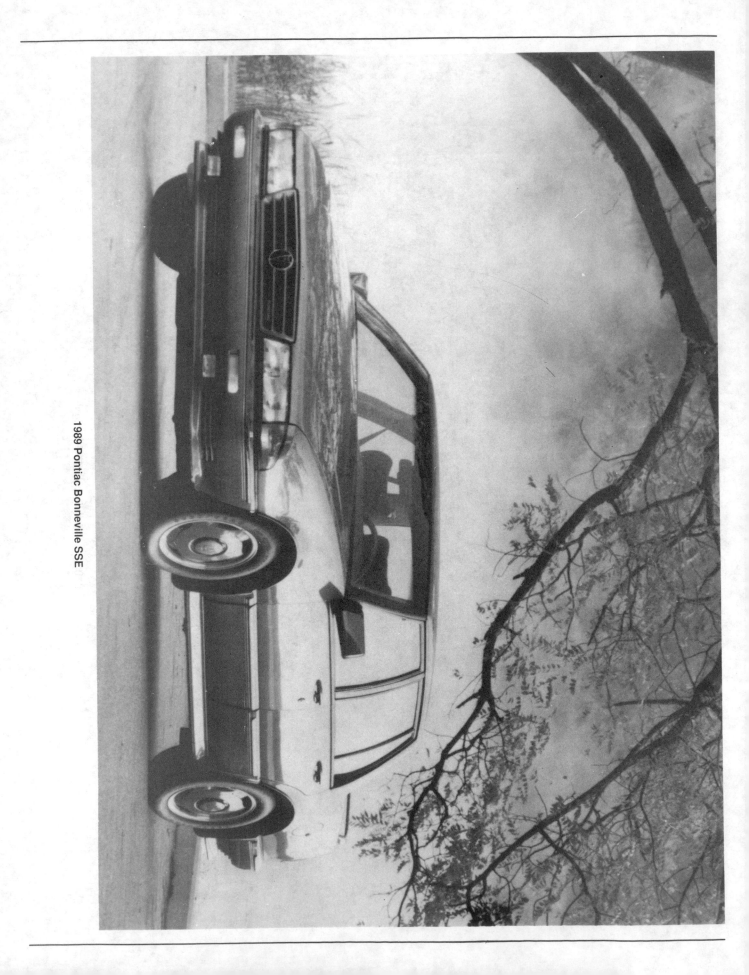

1989 Pontiac Bonneville SSE

About this manual

Its purpose

The purpose of this manual is to help you get the best value from your vehicle. It can do so in several ways. It can help you decide what work must be done, even if you choose to have it done by a dealer service department or a repair shop; it provides information and procedures for routine maintenance and servicing; and it offers diagnostic and repair procedures to follow when trouble occurs.

We hope you use the manual to tackle the work yourself. For many simpler jobs, doing it yourself may be quicker than arranging an appointment to get the vehicle into a shop and making the trips to leave it and pick it up. More importantly, a lot of money can be saved by avoiding the expense the shop must pass on to you to cover its labor and overhead costs. An added benefit is the sense of satisfaction and accomplishment that you feel after doing the job yourself.

Using the manual

The manual is divided into Chapters. Each Chapter is divided into numbered Sections, which are headed in bold type between horizontal lines. Each Section consists of consecutively numbered paragraphs.

At the beginning of each numbered section you will be referred to any illustrations which apply to the procedures in that section. The reference numbers used in illustration captions pinpoint the pertinent Section and the Step within that section. That is, illustration 3.2 means the illustration refers to Section 3 and Step (or paragraph) 2 within that Section.

Procedures, once described in the text, are not normally repeated. When it's necessary to refer to another Chapter, the reference will be given as Chapter and Section number. Cross references given without use of the word "Chapter" apply to Sections and/or paragraphs in the same Chapter. For example, "see Section 8" means in the same Chapter.

References to the left or right side of the vehicle assume you are sitting in the driver's seat, facing forward.

Even though we have prepared this manual with extreme care, neither the publisher nor the author can accept responsibility for any errors in, or omissions from, the information given.

NOTE

A **Note** provides information necessary to properly complete a procedure or information which will make the procedure easier to understand.

CAUTION

A **Caution** provides a special procedure or special steps which must be taken while completing the procedure where the **Caution** is found. Not heeding a **Caution** can result in damage to the assembly being worked on.

WARNING

A **Warning** provides a special procedure or special steps which must be taken while completing the procedure where the **Warning** is found. Not heeding a **Warning** can result in personal injury.

Introduction to the Buick, Oldsmobile and Pontiac full-size, front-wheel drive models

The full-size General Motors models covered by this manual are front engine/front-wheel drive "C" and "H" body vehicles only. Most are four-door sedans, although some two-door models are available.

All models are powered by a transversely-mounted V6 engine which drives the front wheels through an automatic transaxle and independent driveaxles.

Independent suspension, featuring coil springs and struts or shock absorbers, is used at all four wheels. The rack and pinion steering unit is mounted behind the engine.

The brakes are disc at the front and drums at the rear, with power assist standard.

Vehicle identification numbers

Modifications are a continuing and unpublicized part of vehicle manufacturing. Since spare parts manuals and lists are compiled on a numerical basis, the individual vehicle numbers are essential to correctly identify the component required.

Vehicle Identification Number (VIN)

This very important identification number is stamped on a plate attached to the left side of the dashboard and is visible through the driver's side of the windshield **(see illustration)**. The VIN also appears on the Vehicle Certificate of Title and Registration. It contains information such as where and when the vehicle was manufactured, the model year and the body style.

Vehicle Certification Plate

The Vehicle Certification Plate (VC label) is affixed to the rear of the left front door. The plate contains the name of the manufacturer, the month and year of production, the Gross Vehicle Weight Rating (GVWR) and the certification statement.

The Vehicle Identification Number (VIN) is on a plate attached to the left side of the dashboard where it can be seen from outside the vehicle

Body identification plate

The body identification plate is located in the engine compartment on the upper surface of the radiator support. Like the VIN, it contains valuable information concerning the production of the vehicle, as well as information on the options with which it is equipped. This plate is especially useful for matching the color and type of paint for repair work.

Engine identification number

The engine ID number is located on a pad at the drivebelt (right) end of the engine block, adjacent to the water pump or on the front surface of the block at the transaxle (left) end, adjacent to the starter (see illustration).

Service parts identification label

This label is located inside the trunk (see illustration). It lists the VIN number, wheelbase, paint number, options and other information specific to your vehicle. Always refer to this label when ordering parts.

Transaxle identification number

The transaxle identification number is located on the right rear side of the transaxle (see illustration).

Vehicle Emissions Control Information label

The Vehicle Emissions Control Information label is under the hood, often attached to the left shock tower (see Chapter 6 for more information and an illustration of the label).

The engine identification number is in one of two places: at the right end of the block, adjacent to the water pump or at the front side of the block, adjacent to the starter

The service parts identification label is located on the inside of the trunk lid

The transaxle identification number is on the right rear side of the transaxle

Buying parts

Replacement parts are available from many sources, which generally fall into one of two categories – authorized dealer parts departments and independent retail auto parts stores. Our advice concerning these parts is as follows:

Retail auto parts stores: Good auto parts stores will stock frequently needed components which wear out relatively fast, such as clutch components, exhaust systems, brake parts, tune-up parts, etc. These stores often supply new or reconditioned parts on an exchange basis, which can save a considerable amount of money. Discount auto parts stores are often very good places to buy materials and parts needed for general vehicle maintenance such as oil, grease, filters, spark plugs, belts, touch-up paint, bulbs, etc. They also usually sell tools and general accessories, have con-venient hours, charge lower prices and can often be found not far from home.

Authorized dealer parts department: This is the best source for parts which are unique to the vehicle and not generally available elsewhere (such as major engine parts, transmission parts, trim pieces, etc.).

Warranty information: If the vehicle is still covered under warranty, be sure that any replacement parts purchased – regardless of the source – do not invalidate the warranty!

To be sure of obtaining the correct parts, have engine and chassis numbers available and, if possible, take the old parts along for positive identification.

Maintenance techniques, tools and working facilities

Maintenance techniques

There are a number of techniques involved in maintenance and repair that will be referred to throughout this manual. Application of these techniques will enable the home mechanic to be more efficient, better organized and capable of performing the various tasks properly, which will ensure that the repair job is thorough and complete.

Fasteners

Fasteners are nuts, bolts, studs and screws used to hold two or more parts together. There are a few things to keep in mind when working with fasteners. Almost all of them use a locking device of some type, either a lockwasher, locknut, locking tab or thread adhesive. All threaded fasteners should be clean and straight, with undamaged threads and undamaged corners on the hex head where the wrench fits. Develop the habit of replacing all damaged nuts and bolts with new ones. Special locknuts with nylon or fiber inserts can only be used once. If they are removed, they lose their locking ability and must be replaced with new ones.

Rusted nuts and bolts should be treated with a penetrating fluid to ease removal and prevent breakage. Some mechanics use turpentine in a spout-type oil can, which works quite well. After applying the rust penetrant, let it work for a few minutes before trying to loosen the nut or bolt. Badly rusted fasteners may have to be chiseled or sawed off or removed with a special nut breaker, available at tool stores.

If a bolt or stud breaks off in an assembly, it can be drilled and removed with a special tool commonly available for this purpose. Most automotive machine shops can perform this task, as well as other repair procedures, such as the repair of threaded holes that have been stripped out.

Flat washers and lockwashers, when removed from an assembly, should always be replaced exactly as removed. Replace any damaged washers with new ones. Never use a lockwasher on any soft metal surface (such as aluminum), thin sheet metal or plastic.

Fastener sizes

For a number of reasons, automobile manufacturers are making wider and wider use of metric fasteners. Therefore, it is important to be able to tell the difference between standard (sometimes called U.S. or SAE) and metric hardware, since they cannot be interchanged.

All bolts, whether standard or metric, are sized according to diameter, thread pitch and length. For example, a standard 1/2 – 13 x 1 bolt is 1/2 inch in diameter, has 13 threads per inch and is 1 inch long. An M12 – 1.75 x 25 metric bolt is 12 mm in diameter, has a thread pitch of 1.75 mm (the distance between threads) and is 25 mm long. The two bolts are nearly identical, and easily confused, but they are not interchangeable.

In addition to the differences in diameter, thread pitch and length, metric and standard bolts can also be distinguished by examining the bolt heads. To begin with, the distance across the flats on a standard bolt head is measured in inches, while the same dimension on a metric bolt is sized in millimeters (the same is true for nuts). As a result, a standard wrench should not be used on a metric bolt and a metric wrench should not be used on a standard bolt. Also, most standard bolts have slashes radiating out from the center of the head to denote the grade or strength of the bolt, which is an indication of the amount of torque that can be applied to it. The greater the number of slashes, the greater the strength of the bolt. Grades 0 through 5 are commonly used on automobiles. Metric bolts have a property class (grade) number, rather than a slash, molded into their heads to indicate bolt strength. In this case, the higher the number, the stronger the bolt. Property class numbers 8.8, 9.8 and 10.9 are commonly used on automobiles.

Strength markings can also be used to distinguish standard hex nuts from metric hex nuts. Many standard nuts have dots stamped into one side, while metric nuts are marked with a number. The greater the number of dots, or the higher the number, the greater the strength of the nut.

Metric studs are also marked on their ends according to property class (grade). Larger studs are numbered (the same as metric bolts), while smaller studs carry a geometric code to denote grade.

Grade 1 or 2   Grade 5   Grade 8

Bolt strength markings (top – standard/SAE/USS; bottom – metric)

Grade	Identification
Hex Nut Grade 5	3 Dots
Hex Nut Grade 8	6 Dots

Standard hex nut strength markings

Class	Identification
Hex Nut Property Class 9	Arabic 9
Hex Nut Property Class 10	Arabic 10

Metric hex nut strength markings

CLASS 10.9   CLASS 9.8   CLASS 8.8

Metric stud length markings

It should be noted that many fasteners, especially Grades 0 through 2, have no distinguishing marks on them. When such is the case, the only way to determine whether it is standard or metric is to measure the thread pitch or compare it to a known fastener of the same size.

Standard fasteners are often referred to as SAE, as opposed to metric. However, it should be noted that SAE technically refers to a non-metric *fine thread* fastener only. Coarse thread non-metric fasteners are referred to as USS sizes.

Since fasteners of the same size (both standard and metric) may have different strength ratings, be sure to reinstall any bolts, studs or nuts removed from your vehicle in their original locations. Also, when replacing a fastener with a new one, make sure that the new one has a strength rating equal to or greater than the original.

Tightening sequences and procedures

Most threaded fasteners should be tightened to a specific torque value (torque is the twisting force applied to a threaded component such as a nut or bolt). Overtightening the fastener can weaken it and cause it to break, while undertightening can cause it to eventually come loose. Bolts, screws and studs, depending on the material they are made of and their thread diameters, have specific torque values, many of which are noted in the Specifications at the beginning of each Chapter. Be sure to follow the torque recommendations closely. For fasteners not assigned a specific torque, a general torque value chart is presented here as a guide. These torque values are for dry (unlubricated) fasteners threaded into steel or cast iron (not aluminum). As was previously mentioned, the size and grade of a fastener determine the amount of torque that can safely

Metric thread sizes	Ft-lbs	Nm
M-6	6 to 9	9 to 12
M-8	14 to 21	19 to 28
M-10	28 to 40	38 to 54
M-12	50 to 71	68 to 96
M-14	80 to 140	109 to 154

Pipe thread sizes		
1/8	5 to 8	7 to 10
1/4	12 to 18	17 to 24
3/8	22 to 33	30 to 44
1/2	25 to 35	34 to 47

U.S. thread sizes		
1/4 – 20	6 to 9	9 to 12
5/16 – 18	12 to 18	17 to 24
5/16 – 24	14 to 20	19 to 27
3/8 – 16	22 to 32	30 to 43
3/8 – 24	27 to 38	37 to 51
7/16 – 14	40 to 55	55 to 74
7/16 – 20	40 to 60	55 to 81
1/2 – 13	55 to 80	75 to 108

Standard (SAE and USS) bolt dimensions/grade marks

     G   Grade marks (bolt length)
     L   Length (in inches)
     T   Thread pitch (number of threads per inch)
     D   Nominal diameter (in inches)

Metric bolt dimensions/grade marks

     P   Property class (bolt strength)
     L   Length (in millimeters)
     T   Thread pitch (distance between threads in millimeters)
     D   Diameter

be applied to it. The figures listed here are approximate for Grade 2 and Grade 3 fasteners. Higher grades can tolerate higher torque values.

Fasteners laid out in a pattern, such as cylinder head bolts, oil pan bolts, differential cover bolts, etc., must be loosened or tightened in sequence to avoid warping the component. This sequence will normally be shown in the appropriate Chapter. If a specific pattern is not given, the following procedures can be used to prevent warping.

Initially, the bolts or nuts should be assembled finger-tight only. Next, they should be tightened one full turn each, in a criss-cross or diagonal pattern. After each one has been tightened one full turn, return to the first one and tighten them all one-half turn, following the same pattern. Finally, tighten each of them one-quarter turn at a time until each fastener has been tightened to the proper torque. To loosen and remove the fasteners, the procedure would be reversed.

Component disassembly

Component disassembly should be done with care and purpose to help ensure that the parts go back together properly. Always keep track of the sequence in which parts are removed. Make note of special characteristics or marks on parts that can be installed more than one way, such as a grooved thrust washer on a shaft. It is a good idea to lay the disassembled parts out on a clean surface in the order that they were removed. It may also be helpful to make sketches or take instant photos of components before removal.

When removing fasteners from a component, keep track of their locations. Sometimes threading a bolt back in a part, or putting the washers and nut back on a stud, can prevent mix-ups later. If nuts and bolts cannot be returned to their original locations, they should be kept in a compartmented box or a series of small boxes. A cupcake or muffin tin is ideal for this purpose, since each cavity can hold the bolts and nuts from a particular area (i.e. oil pan bolts, valve cover bolts, engine mount bolts, etc.). A pan of this type is especially helpful when working on assemblies with very small parts, such as the carburetor, alternator, valve train or interior dash and trim pieces. The cavities can be marked with paint or tape to identify the contents.

Whenever wiring looms, harnesses or connectors are separated, it is a good idea to identify the two halves with numbered pieces of masking tape so they can be easily reconnected.

Gasket sealing surfaces

Throughout any vehicle, gaskets are used to seal the mating surfaces between two parts and keep lubricants, fluids, vacuum or pressure contained in an assembly.

Many times these gaskets are coated with a liquid or paste-type gasket sealing compound before assembly. Age, heat and pressure can sometimes cause the two parts to stick together so tightly that they are very difficult to separate. Often, the assembly can be loosened by striking it with a soft-face hammer near the mating surfaces. A regular hammer can be used if a block of wood is placed between the hammer and the part. Do not hammer on cast parts or parts that could be easily damaged. With any particularly stubborn part, always recheck to make sure that every fastener has been removed.

Avoid using a screwdriver or bar to pry apart an assembly, as they can easily mar the gasket sealing surfaces of the parts, which must remain smooth. If prying is absolutely necessary, use an old broom handle, but keep in mind that extra clean up will be necessary if the wood splinters.

After the parts are separated, the old gasket must be carefully scraped off and the gasket surfaces cleaned. Stubborn gasket material can be soaked with rust penetrant or treated with a special chemical to soften it so it can be easily scraped off. A scraper can be fashioned from a piece of copper tubing by flattening and sharpening one end. Copper is recommended because it is usually softer than the surfaces to be scraped, which reduces the chance of gouging the part. Some gaskets can be removed with a wire brush, but regardless of the method used, the mating surfaces must be left clean and smooth. If for some reason the gasket surface is gouged, then a gasket sealer thick enough to fill scratches will have to be used during reassembly of the components. For most applications, a non-drying (or semi-drying) gasket sealer should be used.

Hose removal tips

Warning: *If the vehicle is equipped with air conditioning, do not disconnect any of the A/C hoses without first having the system depressurized by a dealer service department or a service station.*

Hose removal precautions closely parallel gasket removal precautions. Avoid scratching or gouging the surface that the hose mates against or the connection may leak. This is especially true for radiator hoses. Because of various chemical reactions, the rubber in hoses can bond itself to the metal spigot that the hose fits over. To remove a hose, first loosen the hose clamps that secure it to the spigot. Then, with slip-joint pliers, grab the hose at the clamp and rotate it around the spigot. Work it back and forth until it is completely free, then pull it off. Silicone or other lubricants will ease removal if they can be applied between the hose and the outside of the spigot. Apply the same lubricant to the inside of the hose and the outside of the spigot to simplify installation.

As a last resort (and if the hose is to be replaced with a new one anyway), the rubber can be slit with a knife and the hose peeled from the spigot. If this must be done, be careful that the metal connection is not damaged.

If a hose clamp is broken or damaged, do not reuse it. Wire-type clamps usually weaken with age, so it is a good idea to replace them with screw-type clamps whenever a hose is removed.

Tools

A selection of good tools is a basic requirement for anyone who plans to maintain and repair his or her own vehicle. For the owner who has few tools, the initial investment might seem high, but when compared to the spiraling costs of professional auto maintenance and repair, it is a wise one.

Micrometer set

Dial indicator set

Dial caliper

Hand-operated vacuum pump

Timing light

Compression gauge with spark plug
hole adapter

Damper/steering wheel puller

General purpose puller

Hydraulic lifter removal tool

Valve spring compressor

Valve spring compressor

Ridge reamer

Piston ring groove cleaning tool

Ring removal/installation tool

Ring compressor

Cylinder hone

Brake hold-down spring tool

Brake cylinder hone

Clutch plate alignment tool

Tap and die set

To help the owner decide which tools are needed to perform the tasks detailed in this manual, the following tool lists are offered: *Maintenance and minor repair, Repair/overhaul* and *Special.*

The newcomer to practical mechanics should start off with the maintenance and minor repair tool kit, which is adequate for the simpler jobs performed on a vehicle. Then, as confidence and experience grow, the owner can tackle more difficult tasks, buying additional tools as they are needed. Eventually the basic kit will be expanded into the repair and overhaul tool set. Over a period of time, the experienced do-it-yourselfer will assemble a tool set complete enough for most repair and overhaul procedures and will add tools from the special category when it is felt that the expense is justified by the frequency of use.

Maintenance and minor repair tool kit

The tools in this list should be considered the minimum required for performance of routine maintenance, servicing and minor repair work. We recommend the purchase of combination wrenches (box-end and open-end combined in one wrench). While more expensive than open end wrenches, they offer the advantages of both types of wrench.

Combination wrench set (1/4-inch to 1 inch or 6 mm to 19 mm)
Adjustable wrench, 8 inch
Spark plug wrench with rubber insert
Spark plug gap adjusting tool
Feeler gauge set
Brake bleeder wrench
Standard screwdriver (5/16-inch x 6 inch)
Phillips screwdriver (No. 2 x 6 inch)
Combination pliers – 6 inch
Hacksaw and assortment of blades
Tire pressure gauge
Grease gun
Oil can
Fine emery cloth
Wire brush

Battery post and cable cleaning tool
Oil filter wrench
Funnel (medium size)
Safety goggles
Jackstands(2)
Drain pan

Note: *If basic tune-ups are going to be part of routine maintenance, it will be necessary to purchase a good quality stroboscopic timing light and combination tachometer/dwell meter. Although they are included in the list of special tools, it is mentioned here because they are absolutely necessary for tuning most vehicles properly.*

Repair and overhaul tool set

These tools are essential for anyone who plans to perform major repairs and are in addition to those in the maintenance and minor repair tool kit. Included is a comprehensive set of sockets which, though expensive, are invaluable because of their versatility, especially when various extensions and drives are available. We recommend the 1/2-inch drive over the 3/8-inch drive. Although the larger drive is bulky and more expensive, it has the capacity of accepting a very wide range of large sockets. Ideally, however, the mechanic should have a 3/8-inch drive set and a 1/2-inch drive set.

Socket set(s)
Reversible ratchet
Extension – 10 inch
Universal joint
Torque wrench (same size drive as sockets)
Ball peen hammer – 8 ounce
Soft-face hammer (plastic/rubber)
Standard screwdriver (1/4-inch x 6 inch)
Standard screwdriver (stubby – 5/16-inch)
Phillips screwdriver (No. 3 x 8 inch)
Phillips screwdriver (stubby – No. 2)

Pliers – vise grip
Pliers – lineman's
Pliers – needle nose
Pliers – snap-ring (internal and external)
Cold chisel – 1/2-inch
Scribe
Scraper (made from flattened copper tubing)
Centerpunch
Pin punches (1/16, 1/8, 3/16-inch)
Steel rule/straightedge – 12 inch
Allen wrench set (1/8 to 3/8-inch or 4 mm to 10 mm)
A selection of files
Wire brush (large)
Jackstands (second set)
Jack (scissor or hydraulic type)

Note: *Another tool which is often useful is an electric drill with a chuck capacity of 3/8-inch and a set of good quality drill bits.*

Special tools

The tools in this list include those which are not used regularly, are expensive to buy, or which need to be used in accordance with their manufacturer's instructions. Unless these tools will be used frequently, it is not very economical to purchase many of them. A consideration would be to split the cost and use between yourself and a friend or friends. In addition, most of these tools can be obtained from a tool rental shop on a temporary basis.

This list primarily contains only those tools and instruments widely available to the public, and not those special tools produced by the vehicle manufacturer for distribution to dealer service departments. Occasionally, references to the manufacturer's special tools are included in the text of this manual. Generally, an alternative method of doing the job without the special tool is offered. However, sometimes there is no alternative to their use. Where this is the case, and the tool cannot be purchased or borrowed, the work should be turned over to the dealer service department or an automotive repair shop.

Valve spring compressor
Piston ring groove cleaning tool
Piston ring compressor
Piston ring installation tool
Cylinder compression gauge
Cylinder ridge reamer
Cylinder surfacing hone
Cylinder bore gauge
Micrometers and/or dial calipers
Hydraulic lifter removal tool
Balljoint separator
Universal-type puller
Impact screwdriver
Dial indicator set
Stroboscopic timing light (inductive pick-up)
Hand operated vacuum/pressure pump
Tachometer/dwell meter
Universal electrical multimeter
Cable hoist
Brake spring removal and installation tools
Floor jack

Buying tools

For the do-it-yourselfer who is just starting to get involved in vehicle maintenance and repair, there are a number of options available when purchasing tools. If maintenance and minor repair is the extent of the work to be done, the purchase of individual tools is satisfactory. If, on the other hand, extensive work is planned, it would be a good idea to purchase a modest tool set from one of the large retail chain stores. A set can usually be bought at a substantial savings over the individual tool prices, and they often come with a tool box. As additional tools are needed, add–on sets, individual tools and a larger tool box can be purchased to expand the tool selection. Building a tool set gradually allows the cost of the tools to be spread over a longer period of time and gives the mechanic the freedom to choose only those tools that will actually be used.

Tool stores will often be the only source of some of the special tools that are needed, but regardless of where tools are bought, try to avoid cheap ones, especially when buying screwdrivers and sockets, because they won't last very long. The expense involved in replacing cheap tools will eventually be greater than the initial cost of quality tools.

Care and maintenance of tools

Good tools are expensive, so it makes sense to treat them with respect. Keep them clean and in usable condition and store them properly when not in use. Always wipe off any dirt, grease or metal chips before putting them away. Never leave tools lying around in the work area. Upon completion of a job, always check closely under the hood for tools that may have been left there so they won't get lost during a test drive.

Some tools, such as screwdrivers, pliers, wrenches and sockets, can be hung on a panel mounted on the garage or workshop wall, while others should be kept in a tool box or tray. Measuring instruments, gauges, meters, etc. must be carefully stored where they cannot be damaged by weather or impact from other tools.

When tools are used with care and stored properly, they will last a very long time. Even with the best of care, though, tools will wear out if used frequently. When a tool is damaged or worn out, replace it. Subsequent jobs will be safer and more enjoyable if you do.

Working facilities

Not to be overlooked when discussing tools is the workshop. If anything more than routine maintenance is to be carried out, some sort of suitable work area is essential.

It is understood, and appreciated, that many home mechanics do not have a good workshop or garage available, and end up removing an engine or doing major repairs outside. It is recommended, however, that the overhaul or repair be completed under the cover of a roof.

A clean, flat workbench or table of comfortable working height is an absolute necessity. The workbench should be equipped with a vise that has a jaw opening of at least four inches.

As mentioned previously, some clean, dry storage space is also required for tools, as well as the lubricants, fluids, cleaning solvents, etc. which soon become necessary.

Sometimes waste oil and fluids, drained from the engine or cooling system during normal maintenance or repairs, present a disposal problem. To avoid pouring them on the ground or into a sewage system, pour the used fluids into large containers, seal them with caps and take them to an authorized disposal site or recycling center. Plastic jugs, such as old antifreeze containers, are ideal for this purpose.

Always keep a supply of old newspapers and clean rags available. Old towels are excellent for mopping up spills. Many mechanics use rolls of paper towels for most work because they are readily available and disposable. To help keep the area under the vehicle clean, a large cardboard box can be cut open and flattened to protect the garage or shop floor.

Whenever working over a painted surface, such as when leaning over a fender to service something under the hood, always cover it with an old blanket or bedspread to protect the finish. Vinyl covered pads, made especially for this purpose, are available at auto parts stores.

Booster battery (jump) starting

Observe these precautions when using a booster battery to start a vehicle:

a) Before connecting the booster battery, make sure the ignition switch is in the Off position.
b) Turn off the lights, heater and other electrical loads.
c) Your eyes should be shielded. Safety goggles are a good idea.
d) Make sure the booster battery is the same voltage as the dead one in the vehicle.
e) The two vehicles MUST NOT TOUCH each other!
f) Make sure the transmission is in Neutral (manual) or Park (automatic).
g) If the booster battery is not a maintenance-free type, remove the vent caps and lay a cloth over the vent holes.

Connect the red jumper cable to the positive (+) terminals of each battery.

Connect one end of the black jumper cable to the negative (−) terminal of the booster battery. The other end of this cable should be connected to a good ground on the vehicle to be started, such as a bolt or bracket on the engine block **(see illustrations)**. Make sure the cable will not come into contact with the fan, drivebelts or other moving parts of the engine.

Start the engine using the booster battery, then, with the engine running at idle speed, disconnect the jumper cables in the reverse order of connection.

Adapters designed to make jumper cable connections to side terminal batteries safer and easier are available at auto parts stores

Make the booster battery cable connections in the numerical order shown (note that the negative cable of the booster battery is NOT attached to the negative terminal of the dead battery)

Jacking and towing

Jacking

Warning: *The jack supplied with the vehicle should only be used for raising the vehicle when changing a tire or placing jackstands under the frame. Never work under the vehicle or start the engine while the jack is being used as the only means of support.*

The vehicle must be on a level surface with the wheels blocked and the transaxle in Park. Apply the parking brake if the front of the vehicle must be raised. Make sure no one is in the vehicle as it's being raised with the jack.

Remove the jack, lug nut wrench and spare tire (if needed) from the vehicle. If a tire is being replaced, use the lug wrench to remove the wheel cover. **Warning:** *Wheel covers may have sharp edges – be very careful not to cut yourself.* Loosen the lug nuts one-half turn, but leave them in place until the tire is raised off the ground. Position the jack under the vehicle at the indicated jacking point. There's a front and rear jacking point on each side of the vehicle **(see illustration)**.

Turn the jack handle clockwise until the tire clears the ground. Remove the lug nuts, pull the tire off and replace it with the spare. Replace the lug nuts with the beveled edges facing in and tighten them snugly. Don't attempt to tighten them completely until the vehicle is lowered or it could slip off the jack.

Turn the jack handle counterclockwise to lower the vehicle. Remove the jack and tighten the lug nuts in a criss-cross pattern. If possible, tighten the nuts with a torque wrench (see Chapter 1 for the torque figures). If you don't have access to a torque wrench, have the nuts checked by a service station or repair shop as soon as possible.

Stow the tire, jack and wrench and unblock the wheels.

Towing

As a general rule, these vehicles should be towed with the front (drive) wheels off the ground. You may tow the vehicle with the front wheels on the ground for distances up to 500 miles provided speed does not exceed 55 mph. These vehicles should not be towed with all four wheels on the ground.

Be sure to release the parking brake. If the vehicle is being towed with the front wheels on the ground, place the transaxle in Neutral. Also, the ignition key must be in the ACC position, since the steering lock mechanism isn't strong enough to hold the front wheels straight while towing.

Equipment specifically designed for towing should be used. It must be attached to the main structural members of the vehicle, not the bumpers or brackets.

Safety is a major consideration when towing and all applicable state and local laws must be obeyed. A safety chain must be used at all times. Remember that power steering and brakes won't work with the engine off.

10 INCHES (254mm)   8 INCHES (203mm)

Jacking points

Automotive chemicals and lubricants

A number of automotive chemicals and lubricants are available for use during vehicle maintenance and repair. They include a wide variety of products ranging from cleaning solvents and degreasers to lubricants and protective sprays for rubber, plastic and vinyl.

Cleaners

Carburetor cleaner and choke cleaner is a strong solvent for gum, varnish and carbon. Most carburetor cleaners leave a dry-type lubricant film which will not harden or gum up. Because of this film it is not recommended for use on electrical components.

Brake system cleaner is used to remove grease and brake fluid from the brake system, where clean surfaces are absolutely necessary. It leaves no residue and often eliminates brake squeal caused by contaminants.

Electrical cleaner removes oxidation, corrosion and carbon deposits from electrical contacts, restoring full current flow. It can also be used to clean spark plugs, carburetor jets, voltage regulators and other parts where an oil-free surface is desired.

Demoisturants remove water and moisture from electrical components such as alternators, voltage regulators, electrical connectors and fuse blocks. They are non-conductive, non-corrosive and non-flammable.

Degreasers are heavy-duty solvents used to remove grease from the outside of the engine and from chassis components. They can be sprayed or brushed on and, depending on the type, are rinsed off either with water or solvent.

Lubricants

Motor oil is the lubricant formulated for use in engines. It normally contains a wide variety of additives to prevent corrosion and reduce foaming and wear. Motor oil comes in various weights (viscosity ratings) from 5 to 80. The recommended weight of the oil depends on the season, temperature and the demands on the engine. Light oil is used in cold climates and under light load conditions. Heavy oil is used in hot climates and where high loads are encountered. Multi-viscosity oils are designed to have characteristics of both light and heavy oils and are available in a number of weights from 5W-20 to 20W-50.

Gear oil is designed to be used in differentials, manual transmissions and other areas where high-temperature lubrication is required.

Chassis and wheel bearing grease is a heavy grease used where increased loads and friction are encountered, such as for wheel bearings, balljoints, tie-rod ends and universal joints.

High-temperature wheel bearing grease is designed to withstand the extreme temperatures encountered by wheel bearings in disc brake equipped vehicles. It usually contains molybdenum disulfide (moly), which is a dry-type lubricant.

White grease is a heavy grease for metal-to-metal applications where water is a problem. White grease stays soft under both low and high temperatures (usually from −100 to +190-degrees F), and will not wash off or dilute in the presence of water.

Assembly lube is a special extreme pressure lubricant, usually containing moly, used to lubricate high-load parts (such as main and rod bearings and cam lobes) for initial start-up of a new engine. The assembly lube lubricates the parts without being squeezed out or washed away until the engine oiling system begins to function.

Silicone lubricants are used to protect rubber, plastic, vinyl and nylon parts.

Graphite lubricants are used where oils cannot be used due to contamination problems, such as in locks. The dry graphite will lubricate metal parts while remaining uncontaminated by dirt, water, oil or acids. It is electrically conductive and will not foul electrical contacts in locks such as the ignition switch.

Moly penetrants loosen and lubricate frozen, rusted and corroded fasteners and prevent future rusting or freezing.

Heat-sink grease is a special electrically non-conductive grease that is used for mounting electronic ignition modules where it is essential that heat is transferred away from the module.

Sealants

RTV sealant is one of the most widely used gasket compounds. Made from silicone, RTV is air curing, it seals, bonds, waterproofs, fills surface irregularities, remains flexible, doesn't shrink, is relatively easy to remove, and is used as a supplementary sealer with almost all low and medium temperature gaskets.

Anaerobic sealant is much like RTV in that it can be used either to seal gaskets or to form gaskets by itself. It remains flexible, is solvent resistant and fills surface imperfections. The difference between an anaerobic sealant and an RTV-type sealant is in the curing. RTV cures when exposed to air, while an anaerobic sealant cures only in the absence of air. This means that an anaerobic sealant cures only after the assembly of parts, sealing them together.

Thread and pipe sealant is used for sealing hydraulic and pneumatic fittings and vacuum lines. It is usually made from a teflon compound, and comes in a spray, a paint-on liquid and as a wrap-around tape.

Chemicals

Anti–seize compound prevents seizing, galling, cold welding, rust and corrosion in fasteners. High-temperature anti-seize, usually made with copper and graphite lubricants, is used for exhaust system and exhaust manifold bolts.

Anaerobic locking compounds are used to keep fasteners from vibrating or working loose and cure only after installation, in the absence of air. Medium strength locking compound is used for small nuts, bolts and screws that may be removed later. High-strength locking compound is for large nuts, bolts and studs which aren't removed on a regular basis.

Oil additives range from viscosity index improvers to chemical treatments that claim to reduce internal engine friction. It should be noted that most oil manufacturers caution against using additives with their oils.

Gas additives perform several functions, depending on their chemical makeup. They usually contain solvents that help dissolve gum and varnish that build up on carburetor, fuel injection and intake parts. They also serve to break down carbon deposits that form on the inside surfaces of the combustion chambers. Some additives contain upper cylinder lubricants for valves and piston rings, and others contain chemicals to remove condensation from the gas tank.

Miscellaneous

Brake fluid is specially formulated hydraulic fluid that can withstand the heat and pressure encountered in brake systems. Care must be taken so this fluid does not come in contact with painted surfaces or plastics. An opened container should always be resealed to prevent contamination by water or dirt.

Weatherstrip adhesive is used to bond weatherstripping around doors, windows and trunk lids. It is sometimes used to attach trim pieces.

Undercoating is a petroleum-based, tar-like substance that is designed to protect metal surfaces on the underside of the vehicle from corrosion. It also acts as a sound-deadening agent by insulating the bottom of the vehicle.

Waxes and polishes are used to help protect painted and plated surfaces from the weather. Different types of paint may require the use of different types of wax and polish. Some polishes utilize a chemical or abrasive cleaner to help remove the top layer of oxidized (dull) paint on older vehicles. In recent years many non-wax polishes that contain a wide variety of chemicals such as polymers and silicones have been introduced. These non-wax polishes are usually easier to apply and last longer than conventional waxes and polishes.

Safety first!

Regardless of how enthusiastic you may be about getting on with the job at hand, take the time to ensure that your safety is not jeopardized. A moment's lack of attention can result in an accident, as can failure to observe certain simple safety precautions. The possibility of an accident will always exist, and the following points should not be considered a comprehensive list of all dangers. Rather, they are intended to make you aware of the risks and to encourage a safety conscious approach to all work you carry out on your vehicle.

Essential DOs and DON'Ts

DON'T rely on a jack when working under the vehicle. Always use approved jackstands to support the weight of the vehicle and place them under the recommended lift or support points.

DON'T attempt to loosen extremely tight fasteners (i.e. wheel lug nuts) while the vehicle is on a jack – it may fall.

DON'T start the engine without first making sure that the transmission is in Neutral (or Park where applicable) and the parking brake is set.

DON'T remove the radiator cap from a hot cooling system – let it cool or cover it with a cloth and release the pressure gradually.

DON'T attempt to drain the engine oil until you are sure it has cooled to the point that it will not burn you.

DON'T touch any part of the engine or exhaust system until it has cooled sufficiently to avoid burns.

DON'T siphon toxic liquids such as gasoline, antifreeze and brake fluid by mouth, or allow them to remain on your skin.

DON'T inhale brake lining dust – it is potentially hazardous (see Asbestos below)

DON'T allow spilled oil or grease to remain on the floor – wipe it up before someone slips on it.

DON'T use loose fitting wrenches or other tools which may slip and cause injury.

DON'T push on wrenches when loosening or tightening nuts or bolts. Always try to pull the wrench toward you. If the situation calls for pushing the wrench away, push with an open hand to avoid scraped knuckles if the wrench should slip.

DON'T attempt to lift a heavy component alone – get someone to help you.

DON'T rush or take unsafe shortcuts to finish a job.

DON'T allow children or animals in or around the vehicle while you are working on it.

DO wear eye protection when using power tools such as a drill, sander, bench grinder, etc. and when working under a vehicle.

DO keep loose clothing and long hair well out of the way of moving parts.

DO make sure that any hoist used has a safe working load rating adequate for the job.

DO get someone to check on you periodically when working alone on a vehicle.

DO carry out work in a logical sequence and make sure that everything is correctly assembled and tightened.

DO keep chemicals and fluids tightly capped and out of the reach of children and pets.

DO remember that your vehicle's safety affects that of yourself and others. If in doubt on any point, get professional advice.

Asbestos

Certain friction, insulating, sealing, and other products – such as brake linings, brake bands, clutch linings, torque converters, gaskets, etc. – contain asbestos. *Extreme care must be taken to avoid inhalation of dust from such products since it is hazardous to health.* If in doubt, assume that they *do* contain asbestos.

Fire

Remember at all times that gasoline is highly flammable. Never smoke or have any kind of open flame around when working on a vehicle. But the risk does not end there. A spark caused by an electrical short circuit, by two metal surfaces contacting each other, or even by static electricity built up in your body under certain conditions, can ignite gasoline vapors, which in a confined space are highly explosive. Do not, under any circumstances, use gasoline for cleaning parts. Use an approved safety solvent.

Always disconnect the battery ground (–) cable *at the battery* before working on any part of the fuel system or electrical system. Never risk spilling fuel on a hot engine or exhaust component.

It is strongly recommended that a fire extinguisher suitable for use on fuel and electrical fires be kept handy in the garage or workshop at all times. Never try to extinguish a fuel or electrical fire with water.

Fumes

Certain fumes are highly toxic and can quickly cause unconsciousness and even death if inhaled to any extent. Gasoline vapor falls into this category, as do the vapors from some cleaning solvents. Any draining or pouring of such volatile fluids should be done in a well ventilated area.

When using cleaning fluids and solvents, read the instructions on the container carefully. Never use materials from unmarked containers.

Never run the engine in an enclosed space, such as a garage. Exhaust fumes contain carbon monoxide, which is extremely poisonous. If you need to run the engine, always do so in the open air, or at least have the rear of the vehicle outside the work area.

If you are fortunate enough to have the use of an inspection pit, never drain or pour gasoline and never run the engine while the vehicle is over the pit. The fumes, being heavier than air, will concentrate in the pit with possibly lethal results.

The battery

Never create a spark or allow a bare light bulb near a battery. They normally give off a certain amount of hydrogen gas, which is highly explosive.

Always disconnect the battery ground (–) cable *at the battery* before working on the fuel or electrical systems.

If possible, loosen the filler caps or cover when charging the battery from an external source (this does not apply to sealed or maintenancefree batteries). Do not charge at an excessive rate or the battery may burst.

Take care when adding water to a non maintenance–free battery and when carrying a battery. The electrolyte, even when diluted, is very corrosive and should not be allowed to contact clothing or skin.

Always wear eye protection when cleaning the battery to prevent the caustic deposits from entering your eyes.

Household current

When using an electric power tool, inspection light, etc., which operates on household current, always make sure that the tool is correctly connected to its plug and that, where necessary, it is properly grounded. Do not use such items in damp conditions and, again, do not create a spark or apply excessive heat in the vicinity of fuel or fuel vapor.

Secondary ignition system voltage

A severe electric shock can result from touching certain parts of the ignition system (such as the spark plug wires) when the engine is running or being cranked, particularly if components are damp or the insulation is defective. In the case of an electronic ignition system, the secondary system voltage is much higher and could prove fatal.

Conversion factors

Length (distance)

Inches (in)	X 25.4	= Millimetres (mm)	X 0.0394	= Inches (in)
Feet (ft)	X 0.305	= Metres (m)	X 3.281	= Feet (ft)
Miles	X 1.609	= Kilometres (km)	X 0.621	= Miles

Volume (capacity)

Cubic inches (cu in; in³)	X 16.387	= Cubic centimetres (cc; cm³)	X 0.061	= Cubic inches (cu in; in³)
Imperial pints (Imp pt)	X 0.568	= Litres (l)	X 1.76	= Imperial pints (Imp pt)
Imperial quarts (Imp qt)	X 1.137	= Litres (l)	X 0.88	= Imperial quarts (Imp qt)
Imperial quarts (Imp qt)	X 1.201	= US quarts (US qt)	X 0.833	= Imperial quarts (Imp qt)
US quarts (US qt)	X 0.946	= Litres (l)	X 1.057	= US quarts (US qt)
Imperial gallons (Imp gal)	X 4.546	= Litres (l)	X 0.22	= Imperial gallons (Imp gal)
Imperial gallons (Imp gal)	X 1.201	= US gallons (US gal)	X 0.833	= Imperial gallons (Imp gal)
US gallons (US gal)	X 3.785	= Litres (l)	X 0.264	= US gallons (US gal)

Mass (weight)

Ounces (oz)	X 28.35	= Grams (g)	X 0.035	= Ounces (oz)
Pounds (lb)	X 0.454	= Kilograms (kg)	X 2.205	= Pounds (lb)

Force

Ounces-force (ozf; oz)	X 0.278	= Newtons (N)	X 3.6	= Ounces-force (ozf; oz)
Pounds-force (lbf; lb)	X 4.448	= Newtons (N)	X 0.225	= Pounds-force (lbf; lb)
Newtons (N)	X 0.1	= Kilograms-force (kgf; kg)	X 9.81	= Newtons (N)

Pressure

Pounds-force per square inch (psi; lbf/in²; lb/in²)	X 0.070	= Kilograms-force per square centimetre (kgf/cm²; kg/cm²)	X 14.223	= Pounds-force per square inch (psi; lbf/in²; lb/in²)
Pounds-force per square inch (psi; lbf/in²; lb/in²)	X 0.068	= Atmospheres (atm)	X 14.696	= Pounds-force per square inch (psi; lbf/in²; lb/in²)
Pounds-force per square inch (psi; lbf/in²; lb/in²)	X 0.069	= Bars	X 14.5	= Pounds-force per square inch (psi; lbf/in²; lb/in²)
Pounds-force per square inch (psi; lbf/in²; lb/in²)	X 6.895	= Kilopascals (kPa)	X 0.145	= Pounds-force per square inch (psi; lbf/in²; lb/in²)
Kilopascals (kPa)	X 0.01	= Kilograms-force per square centimetre (kgf/cm²; kg/cm²)	X 98.1	= Kilopascals (kPa)
Millibar (mbar)	X 100	= Pascals (Pa)	X 0.01	= Millibar (mbar)
Millibar (mbar)	X 0.0145	= Pounds-force per square inch (psi; lbf/in²; lb/in²)	X 68.947	= Millibar (mbar)
Millibar (mbar)	X 0.75	= Millimetres of mercury (mmHg)	X 1.333	= Millibar (mbar)
Millibar (mbar)	X 0.401	= Inches of water (inH₂O)	X 2.491	= Millibar (mbar)
Millimetres of mercury (mmHg)	X 0.535	= Inches of water (inH₂O)	X 1.868	= Millimetres of mercury (mmHg)
Inches of water (inH₂O)	X 0.036	= Pounds-force per square inch (psi; lbf/in²; lb/in²)	X 27.68	= Inches of water (inH₂O)

Torque (moment of force)

Pounds-force inches (lbf in; lb in)	X 1.152	= Kilograms-force centimetre (kgf cm; kg cm)	X 0.868	= Pounds-force inches (lbf in; lb in)
Pounds-force inches (lbf in; lb in)	X 0.113	= Newton metres (Nm)	X 8.85	= Pounds-force inches (lbf in; lb in)
Pounds-force inches (lbf in; lb in)	X 0.083	= Pounds-force feet (lbf ft; lb ft)	X 12	= Pounds-force inches (lbf in; lb in)
Pounds-force feet (lbf ft; lb ft)	X 0.138	= Kilograms-force metres (kgf m; kg m)	X 7.233	= Pounds-force feet (lbf ft; lb ft)
Pounds-force feet (lbf ft; lb ft)	X 1.356	= Newton metres (Nm)	X 0.738	= Pounds-force feet (lbf ft; lb ft)
Newton metres (Nm)	X 0.102	= Kilograms-force metres (kgf m; kg m)	X 9.804	= Newton metres (Nm)

Power

Horsepower (hp)	X 745.7	= Watts (W)	X 0.0013	= Horsepower (hp)

Velocity (speed)

Miles per hour (miles/hr; mph)	X 1.609	= Kilometres per hour (km/hr; kph)	X 0.621	= Miles per hour (miles/hr; mph)

Fuel consumption*

Miles per gallon, Imperial (mpg)	X 0.354	= Kilometres per litre (km/l)	X 2.825	= Miles per gallon, Imperial (mpg)
Miles per gallon, US (mpg)	X 0.425	= Kilometres per litre (km/l)	X 2.352	= Miles per gallon, US (mpg)

Temperature

Degrees Fahrenheit = (°C x 1.8) + 32   Degrees Celsius (Degrees Centigrade; °C) = (°F - 32) x 0.56

*It is common practice to convert from miles per gallon (mpg) to litres/100 kilometres (l/100km), where mpg (Imperial) x l/100 km = 282 and mpg (US) x l/100 km = 235

Troubleshooting

Contents

This section provides an easy reference guide to the more common problems which may occur during the operation of your vehicle. Various symptoms and their possible causes are grouped under headings denoting components or systems, such as *Engine, Cooling system,* etc. They also refer to the Chapter and/or Section that deals with the problem.

Remember that successful troubleshooting isn't a mysterious "black art" practiced only by professional mechanics. It's simply the result of knowledge combined with an intelligent, systematic approach to a problem. Always use a process of elimination, starting with the simplest solution and working through to the most complex – and never overlook the obvious. Anyone can run the gas tank dry or leave the lights on overnight, so don't assume that you're exempt from such oversights.

Finally, always establish a clear idea why a problem has occurred and take steps to ensure that it doesn't happen again. If the electrical system fails because of a poor connection, check all other connections in the system to make sure they don't fail as well. If a particular fuse continues to blow, find out why – don't just go on replacing fuses. Remember, failure of a small component can often be indicative of potential failure or incorrect functioning of a more important component or system.

Engine and performance

1 Engine will not rotate when attempting to start

1 Battery terminal connections loose or corroded (Chapter 1).
2 Battery discharged or faulty (Chapter 1).
3 Automatic transaxle not completely engaged in Park (Chapter 7).
4 Broken, loose or disconnected wiring in the starting circuit (Chapters 5 and 12).
5 Starter motor pinion jammed in flywheel ring gear (Chapter 5).
6 Starter solenoid faulty (Chapter 5).
7 Starter motor faulty (Chapter 5).
8 Ignition switch faulty (Chapter 12).
9 Starter pinion or driveplate teeth worn or broken (Chapter 5).

2 Engine rotates but will not start

1 Fuel tank empty.
2 Battery discharged (engine rotates slowly) (Chapter 5).
3 Battery terminal connections loose or corroded (Chapter 1).
4 Leaking fuel injector(s), fuel pump, pressure regulator, etc. (Chapter 4).
5 Fuel not reaching fuel injection system (Chapter 4).
6 Ignition components damp or damaged (Chapter 5).
7 Worn, faulty or incorrectly gapped spark plugs (Chapter 1).
8 Broken, loose or disconnected wiring in the starting circuit (Chapter 5).
9 Broken, loose or disconnected wires at the ignition coil(s) or faulty coil(s) (Chapter 5).

3 Engine hard to start when cold

1 Battery discharged or low (Chapter 1).
2 Fuel system malfunctioning (Chapter 4).
3 Injector(s) leaking (Chapter 4).

4 Engine hard to start when hot

1 Air filter clogged (Chapter 1).
2 Fuel not reaching the fuel injection system (Chapter 4).
3 Corroded battery connections, especially ground (Chapter 1).

5 Starter motor noisy or excessively rough in engagement

1 Pinion or driveplate gear teeth worn or broken (Chapter 5).
2 Starter motor mounting bolts loose or missing (Chapter 5).

6 Engine starts but stops immediately

1 Loose or faulty electrical connections at coil pack or alternator (Chapter 5).
2 Insufficient fuel reaching the fuel injectors (Chapter 4).
3 Vacuum leak at the gasket between the intake manifold/plenum and throttle body (Chapters 1 and 4).

7 Oil puddle under engine

1 Oil pan gasket and/or oil pan drain bolt seal leaking (Chapters 1 and 2).
2 Oil pressure sending unit leaking (Chapter 2).
3 Rocker arm cover gaskets leaking (Chapter 2).
4 Engine oil seals leaking (Chapter 2).
5 Timing cover sealant or sealing flange leaking (Chapter 2).

8 Engine lopes while idling or idles erratically

1 Vacuum leakage (Chapter 4).
2 Leaking EGR valve or plugged PCV valve (Chapters 1 and 6).
3 Air filter clogged (Chapter 1).
4 Fuel pump not delivering sufficient fuel to the fuel injection system (Chapter 4).
5 Leaking head gasket (Chapter 2).
6 Timing chain and/or gears worn (Chapter 2).
7 Camshaft lobes worn (Chapter 2).

9 Engine misses at idle speed

1 Spark plugs worn or not gapped properly (Chapter 1).
2 Faulty spark plug wires (Chapter 1).
3 Vacuum leaks (Chapters 1 and 4).
4 Incorrect ignition timing (Chapter 5).
5 Uneven or low compression (Chapter 2).

10 Engine misses throughout driving speed range

1 Fuel filter clogged and/or impurities in the fuel system (Chapters 1 and 4).
2 Low fuel output at the injector (Chapter 4).
3 Faulty or incorrectly gapped spark plugs (Chapter 1).
4 Incorrect ignition timing (Chapter 5).

5 Leaking spark plug wires (Chapter 1).
6 Faulty emission system components (Chapter 6).
7 Low or uneven cylinder compression pressures (Chapter 2).
8 Weak or faulty ignition system (Chapter 5).
9 Vacuum leak in fuel injection system, intake manifold or vacuum hoses (Chapter 4).

11 Engine stumbles on acceleration

1 Spark plugs fouled (Chapter 1).
2 Fuel injection system needs adjustment or repair (Chapter 4).
3 Fuel filter clogged (Chapter 1).
4 Incorrect ignition timing (Chapter 5).
5 Intake manifold air leak (Chapter 4).

12 Engine surges while holding accelerator steady

1 Intake air leak (Chapter 4).
2 Fuel pump faulty (Chapter 4).
3 Loose fuel injector harness connections (Chapter 4).
4 Defective ECM (Chapter 6).

13 Engine stalls

1 Idle speed incorrect (Chapters 1 and 4).
2 Fuel filter clogged and/or water and impurities in the fuel system (Chapters 1 and 4).
3 Ignition components damp or damaged (Chapter 5).
4 Faulty emissions system components (Chapter 6).
5 Faulty or incorrectly gapped spark plugs (Chapter 1).
6 Faulty spark plug wires (Chapter 1).
7 Vacuum leak in the fuel injection system, intake manifold or vacuum hoses (Chapter 4).

14 Engine lacks power

1 Incorrect ignition timing (Chapter 5).
2 Faulty or incorrectly gapped spark plugs (Chapter 1).
3 Fuel injection system out of adjustment or malfunctioning (Chapter 4).
4 Faulty coil(s) (Chapter 5).
5 Brakes binding (Chapter 1).
6 Automatic transaxle fluid level incorrect (Chapter 1).
7 Fuel filter clogged and/or impurities in the fuel system (Chapter 1).
8 Emission control system not functioning properly (Chapter 6).
9 Low or uneven cylinder compression pressures (Chapter 2).

15 Engine backfires

1 Emissions system not functioning properly (Chapter 6).
2 Ignition timing incorrect (Chapter 5).
3 Faulty secondary ignition system (Chapter 5).
4 Fuel injection system in need of adjustment or worn excessively (Chapter 4).
5 Vacuum leak at fuel injectors, intake manifold or vacuum hoses (Chapter 4).
6 Valves sticking (Chapter 2).

16 Pinging or knocking engine sounds during acceleration or uphill

1 Incorrect grade of fuel.
2 Ignition timing incorrect (Chapter 5).
3 Fuel injection system in need of adjustment (Chapter 4).
4 Improper or damaged spark plugs or wires (Chapter 1).
5 Worn or damaged ignition components (Chapter 5).
6 Faulty emissions system (Chapter 6).
7 Vacuum leak (Chapter 4).

17 Engine runs with oil pressure light on

1 Low oil level (Chapter 1).
2 Idle rpm below specification (Chapter 1).
3 Short in wiring circuit (Chapter 12).
4 Faulty oil pressure sender (Chapter 2).
5 Oil viscosity too low or oil diluted.
6 Worn engine bearings and/or oil pump (Chapter 2).

18 Engine diesels (continues to run) after switching off

1 Idle speed too high (Chapters 1 and 4).
2 Excessive engine operating temperature (Chapter 3).
3 Hot spots and/or carbon deposits in the combustion chamber(s).

Engine electrical system

19 Battery will not hold a charge

1 Alternator drivebelt defective or not adjusted properly (Chapter 1).
2 Battery terminals loose or corroded (Chapter 1).
3 Alternator not charging properly (Chapter 5).
4 Loose, broken or faulty wiring in the charging circuit (Chapter 5).
5 Short in vehicle wiring (Chapters 5 and 12).
6 Internally defective battery (Chapters 1 and 5).

20 Voltage warning light fails to go out

1 Faulty alternator or charging circuit (Chapter 5).
2 Alternator drivebelt defective or out of adjustment (Chapter 1).
3 Alternator voltage regulator inoperative (Chapter 5).

21 Voltage warning light fails to come on when key is turned on

1 Warning light bulb defective (Chapter 12).
2 Fault in the printed circuit, dash wiring or bulb holder (Chapter 12).

Fuel system

22 Excessive fuel consumption

1 Dirty or clogged air filter element (Chapter 1).
2 Incorrectly set ignition timing (Chapter 5).

3   Emissions system not functioning properly (Chapter 6).
4   Fuel injection internal parts worn or damaged (Chapter 4).
5   Low tire pressure or incorrect tire size (Chapter 1).

23   Fuel leakage and/or fuel odor

1   Leak in a fuel feed or vent line (Chapter 4).
2   Tank overfilled.
3   Evaporative canister filter clogged (Chapters 1 and 6).
4   Fuel injector internal parts excessively worn (Chapter 4).

Cooling system

24   Overheating

1   Insufficient coolant in system (Chapter 1).
2   Water pump drivebelt defective or out of adjustment (Chapter 1).
3   Radiator core blocked or grille restricted (Chapter 3).
4   Thermostat faulty (Chapter 3).
5   Electric cooling fan blades broken or cracked (Chapter 3).
6   Radiator cap not maintaining proper pressure (Chapter 3).
7   Ignition timing incorrect (Chapter 5).

25   Overcooling

Incorrect (opening temperature too low) or faulty thermostat (Chapter 3).

26   External coolant leakage

1   Deteriorated/damaged hoses or loose clamps (Chapters 1 and 3).
2   Water pump seal defective (Chapters 1 and 3).
3   Leakage from radiator core or header tank (Chapter 3).
4   Engine drain or water jacket core plugs leaking (Chapter 2).

27   Internal coolant leakage

1   Leaking cylinder head gasket (Chapter 2).
2   Cracked cylinder bore or cylinder head (Chapter 2).

28   Coolant loss

1   Too much coolant in system (Chapter 1).
2   Coolant boiling away because of overheating (Chapter 3).
3   Internal or external leakage (Chapter 3).
4   Faulty radiator cap (Chapter 3).

29   Poor coolant circulation

1   Inoperative water pump (Chapter 3).
2   Restriction in cooling system (Chapters 1 and 3).
3   Water pump drivebelt defective or out of adjustment (Chapter 1).
4   Thermostat sticking (Chapter 3).

Automatic transaxle

Note: *Due to the complexity of the automatic transaxle, it's difficult for the home mechanic to properly diagnose and service this component. For problems other than the following, the vehicle should be taken to a dealer service department or a transmission shop.*

30   Fluid leakage

1   Automatic transmission fluid is a deep red color. Fluid leaks should not be confused with engine oil, which can easily be blown by air flow to the transaxle.
2   To pinpoint a leak, first remove all built-up dirt and grime from the transaxle housing with degreasing agents and/or steam cleaning. Drive the vehicle at low speeds so air flow will not blow the leak far from its source. Raise the vehicle and determine where the leak is coming from. Common areas of leakage are:
   a) Pan (Chapters 1 and 7)
   b) Filler pipe (Chapter 7)
   c) Fluid cooler lines (Chapter 7)
   d) Speedometer gear or sensor (Chapter 7)

31   Transaxle fluid brown or has a burned smell

Transaxle overheated. Change fluid (Chapter 1).

32   General shift mechanism problems

1   Chapter 7 deals with checking and adjusting the shift linkage on automatic transaxles. Common problems which may be attributed to poorly adjusted linkage are:
   a) Engine starting in gears other than Park or Neutral.
   b) Indicator on shifter pointing to a gear other than the one actually being used.
   c) Vehicle moves when in Park.
2   Refer to Chapter 7 for the shift linkage adjustment procedure.

33   Transaxle will not downshift with accelerator pedal pressed to the floor

Throttle valve (TV) cable out of adjustment (Chapter 7).

34   Engine will start in gears other than Park or Neutral

Starter safety switch malfunctioning (Chapter 7).

35   Transaxle slips, shifts roughly, is noisy or has no drive in forward or reverse gears

There are many probable causes for the above problems, but the home mechanic should be concerned with only one possibility – fluid level. Before taking the vehicle to a repair shop, check the level and condition of the fluid as described in Chapter 1.

Correct the fluid level as necessary or change the fluid and filter if needed. If the problem persists, have a professional diagnose the probable cause.

Driveaxles

36 Clicking noise in turns

Worn or damaged outer CV joint. Check for cut or damaged boots (Chapter 1). Repair as necessary (Chapter 8).

37 Knock or clunk when accelerating after coasting

Worn or damaged outer CV joint. Check for cut or damaged boots (Chapter 1). Repair as necessary (Chapter 8).

38 Shudder or vibration during acceleration

1 Excessive inner CV joint angle. Check and correct as necessary (Chapter 8).
2 Worn or damaged CV joints. Repair or replace as necessary (Chapter 8).
3 Sticking inner joint assembly. Correct or replace as necessary (Chapter 8).

Brakes

Note: *Before assuming that a brake problem exists, make sure . . .*
 a) The tires are in good condition and properly inflated (Chapter 1).
 b) The front end alignment is correct (Chapter 10).
 c) The vehicle isn't loaded with weight in an unequal manner.

39 Vehicle pulls to one side during braking

1 Incorrect tire pressures (Chapter 1).
2 Front end out of line (have the front end aligned).
3 Unmatched tires on same axle.
4 Restricted brake lines or hoses (Chapter 9).
5 Malfunctioning brake assembly (Chapter 9).
6 Loose suspension parts (Chapter 10).
7 Loose brake calipers (Chapter 9).

40 Noise (high-pitched squeal when the brakes are applied)

Front disc brake pads worn out. The noise comes from the wear sensor rubbing against the disc. Replace pads with new ones immediately (Chapter 9).

41 Brake roughness or chatter (pedal pulsates)

1 Excessive front brake disc lateral runout (Chapter 9).
2 Parallelism not within specifications (Chapter 9).
3 Uneven pad wear caused by caliper not sliding due to improper clearance or dirt (Chapter 9).
4 Defective brake disc (Chapter 9).
5 Rear brake drum out-of-round.

42 Excessive pedal effort required to stop vehicle

1 Malfunctioning power brake booster (Chapter 9).
2 Partial system failure (Chapter 9).

3 Excessively worn pads or shoes (Chapter 9).
4 One or more caliper pistons or wheel cylinders seized or sticking (Chapter 9).
5 Brake pads or shoes contaminated with oil or grease (Chapter 9).
6 New pads or shoes installed and not yet seated. It will take a while for the new material to seat.

43 Excessive brake pedal travel

1 Partial brake system failure (Chapter 9).
2 Insufficient fluid in master cylinder (Chapters 1 and 9).
3 Air trapped in system (Chapters 1 and 9).

44 Dragging brakes

1 Master cylinder pistons not returning correctly (Chapter 9).
2 Restricted brakes lines or hoses (Chapters 1 and 9).
3 Incorrect parking brake adjustment (Chapter 9).

45 Grabbing or uneven braking action

1 Malfunction of proportioner valves (Chapter 9).
2 Malfunction of power brake booster unit (Chapter 9).
3 Binding brake pedal mechanism (Chapter 9).

46 Brake pedal feels spongy when depressed

1 Air in hydraulic lines (Chapter 9).
2 Master cylinder mounting bolts loose (Chapter 9).
3 Master cylinder defective (Chapter 9).

47 Brake pedal travels to the floor with little resistance

Little or no fluid in the master cylinder reservoir caused by leaking caliper or wheel cylinder pistons, loose, damaged or disconnected brake lines (Chapter 9).

48 Parking brake does not hold

Parking brake linkage improperly adjusted (Chapter 9).

Suspension and steering systems

Note: *Before attempting to diagnose the suspension and steering systems, perform the following preliminary checks:*
 a) Check the tire pressures and look for uneven wear.
 b) Check the steering universal joints or coupling from the column to the steering gear for loose fasteners and wear.
 c) Check the front and rear suspension and the steering gear assembly for loose and damaged parts.
 d) Look for out-of-round or out-of-balance tires, bent rims and loose and/or rough wheel bearings.

49 Vehicle pulls to one side

1 Mismatched or uneven tires (Chapter 10).
2 Broken or sagging springs (Chapter 10).

3   Wheel alignment incorrect (Chapter 10).
4   Front brakes dragging (Chapter 9).

50   Abnormal or excessive tire wear

1   Front wheel alignment incorrect (Chapter 10).
2   Sagging or broken springs (Chapter 10).
3   Tire out-of-balance (Chapter 10).
4   Worn shock absorber (Chapter 10).
5   Overloaded vehicle.
6   Tires not rotated regularly.

51   Wheel makes a "thumping" noise

1   Blister or bump on tire (Chapter 1).
2   Improper shock absorber action (Chapter 10).

52   Shimmy, shake or vibration

1   Tire or wheel out-of-balance or out-of-round (Chapter 10).
2   Loose or worn wheel bearings (Chapter 10).
3   Worn tie-rod ends (Chapter 10).
4   Worn balljoints (Chapter 10).
5   Excessive wheel runout (Chapter 10).
6   Blister or bump on tire (Chapter 1).

53   Hard steering

1   Lack of lubrication at balljoints, tie-rod ends and steering gear assembly (Chapter 10).
2   Front wheel alignment incorrect (Chapter 10).
3   Low tire pressure (Chapter 1).

54   Steering wheel does not return to center position correctly

1   Lack of lubrication at balljoints and tie-rod ends (Chapter 10).
2   Binding in steering column (Chapter 10).
3   Defective rack-and-pinion assembly (Chapter 10).
4   Front wheel alignment problem (Chapter 10).

55   Abnormal noise at the front end

1   Lack of lubrication at balljoints and tie-rod ends (Chapter 1).
2   Loose upper strut mount (Chapter 10).
3   Worn tie-rod ends (Chapter 10).
4   Loose stabilizer bar (Chapter 10).
5   Loose wheel lug nuts (Chapter 1).
6   Loose suspension bolts (Chapter 10).

56   Wander or poor steering stability

1   Mismatched or uneven tires (Chapter 10).
2   Lack of lubrication at balljoints or tie-rod ends (Chapters 1 and 10).
3   Worn shock absorbers (Chapter 10).

4   Loose stabilizer bar (Chapter 10).
5   Broken or sagging springs (Chapter 10).
6   Front wheel alignment incorrect (Chapter 10).
7   Worn steering gear clamp bushings (Chapter 10).

57   Erratic steering when braking

1   Wheel bearings worn (Chapters 8 and 10).
2   Broken or sagging springs (Chapter 10).
3   Leaking wheel cylinder or caliper (Chapter 9).
4   Warped rotors or brake drums (Chapter 9).
5   Worn steering gear clamp bushings (Chapter 10).

58   Excessive pitching and/or rolling around corners or during braking

1   Loose stabilizer bar (Chapter 10).
2   Worn shock absorbers or mounts (Chapter 10).
3   Broken or sagging springs (Chapter 10).
4   Overloaded vehicle.

59   Suspension bottoms

1   Overloaded vehicle.
2   Worn shock absorbers (Chapter 10).
3   Incorrect, broken or sagging springs (Chapter 10).

60   Cupped tires

1   Front wheel alignment incorrect (Chapter 10).
2   Worn shock absorbers (Chapter 10).
3   Wheel bearings worn (Chapters 8 and 10).
4   Excessive tire or wheel runout (Chapter 10).
5   Worn balljoints (Chapter 10).

61   Excessive tire wear on outside edge

1   Inflation pressures incorrect (Chapter 1).
2   Excessive speed in turns.
3   Wheel alignment incorrect (excessive toe-in or positive camber). Have professionally aligned.
4   Suspension arm bent or twisted (Chapter 10).

62   Excessive tire wear on inside edge

1   Inflation pressures incorrect (Chapter 1).
2   Wheel alignment incorrect (toe-out or excessive negative camber). Have professionally aligned.
3   Loose or damaged steering components (Chapter 10).

63   Tire tread worn in one place

1   Tires out-of-balance.
2   Damaged or buckled wheel. Inspect and replace if necessary.
3   Defective tire (Chapter 1).

64 Excessive play or looseness in steering system

1 Wheel bearings worn (Chapter 10).
2 Tie-rod end loose or worn (Chapter 10).
3 Steering gear loose (Chapter 10).

65 Rattling or clicking noise in rack and pinion

Steering gear clamps loose (Chapter 10).

Chapter 1 Tune-up and routine maintenance

Contents

1

Specifications

Recommended lubricants and fluids

Engine oil	
Type	SG/CC or SG/CD
Viscosity	See accompanying chart
Automatic transaxle fluid	Dexron II, Dexron IIE or Dexron III ATF
Engine coolant	Mixture of water and ethylene glycol-based antifreeze

IF NEITHER SAE 5W-30 NOR SAE 10W-30 GRADE OILS ARE AVAILABLE, SAE 30 GRADE MAY BE USED AT TEMPERATURES ABOVE 40° F (4° C)

For best fuel economy and cold starting, select the lowest SAE viscosity grade oil for the expected temperature range

Recommended lubricants and fluids (continued)

Brake fluid .... Delco Supreme II or DOT 3 fluid
Power steering fluid .... GM power steering fluid or equivalent
Chassis lubrication .... Multi-purpose, lithium-base chassis grease (meeting specification GM-6031M)

Capacities

Engine oil (approximate) .... 4.0 qts (3.8 liters)
Fuel tank .... 18.0 gals (68 liters)
Cooling system .... 13.0 qts (12.5 liters)
Automatic transaxle (approximate)
  1985 through 1996 .... 6 qts (5.8 liters) (when draining pan and replacing filter only)
  1997 on .... 7.4 qts (7.0 liters) (when draining pan and replacing filter only)

ignition system

Spark plug type and gap
  1985 .... AC R44TS8 or equivalent @ 0.080 inch
  1986 and 1987 .... AC R44LTS or equivalent @ 0.045 inch
  1988 to 1991 .... AC R44LTS6 or equivalent @ 0.060 inch
  1992 and 1993 .... AC 41-600 or equivalent @ 0.060 inch
  1994 on .... AC 41-601 or equivalent @ 0.060 inch
Ignition timing
  1985 .... Refer to Vehicle Emission Control Information label in the engine compartment
  1986 on .... Non-adjustable
Firing order 1-6-5-4-3-2
Cylinder locations .... See Chapter 2

1985 3.8L

1989 to 1991
3800

1986 to 1988 3.8L
Type I

1992 and later
3800

Radiator cap pressure rating .... 15 psi

Brakes

Brake pad wear limit .... 1/8 in
Brake shoe wear limit .... 1/16 in

Torque specifications   **Ft-lbs**

Spark plugs 20
Engine oil drain plug
  1985 25
  1986 30
  1987 42
  1988 30
  1989 on 18
Automatic transaxle oil pan bolts .... 8 to 10
Wheel lug nuts 100

1986 to 1988 3.8L
Type II

1   Introduction

Note: *On models equipped with the Delco Loc II audio system, be sure the lockout feature is turned off before performing any procedure which requires disconnecting the battery.*

This Chapter is designed to help home mechanics maintain their vehicles with the goals of maximum performance, economy, safety and reliability in mind.

Included is a master maintenance schedule (page 34), followed by procedures dealing specifically with each item on the schedule. Visual checks, adjustments, component replacement and other helpful items are included. Refer to the accompanying illustrations of the engine compartment and the underside of the vehicle for the locations of various components.

Servicing your vehicle in accordance with the mileage/time maintenance schedule and the step-by-step procedures will result in a planned maintenance program that should produce a long and reliable service life.

Keep in mind that it's a comprehensive plan, so maintaining some items but not others at the specified intervals will not produce the same results.

As you service your vehicle, you'll discover that many of the procedures can – and should – be grouped together because of the nature of the particular procedure you're performing or because of the close proximity of two otherwise unrelated components to one another.

For example, if the vehicle is raised, you should inspect the exhaust, suspension, steering and fuel systems while you're under the vehicle. When you're rotating the tires, it makes good sense to check the brakes since the wheels are already removed. Finally, let's suppose you have to borrow or rent a torque wrench. Even if you only need it to tighten the spark plugs, you might as well check the torque of as many critical fasteners as time allows.

The first step in this maintenance program is to prepare yourself before the actual work begins. Read through all the procedures you're planning to do, then gather up all the parts and tools needed. If it looks like you might run into problems during a particular job, seek advice from a mechanic or an experienced do-it-yourselfer.

Typical engine compartment component layout

1 Power steering dipstick
2 Coolant reservoir
3 Alternator
4 Radiator cap

5 EGR valve
6 Engine oil filler cap
7 Engine oil dipstick
8 Air cleaner assembly

9 Battery
10 Windshield washer fluid reservoir
11 Brake fluid reservoir
12 Automatic transaxle dipstick

1

Underside view of engine/transaxle

1   CV joint boot
2   Automatic transaxle

3   Exhaust pipe
4   Engine oil filter

5   Engine oil drain plug
6   Disc brake caliper

Typical rear underside component layout

1 Fuel tank
2 Fuel tank filler hose and pipe
3 Parking brake cable
4 Muffler

1

2 General Motors Full-size FWD car Maintenance schedule

The following maintenance intervals are based on the assumption that the vehicle owner will be doing the maintenance or service work, as opposed to having a dealer service department do the work. Although the time/mileage intervals are loosely based on factory recommendations, most have been shortened to ensure, for example, that such items as lubricants and fluids are checked/changed at intervals that promote maximum engine/driveline service life. Also, subject to the preference of the individual owner interested in keeping his or her vehicle in peak condition at all times, and with the vehicle's ultimate resale in mind, many of the maintenance procedures may be performed more often than recommended in the following schedule. We encourage such owner initiative.

When the vehicle is new it should be serviced initially by a factory authorized dealer service department to protect the factory warranty. In many cases the initial maintenance check is done at no cost to the owner (check with your dealer service department for more information).

Every 250 miles or weekly, whichever comes first

Check the engine oil level (Section 4)
Check the engine coolant level (Section 4)
Check the windshield washer fluid level (Section 4)
Check the brake fluid level (Section 4)
Check the tires and tire pressures (Section 5)

Every 3000 miles or 3 months, whichever comes first

All items listed above plus:
Change the engine oil and filter (Section 12)*
Check the automatic transaxle fluid level (Section 6)*
Check the power steering fluid level (Section 7)*
Check and service the battery (Section 8)
Check the cooling system (Section 9)
Inspect and replace, if necessary, all underhood hoses (Section 10)
Inspect and replace, if necessary, the windshield wiper blades (Section 11)

Every 6000 miles or 6 months, whichever comes first

Replace the air filter (1995 models) (Section 20)*
Rotate the tires (Section 17).
Lubricate the chassis components (1995 models) (Section 13).

Every 7500 miles or 12 months, whichever comes first

All items listed above plus:
Lubricate the chassis components (1985 through 1994) (Section 13)
Check the driveaxle boots (Section 14)
Inspect the suspension and steering components (Section 15)*
Inspect the exhaust system (Section 16)*
Check the brakes (Section 18)*
Inspect the fuel system (Section 19)
Replace the air filter (1985 through 1994) (Section 20)
Check the engine drivebelts (Section 21)
Check the seat belts (Section 22)
Check the neutral start switch (Section 23)
Check the seatback latch (Section 24)
Check the spare tire and jack (Section 25)

Every 30,000 miles or 24 months, whichever comes first

All items listed above plus:
Replace the fuel filter (Section 26)
Change the automatic transaxle fluid (Section 27)**
Service the cooling system (drain, flush and refill) (Section 28)
Inspect and replace,if necessary, the PCV valve (Section 29)
Inspect the evaporative emissions control system (Section 30)
Check the EGR system (Section 31)
Replace the spark plugs (Section 32)
Inspect the spark plug wires (Section 33)
Inspect the distributor cap and rotor (1985 models only) (Section 34)
Check and adjust, if necessary, the ignition timing (1985 models only) (Section 35)

* This item is affected by "severe" operating conditions as described below. If the vehicle is operated under severe conditions, perform all maintenance indicated with an asterisk (*) at 3000 mile/3 month intervals. Severe conditions are indicated if the vehicle is operated mainly . . .
in dusty areas
while towing a trailer
when allowed to idle for extended periods and/or at low speeds when outside temperatures remain below freezing and most trips are less than four miles long

** If operated under one or more of the following conditions, change the automatic transaxle fluid every 15,000 miles:
In heavy city traffic where the outside temperature regularly reaches 90-degrees F or higher
In hilly or mountainous terrain
Frequent trailer pulling

3 Tune-up general information

The term tune-up is used in this manual to represent a combination of individual operations rather than one specific procedure.

If, from the time the vehicle is new, the routine maintenance schedule is followed closely and frequent checks are made of fluid levels and high wear items, as suggested throughout this manual, the engine will be kept in relatively good running condition and the need for additional work will be minimized.

More likely than not, however, there will be times when the engine is running poorly due to lack of regular maintenance. This is even more likely if a used vehicle, which has not received regular and frequent maintenance checks, is purchased. In such cases, an engine tune-up will be needed outside of the regular routine maintenance intervals.

The first step in any tune-up or diagnostic procedure to help correct a poor running engine is a cylinder compression check. A compression check (see Chapter 2, Part B) will help determine the condition of internal engine components and should be used as a guide for tune-up and repair procedures. If, for instance, a compression check indicates serious internal engine wear, a conventional tune-up won't improve the performance of the engine and would be a waste of time and money. Because of its importance, the compression check should be done by someone with the right equipment and the knowledge to use it properly.

The following procedures are those most often needed to bring a generally poor running engine back into a proper state of tune.

Minor tune-up

    Check all engine related fluids (Section 4)
    Clean, inspect and test the battery (Section 8)
    Check the cooling system (Section 9)
    Check all underhood hoses (Section 10)
    Check the air filter (Section 20)
    Check the drivebelt (Section 21)
    Check the PCV valve (Section 29)
    Replace the spark plugs (Section 32)
    Inspect the spark plug wires (Section 33)
    Inspect the distributor cap and rotor (1985 models only) (Section 34)
    Check and adjust, if necessary, the ignition timing (1985 models only) (Section 35)

Major tune-up

All items listed under Minor tune-up plus . . .
    Check the fuel system (Section 19)
    Replace the air filter (Section 20)
    Check the EGR system (Section 31)

    Check the ignition system (Section 33 and Chapter 5)
    Check the charging system (Chapter 5)
    Replace the spark plug wires (Section 33)
    Replace the distributor cap and rotor (1985 models only) (Section 34)

4 Fluid level checks

Note: *The following are fluid level checks to be done on a 250 mile or weekly basis. Additional fluid level checks can be found in specific maintenance procedures which follow. Regardless of intervals, be alert to fluid leaks under the vehicle which would indicate a problem to be corrected immediately.*

1   Fluids are an essential part of the lubrication, cooling, brake and windshield washer systems. Because the fluids gradually become depleted and/or contaminated during normal operation of the vehicle, they must be periodically replenished. See *Recommended lubricants and fluids* at the beginning of this Chapter before adding fluid to any of the following components. **Note:** *The vehicle must be on level ground when fluid levels are checked.*

Engine oil

Refer to illustrations 4.2 and 4.4
2   The engine oil level is checked with a dipstick **(see illustration)**. The dipstick extends through a metal tube down into the oil pan.
3   The oil level should be checked before the vehicle has been driven, or about 15 minutes after the engine has been shut off. If the oil is checked immediately after driving the vehicle, some of the oil will remain in the upper part of the engine, resulting in an inaccurate reading on the dipstick.
4   Pull the dipstick from the tube and wipe all the oil from the end with a clean rag or paper towel. Insert the clean dipstick all the way back into the tube and pull it out again. Note the oil at the end of the dipstick. Add oil as necessary to keep the level above the ADD mark in the cross-hatched area of the dipstick **(see illustration)**.
5   Do not overfill the engine by adding too much oil since this may result in oil fouled spark plugs, oil leaks or oil seal failures.
6   Oil is added to the engine after removing a twist off cap located on the rocker arm cover **(see illustration 4.2)**. An oil can spout or funnel may help to reduce spills.
7   Checking the oil level is an important preventive maintenance step. A consistently low oil level indicates oil leakage through damaged seals, defective gaskets or past worn rings or valve guides. If the oil looks milky in color or has water droplets in it, the cylinder head gasket may be blown or the head or block may be cracked. The engine should be checked immediately. The condition of the oil should also be checked. Whenever you check the oil level, slide your thumb and index finger up the dipstick before wiping off the oil. If you see small dirt or metal particles clinging to the dipstick, the oil should be changed (Section 12).

4.2 On most models, the engine oil dipstick is clearly marked "ENGINE OIL" (arrow), as is the oil filler cap, which threads into the rocker arm cover (arrow)

4.4 The oil level should be in the cross-hatched area – if it's below the ADD line, add enough oil to bring the level into the cross-hatched area

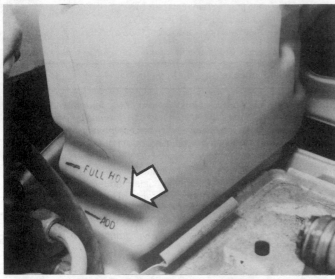

4.9   The coolant level must be maintained between the FULL HOT and ADD marks on the reservoir

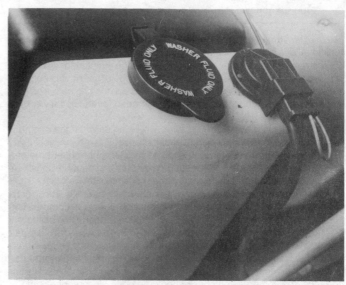

4.14   The reservoir for the windshield washer is located on the right side of the engine compartment (fluid is added after removing the top – how often you use the washers will dictate how often you need to check the reservoir)

Engine coolant

Refer to illustration 4.9

Warning: *Do not allow antifreeze to come in contact with your skin or painted surfaces of the vehicle. Flush contaminated areas immediately with plenty of water. Do not store new coolant or leave old coolant lying around where it's accessible to children or pets – they're attracted by its sweet taste. Ingestion of even a small amount of coolant can be fatal! Wipe up garage floor and drip pan coolant spills immediately. Keep antifreeze containers covered and repair leaks in the cooling system immediately.*

8   All vehicles covered by this manual are equipped with a pressurized coolant recovery system. A plastic coolant reservoir located in the right front corner of the engine compartment is connected by a hose to the radiator filler neck. If the engine overheats, coolant escapes through a valve in the radiator cap and travels through the hose into the reservoir. As the engine cools, the coolant is automatically drawn back into the cooling system to maintain the correct level.

9   The coolant level in the reservoir should be checked regularly. **Warning:** *Do not remove the radiator cap to check the coolant level when the engine is warm.* The level in the reservoir varies with the temperature of the engine. When the engine is cold, the coolant level should be at or slightly above the FULL COLD mark on the reservoir. Once the engine has warmed up, the level should be at or near the FULL HOT mark **(see illustration)**. If it isn't, allow the engine to cool, then unscrew the cap from the reservoir and add a 50/50 mixture of ethylene glycol based antifreeze and water. The coolant and windshield washer reservoirs are similar-looking, so be sure to add the correct fluids; the caps are clearly marked.

10   Drive the vehicle and recheck the coolant level. If only a small amount of coolant is required to bring the system up to the proper level, water can be used. However, repeated additions of water will dilute the antifreeze and water solution. In order to maintain the proper ratio of antifreeze and water, always top up the coolant level with the correct mixture. An empty plastic milk jug or bleach bottle makes an excellent container for mixing coolant. Do not use rust inhibitors or additives.

11   If the coolant level drops consistently, there may be a leak in the system. Inspect the radiator, hoses, filler cap, drain plugs and water pump (see Section 9). If no leaks are noted, have the radiator cap pressure

tested by a service station.

12   If you have to remove the radiator cap, wait until the engine has cooled completely, then wrap a thick cloth around the cap and turn it to the first stop. If coolant or steam escapes, let the engine cool down longer, then remove the cap.

13   Check the condition of the coolant as well. It should be relatively clear. If it is brown or rust colored, the system should be drained, flushed and refilled. Even if the coolant appears to be normal, the corrosion inhibitors wear out, so it must be replaced at the specified intervals.

Windshield washer fluid

Refer to illustration 4.14

14   Fluid for the windshield washer system is located in a plastic reservoir on the right side of the engine compartment **(see illustration)**. In milder climates, plain water can be used in the reservoir, but it should be kept no more than two-thirds full to allow for expansion if the water freezes. In colder climates, use windshield washer system antifreeze, available at any auto parts store, to lower the freezing point of the fluid. Mix the antifreeze with water in accordance with the manufacturer's directions on the container. **Caution:** *Do not use cooling system antifreeze – it will damage the vehicle's paint.*

15   To help prevent icing in cold weather, warm the windshield with the defroster before using the washer.

Battery electrolyte

16   All vehicles covered by this manual are equipped with a battery which is permanently sealed (except for vent holes) and has no filler caps. Water does not have to be added to these batteries at any time.

4.18a   **Anti-lock brake systems have a reservoir with a threaded cap**

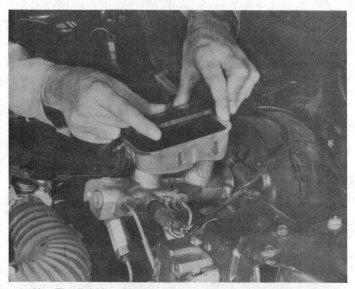

4.18b   **The fluid level inside the white plastic brake reservoir is easily checked through the inspection windows (when adding fluid, grasp the tabs and rotate the cover up as shown)**

1

Brake fluid

Refer to illustrations 4.18a and 4.18b

17   The brake master cylinder is mounted on the front of the power booster unit in the engine compartment.

18   On anti-lock brake reservoirs, unscrew the cap and make sure the fluid level is even with the bottom of the filler neck slot **(see illustration)**. On translucent white plastic reservoirs, the fluid inside is readily visible **(see illustration)**. If a low level is indicated, be sure to clean the reservoir cap, to prevent contamination of the brake system, before removing it.

19   When adding fluid, pour it carefully into the reservoir to avoid spilling it on surrounding painted surfaces. Be sure the specified fluid is used, since mixing different types of brake fluid can cause damage to the system. See *Recommended lubricants and fluids* at the front of this Chapter or your owner's manual. **Warning:** *Brake fluid can harm your eyes and damage painted surfaces, so use extreme caution when handling or pouring it. Do not use brake fluid that has been standing open or is more than one year old. Brake fluid absorbs moisture from the air. Excess moisture can cause a dangerous loss of braking effectiveness.*

20   At this time the fluid and master cylinder can be inspected for contamination. The system should be drained and refilled if deposits, dirt particles or contamination are seen in the fluid.

21   After filling the reservoir to the proper level, make sure the cap is on tight to prevent fluid leakage.

22   The brake fluid level in the master cylinder will drop slightly as the pads and the brake shoes at each wheel wear down during normal operation. If the master cylinder requires repeated replenishing to keep it at the proper level, this is an indication of leakage in the brake system, which should be corrected immediately. Check all brake lines and connections (see Section 18 for more information).

23   If, when checking the master cylinder fluid level, you discover one or both reservoirs empty or nearly empty, the brake system should be bled (see Chapter 9) and the cause of the fluid loss found.

5   Tire and tire pressure checks

Refer to illustrations 5.2, 5.3, 5.4a, 5.4b and 5.8

1   Periodic inspection of the tires may spare you the inconvenience of being stranded with a flat tire. It can also provide you with vital information

regarding possible problems in the steering and suspension systems before major damage occurs.

2   The original tires on this vehicle are equipped with 1/2-inch side bands that appear when tread depth reaches 1/16-inch, but they don't appear until the tires are worn out. Tread wear can be monitored with a simple, inexpensive device known as a tread depth indicator **(see illustration)**.

3   Note any abnormal tread wear **(see illustration on next page)**. Tread pattern irregularities such as cupping, flat spots and more wear on one side than the other are indications of front end alignment and/or balance problems. If any of these conditions are noted, take the vehicle to a tire shop or service station to correct the problem.

5.2   **Use a tire tread depth indicator to monitor tire wear – they are available at auto parts stores and service stations and cost very little**

Condition	Probable cause	Corrective action	Condition	Probable cause	Corrective action
Shoulder wear	• Underinflation (both sides wear) • Incorrect wheel camber (one side wear) • Hard cornering • Lack of rotation	• Measure and adjust pressure. • Repair or replace axle and suspension parts. • Reduce speed. • Rotate tires.	Feathered edge Toe wear	• Incorrect toe	• Adjust toe-in.
Center wear	• Overinflation • Lack of rotation	• Measure and adjust pressure. • Rotate tires.	Uneven wear	• Incorrect camber or caster • Malfunctioning suspension • Unbalanced wheel • Out-of-round brake drum • Lack of rotation	• Repair or replace axle and suspension parts. • Repair or replace suspension parts. • Balance or replace. • Turn or replace. • Rotate tires.

5.3   This chart will help you determine the condition of the tires, the probable cause(s) of abnormal wear and the corrective action necessary

4   Look closely for cuts, punctures and embedded nails or tacks. Sometimes a tire will hold air pressure for a short time or leak down very slowly after a nail has embedded itself in the tread. If a slow leak persists, check the valve stem core to make sure it's tight **(see illustration)**. Examine the tread for an object that may have embedded itself in the tire or for a "plug" that may have begun to leak (radial tire punctures are repaired with a plug that's installed in a puncture). If a puncture is suspected, it can be easily verified by spraying a solution of soapy water onto the suspected area **(see illustration)**. The soapy solution will bubble if there's a leak. Unless

the puncture is unusually large, a tire shop or service station can usually repair the tire.

5   Carefully inspect the inner sidewall of each tire for evidence of brake fluid. If you see any, inspect the brakes immediately.

6   Correct air pressure adds miles to the lifespan of the tires, improves mileage and enhances overall ride quality. Tire pressure cannot be accurately estimated by looking at a tire, especially if it's a radial. A tire pressure gauge is essential. Keep an accurate gauge in the vehicle. The pressure gauges attached to the nozzles of air hoses at gas stations are often inac-

5.4a   If a tire loses air on a steady basis, check the valve core first to make sure it's snug (special inexpensive wrenches are commonly available at hardware and auto parts stores)

5.4b   If the valve core is tight, raise the corner of the vehicle with the low tire and spray a soapy water solution onto the tread as the tire is turned slowly – leaks will cause small bubbles to appear

5.8   To extend the life of the tires, check the air pressure at least once a week with an accurate gauge (don't forget the spare!)

6.3   The automatic transaxle fluid dipstick is clearly marked ("TRANS FLUID") and is located at the rear of the engine compartment

curate.

7   Always check tire pressure when the tires are cold. Cold, in this case, means the vehicle has not been driven over a mile in the three hours preceding a tire pressure check. A pressure rise of four to eight pounds is not uncommon once the tires are warm.

8   Unscrew the valve cap protruding from the wheel or hubcap and push the gauge firmly onto the valve stem **(see illustration)**. Note the reading on the gauge and compare the figure to the recommended tire pressure shown on the label attached to the rear edge of the driver's door. Be sure to reinstall the valve cap to keep dirt and moisture out of the valve stem mechanism. Check all four tires and, if necessary, add enough air to bring them up to the recommended pressure.

9   Don't forget to keep the spare tire inflated to the specified pressure (refer to your owner's manual or the tire sidewall).

6   Automatic transaxle fluid level check

Refer to illustrations 6.3 and 6.6

1   The automatic transaxle fluid level should be carefully maintained. Low fluid level can lead to slipping or loss of drive, while overfilling can cause foaming and loss of fluid.

2   With the parking brake set, start the engine, then move the shift lever through all the gear ranges, ending in Park. The fluid level must be checked with the vehicle level and the engine running at idle. **Note:** *Incorrect fluid level readings will result if the vehicle has just been driven at high speeds for an extended period, in hot weather in city traffic, or if it has been pulling a trailer. If any of these conditions apply, wait until the fluid has cooled (about 30 minutes).*

3   With the transaxle at normal operating temperature, remove the dipstick from the filler tube. The dipstick is located at the rear of the engine compartment **(see illustration)**.

4   Carefully touch the fluid at the end of the dipstick to determine if the fluid is cool, warm or hot. Wipe the fluid from the dipstick with a clean rag and push it back into the filler tube until the cap seats.

5   Pull the dipstick out again and note the fluid level.

6   If the fluid felt cool, the level should be about 1/8-to-3/8 inch below the "ADD 1 PT" mark **(see illustration)**. If it felt warm, the level should be close to the "ADD 1 PT" mark. If the fluid was hot, the level should be within the cross-hatched area. If additional fluid is required, pour it directly into

the tube using a funnel. It takes about one pint to raise the level from the ADD mark to the upper edge of the cross-hatched area with a hot transaxle, so add the fluid a little at a time and keep checking the level until it's correct.

7   The condition of the fluid should also be checked along with the level. If the fluid at the end of the dipstick is a dark reddish-brown color, or if the fluid has a burned smell, the fluid should be changed. If you're in doubt about the condition of the fluid, purchase some new fluid and compare the two for color and smell.

7   Power steering fluid level check

Refer to illustrations 7.2 and 7.6

1   The power steering system relies on fluid which may, over a period of time, require replenishing.

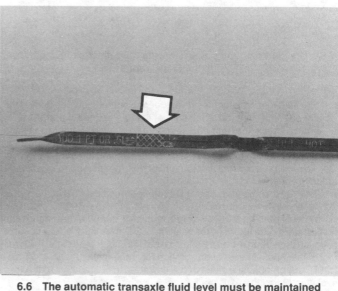

6.6   The automatic transaxle fluid level must be maintained within the cross-hatched area on the dipstick

7.2   The power steering fluid reservoir is located near the front (drivebelt end) of the engine; turn the cap clockwise for removal

8.1   Tools and materials required for battery maintenance

1   *Face shield/safety goggles – When removing corrosion with a brush, the acidic particles can easily fly up into your eyes*
2   *Rubber gloves – Another safety item to consider when servicing the battery; remember that's acid inside the battery!*
3   *Battery terminal cable cleaner – This wire brush cleaning tool will remove all traces of corrosion from the battery and cable*
4   *Treated felt washers – Placing one of these on each terminal, directly under the cable end, will help prevent corrosion (be sure to get the correct type for side terminal batteries)*
5   *Baking soda – A solution of baking soda and water can be used to neutralize corrosion*
6   *Petroleum jelly – A layer of this on the battery terminal bolts will help prevent corrosion*

7.6   The marks on the power steering fluid dipstick indicate the safe fluid level range

2   The fluid reservoir for the power steering pump is located behind the radiator near the front (drivebelt end) of the engine **(see illustration)**.
3   For the check, the front wheels should be pointed straight ahead and the engine should be off.
4   Use a clean rag to wipe off the reservoir cap and the area around the cap. This will help prevent any foreign matter from entering the reservoir during the check.
5   Twist off the cap and check the temperature of the fluid at the end of the dipstick with your finger.
6   Wipe off the fluid with a clean rag, reinsert it, then withdraw it and read the fluid level. The level should be at the HOT mark if the fluid was hot to the touch **(see illustration)**. It should be at the COLD mark if the fluid was cool to the touch. Note that on some models the marks (FULL HOT and COLD) are on opposite sides of the dipstick. At no time should the fluid level drop below the ADD mark.
7   If additional fluid is required, pour the specified type directly into the reservoir, using a funnel to prevent spills.

8   If the reservoir requires frequent fluid additions, all power steering hoses, hose connections, the power steering pump and the rack and pinion assembly should be carefully checked for leaks.

---

8   Battery check and maintenance

Refer to illustration 8.1
Warning: *Certain precautions must be followed when checking and servicing the battery. Hydrogen gas, which is highly flammable, is always present in the battery cells, so keep lighted tobacco and all other open flames and sparks away from the battery. The electrolyte inside the battery is actually dilute sulfuric acid, which will cause injury if splashed on your skin or in your eyes. It will also ruin clothes and painted surfaces. When removing the battery cables, always detach the negative cable first and hook it up last!*

ALWAYS CHECK hose for chafed or burned areas that may cause an untimely and costly failure.

SOFT hose indicates inside deterioration. This deterioration can contaminate the cooling system and cause particles to clog the radiator.

HARDENED hose can fail at any time. Tightening hose clamps will not seal the connection or stop leaks.

SWOLLEN hose or oil soaked ends indicate danger and possible failure from oil or grease contamination. Squeeze the hose to locate cracks and breaks that cause leaks.

9.4 Hoses, like drivebelts, have a habit of failing at the worst possible time – to prevent the inconvenience of a blown radiator or heater hose, inspect them carefully as shown here

1   Battery maintenance is an important procedure which will help ensure you aren't stranded because of a dead battery. Several tools are required for this procedure (**see illustration**).

2   A sealed battery is standard equipment on all vehicles covered by this manual. Although this type of battery has many advantages over the older, capped cell type, and never requires the addition of water, it should still be routinely maintained according to the procedure which follows.

3   The battery is located on the right side of the engine compartment. The exterior of the battery should be inspected periodically for damage such as a cracked case or cover.

4   Check the tightness of the battery cable bolts to ensure good electrical connections and check the entire length of each cable for cracks and frayed conductors.

5   If corrosion (visible as white, fluffy deposits) is evident, remove the cables from the terminals, clean them with a battery brush and reinstall the cables. Corrosion can be kept to a minimum by using special treated fiber washers available at auto parts stores or by applying a layer of petroleum jelly to the terminals and cables after they are assembled.

6   Make sure that the battery tray is in good condition and the hold-down clamp bolt is tight. If the battery is removed from the tray, make sure no parts remain in the bottom of the tray when the battery is reinstalled. When reinstalling the hold-down clamp bolt, do not overtighten it.

7   Corrosion on the hold-down components, battery case and surrounding areas can be removed with a solution of water and baking soda. Thoroughly rinse all cleaned areas with plain water.

8   Any metal parts of the vehicle damaged by corrosion should be covered with a zinc-based primer then painted.

9   Further information on the battery, charging and jump starting can be found in Chapter 5 and at the front of this manual.

9   Cooling system check

Refer to illustration 9.4

1   Many major engine failures can be attributed to a faulty cooling system. The cooling system also cools the transaxle fluid and plays an impor-

tant role in prolonging transaxle life.

2   The cooling system should be checked with the engine cold. Do this before the vehicle is driven for the day or after the engine has been shut off for at least three hours.

3   Remove the radiator cap by turning it to the left until it reaches a stop. If you hear any hissing sounds (indicating there is still pressure in the system), wait until it stops. Now press down on the cap with the palm of your hand and continue turning to the left until the cap can be removed. Thoroughly clean the cap, inside and out, with clean water. Also clean the filler neck on the radiator. All traces of corrosion should be removed. The coolant inside the radiator should be relatively transparent. If it is rust colored, the system should be drained and refilled (Section 28). If the coolant level is not up to the top, add additional antifreeze/coolant mixture (Section 4).

4   Carefully check the large upper and lower radiator hoses along with any smaller diameter heater hoses which run from the engine to the firewall. Inspect each hose along its entire length, replacing any hose which is cracked, swollen or shows signs of deterioration. Cracks may become more apparent if the hose is squeezed (**see illustration**).

5   Make sure all hose connections are tight. A leak in the cooling system will usually show up as white or rust colored deposits on the areas adjoining the leak. If wire-type clamps are used at the ends of the hoses, it may be wise to replace them with more secure screw-type clamps.

6   Use compressed air or a soft brush to remove bugs, leaves, etc. from the front of the radiator or air conditioning condenser. Be careful not to damage the delicate cooling fins or cut yourself on them.

7   Every other inspection, or at the first indication of cooling system problems, have the cap and system pressure tested. If you don't have a pressure tester, most gas stations and repair shops will do this for a minimal charge.

10   Underhood hose check and replacement

General

Refer to illustration 10.1

1   **Caution:** *Replacement of air conditioning hoses must be left to a dealer service department or air conditioning shop that has the equipment to depressurize the system safely. Never remove air conditioning components or hoses* (**see illustration**) *until the system has been depressurized.*

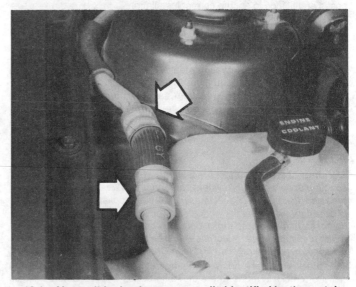

10.1   Air conditioning hoses are easily identified by the metal tubes used at all bends (arrows) – DO NOT disconnect or accidentally damage the air conditioning hoses (the system is under high pressure)

11.5a   Using a small screwdriver, gently pry on the spring at the center of the windshield wiper arm . . .

11.5b   . . . while pulling the blade assembly away from the arm

2   High temperatures under the hood can cause the deterioration of the rubber and plastic hoses used for engine, accessory and emission systems operation. Periodic inspection should be made for cracks, loose clamps, material hardening and leaks. Information specific to the cooling system hoses can be found in Section 9.

3   Some, but not all, hoses are secured to the fittings with clamps. Where clamps are used, check to be sure they haven't lost their tension, allowing the hose to leak. If clamps aren't used, make sure the hose hasn't expanded and/or hardened where it slips over the fitting, allowing it to leak.

Vacuum hoses

4   It's quite common for vacuum hoses, especially those in the emissions system, to be color coded or identified by colored stripes molded into each hose. Various systems require hoses with different wall thicknesses, collapse resistance and temperature resistance. When replacing hoses, be sure the new ones are made of the same material.

5   Often the only effective way to check a hose is to remove it completely from the vehicle. If more than one hose is removed, be sure to label the hoses and fittings to ensure correct installation.

6   When checking vacuum hoses, be sure to include any plastic T-fittings in the check. Inspect the fittings for cracks and the hose where it fits over the fitting for distortion, which could cause leakage.

7   A small piece of vacuum hose (1/4-inch inside diameter) can be used as a stethoscope to detect vacuum leaks. Hold one end of the hose to your ear and probe around vacuum hoses and fittings, listening for the "hissing" sound characteristic of a vacuum leak. **Warning:** *When probing with the vacuum hose stethoscope, be careful not to allow your body or the hose to come into contact with moving engine components such as the drivebelt, cooling fan, etc.*

Fuel hose

Warning: *There are certain precautions which must be taken when inspecting or servicing fuel system components. Work in a well ventilated area and do not allow open flames (cigarettes, appliance pilot lights, etc.) or bare light bulbs near the work area. Mop up any spills immediately and do not store fuel soaked rags where they could ignite. The fuel system is under pressure, so if any fuel lines must be disconnected, the pressure in the system must be relieved first (see Chapter 4 for more information).*

8   Check all rubber fuel lines for deterioration and chafing. Check especially for cracks in areas where the hose bends and just before fittings, such as where a hose attaches to the fuel filter and fuel injection unit.

9   High quality fuel line, usually identified by the word Fluroelastomer printed on the hose, should be used for fuel line replacement. Never, under any circumstances, use unreinforced vacuum line, clear plastic tubing or water hose for fuel lines.

10   Spring-type clamps are commonly used on fuel lines. These clamps often lose their tension over a period of time, and can be "sprung" during the removal process. As a result spring-type clamps be replaced with screw-type clamps whenever a hose is replaced.

Metal lines

11   Sections of steel tubing often used for fuel line between the fuel pump and fuel injection unit. Check carefully for cracks, kinks and flat spots in the line.

12   If a section of metal fuel line must be replaced, only seamless steel tubing should be used, since copper and aluminum tubing do not have the strength necessary to withstand normal engine vibration.

13   Check the metal brake lines where they enter the master cylinder and brake proportioning unit (if used) for cracks in the lines and loose fittings. Any sign of brake fluid leakage calls for an immediate thorough inspection of the brake system.

---

11   Windshield wiper blade inspection and replacement

Refer to illustrations 11.5a, 11.5b and 11.7

1   The windshield wiper and blade assembly should be inspected periodically for damage, loose components and cracked or worn blade elements.

2   Road film can build up on the wiper blades and affect their efficiency, so they should be washed regularly with a mild detergent solution.

3   The action of the wiping mechanism can loosen the bolts, nuts and fasteners, so they should be checked and tightened, as necessary, at the same time the wiper blades are checked.

4   If the wiper blade elements (sometimes called inserts) are cracked, worn or warped, they should be replaced with new ones.

5   On 1997 and later Park Avenue models, push in on the button of the wiper blade assembly clip and remove the blade assembly from the wiper arm. Carefully withdraw the blade assembly from the wiper arm. On all other models, remove the wiper blade assembly from the wiper arm by inserting a small screwdriver into the opening and gently prying on the spring while pulling on the blade to release it **(see illustrations)**.

6   With the blade removed from the vehicle, you can remove the rubber element from the blade.

7   Using pliers, pinch the metal backing of the element **(see illustration)**, then slide the element out of the blade assembly.

8   Compare the new element with the old for length, design, etc.

9   Slide the new element into place. It will automatically lock at the correct location.

10   Reinstall the blade assembly on the arm, wet the windshield glass and test for proper operation.

11.7 The rubber element is retained in the blade by small clips – the metal backing of the rubber element can be compressed at one end with pliers, allowing the element to slide out of the clips

12 Engine oil and filter change

Refer to illustrations 12.3, 12.9, 12.14 and 12.18

1   Frequent oil changes are the most important preventive maintenance procedures that can be done by the home mechanic. As engine oil ages, it becomes diluted and contaminated, which leads to premature engine wear.

2   Although some sources recommend oil filter changes every other oil change, we feel that the minimal cost of an oil filter and the relative ease with which it is installed dictate that a new filter be used every time the oil is changed.

3   Gather together all necessary tools and materials before beginning the procedure **(see illustration)**.

4   In addition, you should have plenty of clean rags and newspapers handy to mop up any spills. Access to the underside of the vehicle is greatly improved if the vehicle can be lifted on a hoist, driven onto ramps or supported by jackstands. **Warning:** *Do not work under a vehicle which is supported only by a bumper, hydraulic or scissors-type jack.*

5   If this is your first oil change, get under the vehicle and familiarize yourself with the locations of the oil drain plug and the oil filter. The engine and exhaust components will be warm during the actual work, so note how they are situated to avoid touching them when working under the vehicle.

6   Warm the engine to normal operating temperature. If the new oil or any tools are needed, use this warm-up time to gather everything necessary for the job. The correct type of oil for your application can be found in *Recommended lubricants and fluids* at the beginning of this Chapter.

7   With the engine oil warm (warm engine oil will drain better and more built-up sludge will be removed with the oil), raise and support the vehicle. Make sure it's safely supported.

8   Move all necessary tools, rags and newspapers under the vehicle. Position the drain pan under the drain plug. Keep in mind that the oil will initially flow from the pan with some force, so place the pan accordingly.

9   Being careful not to touch any of the hot exhaust components, remove the drain plug at the bottom of the oil pan **(see illustration)**. Depending on how hot the oil is, you may want to wear gloves while unscrewing the plug the final few turns.

10   Allow the old oil to drain into the pan. It may be necessary to move the pan farther under the engine as the oil flow slows to a trickle.

11   After all the oil has drained, wipe off the drain plug with a clean rag. Small metal particles may cling to the plug which would immediately contaminate the new oil.

12.3 These tools are required when changing the engine oil and filter

1   *Drain pan* – *It should be fairly shallow in depth, but wide to prevent spills*

2   *Rubber gloves* – *When removing the drain plug and filter, you will get oil on your hands (the gloves will prevent burns)*

3   *Breaker bar* – *Sometimes the oil drain plug is tight and a long breaker bar is needed to loosen it*

4   *Socket* – *To be used with the breaker bar or a ratchet (must be the correct size to fit the drain plug – 6-point preferred)*

5   *Filter wrench* – *This is a metal band-type wrench, which requires clearance around the filter to be effective*

6   *Filter wrench* – *This type fits on the bottom of the filter and can be turned with a ratchet or breaker bar (different size wrenches are available for different types of filters)*

12.9 The engine oil drain plug is located at the rear of the oil pan – it's usually very tight, so use a box-end wrench to avoid rounding off the hex

12.14   The oil filter is usually on very tight as well and will require a special wrench for removal – DO NOT use the wrench to tighten the new filter!

12.18   Lubricate the oil filter gasket with clean engine oil before installing the filter on the engine

12   Clean the area around the drain plug opening and reinstall the plug. Tighten the plug securely with the wrench. If a torque wrench is available, use it to tighten the plug.

13   Move the drain pan into position under the oil filter.

14   Use the filter wrench to loosen the oil filter **(see illustration)**. Chain or metal band filter wrenches may distort the filter canister, but this is of no concern as the filter will be discarded anyway.

15   Completely unscrew the old filter. Be careful – it's full of oil. Empty the oil inside the filter into the drain pan.

16   Compare the old filter with the new one to make sure they are the same type.

17   Use a clean rag to remove all oil, dirt and sludge from the area where the oil filter mounts on the engine. Check the old filter to make sure the rubber gasket isn't stuck to the engine. If the gasket is stuck to the engine (use a flashlight if necessary), remove it.

18   Apply a light coat of oil to the rubber gasket on the new oil filter **(see illustration)**. Open a container of oil and partially fill the oil filter with fresh oil. Oil pressure will not build in the engine until the oil pump has filled the filter with oil, so partially filling it at this time will reduce the amount of time the engine runs with no oil pressure.

19   Attach the new filter to the engine, following the tightening directions printed on the filter canister or box. Most filter manufacturers recommend against using a filter wrench due to the possibility of overtightening and damage to the seal.

20   Remove all tools, rags, etc. from under the vehicle, being careful not to spill the oil in the drain pan, then lower the vehicle.

21   Move to the engine compartment and locate the oil filler cap.

22   Pour the fresh oil through the filler opening. A funnel can be used.

23   Pour three quarts of fresh oil into the engine. Wait a few minutes to allow the oil to drain into the pan, then check the level on the dipstick (see Section 4 if necessary). If the oil level is above the ADD mark, start the engine and allow the new oil to circulate.

24   Run the engine for only about a minute and then shut it off. Immediately look under the vehicle and check for leaks at the oil pan drain plug and around the oil filter. If either is leaking, tighten with a bit more force.

25   With the new oil circulated and the filter now completely full, recheck the level on the dipstick and add more oil as necessary.

26   During the first few trips after an oil change, make it a point to check frequently for leaks and proper oil level.

27   The old oil drained from the engine cannot be reused in its present state and should be disposed of. Oil reclamation centers, auto repair shops and gas stations will normally accept the oil, which can be refined and used again. After the oil has cooled it can be drained into a container (capped plastic jugs, topped bottles, milk cartons, etc.) for transport to a disposal site.

13   Chassis lubrication

Refer to illustrations 13.1, 13.5 and 13.6

1   Refer to *Recommended lubricants and fluids* at the front of this Chapter to obtain the necessary lubricants. You'll also need a grease gun **(see illustration)**. Occasionally plugs will be installed rather than grease fittings. If so, grease fittings will have to be purchased and installed.

2   Look under the vehicle and see if grease fittings or plugs are installed in the balljoints and tie-rod ends. If there are plugs, remove them and buy grease fittings, which will thread into the component. A dealer or auto parts store will be able to supply the correct fittings. Straight, as well as angled, fittings are available.

3   For easier access under the vehicle, raise it with a jack and place jackstands under the frame. Make sure it's securely supported by the stands. If the wheels are being removed at this interval for rotation or brake inspection, loosen the lug nuts slightly while the vehicle is still on the ground.

4   Before beginning, force a little grease out of the nozzle to remove any dirt from the end of the gun. Wipe the nozzle clean with a rag.

5   With the grease gun and plenty of clean rags, crawl under the vehicle and begin lubricating the components **(see illustration)**.

6   Wipe off the grease fitting and push the nozzle firmly over it **(see illustration)**. Squeeze the trigger on the grease gun to force grease into the component. The balljoints and tie-rod ends should be lubricated until each rubber seal is firm to the touch. Do not pump too much grease into the fitting or it could rupture the seal. If the grease escapes around the grease gun nozzle, the fitting is clogged or the nozzle isn't completely seated on the fitting. Resecure the gun nozzle to the fitting and try again. If necessary, replace the fitting with a new one.

7   Wipe the excess grease off the components and the grease fitting. Repeat the procedure for the remaining fittings.

8   Lubricate the shift linkage with a little multi-purpose grease. While you are under the vehicle, clean and lubricate the parking brake cable along with the cable guides and levers. This can be done by smearing some of the chassis grease onto the cable and its related parts with your fingers.

13.1   Materials required for chassis and body lubrication

1   **Engine oil** – Light engine oil in a can like this can be used for door and hood hinges
2   **Graphite spray** – Used to lubricate lock cylinders
3   **Grease** – Grease, in a variety of types and weights, is available for use in a grease gun. Check the Specifications for your requirements.
4   **Grease gun** – A common grease gun, shown here with a detachable hose and nozzle, is needed for chassis lubrication. After use, clean it thoroughly!

13.6   After cleaning the grease fitting, push the gun nozzle firmly into place and pump the grease into the component (usually about two pumps will be sufficient)

9   Open the hood and smear a little chassis grease on the hood latch mechanism. Have an assistant pull the hood release lever from inside the vehicle as you lubricate the cable at the latch.
10   Lubricate all the hinges (door, hood, etc.) with engine oil.
11   The key lock cylinders can be lubricated with spray-on graphite or silicone lubricant, which is available at auto parts stores. **Caution:** *The manufacturer doesn't recommend using oil in black plastic lock cylinders – it could damage them by washing out the factory-applied lubricant.*
12   Lubricate the door weatherstripping with silicone spray. This will reduce chafing and retard wear.

14   Driveaxle boot check

Refer to illustration 14.2
1   The driveaxle boots are very important because they prevent dirt, water and foreign material from entering and damaging the constant velocity (CV) joints.

13.5   There are eight grease fittings on the chassis

1   *Front balljoint*
2   *Front tie-rod end*
3   *Toe link end*
4   *Rear balljoint*

14.2   Push on the driveaxle boots to check for cracks

17.2   Tire rotation diagram

2   Inspect the boots for tears and cracks as well as loose clamps **(see illustration)**. If there is any evidence of cracks or leaking lubricant, they must be replaced as described in Chapter 8.

15   Suspension and steering check

1   Raise the front of the vehicle periodically and visually check the suspension and steering components for wear.
2   Be alert for excessive play in the steering wheel before the front wheels react, excessive sway around corners, body movement over rough roads and binding at some point as the steering wheel is turned. If you notice any of the above symptoms, the steering and suspension systems should be checked.
3   Support the vehicle on jackstands placed under the frame rails. Because of the work to be done, make sure the vehicle cannot fall off the stands.
4   Check the front wheel hub nuts and make sure they are securely locked in place.
5   Working under the vehicle, check for loose bolts, broken or disconnected parts and deteriorated rubber bushings on all suspension and steering components. Look for grease or fluid leaking from the steering assembly. Check the power steering hoses and connections for leaks.
6   Have an assistant turn the steering wheel from side-to-side and check the steering components for free movement, chafing and binding. If the steering doesn't react with the movement of the steering wheel, try to determine where the slack is located.

16   Exhaust system check

1   With the engine cold (at least three hours after the vehicle has been driven), check the complete exhaust system from the engine to the end of the tailpipe. Ideally, the inspection should be done with the vehicle on a hoist to permit unrestricted access. If a hoist is not available, raise the vehicle and support it securely on jackstands.
2   Check the exhaust pipes and connections for evidence of leaks, severe corrosion and damage. Make sure that all brackets and hangers are in good condition and tight.
3   At the same time, inspect the underside of the body for holes, corrosion, open seams, etc. which may allow exhaust gases to enter the interior. Seal all body openings with silicone or body putty.
4   Rattles and other noises can often be traced to the exhaust system, especially the mounts and hangers. Try to move the pipes, muffler and catalytic converter. If the components can come in contact with the body or suspension parts, secure the exhaust system with new mounts.
5   Check the running condition of the engine by inspecting inside the end of the tailpipe. The exhaust deposits here are an indication of engine state-of-tune. If the pipe is black and sooty or coated with white deposits, the engine is in need of a tune-up, including a thorough fuel system inspection and adjustment.

17   Tire rotation

Refer to illustration 17.2

1   The tires should be rotated at the specified intervals and whenever uneven wear is noticed.
2   Front wheel drive vehicles require a special tire rotation pattern **(see illustration)**.
3   Refer to the information in *Jacking and towing* at the front of this manual for the proper procedures to follow when raising the vehicle and changing a tire. If the brakes are going to be checked, don't apply the parking brake as stated. Make sure the tires are blocked to prevent the vehicle from rolling as it's raised.
4   The entire vehicle should be raised at the same time. This can be done on a hoist or by jacking up each corner and then lowering the vehicle onto jackstands placed under the frame rails. Always use four jackstands and make sure the vehicle is safely supported.
5   After rotation, check and adjust the tire pressures as necessary and be sure to check the lug nut tightness.

18.3   The brake pad wear indicator (arrow) will contact the disc and make a squealing noise when the pad is worn

18.5   Look through the opening in the front of the caliper to check the brake pads (arrows) – the pad lining, which rubs against the disc, can also be inspected by looking through each end of the caliper

18   Brake check

Note: *For detailed photographs of the brake system, refer to Chapter 9.*

Warning: *Brake system dust contains asbestos, which is hazardous to your health. DO NOT blow it out with compressed air or inhale it. DO NOT use gasoline or solvents to remove the dust. Use brake system cleaner or denatured alcohol only.*

1   In addition to the specified intervals, the brakes should be inspected every time the wheels are removed or whenever a defect is suspected. Raise the vehicle and place it securely on jackstands. Remove the wheels (see Jacking and towing at the front of this manual, if necessary).

Disc brakes

Refer to illustrations 18.3 and 18.5

2   Disc brakes are used on the front of this vehicle. Extensive rotor damage can occur if the pads are not replaced when needed.

3   The disc brake pads have built-in wear indicators which make a high-pitched squealing or cricket-like warning sound when the pads are worn **(see illustration). Caution:** *Expensive rotor damage can result if the pads are not replaced soon after the wear indicators start squealing.*

4   The disc brake calipers, which contain the pads, are now visible. There is an outer pad and an inner pad in each caliper. All pads should be inspected.

5   Each caliper has an opening to inspect the pads **(see illustration)**. If the pad material has worn to about 1/8-inch thick or less, the pads should be replaced.

6   If you're unsure about the exact thickness of the remaining lining material, remove the pads for further inspection or replacement (refer to Chapter 9).

7   Before installing the wheels, check for leakage and/or damage at the brake hoses and connections. Replace the hose or fittings as necessary, referring to Chapter 9.

8   Check the condition of the brake rotor. Look for score marks, deep scratches and overheated areas (they will appear blue or discolored). If damage or wear is noted, the rotor can be removed and resurfaced by an automotive machine shop or replaced with a new one. Refer to Chapter 9 for more detailed inspection and repair procedures.

Drum brakes

Refer to illustrations 18.11 and 18.12

9   Using a scribe or chalk, mark the drum and hub so the drum can be reinstalled in the same position on the hub.

10   Remove and discard the retaining clip (if equipped) and pull the brake drum off the hub and brake assembly. If this proves difficult, make sure the parking brake is released, then squirt some penetrating oil around the center hub area. Allow the oil to soak in and try to pull the drum off again.

11   If the drum still cannot be pulled off, the brake shoes will have to be adjusted in. This is done by first removing the cover in the brake drum. Pull the self-adjusting lever off the star wheel and use a small screwdriver to turn the wheel, which will move the shoes away from the drum **(see illustration)**. With the drum removed, carefully brush away the accumulations of dirt and dust (see **Warning** above).

18.11   Knock out the access hole cover in the brake drum, push the self-adjusting lever aside and turn the star wheel

18.12   Measure the depth of the rivet hole (arrow) to determine the thickness of remaining brake shoe material

20.2a   On 1985 through 1991 models, remove the air cleaner cover screws (arrows) and detach the cover (two screws are located on the side, not visible in this photo), . . .

20.2b   . . . then pull the air filter element out of the housing

12   Note the thickness of the lining material on the brake shoes. If the material is worn to within 1/16-inch of the recessed rivets or metal backing, the shoes should be replaced **(see illustration)**. The shoes should also be replaced if they are cracked, glazed, (shiny surface) or contaminated with brake fluid.

13   Check to make sure all the brake assembly springs are connected and in good condition.

14   Check the brake components for signs of fluid leakage. Carefully pry back the rubber cups on the wheel cylinder, located at the top of the backing plate. Any leakage is an indication that the wheel cylinders should be replaced or overhauled immediately (Chapter 9). Also check the hoses and connections for signs of leakage.

15   Wipe the inside of the drum with a clean rag and brake cleaner or denatured alcohol.

16   Check the inside of the drum for cracks, scoring, deep scratches and hard spots, which will appear as small discolored areas. If imperfections cannot be removed with fine emery cloth, the drum must be taken to a machine shop for resurfacing.

17   After the inspection process is complete, and if all the components are in good condition, reinstall the brake drums. Install the wheels and lower the vehicle to the ground.

Parking brake

18   The parking brake is operated by a hand lever and locks the rear drum brake system. The easiest, and perhaps most obvious, method of periodically checking the operation of the parking brake assembly is to park the vehicle on a steep hill with the parking brake set and the transaxle in Neutral. If the parking brake cannot prevent the vehicle from rolling, it is in need of adjustment (see Chapter 9).

19   Fuel system check

Warning: *Certain precautions must be taken when inspecting or servicing fuel system components. Work in a well ventilated area and don't allow open flames (cigarettes, appliance pilot lights, etc.) near the work area. Mop up spills immediately and do not store fuel soaked rags where they could ignite. The fuel system is under pressure – nothing should be disconnected until the pressure is relieved (see Chapter 4).*

1   The fuel system is most easily checked with the vehicle raised on a hoist so the components underneath the vehicle are readily visible and accessible.

2   If the smell of gasoline is noticed while driving or after the vehicle has been in the sun, the system should be thoroughly inspected immediately.

3   Remove the gas tank cap and check for damage, corrosion and an unbroken sealing imprint on the gasket. Replace the cap with a new one if necessary.

4   With the vehicle raised, inspect the gas tank and filler neck for punctures, cracks and other damage. The connection between the filler neck and tank is especially critical. Sometimes a rubber filler neck will leak due to loose clamps or deteriorated rubber, problems a home mechanic can usually rectify. **Warning:** *Do not, under any circumstances, try to repair a fuel tank yourself (except rubber components). A welding torch or any open flame can easily cause the fuel vapors to explode if the proper precautions are not taken.*

5   Carefully check all rubber hoses and metal lines leading away from the fuel tank. Check for loose connections, deteriorated hoses, crimped lines and other damage. Follow the lines to the front of the vehicle, carefully inspecting them all the way. Repair or replace damaged sections as necessary.

20   Air filter replacement

Refer to illustrations 20.2a and 20.2b

1   At the specified intervals, the air filter should be replaced with a new one. The air filter housing is located on the left (driver's side) of the engine compartment.

2   On 1985 through 1991 models, remove the screws, lift the top cover off and withdraw the air filter **(see illustration)**.

3   On 1992 through 1997 models, loosen the hose clamp and unhook the rear air intake duct from the throttle body. Remove the wing screws or release the clips, then remove the rear of the cover. Withdraw the air filter.

4   On 1998 models, disconnect the electrical connector from the intake temperature sensor. Loosen the hose clamp and unhook the air intake duct from the throttle body. Remove the screws, then remove the front air intake duct from the housing. Withdraw the air filter.

5   While the filter housing cover is off, be careful not to drop anything down into the air duct or air filter assembly.

6   Wipe out the inside of the air filter housing with a clean rag.

7   Place a new air filter in the air filter housing. Make sure it seats properly in the bottom of the housing.

8   On 1985 through 1991 models, install the cover and tighten the screws.

9   On 1992 through 1997, install the cover and clips or tighten the screws. Install the rear air intake duct onto the throttle body and tighten the hose clamp securely.

10   On 1998 models, install the front air intake duct onto the housing and tighten the screws. Install the air intake duct onto the throttle body and tighten the hose clamp securely. Connect the electrical connector onto the intake temperature sensor.

21   Drivebelt check, adjustment and replacement

1985 models

Refer to illustrations 21.3 and 21.4

1   The drivebelts, or V-belts as they are often called, are located at the front of the engine and play an important role in the overall operation of the vehicle and its components. Due to their function and material make-up,

Common spark plug conditions

NORMAL

Symptoms: Brown to grayish-tan color and slight electrode wear. Correct heat range for engine and operating conditions.

Recommendation: When new spark plugs are installed, replace with plugs of the same heat range.

WORN

Symptoms: Rounded electrodes with a small amount of deposits on the firing end. Normal color. Causes hard starting in damp or cold weather and poor fuel economy.

Recommendation: Plugs have been left in the engine too long. Replace with new plugs of the same heat range. Follow the recommended maintenance schedule.

CARBON DEPOSITS

Symptoms: Dry sooty deposits indicate a rich mixture or weak ignition. Causes misfiring, hard starting and hesitation.

Recommendation: Make sure the plug has the correct heat range. Check for a clogged air filter or problem in the fuel system or engine management system. Also check for ignition system problems.

ASH DEPOSITS

Symptoms: Light brown deposits encrusted on the side or center electrodes or both. Derived from oil and/or fuel additives. Excessive amounts may mask the spark, causing misfiring and hesitation during acceleration.

Recommendation: If excessive deposits accumulate over a short time or low mileage, install new valve guide seals to prevent seepage of oil into the combustion chambers. Also try changing gasoline brands.

OIL DEPOSITS

Symptoms: Oily coating caused by poor oil control. Oil is leaking past worn valve guides or piston rings into the combustion chamber. Causes hard starting, misfiring and hesitation.

Recommendation: Correct the mechanical condition with necessary repairs and install new plugs.

GAP BRIDGING

Symptoms: Combustion deposits lodge between the electrodes. Heavy deposits accumulate and bridge the electrode gap. The plug ceases to fire, resulting in a dead cylinder.

Recommendation: Locate the faulty plug and remove the deposits from between the electrodes.

TOO HOT

Symptoms: Blistered, white insulator, eroded electrode and absence of deposits. Results in shortened plug life.

Recommendation: Check for the correct plug heat range, over-advanced ignition timing, lean fuel mixture, intake manifold vacuum leaks, sticking valves and insufficient engine cooling.

PREIGNITION

Symptoms: Melted electrodes. Insulators are white, but may be dirty due to misfiring or flying debris in the combustion chamber. Can lead to engine damage.

Recommendation: Check for the correct plug heat range, over-advanced ignition timing, lean fuel mixture, insufficient engine cooling and lack of lubrication.

HIGH SPEED GLAZING

Symptoms: Insulator has yellowish, glazed appearance. Indicates that combustion chamber temperatures have risen suddenly during hard acceleration. Normal deposits melt to form a conductive coating. Causes misfiring at high speeds.

Recommendation: Install new plugs. Consider using a colder plug if driving habits warrant.

DETONATION

Symptoms: Insulators may be cracked or chipped. Improper gap setting techniques can also result in a fractured insulator tip. Can lead to piston damage.

Recommendation: Make sure the fuel anti-knock values meet engine requirements. Use care when setting the gaps on new plugs. Avoid lugging the engine.

MECHANICAL DAMAGE

Symptoms: May be caused by a foreign object in the combustion chamber or the piston striking an incorrect reach (too long) plug. Causes a dead cylinder and could result in piston damage.

Recommendation: Repair the mechanical damage. Remove the foreign object from the engine and/or install the correct reach plug.

1

21.3   Here are some of the more common problems associated with drivebelts (check the belts carefully to prevent an untimely breakdown)

21.4   Drivebelt tension can be checked with a straightedge and ruler

21.10   Check the belt for signs of wear like these – if the belt looks worn, replace it

21.12a   The belt tension indicator must be between the maximum and minimum marks (all except VIN K)

21.12b   The belt tension indicator must be between the maximum and minimum marks (VIN K)

1   Belt tensioner pulley
2   Belt
3   Belt tension indicator
4   Minimum tension
5   Maximum tension

the belts are prone to failure after a period of time and should be inspected and adjusted periodically to prevent major engine damage.

2   The number of belts used on a particular vehicle depends on the accessories installed. Drivebelts are used to turn the alternator, power steering pump, water pump and air-conditioning compressor. Depending on the pulley arrangement, more than one of these components may be driven by a single belt.

3   With the engine off, open the hood and locate the various belts at the front of the engine. Using your fingers (and a flashlight, if necessary), move along the belts checking for cracks and separation of the belt plies. Also check for fraying and glazing, which gives the belt a shiny appearance. Both sides of the belt should be inspected **(see illustration)**.

4   The tension of each belt is checked by pushing on the belt at a distance halfway between the pulleys. Push firmly with your thumb and see how much the belt deflects. If the distance between pulley center to pulley center is between 7 and 11 inches, the belt should deflect 1/4 inch. If the belt travels between pulleys 12 to 16 inches apart, the belt should deflect 1/2 inch **(see illustration)**.

5   If it is necessary to adjust the belt tension, either to make the belt tighter or looser, it is done by moving the belt driven accessory on its mounting brackets.

6   For each component there will be an adjusting bolt and a pivot bolt. Both bolts must be loosened slightly to enable you to move the component.

7   After the two bolts have been loosened, move the component away from engine to tighten the belt or toward the engine to loosen the belt. Hold the accessory in position and check the belt tension. If it is correct, tighten the two bolts until just snug, then recheck the tension. If the tension is correct, tighten the bolts securely.

8   It will often be necessary to use some sort of prybar to move the accessory while the belt is adjusted. If this must be done to gain the proper leverage, be very careful not to damage the component being moved or the part being pried against.

1986 and later models

Refer to illustrations 21.10, 21.12a, 21.12b, 21.13, and 21.15

9   A single serpentine drivebelt is located at the front of the engine and plays an important role in the overall operation of the engine and its com-

ponents. Due to its function and material make up, the belt is prone to wear and should be periodically inspected. The serpentine belt drives the alternator, power steering pump, water pump and air conditioning compressor (if equipped).

10   With the engine off, open the hood and use your fingers (and a flashlight, if necessary), to move along the belt checking for cracks and separation of the belt plies. Also check for fraying and glazing, which gives the belt a shiny appearance. Both sides of the belt should be inspected, which means you will have to twist the belt to check the underside **(see illustration)**.

11   Check the ribs on the underside of the belt. They should all be the same depth, with none of the surface uneven.

12   The tension of the belt is checked visually. Locate the belt tensioner at the front of the engine under the power steering pump on the right (passenger) side, then find the tensioner operating marks **(see illustration)** located on the side of the tensioner. If the indicator mark is outside of the operating range, the belt should be replaced.

13   To replace the belt, rotate the tensioner counterclockwise to release belt tension **(see illustrations)**. The tensioner will swing down once the tension of the belt is released.

21.13 Rotate the tensioner counterclockwise to remove or install the drivebelt (air conditioned model shown)

14 Remove the belt from the auxiliary components and carefully release the tensioner.
15 Route the new belt over the various pulleys, again rotating the tensioner to allow the belt to be installed, then release the belt tensioner. **Note:** *Most models have a drivebelt routing decal on the upper radiator panel to help during drivebelt installation* **(see illustration)**.

22 Seat belt check

1 Check the seat belts, buckles, latch plates and guide loops for obvious damage and signs of wear.
2 See if the seat belt reminder light comes on when the key is turned to the Run or Start position. A chime should also sound.
3 The seat belts are designed to lock up during a sudden stop or impact, yet allow free movement during normal driving. Make sure the retractors return the belt against your chest while driving and rewind the belt fully when the buckle is unlatched.
4 If any of the above checks reveal problems with the seat belt system, replace parts as necessary.

23 Neutral start switch check

Warning: *During the following checks there's a chance the vehicle could lunge forward, possibly causing damage or injuries. Allow plenty of room around the vehicle, apply the parking brake and hold down the regular brake pedal during the checks.*
1 Try to start the engine in each gear. The engine should crank only in Park or Neutral.
2 Make sure the steering column lock allows the key to go into the Lock position only when the shift lever is in Park.
3 The ignition key should come out only in the Lock position.

24 Seatback latch check (two-door models only)

1 It's important to periodically check the seatback latch mechanism to prevent the seatback from moving forward during a sudden stop or an accident.
2 Grasping the top of the seat, attempt to tilt it forward. It should tilt only when the latch on the rear of the seat is pulled up. Note that there is a certain amount of free play built into the latch mechanism.
3 When returned to the upright position, the seatback should latch securely.

21.15 Most models have a drivebelt routing decal on the upper radiator panel

25 Spare tire and jack check

1 Periodically checking the security and condition of the spare tire and jack will help to familiarize you with the procedures necessary for emergency tire replacement and also ensure that no components work loose during normal vehicle operation.
2 Following the instructions in your owner's manual or under Jacking and towing near the front of this manual, remove the spare tire and jack.
3 Using a reliable air pressure gauge, check the pressure in the spare tire. It should be kept at the pressure marked on the tire sidewall.
4 Make sure the jack operates freely and all components are undamaged.
5 When finished, make sure the wing nuts hold the jack and tire securely in place.

26 Fuel filter replacement

Refer to illustrations 26.3 and 26.4
Warning: *Gasoline is extremely flammable, so extra precautions must be taken when working on any part of the fuel system. Don't smoke or allow open flames or unshielded light bulbs in or near the work area. Also, don't work in a garage where a natural gas appliance (clothes dryer or water heater) with a pilot light is present. Have a fire extinguisher rated for gasoline fires handy and know how to use it!*

1985 through 1992 models

1 Relieve the fuel system pressure (see Chapter 4).
2 Raise the vehicle and support it securely on jackstands.
3 Unscrew the fuel line-to-fuel filter fittings **(see illustration)**. Use a back-up wrench to keep from twisting the line.

26.3 To remove the fuel filter, use two wrenches to unscrew the fuel line fittings from both ends of the filter

26.4   Fuel filter and related components

1	Fuel filter	A	Use a back-up wrench
2	Fuel feed line		at this location
3	O-ring	B	Be sure to replace this O-ring
4	Feed line fitting	C	Fuel tank

27.11   Automatic transaxle filter installation details

1	O-ring	4	Pan
2	Filter	5	Bolt
3	Pan gasket		

4   Remove the filter from the clip **(see illustration)**.
5   Snap the new filter securely into the clip. Make sure the arrow on the filter points toward the engine.
6   Reattach the fuel lines to the filter, using new O-ring seals. **Note:** *The fuel line and/or filter must be replaced with new ones if they are scratched or damaged during installation.*
7   Start the engine and check for fuel leaks

1993 and later models

8   Relieve the fuel system pressure (see Chapter 4).
9   Raise the vehicle and support it securely on jackstands.
10   Twist the connector 1/4 turn in each direction to loosen any debris within the connector, then blow out the debris from the connector. Squeeze the plastic tabs on the male end of the connector and pull the connector apart. Repeat for the other connector.
11   Remove the filter mounting bolt, unhook the tab from the receptacle in the frame and remove the filter.
12   Wipe off the male end of both connectors, then apply a drop of clean engine oil onto the fuel filter male connectors where they are inserted into the female connector. Position the new filter so the arrow on the filter points toward the engine.
13   Insert the fuel line female connectors onto the fuel filter's male connectors and push them on until the plastic tabs snap and lock into place.
14   Pull on the female end of each connector to make sure it is securely locked into place.
15   Move the filter into place and install the bolt.
16   Start the engine and check for fuel leaks.

---

27   Automatic transaxle fluid and filter change

Refer to illustration 27.11

1   At the specified time intervals, the transaxle fluid should be drained and replaced. Since the fluid will remain hot long after driving, perform this procedure only after everything has cooled down completely.
2   Before beginning work, purchase the specified transaxle fluid (see *Recommended lubricants and fluids* at the front of this Chapter) and a new filter.
3   Other tools necessary for this job include jackstands to support the vehicle in a raised position, a drain pan capable of holding several quarts, newspapers and clean rags.
4   Raise and support the vehicle on jackstands.
5   With a drain pan in place, remove the front and side oil pan mounting bolts.

6   Loosen the rear pan bolts approximately four turns.
7   Carefully pry the transaxle oil pan loose with a screwdriver, allowing the fluid to drain.
8   Remove the remaining bolts, pan and gasket. Carefully clean the gasket surface of the transaxle to remove all traces of the old gasket and sealant.
9   Drain the fluid from the transaxle oil pan, clean the pan with solvent and dry it with compressed air. **Warning:** *Wear eye protection.* Be careful not to lose the magnet.
10   Remove the filter from the mount inside the transaxle.
11   Install the new filter and o-ring or seal **(see illustration)**. Apply a light coat of petroleum jelly (Vaseline) to the seal prior to installation. Install the seal with the smaller diameter end going in first.
12   Make sure the gasket surface on the transaxle oil pan is clean, then install a new gasket. Put the pan in place against the transaxle and install the bolts. Working around the pan, tighten each bolt a little at a time until the final torque figure is reached.
13   Lower the vehicle and add about seven pints of the specified type of automatic transaxle fluid through the filler tube (see Section 6).
14   With the shift lever in Park and the parking brake set, run the engine at a fast idle, but don't race it.
15   Move the shift lever through each gear and back to Park. Check the fluid level. You'll probably have to add about a pint of fluid.
16   Check under the vehicle for leaks during the first few trips.

---

28   Cooling system servicing (draining, flushing and refilling)

Refer to illustrations 28.6a, 28.6b and 28.6c

1   Periodically, the cooling system should be drained, flushed and re-filled to replenish the antifreeze mixture and prevent formation of rust and corrosion, which can impair the performance of the cooling system and cause engine damage.
2   At the same time the cooling system is serviced, all hoses and the radiator cap should be inspected and replaced if defective (see Section 9).
3   Since antifreeze is a corrosive and poisonous solution, be careful not to spill any of the coolant mixture on the vehicle's paint or your skin. If this happens, rinse it off immediately with plenty of clean water. Consult local authorities about the dumping of antifreeze before draining the cooling system. In many areas, reclamation centers have been set up to collect automobile oil and drained antifreeze/water mixtures, rather than allowing them to be added to the sewage system.
4   With the engine cold, remove the radiator cap.

28.6a   The radiator petcock (arrow) is located at the left lower corner of the radiator (viewed from below)

28.6b   The front engine block drain plug (arrow) is located adjacent to the starter

28.6c   The rear engine block drain plug (arrow) is located near the middle of the block

5   Move a large container under the radiator to catch the coolant as it's drained.

6   Drain the radiator by unscrewing the petcock **(see illustration)** at the bottom on the left side. If it's corroded and can't be turned easily, or if the radiator isn't equipped with a petcock, disconnect the lower radiator hose to allow the coolant to drain. Be careful not to get antifreeze on your skin or in your eyes. **Note:** *To drain the engine block, remove the front and rear drain plugs* **(see illustrations)**.

7   Disconnect the hose from the coolant reservoir and remove the reservoir. Flush it out with clean water.

8   Place a garden hose in the radiator filler neck and flush the system until the water runs clear at all drain points.

9   In severe cases of contamination or clogging of the radiator, remove it (see Chapter 3) and reverse flush it. This involves inserting the hose in the bottom radiator outlet to allow the water to run against the normal flow, draining through the top. A radiator repair shop should be consulted if further cleaning or repair is necessary.

10   When the coolant is regularly drained and the system refilled with the correct antifreeze/water mixture, there should be no need to use chemical cleaners or descalers.

11   To refill the system, reconnect the radiator hoses and install the reservoir and the overflow hose.

12   Fill the radiator with the recommended mixture of antifreeze and water (see Section 4) to the base of the filler neck and then add more coolant to the reservoir until it reaches the lower mark.

13   With the radiator cap still removed, start the engine and run it until normal operating temperature is reached. With the engine idling, add additional coolant to the radiator and the reservoir. Install the radiator and reservoir caps.

14   Keep a close watch on the coolant level and the cooling system hoses during the first few miles of driving. Tighten the hose clamps and/or add more coolant as necessary. The coolant level should be at the FULL HOT mark with the engine at normal operating temperature.

29   Positive Crankcase Ventilation (PCV) valve check and replacement

1985 through 1991 models

Refer to illustration 29.1

1   With the engine idling at normal operating temperature, pull the valve (with hose attached) out of the rubber grommet in the rocker arm cover or intake manifold **(see illustration)**.

2   Place your finger over the end of the valve. If there is no vacuum at the valve, check for a plugged hose, manifold port, or the valve itself. Replace any plugged or deteriorated hoses.

3   Turn off the engine and shake the PCV valve, listening for a rattle. If the valve doesn't rattle, replace it with a new one.

4   To replace the valve, pull it out of the end of the hose, noting its installed position and direction.

5   When purchasing a replacement PCV valve, make sure it's for your particular vehicle, model year and engine size. Compare the old valve with the new one to make sure they are the same.

6   Push the valve into the end of the hose until it's seated.

7   Inspect the rubber grommet for damage and replace it with a new one if necessary.

8   Push the PCV valve and hose securely into position in the rocker arm cover or intake manifold.

1992 and 1993 models

Refer to illustration 29.10

9   The PCV valve on these models is located in the intake manifold under a cover. Remove the three bolts and detach the cover.

29.1   The PCV valve plugs into the rocker arm cover or intake manifold; pull it out, then feel for suction at the end of the valve and shake it, listening for a clicking sound

29.10   Use needle-nose pliers to remove the PCV valve and spring from the cavity in the intake manifold

10   Use needle-nose pliers to withdraw the PCV valve and spring from the manifold **(see illustration)**. Be careful not to lose the O-ring at the end of the valve.
11   Shake the PCV valve, listening for a rattle. If the valve doesn't rattle, replace it with a new one. Make sure the new PCV valve is for your particular vehicle, model year and engine size. Compare the old valve with the new one to make sure they are the same.
12   Insert the new O-ring, PCV valve and spring into position and install the cover (be sure to use a new gasket) and bolts, tightening the bolts securely.

1994 and later models

Refer to illustration 29.16
13   Remove the sight shield from the fuel rail and intake manifold.
14   Using a 1/2-inch socket, press the cover down and rotate it 1/4 of a turn counterclockwise.
15   Slowly lift the cover and O-ring off the housing.
16   Remove the O-ring, spring (VIN L engine) and valve from the intake manifold **(see illustration)**.
17   Shake the valve, listening for a rattle. If the valve doesn't rattle, replace it with a new one. Make sure the new valve is for your particular vehicle, model year and engine size. Compare the old valve with the new one to make sure they are the same.
18   Insert a new O-ring, valve and spring (VIN L engine) into position and install the cover. Rotate the cover clockwise and lock the cover in place.

---

30   Evaporative emissions control system check

Refer to illustration 30.2
1   The function of the evaporative emissions control system is to draw

29.16   PCV valve (1994 and later models) – exploded view

1	*Cover*	4	*PCV valve*
2	*Cover O-ring*	5	*O-ring*
3	*Spring (VIN L only)*		

fuel vapors from the gas tank and fuel system, store them in a charcoal canister and then burn them during normal engine operation.
2   The most common symptom of a fault in the evaporative emissions system is a strong fuel odor in the engine compartment. If a fuel odor is detected, inspect the charcoal canister, located at the front of the engine compartment **(see illustration)**. Check the canister and all hoses for damage and deterioration.
3   The evaporative emissions control system is explained in more detail in Chapter 6.

---

31   Exhaust Gas Recirculation (EGR) system check

Refer to illustrations 31.2a and 31.2b
Note: *The following procedure applies only to models equipped with conventional-type EGR valves. Some models are equipped with a newer digital or linear EGR valve that does not have a diaphragm (see Chapter 6).*
1   The EGR valve is located on the intake manifold. Most of the time, when a problem develops in the emissions system, it's due to a stuck or corroded EGR valve.
2   With the engine cold to prevent burns, reach under the valve and push on the diaphragm **(see illustrations)**. Using moderate pressure, you should be able to move the diaphragm.
3   If the diaphragm doesn't move or moves only with much effort, replace the EGR valve with a new one. If in doubt about the condition of the valve, compare the free movement with a new valve.
4   Refer to Chapter 6 for more information on the EGR system.

30.2   The charcoal canister is located at the left (driver's side) front corner of the engine compartment (shown with air intake duct removed for clarity)

31.2a   Some EGR valves have plastic covers which you can pull off with your fingers

31.2b   The diaphragm, reached from under the EGR valve, should move easily with finger pressure

32.2   Tools required for changing spark plugs

1 **Spark plug socket** – *This will have special padding inside to protect the spark plug's porcelain insulator*
2 **Torque wrench** – *Although not mandatory, using this tool is the best way to ensure the plugs are tightened properly*
3 **Ratchet** – *Standard hand tool to fit the spark plug socket*
4 **Extension** – *Depending on model and accessories, you may need special extensions and universal joints to reach one or more of the plugs*
5 **Spark plug gap gauge** – *This gauge for checking the gap comes in a variety of styles. Make sure the gap for your engine is included.*

TWIST AND PULL

32.6   When removing a spark plug wire from a spark plug, pull only on the boot and twist it back-and forth – don't pull on the wire

32   Spark plug replacement

Refer to illustrations 32.2, 32.5a, 32.5b, 32.6 and 32.10

1   Three spark plugs are located at the front and three at the rear (fire-wall) side of the engine.
2   In most cases, the tools necessary for spark plug replacement included a spark plug socket which fits onto a ratchet (spark plug sockets are padded inside to prevent damage to the porcelain insulators on the new plugs), various extensions and a gap gauge to check and adjust the gaps on the new plugs **(see illustration)**. A special plug wire removal tool is available for separating the wire boots from the spark plugs, but it isn't ab-solutely necessary. A torque wrench should be used to tighten the new plugs. Because the aluminum cylinder heads used on these models are easily damaged, allow the engine to cool before removing or installing the spark plugs.
3   The best approach when replacing the spark plugs is to purchase the new ones in advance, adjust them to the proper gap and replace the plugs one at a time. When buying the new spark plugs, be sure to obtain the cor-rect plug type for your particular engine. The plug type can be found on the Emission Control Information label located under the hood and on the ref-erence chart at the store where you buy the plugs. If differences exist be-tween the plug specified on the emissions label and other sources, assume the emissions label is correct.
4   Allow the engine to cool completely before attempting to remove any of the plugs. While you are waiting for the engine to cool, check the new plugs for defects and adjust the gaps.

32.5a   Spark plug manufacturers recommend using a wire type gauge when checking the gap – if the wire does not slide between the electrodes with a slight drag, adjustment is required

32.5b   To change the gap, bend the side electrode only, as indicated by the arrows, and be very careful not to crack or chip the porcelain insulator surrounding the center electrode

5   The gap is checked by inserting the proper thickness gauge between the electrodes at the tip of the plug **(see illustration)**. The gap between the electrodes should be the same as the one specified on the Emissions Control Information label. The wire should just slide between the elec-trodes with a slight amount of drag. If the gap is incorrect, use the adjuster on the gauge body to bend the curved side electrode slightly until the prop-er gap is obtained **(see illustration)**. If the side electrode is not exactly over the center electrode, bend it with the adjuster until it is. Check for cracks in the porcelain insulator (if any are found, the plug should not be used).
6   With the engine cool, remove the spark plug wire from one spark plug. Pull only on the boot at the end of the wire – do not pull on the wire **(see illustration on page 56)**. A plug wire removal tool should be used if avail-able.
7   If compressed air is available, use it to blow any dirt or foreign material away from the spark plug hole. A common bicycle pump will also work. The idea here is to eliminate the possibility of debris falling into the cylinder as the spark plug is removed.
8   Place the spark plug socket over the plug and remove it from the en-gine by turning it in a counterclockwise direction.
9   Compare the spark plug to those shown in the accompanying photos to get an indication of the general running condition of the engine.
10   Thread one of the new plugs into the hole until you can no longer turn it with your fingers, then tighten it with a torque wrench (if available) or the ratchet. It might be a good idea to slip a short length of rubber hose over the end of the plug to use as a tool to thread it into place **(see illustration)**. The hose will grip the plug well enough to turn it, but will start to slip if the plug begins to cross-thread in the hole – this will prevent damaged threads and

1

32.10   A short length of 3/16-inch ID rubber hose will prevent damaged threads when installing the spark plugs

34.3   Inspect the distributor cap for cracks and carbon tracks and the terminals (arrow) for corrosion and damage

35.2   Location of a typical timing scale

the accompanying repair costs.

11   Before pushing the spark plug wire onto the end of the plug, inspect it following the procedures outlined in Section 33.

12   Attach the plug wire to the new spark plug, again using a twisting motion on the boot until it's seated on the spark plug.

13   Repeat the procedure for the remaining spark plugs, replacing them one at a time to prevent mixing up the spark plug wires.

---

33   Spark plug wire check and replacement

1   The spark plug wires should be checked at the recommended intervals and whenever new spark plugs are installed in the engine.

2   The wires should be inspected one at a time to prevent mixing up the order, which is essential for proper engine operation

3   Disconnect the plug wire from the spark plug. To do this, grab the rubber boot, twist slightly and pull the wire off. Do not pull on the wire itself, only on the rubber boot.

4   Check inside the boot for corrosion, which will look like a white crusty powder. Push the wire and boot back onto the end of the spark plug. It should be a tight fit on the plug. If it isn't, remove the wire and use pliers to carefully crimp the metal connector inside the boot until it fits securely on the end of the spark plug.

5   Using a clean rag, wipe the entire length of the wire to remove any built-up dirt and grease. Once the wire is clean, check for burns, cracks and other damage. Do not bend the wire excessively or pull the wire lengthwise – the conductor inside might break.

6   Disconnect the wire from the coil or distributor. Again, pull only on the rubber boot. Check for corrosion and a tight fit in the same manner as the spark plug end. Replace the wire at the coil or distributor.

7   Check the remaining spark plug wires one at a time, making sure they are securely fastened at the ignition coil or distributor and the spark plug when the check is complete.

8   If new spark plug wires are required, purchase a set for your specific engine model. Wire sets are available pre-cut, with the rubber boots already installed. Remove and replace the wires one at a time to avoid mixups in the firing order.

---

34   Distributor cap and rotor check and replacement (1985 models only)

Refer to illustration 34.3

1   At the distributor cap, disconnect the electrical connector to the coil.

2   Remove the distributor cap by placing a screwdriver on the slotted head of each latch, press down and turn each latch 90 degrees to release the hook. When all the latches are disengaged, separate the cap from the distributor with the spark plug wires still attached.

3   Inspect the cap for cracks and other damage. Closely examine the terminals on the inside of the cap for excessive corrosion **(see illustration)**. Slight pitting is normal. Deposits on the terminals may be removed

with a small file.

4   The rotor is visible, with the cap removed, at the top of the distributor shaft. Remove the two retaining screws and remove the rotor.

5   Inspect the rotor for cracks and other damage. Carefully check the condition of the rotor tip and the metal contact at the top of the rotor for excessive burning or pitting. Check the top of the rotor for carbon tracks, replace the rotor if carbon tracks are visible.

6   Install the rotor (either new or original). Note that the slot in the rotor engages the tab on the distributor shaft when the rotor is properly seated. Tighten the screws securely.

7   If a new cap is being installed, release the locking tabs to the spark plug wire retaining ring and remove the ring with the wires attached (this will prevent mixing the wires). If the ring is missing, or the wires have been previously replaced with a type that does not attach to the ring, make sure you label the wires and mark the cap before removing so they can be reinstalled in their original locations. Transfer the ignition coil to the new cap (see Chapter 5).

8   Install the cap to the distributor. Note that the tab on the cap engages the slot in the distributor housing when the cap is properly seated. Engage the latches, by pushing down and rotating 90 degrees. Connect the electrical connector to the coil.

---

35   Ignition timing check and adjustment (1985 models only)

Refer to illustration 35.2

Note: *It is imperative that the procedures included on the Vehicle Emission Control Information label be followed when adjusting the ignition timing. The label will include all information concerning preliminary steps to be performed before adjusting the timing as well as the timing specifications.*

1   Locate the VECI label under the hood and read through and perform the preliminary instructions.

2   Locate the timing scale, near the crankshaft pulley, and the notch on the crankshaft pulley **(see illustration)**. Clean the timing scale and mark the notch with a dab of white paint.

3   Connect the pick-up lead of the timing light to the number one spark plug wire and the power leads to the battery, according to the manufactures instructions.

4   Start the engine and allow it to reach normal operating temperature. Aim the timing light at the timing scale and note at what point on the scale the notch is lined up with. The numbers on the scale represent degrees of advance (BTDC) or retard (ATDC), with the zero representing TDC.

5   If the notch is not lined up at the correct point, according to the specifications on the VECI label, Loosen the distributor hold-down bolt slightly, and while watching the scale rotate the distributor until the notch lines up with the correct mark.

6   Tighten the distributor hold-down bolt and recheck the timing.

7   Turn off the engine, remove the timing light and return the engine to the normal operating mode.

Chapter 2 Part A Engine

Contents

Specifications

General

1985 3.8L

1989 to 1991
3800

1986 to 1988 3.8L
Type I

1992 and later
3800

1986 to 1988 3.8L
Type II

Cylinder numbers (drivebelt end-to-transaxle end)

Front bank (radiator side) 1-3-5
Rear bank 2-4-6
Firing order 1-6-5-4-3-2

Valve lifters

Diameter . . . . 0.8420 to 0.8427 in
Lifter-to-bore clearance . . . . 0.0008 to 0.0025 in

Oil pump

1985 models
  Gear lash . . . . 0.0015 to 0.003
  Side clearance . . . . 0.003 to 0.005
  End clearance . . . . 0.002 to 0.006
1986 and later models
  Outer gear-to-housing clearance . . . . 0.008 to 0.015 in
  Inner gear-to-outer gear clearance . . . . 0.006 in
  Gear end clearance . . . . 0.001 to 0.0035 in
  Pump cover warpage limit . . . . 0.002 in

Torque specifications

Ft-lbs (unless otherwise indicated)

Camshaft sprocket bolts
  1985 through 1987 31
  1988 through 1991 26
  1992
    Step one 74
    Step two . . . . Turn an additional 105-degrees
  1993 on
    Step one 74
    Step two . . . . Turn an additional 90-degrees
Cylinder head bolts
  1985 80
  1986 through 1988
    Step one 25
    Step two . . . . Turn an additional 90-degrees
    Step three . . . . Turn an additional 90-degrees
  1989-on
    Step one 35
    Step two . . . . Turn an additional 130-degrees
    Step three . . . . Turn an additional 30-degrees

Driveplate-to-crankshaft bolts
   1985 through 1991 60
   1992 on
      Step one 11
      Step two .... Turn an additional 50-degrees
Exhaust manifold-to-cylinder head bolts
   1985 through 1987 37
   1988 through 1990 41
   1991 on 38
Intake manifold-to-cylinder head bolts/nuts
   1985 through 1987 32
   1988 through 1990 10
   1991 through 1995 .... 88 in-lbs
   1996 on .... 132 in-lbs
Intake manifold, upper to lower bolts
   1994 through 1995 .... 88 in-lbs
   1996 on .... 132 in-lbs
Oil pan bolts
   1985 through 1987 8
   1988-on 10
Oil filter adapter-to-timing chain cover bolts
   1986 30
   1987-on 24
Oil pump
   Cover-to-timing chain cover bolts 8
   Pickup tube and screen assembly bolts 8
Rear main oil seal corner bolts 22
Rocker arm cover nuts/bolts .... 88 in-lbs
Rocker arm pivot bolts
   1985 30
   1986 and 1987 43
   1988 through 1992 28
   1993 on
      Step one 18
      Step two .... Turn an additional 70-degrees
Timing chain cover bolts 22
Vibration damper-to-crankshaft bolt
   1985 and 1986 200
   1987 through 1990 219
   1991
      Step one 105
      Step two .... Turn an additional 56-degrees
   1992 on
      Step one 110
      Step two .... Turn an additional 76-degrees

1   General information

Note: *On models equipped with the Delco Loc II audio system, be sure the lockout feature is turned off before performing any procedure which requires disconnecting the battery.*

This Part of Chapter 2 is devoted to in-vehicle repair procedures for the 3.0 and 3.8 liter V6 engines. Some 3.8 liter engines (VIN code C, K and L) are equipped with a balance shaft; they will be referred to as "3800" engines to avoid confusion with the non-balance shaft equipped 3.8 liter engines.

Information concerning camshaft, balance shaft and engine removal and installation, as well as engine block and cylinder head overhaul, is in Part B of this Chapter.

The following repair procedures are based on the assumption the engine is installed in the vehicle. If the engine has been removed from the vehicle and mounted on a stand, many of the steps included in this Part of Chapter 2 will not apply.

The Specifications included in this Part of Chapter 2 apply only to the procedures in this Part. The Specifications necessary for rebuilding the block and cylinder heads are found in Part B.

2   Repair operations possible with the engine in the vehicle

Many major repair operations can be accomplished without removing the engine from the vehicle.

Clean the engine compartment and the exterior of the engine with some type of pressure washer before any work is done. A clean engine will make the job easier and will help keep dirt out of the internal areas of the engine.

Depending on the components involved, it may be a good idea to remove the hood to improve access to the engine as repairs are performed (refer to Chapter 11 if necessary).

If vacuum, exhaust, oil or coolant leaks develop, indicating a need for gasket or seal replacement, the repairs can generally be made with the engine in the vehicle. The intake and exhaust manifold gaskets, oil pan gasket and cylinder head gaskets are all accessible with the engine in place.

Exterior engine components such as the intake and exhaust manifolds, the oil pan, the oil pump, the water pump, the starter motor, the alternator and the fuel injection system can be removed for repair with the engine in place. The timing chain and sprockets can also be replaced with the engine in the vehicle, but the camshaft (and balance shaft, if equipped) cannot be removed with the engine in place.

Since the cylinder heads can be removed without pulling the engine, valve component servicing can also be accomplished with the engine in the vehicle.

In extreme cases caused by a lack of necessary equipment, repair or replacement of piston rings, pistons, connecting rods and rod bearings is possible with the engine in the vehicle. However, this practice is not

3.6 Hold a finger over the spark plug opening until you feel air escaping, . . .

3.8 . . . then insert a soft plastic pen into the hole to detect piston movement

recommended because of the cleaning and preparation work that must be done to the components involved.

3 Top Dead Center (TDC) for number one piston – locating

Refer to illustrations 3.6 and 3.8

1   Top Dead Center (TDC) is the highest point in the cylinder each piston reaches as it travels up-and-down when the crankshaft turns. Each piston reaches TDC on the compression stroke and again on the exhaust stroke, but TDC generally refers to piston position on the compression stroke.

2   Positioning the piston(s) at TDC is an essential part of certain procedures such as timing chain/sprocket removal and camshaft removal.

3   Before beginning this procedure, be sure to place the transaxle in Park, apply the parking brake and block the rear wheels. Raise the front of the vehicle and support it securely on jackstands.

4   Remove the spark plugs (see Chapter 1).

5   When looking at the drivebelt end of the engine, normal crankshaft rotation is clockwise. In order to bring any piston to TDC, the crankshaft must be turned with a socket and ratchet attached to the bolt threaded into the center of the vibration damper on the crankshaft.

Models with distributorless (C3I) ignition

6   Have an assistant turn the crankshaft with a socket and ratchet as described above while you hold a finger over the number one spark plug hole **(see illustration)**. **Note:** *See the cylinder numbering diagram in the specifications for this Chapter.*

7   When the piston approaches TDC, air pressure will be felt at the spark plug hole. Instruct your assistant to turn the crankshaft slowly.

8   Insert a plastic pen into the spark plug hole **(see illustration)**. As the

piston rises the pen will be pushed out. Note the point where the pen stops moving out – this is TDC.

9   After the number one piston has been positioned at TDC on the compression stroke, TDC for any of the remaining pistons can be located by repeating the procedure described above and following the firing order.

Models with distributor (HEI) ignition

10   Make a mark on the distributor housing directly below the number one spark plug wire terminal on the distributor cap. **Note:** *The terminal numbers are usually marked on the spark plug wires, near the distributor. Remove the distributor cap.*

11   Turn the crankshaft with a socket and ratchet (see Step 5) until the line on the vibration damper is aligned with the zero mark on the timing scale.

12   The rotor should now be pointing directly at the mark on the distributor housing. If it isn't, the piston is at TDC on the exhaust stroke – to get the piston on the compression stroke, turn the crankshaft one complete turn (360-degrees) clockwise. When the rotor is pointing at the number one spark plug wire terminal in the distributor cap (which is indicated by the mark on the housing) and the ignition timing marks are aligned, the number one piston is at TDC on the compression stroke.

4 Rocker arm covers – removal and installation

Refer to illustrations 4.2a, 4.2b, 4.3, 4.5a, 4.5b, 4.8 and 4.12

Front cover removal

1   Disconnect the negative battery cable from the battery.

2   Remove the spark plug wires from the spark plugs and remove the harness cover **(see illustrations)**. Number each wire before removal to ensure correct reinstallation.

4.2a Unclip the harness cover

4.2b Front rocker arm cover details – 3800 engine shown

1   *Coil module*   2   *Spark plug wire holder*

2A

4.3   Detach the PCV tube (except 3800 engine)

1   *PCV tube*   2   *Mounting nuts*

3   Remove the PCV tube **(see illustration)** from the cover (except 3800 engine).
4   On 3800 engines, remove the drivebelt (see Chapter 1) and the alternator brace.
5   Remove the rocker arm cover mounting bolts/nuts **(see illustrations)**.
6   Detach the rocker arm cover. **Note:** *If the cover sticks to the cylinder head, use a soft-face hammer to dislodge it.*

Rear cover removal

7   Disconnect the negative battery cable from the battery.

8   Remove the spark plug wires from the spark plugs and remove the wire holder **(see illustration)**. Be sure each wire is labeled before removal to ensure correct reinstallation.
9   Remove the serpentine drivebelt (see Chapter 1).
10   Remove the power steering pump, if necessary (see Chapter 10).

3.0 and 3.8 liter engines
11   Remove the ignition coil assembly (see Chapter 5).
12   Remove the drivebelt tensioner **(see illustration)**.
13   Remove the alternator, if necessary (see Chapter 5).
14   Remove the engine lift bracket and rear alternator brace.
15   Drain the coolant (see Chapter 1) and remove the throttle body coolant hoses.

3800 engines
16   Remove the EGR pipe, valve and adapter (see Chapter 6).

All engines
17   Remove the rocker arm cover mounting bolts/nuts.
18   Detach the rocker arm cover. **Note:** *If the cover sticks to the cylinder head, use a soft-face hammer to dislodge it.*

Installation

19   The mating surfaces of the cylinder head and rocker arm cover must be perfectly clean when the covers are installed. Use a gasket scraper to remove all traces of sealant or old gasket, then clean the mating surfaces with lacquer thinner or acetone (if there's sealant or oil on the mating surfaces when the cover is installed, oil leaks may develop). The rocker arm covers are made of aluminum, so be extra careful not to nick or gouge the mating surfaces with the scraper.

4.5a   Rocker arm cover mounting details – exploded view (except 3800 engine)

| 1 | Nut | 3 | Rubber grommet |
| 2 | Washer | 4 | Gasket |

4.5b   Rocker arm cover mounting details – exploded view (3800 engine)

| 1 | Cover | 3 | Gasket |
| 2 | Bolt | | |

4.8   Rear rocker arm cover mounting details – 3800 engine

1   *Spark plug wires*   2   *Spark plug wire holder*

4.12   Drivebelt tensioner mounting details – exploded view

1   *Tensioner*   2   *Bolts*

5.2a   1985 model intake and exhaust rocker arms are different and are marked to prevent mix-up

5.2b   Positions of the earlier rocker arms when installed correctly on the engine (1985 models)

5.4   Rocker arm components – exploded view (1986 and later VIN C and VIN L engines)

1	Bolt	3	Rocker arm
2	Rocker arm pivot	4	Pushrod guide

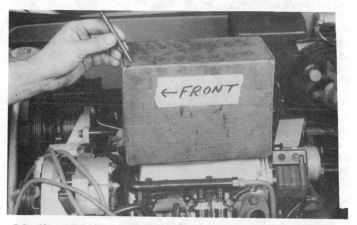

5.6   If more than one pushrod is being removed, store them in a perforated cardboard box to prevent mix-ups during installation – note the label indicating the front of the engine

20   On 3800 engines, apply GM no. 12345493 (or equivalent) to the mounting bolt threads. Place the rocker arm cover and new gasket in position, then (on 3800 engines) install the bolts or (on 3.0 and 3.8 liter engines) washers, mounting nuts and new rubber grommets.

21   Tighten the bolts/nuts in several steps to the torque listed in this Chapter's specifications.

22   Complete the installation by reversing the removal procedure. Be sure to add coolant if it was drained.

23   Start the engine and check for oil leaks at the rocker arm cover-to-head joints.

5   Rocker arms and pushrods – removal, inspection and installation

Refer to illustrations 5.2a, 5.2b, 5.2c and 5.3

Note: Store each set of rocker components separately in a marked plastic bag to ensure that they're installed in their original locations.

1   Refer to Section 4 and detach the rocker arm covers from the cylinder heads.

2   On models with rocker arm shafts, loosen the three bolts on each shaft a little at a time, working from the center out. On 3.0 and 3.8 liter engines, note the locations of the rocker arm cover mounting studs for correct location. Remove the nylon retainers with pliers and slide the rocker arms off the shafts. Keep track of the rocker arm positions, since they must be returned to the same locations **(see illustrations)**.

3   On Vin K engines, loosen the rocker arm pivot bolts one at a time and detach the rocker arms and bolts.

4   On Vin C and VIN L engines, loosen the rocker arm pivot bolts one at a time and detach the rocker arms, bolts, pivots and pivot retainers **(see illustration)**.

5   If necessary, remove the pushrod guide from the cylinder head.

6   Remove the pushrods and store them separately to make sure they don't get mixed up during installation **(see illustration)**.

Inspection

7   Check each rocker arm for wear, cracks and other damage, especially where the pushrods and valve stems contact the rocker arm.

8   Check the pivot seat in each rocker arm and the pivot faces. Look for galling, stress cracks and unusual wear patterns. If the rocker arms are worn or damaged, replace them with new ones and install new pivots or shafts as well.

9   Make sure the hole at the pushrod end of each rocker arm is open.

10   Inspect the pushrods for cracks and excessive wear at the ends. Roll each pushrod across a piece of plate glass to see if it's bent (if it wobbles, it's bent).

6.4   This is what the air hose adapter that threads into the spark plug hole looks like – they're commonly available from auto parts stores

Installation

11   Lubricate the lower end of each pushrod with clean engine oil or moly-base grease and install them in their original locations. Make sure each pushrod seats completely in the lifter socket.

12   Apply moly-base grease to the ends of the valve stems, the upper ends of the pushrods and to the pivot faces to prevent damage to the mating surfaces before engine oil pressure builds up.

13   If removed, install the pushrod guide onto the cylinder head.

14   Coat the rocker arm pivot bolt threads with GM thread lock compound no. 12345493 (or equivalent).

15   On models with rocker arm shafts, tighten the three bolts on each shaft a little at a time, working from the center out until the torque listed in this Chapter's Specifications is reached.

16   On Vin K engines, install the rocker arms and bolts. On Vin C and VIN L engines, install the pivot retainers, pivots rocker arms and bolts. Tighten the bolts to the torque listed in this Chapter's specifications.

17   Install the rocker arm covers (see Section 4).

---

6   Valve springs, retainers and seals – replacement

Refer to illustrations 6.4, 6.8, 6.9 and 6.17

Note: *Broken valve springs and defective valve stem seals can be replaced without removing the cylinder heads. Two special tools and a compressed air source are normally required to perform this operation, so read through this Section carefully and rent or buy the tools before beginning the job. If compressed air is not available, a length of nylon rope can be used to keep the valves from falling into the cylinder during this procedure.*

1   Refer to Section 4 and remove the rocker arm cover from the affected cylinder head. If all of the valve stem seals are being replaced, remove both rocker arm covers.

2   Remove the spark plug from the cylinder which has the defective component. If all of the valve stem seals are being replaced, all of the spark plugs should be removed.

3   Turn the crankshaft until the piston in the affected cylinder is at Top Dead Center on the compression stroke (refer to Section 3 for instructions). If you're replacing all of the valve stem seals, begin with cylinder number one and work on the valves for one cylinder at a time. Move from cylinder-to-cylinder following the firing order sequence (1-6-5-4-3-2).

4   Thread an adapter into the spark plug hole **(see illustration)** and connect an air hose from a compressed air source to it. Most auto parts stores can supply the air hose adapter. **Note:** *Many cylinder compression gauges utilize a screw-in fitting that may work with your air hose quick-disconnect fitting.*

5   Remove the bolt, pivot and rocker arm for the valve with the defective part and pull out the pushrod (see Section 5). If all of the valve stem seals are being replaced, all of the rocker arms and pushrods should be removed.

6   Apply compressed air to the cylinder. The valves should be held in place by the air pressure. If the valve faces or seats are in poor condition,

6.8   After compressing the valve spring, remove the keepers with a magnet (as shown here) or small needle-nose pliers

6.9   Valve components – exploded view

1   *Valve keepers*
2   *Valve spring retainer*
3   *Valve spring*
4   *Valve guide seal*
5   *Cylinder head*
6   *Valve*

leaks may prevent the air pressure from retaining the valves – refer to the alternative procedure below.

7   If you don't have access to compressed air, an alternative method can be used. Position the piston at a point just before TDC on the compression stroke, then feed a long piece of nylon rope through the spark plug hole until it fills the combustion chamber. Be sure to leave the end of the rope hanging out of the engine so it can be removed easily. Use a large breaker bar and socket to rotate the crankshaft in the normal direction of rotation until slight resistance is felt.

8   Stuff shop rags into the cylinder head holes above and below the valves to prevent parts and tools from falling into the engine, then use a valve spring compressor to compress the spring. Remove the keepers with small needle-nose pliers or a magnet **(see illustration)**. **Note:** *A couple of different types of tools are available for compressing the valve springs with the head in place. One type grips the lower spring coils and presses on the retainer as the knob is turned, while the other type, shown here, utilizes the rocker arm bolt for leverage. Both types work very well, although the lever type is usually less expensive.*

9   Remove the spring retainer and valve spring, then remove the guide seal **(see illustration)**. 3.0 and 3.8 liter engines have seals on the intake

6.17 Apply a small dab of grease to each keeper as shown here before installation – it will hold them in place on the valve stem as the spring is released

7.6 Pinch the tabs (arrows) together with pliers to detach the cables from the bracket

7.10 Remove the hoses (arrows) and tubes from the intake manifold (3.8 liter shown, others similar)

7.12 Unplug the electrical connectors (arrows) and move the harness aside

2A

valves only. **Note:** *If air pressure fails to hold the valve in the closed position during this operation, the valve face or seat is probably damaged. If so, the cylinder head will have to be removed for additional repair operations.*

10 Wrap a rubber band or tape around the top of the valve stem so the valve won't fall into the combustion chamber, then release the air pressure. **Note:** *If a rope was used instead of air pressure, turn the crankshaft slightly in the direction opposite normal rotation.*

11 Inspect the valve stem for damage. Rotate the valve in the guide and check the end for eccentric movement, which would indicate that the valve is bent.

12 Move the valve up-and-down in the guide and make sure it doesn't bind. If the valve stem binds, either the valve is bent or the guide is damaged. In either case, the head will have to be removed for repair.

13 Reapply air pressure to the cylinder to retain the valve in the closed position, then remove the tape or rubber band from the valve stem. If a rope was used instead of air pressure, rotate the crankshaft in the normal direction of rotation until slight resistance is felt.

14 Lubricate the valve stem with clean engine oil and install a new valve guide seal. Using a hammer and a deep socket or seal installation tool, gently tap the seal into place until it's completely seated on the guide.

15 Install the spring in position over the valve.

16 Install the valve spring retainer and compress the valve spring.

17 Position the keepers in the upper groove. Apply a small dab of grease to the inside of each keeper to hold it in place if necessary **(see illustration)**. Remove the pressure from the spring tool and make sure the keepers are seated.

18 Disconnect the air hose and remove the adapter from the spark plug hole. If a rope was used in place of air pressure, pull it out of the cylinder.

19 Install the rocker arm(s) and pushrod(s).

20 Install the spark plug(s) and connect the wire(s).

21 Refer to Section 4 and install the rocker arm cover(s).

22 Start and run the engine, then check for oil leaks and unusual sounds coming from the rocker arm cover area.

---

7 Intake manifold – removal and installation

Refer to illustrations 7.6, 7.10, 7.12, 7.13, 7.14, 7.15, 7.34, 7.36a and 7.36b

Removal (one-piece manifold)

1 Relieve the fuel system pressure (see Chapter 4).

2 Disconnect the negative battery cable from the battery.

3 Remove the air intake duct, the mass airflow sensor and the throttle body (see Chapter 4).

4 Remove the power steering pump-to-manifold brace (Chapter 10).

5 Remove the fuel injectors (see Chapter 4).

6 Remove the control cables from their brackets **(see illustration)**.

7 Remove the drivebelt (see Chapter 1).

8 Disconnect and remove the alternator and brackets (see Chapter 5).

9 Drain the cooling system (see Chapter 1).

10 Disconnect the coolant tubes and hoses at the manifold **(see illustration)**.

11 Remove the ignition module assembly or distributor cap and spark plug wires (see Chapters 1 and 5).

12 Label and disconnect the fuel and vacuum lines and electrical wires at the manifold **(see illustration)**. When disconnecting fuel line fittings, be

7.13   Intake manifold mounting bolt locations (arrows) (one–piece manifold shown)

7.14   Carefully pry up on a casting boss – don't pry between gasket surfaces

prepared to catch some fuel, then cap the fittings to prevent contamination.

13   Remove the manifold mounting bolts **(see illustration)**. **Note:** *On 3.0 and 3.8 liter models, one bolt requires a Torx T-50 drive bit (GM tool no. J 24394 – or equivalent).*

14   Separate the manifold from the engine **(see illustration)**. Do not pry between the manifold and heads, as damage to the gasket sealing surfaces may result. If you're installing a new manifold, transfer all fittings and sensors to the new manifold.

Removal (two-piece manifold)

Note: *On VIN L engines, don't disassemble the upper intake manifold from the lower intake manifold unless one of the components requires replacement. On VIN K engines, it is necessary to first remove the upper manifold prior to removing the lower manifold.*

15   Relieve the fuel system pressure (see Chapter 4).
16   Disconnect the negative battery cable from the battery.
17   Remove the fuel injector sight shield and the air intake duct.
18   Disconnect the spark plug wires from the engine and set them aside.
19   Remove the fuel rail and injector assembly (see Chapter 4).
20   Remove the exhaust heat shield.
21   Remove the ignition coil/module assembly (see Chapter 5).
22   Disconnect all hoses from the manifold assembly.
23   Disconnect the throttle cable and remove the cable bracket from the cylinder head.
24   Remove the drivebelt (see Chapter 1).
25   Remove the drivebelt tensioner.
26   Disconnect and remove the alternator and brackets (see Chapter 5).
27   Drain the cooling system (see Chapter 1).
28   Disconnect the coolant hoses and tubes at the manifold. When disconnecting fuel line fittings, be prepared to catch some fuel, then cap the fittings to prevent contamination.
29   Remove the EGR valve outlet pipe.
30   On VIN L engines, perform the following:
    a) Remove the manifold assembly mounting bolts.
    b) Separate the manifold assembly from the engine. Do not pry between the manifold and heads, as damage to the gasket sealing surfaces may result. If you're installing a new manifold assembly, transfer all fittings and sensors to the new manifold assembly. **Caution:** *On VIN K engines, do not try to remove the lower manifold without first removing the upper manifold as there are two additional lower manifold mounting bolts located under the upper manifold.*
31   On VIN K engines, perform the following:
    a) Remove the upper manifold mounting bolts.
    b) Separate the upper manifold from the lower manifold. Do not pry between the upper and lower manifolds, as damage to the gasket sealing surfaces may result.

7.32   Remove all traces of gasket material, but don't gouge the soft aluminum

    c) Remove the two additional lower manifold mounting bolts located at the front and rear corners.
    d) Separate the lower manifold from the engine. Do not pry between the manifold and heads, as damage to the gasket sealing surfaces may result. If you're installing new manifolds, transfer all fittings and sensors to the new manifold assembly.

Installation

Note: *The mating surfaces of the cylinder heads, block and manifold must be perfectly clean when the manifold is installed. Gasket removal solvents in aerosol cans are available at most auto parts stores and may be helpful when removing old gasket material that's stuck to the heads and manifold (since the manifold is made of aluminum, aggressive scraping can cause damage). Be sure to follow the directions printed on the container.*

32   Use a gasket scraper to remove all traces of sealant and old gasket material **(see illustration)**, then clean the mating surfaces with lacquer thinner or acetone. If there's old sealant or oil on the mating surfaces when the manifold is installed, oil or vacuum leaks may develop. Use a vacuum cleaner to remove any gasket material that falls into the intake ports or the lifter valley.

33   Use a tap of the correct size to chase the threads in the bolt holes, then use compressed air (if available) to remove the debris from the holes. **Warning:** *Wear safety glasses or a face shield to protect your eyes when using compressed air.*

34   If steel manifold gaskets are used, apply GM sealant number 1050026 or equivalent to both sides of the gaskets before positioning them on the heads. Apply RTV sealant to the ends of the new manifold-to-block seals, then install them. Make sure the pointed end of the seal fits snugly against both the head and block **(see illustration)**.

7.36a Intake manifold bolt tightening sequence (one-piece manifold)

7.34 Intake manifold mounting details (one-piece manifold) – exploded view

1	Bolt	3	Intake manifold gasket
2	Intake manifold	4	Intake manifold seal

35 Carefully lower the manifold into place. Apply GM thread lock compound no. 12345493 (or equivalent) to the mounting bolt threads and install the bolts finger tight.

36 Tighten the mounting bolts in two stages, following the recommended sequence **(see illustration)**, until they're all at the torque listed in this Chapter's specifications.

37 Install the remaining components in the reverse order of removal.

38 Change the oil and filter and fill the cooling system (see Chapter 1). Start the engine and check for oil and vacuum leaks.

2A

7.36b Intake manifold bolt tightening sequence (two-piece manifold)

8 Valve lifters – removal, inspection and installation

Refer to illustrations 8.6a, 8.6b, 8.6c, 8.7, 8.8, 8.11a, 8.11b, 8.11c and 8.12

1 A noisy valve lifter can be isolated when the engine is idling. Hold a mechanic's stethoscope or a length of hose near the position of each valve while listening at the other end.

2 The most likely causes of noisy valve lifters are dirt trapped between the plunger and the lifter body or lack of oil flow, viscosity or pressure. Before condemning the lifters, we recommend checking the oil for fuel contamination, proper level, cleanliness and correct viscosity.

Removal

3 Remove the rocker arm cover(s) as described in Section 4.

4 Remove the rocker arms and pushrods (see Section 5).

5 Remove the intake manifold(s) as described in Section 7.

6 Earlier models have conventional lifters. Later production engines have roller lifters. Roller lifters are kept from turning by a guide plate and lifter guide **(see illustrations)**, which must be removed to access the lifters.

8.6a The guide plate is held in place by two bolts (arrows)

8.6b The lifter guides slip over the lifters

**8.6c   Roller lifter guide plate details
(1985 through 1991 models) – exploded view**

1	*Bolt*	*3*	*Pushrod*
2	*Guide plate*	*4*	*Lifter guide*

8.7   Many times you can remove the lifters by hand

**8.8   The lifters on an engine that has accumulated many miles
may have to be removed with a special tool – be sure to store the
lifters in an organized manner to make sure they're reinstalled in
their original locations**

7   There are several ways to extract the lifters from the bores. A special tool designed to grip and remove lifters is manufactured by many tool companies and is widely available, but it may not be required in every case **(see illustration)**. On newer engines without a lot of varnish buildup, the lifters can often be removed with a small magnet or even with your fingers. A machinist's scribe with a bent end can be used to pull the lifters out by positioning the point under the retainer ring in the top of each lifter. **Caution:** *Don't use pliers to remove the lifters unless you intend to replace them with new ones. The pliers will damage the precision machined and hardened lifters, rendering them useless.*

8   Before removing the lifters, arrange to store them in a clearly labelled box to ensure that they're reinstalled in their original locations. Remove the lifters and store them where they won't get dirty **(see illustration)**.

Inspection

9   Parts for valve lifters are not available separately. The work required to remove them from the engine again if repair is unsuccessful outweighs any potential savings from repairing them.

**8.11a   If the bottom (foot) of any lifter is
worn concave, scratched or pitted,
replace the entire set with new lifters**

**8.11b   The bottom (foot) of each lifter
should be slightly convex – the side of
another lifter can be used as a
straightedge to check it (if it appears flat,
it's worn and should be discarded)**

**8.11c   Check the pushrod seat (arrow)
in the top of each lifter for wear**

8.12   The roller on roller lifters must turn freely – check for wear and excessive play as well

9.4   The exhaust manifolds are bolted to the crossover pipe (arrows)

10   Clean the lifters with solvent and dry them thoroughly without mixing them up.

Conventional lifters

11   Check each lifter wall, pushrod seat and foot for scuffing, score marks and uneven wear. Each lifter foot (the surface that rides on the cam lobe) must be slightly convex, although this can be difficult to determine by eye. If the base of the lifter is concavo **(see illustrations)**, the lifters and camshaft must be replaced. If the lifter walls are damaged or worn (which isn't very likely), inspect the lifter bores in the engine block as well. If the pushrod seats **(see illustration)** are worn, check the pushrod ends.

Roller lifters

12   Check the rollers carefully for wear and damage and make sure they turn freely without excessive play **(see illustration)**. The inspection procedure for conventional lifters also applies to roller lifters.

Installation

13   Used roller lifters can be reinstalled with a new camshaft and the original camshaft can be used if new lifters are installed.
14   If the conventional lifters are worn, they must be replaced with new ones and the camshaft must be replaced as well – never install used conventional lifters with a new camshaft or new lifters with a used camshaft.
15   When reinstalling used lifters, make sure they're replaced in their original bores. Soak new lifters in oil to remove trapped air. Coat all lifters with moly-base grease or engine assembly lube prior to installation.
16   The remaining installation steps are the reverse of removal.
17   Run the engine and check for oil leaks.

---

9   Exhaust manifolds – removal and installation

Warning: *Allow the engine to cool completely before beginning this procedure.*

Note: *Exhaust system fasteners are frequently difficult to remove – they get frozen in place because of the heating/cooling cycle to which they're constantly exposed. To ease removal, apply penetrating oil to the threads of all exhaust manifold and exhaust pipe fasteners and allow it to soak in.*

Removal – front manifold

Refer to illustrations 9.4, 9.7 and 9.8

1   Disconnect the negative battery cable.
2   Remove the cooling fan for access (see Chapter 3).
3   Remove the mass airflow sensor, air duct and crankcase ventilation pipe, if necessary (see Chapter 4).
4   Unbolt the manifold from the crossover pipe **(see illustration)**.
5   Remove the dipstick tube hold-down nut and wiggle the dipstick tube out of the block.
6   Detach the spark plug wires from the front spark plugs (see Chapter 1).
7   Remove the heat shield, if equipped **(see illustration)**.
8   Unbolt and remove the exhaust manifold **(see illustration)**.

2A

9.7   Typical front exhaust manifold heat shield

1   Shield   3   Nut
2   Washer

9.8   Front exhaust manifold

1   Manifold   2   Bolt

9.18   Typical rear exhaust manifold heat shield

1   Shield   2   Fasteners

9.23   Rear exhaust manifold

1   Manifold   2   Bolt

Removal – rear manifold

Refer to illustrations 9.18 and 9.23

9   Disconnect the negative battery cable.

10   Drain the coolant from the radiator (see Chapter 1).

11   Remove the mass airflow sensor, air duct and crankcase ventilation pipe, if necessary (see Chapter 4).

12   Remove the two nuts attaching the crossover pipe to the rear exhaust manifold.

13   Disconnect the spark plug wires from the rear spark plugs (see Chapter 1).

14   Remove the EGR pipe and transaxle dipstick tube if it's in the way (see Chapters 6 and 7).

15   Unbolt the power steering pump (some models) without removing the hoses and hold it to one side with wire (see Chapter 10).

16   Remove the ignition module bracket nuts and studs (except 3800). On 3800 models, detach the alternator support bracket. Refer to Chapter 5 as necessary.

17   Remove the heater hoses and coolant tube brackets and tubing above the exhaust manifold.

18   Remove the manifold heat shield, if equipped **(see illustration)**.

19   Detach the IAC wiring from the throttle body.

20   Set the parking brake, block the rear wheels and raise the front of the vehicle, supporting it securely on jackstands.

21   Working under the vehicle, remove the two exhaust pipe-to-manifold bolts.

22   Disconnect the oxygen sensor wire (the sensor is threaded into the manifold), then lower the vehicle.

23   Remove the six bolts and detach the manifold from the head **(see illustration)**.

Installation

24   Clean the mating surfaces of the manifold and cylinder head to remove all traces of old gasket material, then check the manifold for warpage and cracks. If the manifold gasket was blown, take the manifold to an automotive machine shop for resurfacing.

25   Place the manifold in position with a new gasket and install the bolts finger tight.

26   Starting in the middle and working out toward the ends, tighten the mounting bolts a little at a time until all of them are at the specified torque.

27   Install the remaining components in the reverse order of removal.

28   Start the engine and check for exhaust leaks between the manifold and cylinder head and between the manifold and exhaust pipe.

---

10   Cylinder heads – removal and installation

Refer to illustrations 10.3a, 10.3b, 10.3c, 10.3d, 10.9, 10.10, 10.13, 10.16 and 10.19

Removal

1   Disconnect the negative battery cable at the battery.

10.3a   The alternator bracket is attached to the cylinder head with two nuts or bolts (arrows)

10.3b   Remove the nut from the exhaust support bracket (3.8 liter shown)

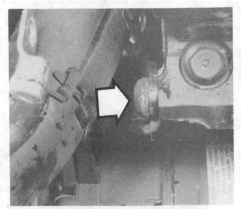

10.3c   The air conditioner compressor bracket is attached to the cylinder head with one Torx T-50 bolt (arrow)

10.3d   Drivebelt tensioner bolt locations (arrows) (typical)

10.9   Cylinder head bolt LOOSENING sequence

2   Disconnect the spark plug wires and remove the spark plugs (see Chapter 1). Be sure to label the plug wires to simplify reinstallation.

3   Remove the nuts/bolts holding the brackets to the head **(see illustrations)**.

4   Disconnect all wires and hoses from the cylinder head(s). Be sure to label them to simplify reinstallation.

5   Remove the intake manifold as described in Section 7.

6   Detach the exhaust manifold(s) from the cylinder head(s) being removed (see Section 9).

7   Remove the rocker arm cover(s) (see Section 4).

8   Remove the rocker arms and pushrods (see Section 5).

9   Loosen the head bolts in 1/4-turn increments until they can be removed by hand. Work from bolt-to-bolt as shown **(see illustration)**.

10   Lift the head off the engine. If resistance is felt, don't pry between the head and block as damage to the mating surfaces will result. Recheck for head bolts that may have been overlooked, then use a hammer and block of wood to tap the head and break the gasket seal. Be careful because there are locating dowels in the block which position each head. As a last resort, pry each head up at the rear corner only and be careful not to damage anything **(see illustration)**. After removal, place the head on blocks of wood to prevent damage to the gasket surfaces.

11   Refer to Chapter 2, Part B, for cylinder head disassembly, inspection and valve service procedures.

Installation

12   The mating surfaces of the cylinder heads and block must be perfectly clean when the heads are installed.

13   Use a gasket scraper to remove all traces of carbon and old gasket material **(see illustration)**, then clean the mating surfaces with lacquer thinner or acetone. If there's oil on the mating surfaces when the heads are installed, the gaskets may not seal correctly and leaks may develop. When working on the block, it's a good idea to cover the lifter valley with shop rags to keep debris out of the engine. Use a shop rag or vacuum cleaner to remove any debris that falls into the cylinders.

14   Check the block and head mating surfaces for nicks, deep scratches and other damage. If damage is slight, it can be removed with a file; if it's excessive, machining may be the only alternative.

15   Use a tap of the correct size to chase the threads in the head bolt holes. Dirt, corrosion, sealant and damaged threads will affect torque readings.

2A

10.10   Pry carefully – don't force a tool between the gasket surfaces

10.13   Carefully remove all traces of old gasket material

10.16 Look for gasket marks (arrow) to ensure correct installation

10.19   Cylinder head bolt TIGHTENING sequence

16   Position the new gaskets over the dowel pins in the block. If steel gaskets are used, apply GM sealant no. 1050026 or equivalent. Install "non-retorquing" type gaskets dry (no sealant), unless the manufacturer states otherwise. Most gaskets are marked UP or TOP **(see illustration)** because they must be installed a certain way.

17   Carefully position the heads on the block without disturbing the gaskets.

18   Use NEW head bolts – don't reinstall the old ones – and apply GM sealant (no. 1052080 or equivalent) to the threads and the undersides of the bolt heads.

19   Tighten the bolts as directed in this Chapter's specifications in the sequence shown **(see illustration)**. This must be done in three steps, following the sequence each time. **Caution:** *On 1986 through 1988 models, if you reach 60 ft-lbs. at any time during the final two steps, stop immediately – DO NOT complete the balance of the 90-degree turn. Go on to the next bolt in the sequence.*

20   The remaining installation steps are the reverse of removal.

21   Change the oil and filter (see Chapter 1).

11   Vibration damper – removal and installation

Refer to illustrations 11.7a, 11.7b, 11.7c and 11.9
Caution: *The vibration damper is serviced as an assembly. Do not attempt to separate the pulley from the balancer hub.*

1   Disconnect the negative cable from the battery.

2   Loosen the lug nuts on the right front wheel.

3   Raise the vehicle and support it securely on jackstands.

4   Remove the right front wheel.

5   Remove the right front fender inner splash shield.

6   Remove the drivebelt (see Chapter 1).

7   Remove the lower bellhousing cover plate and hold the crankshaft with GM tool J 37096, or equivalent. If this tool is unavailable, position a large screwdriver in the ring gear teeth **(see illustrations)** to keep the crankshaft from turning while an assistant removes the crankshaft balancer bolt **(see illustration)**. The bolt is normally quite tight, so use a large breaker bar and a six-point socket.

11.7a   Hold the ring gear from turning with a special tool or . . .

    1   *J 37096*   2   *Ring gear*

11.7b   . . . wedge a large screwdriver in the teeth

11.7c Remove the bolt in the center of the hub (arrow)

11.9 Be sure to align the keyway (arrow) with the key in the crankshaft

8 The damper should pull off the crankshaft by hand. Leave the Woodruff key in place in the end of the crankshaft.

9 Installation is the reverse of removal. Align the keyway with the key **(see illustration)** and avoid bending the metal tabs. Be sure to apply moly-base grease to the seal contact surface on the back side of the damper (if it isn't lubricated, the seal lip could be damaged and oil leakage would result).

10 Apply sealant to the threads and tighten the crankshaft bolt to the torque listed in this Chapter's Specifications.

11 Reinstall the remaining components in the reverse order of removal.

12 Crankshaft front oil seal – replacement

Refer to illustrations 12.2 and 12.5

1 Remove the vibration damper (see Section 11). If there's a groove worn into the seal contact surface on the vibration damper, sleeves are available that fit over the groove, restoring the contact surface to like-new condition. These sleeves are sometimes included with the seal kit. Check with your parts supplier for details.

2 Pry the old oil seal out with a seal removal tool or a screwdriver **(see illustration)**. Be very careful not to nick or otherwise damage the crank-

shaft in the process.

3 Apply a thin coat of RTV-type sealant to the outer edge of the new seal. Lubricate the seal lip with moly-base grease or clean engine oil.

4 Place the seal squarely in position in the bore and press it into place with special tool J 35354, or equivalent. Make sure the seal enters the bore squarely and seats completely.

5 If the special tool is unavailable, carefully guide the seal into place with a large socket or piece of pipe and a hammer **(see illustration)**. The outer diameter of the socket or pipe should be the same size as the seal outer diameter.

6 Install the vibration damper (see Section 11).

7 Reinstall the remaining parts in the reverse order of removal.

8 Start the engine and check for oil leaks at the seal.

13 Timing chain cover – removal and installation

Refer to illustrations 13.9, 13.10, 13.11, 13.12 and 13.16

Note: *A special tool is required to complete this procedure on models equipped with distributorless ignition – read through all steps before beginning. In 1987 a change was made to the timing chain cover and oil*

12.2 Pry out the old seal with a seal removal tool (shown here) or a screwdriver

12.5 Gently drive the new seal into place with a hammer and large socket

2A

13.9   Timing chain cover bolt locations (arrows)

13.10   Timing chain cover and related components – exploded view

1	Front crankshaft oil seal	3 Spring
2	Camshaft button	

pressure relief valve. If excessive wear in the camshaft thrust area or other related problems are noted, refer to Buick Service Bulletin no. 87-6-5, Dec. 86, reference no. 87-036-6.

1   Disconnect the negative battery cable from the battery.

2   Set the parking brake and put the transmission in Park. Raise the front of the vehicle and support it securely on jackstands. Remove the splash shield from the right inner fender.

3   Drain the oil and coolant (see Chapter 1).

4   Remove the coolant hoses from the timing chain cover.

5   Remove the large (8 mm) water pump-to-block bolts, leaving the smaller (6 mm) diameter bolts in place.

6   Remove the vibration damper (see Section 11).

7   Unplug the connectors from the oil pressure, camshaft and crankshaft sensors on distributorless ignition models or remove the distributor, if equipped (see Chapter 5).

8   Remove the oil pan (see Section 17).

9   Remove the timing chain cover-to-engine block bolts **(see illustration)**. Note that two of the bolts also secure the crankshaft sensor. Lift the sensor off when removing these bolts.

10   Separate the cover from the front of the engine. Inside the cam sprocket is a spring and button that controls camshaft end play. If they are missing, look for them in the oil pan **(see illustration)**.

11   Use a gasket scraper to remove all traces of old gasket material and sealant from the cover and engine block **(see illustration)**. The cover is made of aluminum, so be careful not to nick or gouge it. Clean the gasket sealing surfaces with lacquer thinner or acetone.

12   Check the camshaft thrust surface in the cover for excessive wear **(see illustration)**. If it's worn, a new cover will be required (see the note at

the beginning of this Section).

13   On 1986 and later models, the oil pump cover must be removed and the cavity packed with petroleum jelly as described in Section 15 before the cover is installed.

14   Apply a thin layer of RTV sealant to both sides of the new gasket, then position the gasket on the engine block (the dowel pins should keep it in place). Make sure the spring and button are in place in the end of the camshaft (hold them in place with grease), then attach the cover to the engine. The oil pump drive must engage with the crankshaft or distributor gear.

15   Apply GM thread sealant (no. 1052080 or equivalent) to the bolt threads, then install them finger tight. Install the crankshaft sensor, but leave the bolts finger tight until Step 16. Follow a criss-cross pattern when tightening the other bolts and work up to the torque listed in this Chapter's specifications in three steps to avoid warping the cover.

16   Use GM special tool (no. J 37089 or equivalent) to position the crankshaft sensor on the timing cover **(see illustration)**. Tighten the bolts to the torque listed in this Chapter's specifications for the timing chain cover.

17   The remainder of installation is the reverse of removal.

18   Add oil and coolant, start the engine and check for leaks.

---

14   Oil filter adapter and pressure regulator valve – removal and installation (1986 and later models only)

Refer to illustrations 14.3, 14.4 and 14.6

Note: *The oil pressure regulator valve and timing chain cover were changed in 1987. Refer to Buick Service Bulletin no. 87-6-5, Dec. 86, reference no. 87-036-6.*

13.11   Remove all traces of old gasket material

13.12   The camshaft thrust surface on this cover is worn away (arrow) which means that a new cover must be installed

13.16   Slip special tool J37089 over the end of the crankshaft to position the sensor, then tighten the mounting bolts (Distributorless ignition models only)

14.3   Oil filter adapter and pressure regulator (1986 and later models) – exploded view

1	*Oil filter adapter*	*4*	*Oil pressure*
2	*Bolt (4)*		*regulator valve*
3	*Gasket*	*5*	*Spring*

4   Remove the pressure regulator valve and spring **(see illustration)**. Use a gasket scraper to remove all traces of the old gasket.
5   Clean all parts with solvent and dry them with compressed air (if available). **Warning:** *Wear eye protection.* Check for wear, score marks and valve binding.
6   Installation is the reverse of removal. Be sure to use a new gasket. **Caution:** *If a new timing chain cover is being installed on the engine, make sure the oil pressure relief valve supplied with the new cover is used. If the old style relief valve is installed in a new cover, oil pressure problems will result* **(see illustration)**.
7   Tighten the bolts to the torque listed in this Chapter's Specifications.
8   Run the engine and check for oil leaks.

14.4   Remove the pressure regulator valve and spring, then check the valve for wear and damage

1   Remove the oil filter (see Chapter 1).
2   Remove the timing chain cover (see Section 13).
3   Remove the four bolts holding the oil filter adapter to the timing chain cover **(see illustration)**. The cover is spring loaded, so remove the bolts while keeping pressure on the cover, then release the spring pressure carefully.

15   Oil pump – removal, inspection and installation

1985 models

Removal
Refer to illustration 15.3
1   Remove the oil filter.
2   Remove the oil pump cover-to-timing chain cover attaching bolts.

14.6   If the timing chain cover is replaced with a new one, be sure to use the correct pressure relief valve – an early valve will not work in a new timing chain cover!

15.3   Oil pump cover installation details (1985 models)

1	Plug	5	Cover	3	Spring
2	Washer	6	Gasket	4	Relief valve

15.14   The oil pump cover is attached to the inside of the timing chain cover – a T-30 Torx driver is required for removal of the screws

Inspection

5   Clean all the components thoroughly in solvent.

6   Inspect all components for wear or scoring.

7   Temporarily install the oil pump gears back into the body and measure the gear lash and side clearance. Place a straight edge across the gears and pump body and measure the end clearance.

8   Compare the measurements to the specifications, replacing any worn or damaged components. **Note:** *Considering that a malfunctioning oil pump will cause sever engine damage, we recommend replacing the oil pump gears, cover and body if there's any doubt to their condition.*

Installation

9   Pack the pump body with petroleum jelly and install the gears forcing the petroleum jelly into every cavity. Failure to do so could cause the pump to lose its prime when the engine is started, resulting in engine damage from lack of oil pressure.

10   Install the pump cover, using a new gasket. Install the oil filter and add clean oil to the engine as necessary.

15.15   Oil pump components – exploded view

1	Screw	4	Inner gear
2	Oil pump cover	5	Timing chain cover
3	Outer gear		

1986 and later models

Refer to illustrations 15.14, 15.15, 15.20, 15.21 and 15.22

Removal

11   Remove the oil filter (see Chapter 1).

12   Remove the oil filter adapter, pressure regulator valve and spring (see Section 14).

13   Remove the timing chain cover (see Section 13).

14   Remove the oil pump cover-to-timing chain cover bolts **(see illustration)**.

3   Lift off the cover, oil pump drive gear and driven gears as an assembly **(see illustration)**.

4   Do not attempt to remove the oil filter bypass valve and spring – they are staked in place.

15.20   Measuring the outer gear-to-housing clearance with a feeler gauge

15.21   Measuring the inner gear-to-outer gear clearance with a feeler gauge

15.22   Measuring gear end clearance with the special fixture and a dial indicator

15   Lift out the cover and oil pump gears as an assembly **(see illustration)**.

Inspection

16   Clean the parts with solvent and dry them with compressed air (if available). **Warning:** *Wear eye protection!*
17   Inspect all components for wear and score marks. Replace any worn out or damaged parts.
18   Refer to Section 14 for bypass valve information.
19   Reinstall the gears in the timing chain cover.
20   Measure the outer gear-to-housing clearance with a feeler gauge **(see illustration)**.
21   Measure the inner gear-to-outer gear clearance at several points **(see illustration)**.
22   Use a dial indicator or straightedge and feeler gauges to measure the gear end clearance (distance from the gear to the gasket surface of the cover) **(see illustration)**.
23   Check for pump cover warpage by laying a precision straightedge across the cover and trying to slip a feeler gauge between the cover and straightedge.
24   Compare the measurements to this Chapter's Specifications. Replace all worn or damaged components with new ones.

Installation

25   Remove the gears and pack the pump cavity with petroleum jelly.
26   Install the gears – make sure petroleum jelly is forced into every cavity. Failure to do so could cause the pump to lose its prime when the engine is started, causing damage from lack of oil pressure.

27   Install the pump cover, using a new GM gasket only – its thickness is critical for maintaining the correct clearances.
28   Install the pressure regulator spring and valve.
29   Install the timing chain cover.
30   Install the oil filter and check the oil level. Start and run the engine and check for correct oil pressure, then look carefully for oil leaks at the timing chain cover.

16   Timing chain and sprockets – removal and installation

Refer to illustrations 16.1, 16.3, 16.4, 16.5a, 16.5b, 16.5c and 16.6

Removal

1   Remove the timing chain cover (see Section 13), then slide the shim off the nose of the crankshaft **(see illustration)**.
2   The timing chain should be replaced with a new one if the total free play midway between the sprockets exceeds one inch. Failure to replace the timing chain may result in erratic engine performance, loss of power and lowered fuel mileage.
3   Temporarily install the vibration damper bolt and turn the crankshaft clockwise to align the timing marks on the crankshaft and camshaft sprockets directly opposite each other **(see illustration)**.
4   Detach the spring **(see illustration)**, then remove the bolt and separate the timing chain damper from the block.
5   Remove the camshaft sprocket bolts **(see illustrations)**. Try not to turn the camshaft in the process (if you do, realign the timing marks after the bolts are loosened).

2A

16.1   The shim has a notch in it to fit over the key in the crankshaft

16.3   The marks on the crankshaft and camshaft sprockets (arrows) must be aligned adjacent to each other as shown here (the mark on the camshaft sprocket is a dimple – the one on the crankshaft sprocket is a raised dot)

16.4   Carefully release the spring with needle-nose pliers

16.5a   3.0 and 3.8 liter engine timing chain components – exploded view

1	Timing marks (aligned)	4 Crankshaft sprocket
2	Camshaft sprocket bolts	5 Chain dampener components
3	Shim	6 Camshaft flange

16.5b   On 3.0 and 3.8 liter engines, the camshaft position sensor is activated by a small magnet held in place by a special copper-colored bolt – note its location for correct installation later

16.5c   Timing chain components – exploded view (3800 engine only)

1	Camshaft sprocket bolts (3)	6	Chain damper
2	Timing chain	7	Damper bolt
3	Camshaft sprocket	8	Spring
4	Camshaft gear	9	Crankshaft sprocket
5	Key		

11   Install the camshaft sprocket bolts and tighten them to the torque listed in this Chapter's specifications.

12   Attach the timing chain damper assembly to the block and install the spring.

13   Install the camshaft thrust button and spring. Hold it in place with grease.

14   Lubricate the chain and sprocket with clean engine oil and install the timing chain cover (see Section 13).

16.6   Guide the chain and sprockets off as an assembly

6   Alternately pull the camshaft sprocket and then the crankshaft sprocket forward and remove the sprockets and timing chain as an assembly **(see illustration)**.

7   On 3800 engines, remove the camshaft gear.

8   Clean the timing chain components with solvent and dry them with compressed air (if available). **Warning:** *Wear eye protection.*

9   Inspect the components for wear and damage. Look for teeth that are deformed, chipped, pitted, polished or discolored.

Installation

Note: *If the crankshaft has been disturbed, install the sprocket temporarily and turn the crankshaft until the mark on the crankshaft sprocket is exactly at the top. If the camshaft was disturbed, install the sprocket temporarily and turn the camshaft until the timing mark is at the bottom, opposite the mark on the crankshaft sprocket* **(see illustration 16.3).**

10   Assemble the timing chain on the sprockets, then slide the sprocket and chain assembly onto the shafts with the timing marks aligned as shown in illustration 16.3. **Note:** *On 3800 models, be sure to install the camshaft gear. Aligning the gear with the balance shaft gear is covered in Chapter 2B under camshaft and balance shaft installation.*

---

17   Oil pan – removal and installation

Refer to illustrations 17.4 and 17.6

1   Disconnect the cable from the negative battery terminal.

2   Raise the vehicle and place it securely on jackstands. Drain the engine oil and replace the oil filter (refer to Chapter 1 if necessary).

3   Remove the driveplate inspection cover and starter, if necessary for access (refer to Chapter 5). On 1992 and later models, disconnect the electrical connector from the oil lever sensor.

4   Remove the oil pan mounting bolts **(see illustration)** and carefully separate the oil pan from the block. Don't pry between the block and the pan or damage to the sealing surfaces may result and oil leaks may develop. Instead, tap the pan with a soft-face hammer to break the gasket seal.

5   Clean the pan with solvent and remove all old sealant and gasket material from the block and pan mating surfaces. Clean the mating surfaces with lacquer thinner or acetone and make sure the bolt holes in the block are clear. Check the oil pan flange for distortion, particularly around the bolt holes. If necessary, place the pan on a block of wood and use a hammer to flatten and restore the gasket surface.

6   Always use a new gasket whenever the oil pan is installed **(see illustration)**.

7   Place the oil pan in position on the block and install the bolts.

8   After the bolts are installed, tighten them to the torque listed in this Chapter's specifications. Starting at the center, follow a criss-cross pattern and work up to the final torque in three steps.

9   The remaining steps are the reverse of the removal procedure.

10   Refill the engine with oil. Run the engine until normal operating temperature is reached and check for leaks.

17.4   The oil pan bolts (arrows) are located around the perimeter of the oil pan (viewed from below)

17.6   Oil pan mounting details – exploded view

1   Gasket   3   Bolts
2   Oil pan

---

18   Oil pump pickup tube and screen assembly – removal and installation

Refer to illustration 18.2

1   Remove the oil pan (see Section 17).
2   Unbolt the oil pump pickup tube and screen assembly and detach it from the engine **(see illustration)**.
3   Clean the screen and housing assembly with solvent and dry it with compressed air, if available. **Warning:** *Wear eye protection.*
4   If the oil screen is damaged or has metal chips in it, replace it. An abundance of metal chips indicates a major engine problem which must be corrected.
5   Make sure the mating surfaces of the pipe flange and the engine block are clean and free of nicks and install the screen assembly with a new gasket.

6   Install the oil pan (see Section 17).
7   Be sure to refill the engine with oil before starting it.

---

19   Driveplate – removal and installation

Refer to illustration 19.2

1   Refer to Chapter 7 and remove the transaxle.
2   Place a prybar or large screwdriver through a hole in the driveplate to keep the crankshaft from turning, then remove the mounting bolts **(see illustration)**.
3   Pull straight back on the driveplate to detach it from the crankshaft. Inspect the driveplate for cracks and chipped teeth. Replace it if it's damaged.
4   Reinstall the driveplate. The holes in the driveplate are staggered to ensure correct positioning on the crankshaft. Use Locktite on the bolt threads and tighten them to the specified torque in a crisscross pattern.
5   Reinstall the transaxle (see Chapter 7).

2A

18.2   Remove the bolts and lower the pickup tube and screen assembly

19.2   Place a prybar or large screwdriver through one of the holes in the driveplate to keep the crankshaft from turning as the bolts are loosened/tightened

20.3   Packing the seal into the engine block groove with the special tool (arrow)

20.6   Seal installation requires a special tool that bolts to the block

1   Seal   *2   Guide tool*

20.7   Packing the short pieces of rope seal into the guide tool and engine block

1   Packing tool   *2   Guide tool*

20   Crankshaft rear oil seal – replacement

1985 through 1990 models

Refer to illustrations 20.3, 20.6, 20.7, 20.10 and 20.13

Note: *Braided fabric seals inserted into grooves in the engine block and main bearing cap are used to seal against oil leakage around the crankshaft. The upper rear main bearing oil seal can be replaced only with the crankshaft removed (Chapter 2, Part B) but it can be repaired with the crankshaft in place. Two piece rubber seals are available from aftermarket suppliers. Two special tools are required for this procedure.*

1   Remove the oil pan (Section 17).

2   Remove the rear main bearing cap.

3   Using the special GM tool (no. J-21526-2), drive the upper seal gently back into the groove in the engine block, packing it tightly. It will pack in to a depth of between 1/4-inch and 3/4-inch **(see illustration)**.

4   Repeat the procedure on the other end of the seal.

5   Measure how far the seal was driven up in the groove on each side and add 1/16-inch. Remove the old seal from the main bearing cap. Use the main bearing cap as a fixture and cut two pieces of the old seal to the predetermined lengths.

6   Install the special GM tool (no. J-21526-1) on the engine block **(see illustration)**.

7   Using the packing tool (no. J-21526-2), work the short pieces of the previously cut seal into the guide tool (J-21526-1) and pack them into the engine block groove. The guide and packing tools have been machined to provide a built-in stop. Lubricate the seal with oil to ease installation **(see illustration)**.

20.10   Rear main bearing cap oil seal installation details

20.13   Sealant must be applied to the main bearing cap parting line

20.18 Carefully pry the old oil seal out

20.20 GM special tool J-34924 is recommended for seal installation

8 Remove the guide tool.
9 Place a new seal in the main bearing cap groove with both ends projecting an equal amount above the parting surface of the cap.
10 Use the handle of a hammer or similar tool to force the seal into the groove until it projects no more than 1/16-inch. Cut the ends of the seal flush with the surface of the cap with a single-edge razor blade **(see illustration)**.
11 Soak the neoprene seals which fit into the side grooves in the bearing cap in light oil or kerosene for one or two minutes.
12 Install the neoprene seals in the groove between the bearing cap and the block. The seals are slightly undersize and swell in the presence of heat and oil. They are slightly longer than the groove in the bearing cap and must be cut to fit.
13 Apply a small amount of RTV sealant to the joint where the bearing cap meets the block to help eliminate oil leakage. A very thin coat is all that's necessary **(see illustration)**.
14 Install the main bearing cap on the block. Force the seals up into the bearing cap with a blunt instrument to be sure of a good seal at the upper parting line. Install the bolts and tighten them to the torque listed in the Chapter 2B specifications.
15 Install the oil pan.

1991 and later VIN C and VIN L models

Refer to illustrations 20.18 and 20.20

16 Remove the transaxle (see Chapter 7).
17 Remove the driveplate (see Section 19).
18 Using a thin screwdriver or seal removal tool, carefully remove the oil seal from the engine block **(see illustration)**. Be very careful not to damage the crankshaft surface while prying the seal out.
19 Clean the bore in the block and the seal contact surface on the crankshaft. Check the seal contact surface on the crankshaft for scratches and nicks that could damage the new seal lip and cause oil leaks – if the crankshaft is damaged, the only alternative is a new or different crankshaft. Inspect the seal bore for nicks and scratches. Carefully smooth if with a fine file if necessary, but don't nick the crankshaft in the process.
20 A special tool is recommended to install the new oil seal **(see illustration)**. Lubricate the lips of the seal with clean engine oil. Slide the seal onto the mandril until the dust lip bottoms squarely against the collar of the tool. **Note:** If the special tool isn't available, carefully work the seal lip over the crankshaft and tap it into place with a hammer and punch.
21 Align the dowel pin on the tool with the dowel pin hole in the crankshaft and attach the tool to the crankshaft by hand-tightening the bolts.
22 Turn the tool handle until the collar bottoms against the case, seating the seal.
23 Loosen the tool handle and remove the bolts. Remove the tool.
24 Check the seal and make sure it's seated squarely in the bore.
25 Install the driveplate (see Section 19).
26 Install the transaxle (see Chapter 7).

21 Rear main oil seal carrier (VIN K engine) – removal and installation

Note: *The rear main oil seal carrier on these engines does not have to be removed for oil seal replacement. Rear main oil seal replacement is the same as on all other models.*

Removal

1 Remove the oil pan (see Section 17).
2 Remove the driveplate (see Section 19).
3 Remove the rear main oil seal carrier mounting bolts.
4 Separate the rear main oil seal carrier from the engine.

Installation

Caution: *Correct alignment of the rear main oil seal carrier to the back surface of the engine is critical to make sure the rear main oil seal and oil pan seal correctly.*

5 If still in place, remove the rear main oil seal from the carrier.
6 Install the rear main oil seal carrier and mounting bolts. Tighten the bolts only enough to hold the carrier in place. The carrier must be able to move so it can be adjusted in the following steps.
7 Use GM special tool (no. J-41349) to position the carrier onto the crankshaft. Apply a light coat of engine oil to both sides of the special tool and slip the tool onto the end of the crankshaft. If necessary, twist and turn the special tool while installing it and push it on until it stops.
8 Tighten the bolts to the torque listed in this Chapter's specifications.
9 Remove the special tool.
10 Place a straight edge on the cylinder block oil pan flange and the rear main oil seal carrier flange. Place a flat feeler gauge between the straight edge and the flanges and make sure there is no more than a 0.004-inch step, either high or low, between the two parts. If out of specification, repeat Steps 7 through 10 and measure again. If excessive clearance is still present, replace the rear main oil seal carrier.
11 Install the rear main oil seal (see section 20).
12 Install the driveplate (see Section 19).
13 Install the oil pan (see Section 17).

22 Engine mount – check and replacement

Refer to illustrations 22.4, 22.8a and 22.8b
Note: *See Chapter 7 for transaxle mount information.*
Warning: *A special tool (GM no. J28467) is available to support the engine during repair operations. Similar fixtures are available from rental yards. Improper lifting methods or devices are hazardous and could result in severe injury or death. DO NOT place any part of your body under the engine/transaxle when it's supported only by a jack. Failure of the lifting device could result in serious injury or death.*

2A

22.4   Broken engine mount (removed from vehicle for clarity)

1   Engine mounts seldom require attention, but broken or deteriorated mounts should be replaced immediately or the added strain placed on the driveline components may cause damage or wear.

Check

2   During the check, the engine must be raised slightly to remove the weight from the mounts.
3   Raise the vehicle and support it securely on jackstands, then position a jack under the engine oil pan. Place a large block of wood between the jack head and the oil pan, then carefully raise the engine just enough to take the weight off the mounts. **Warning:** *DO NOT place any part of your body under the engine when it's supported only by a jack!*
4   Check the mounts to see if the rubber is cracked, hardened or separated from the metal plates **(see illustration)**. Sometimes the rubber will split right down the center.
5   Check for relative movement between the mount plates and the engine or frame (use a large screwdriver or prybar to attempt to move the mounts). If movement is noted, lower the engine and tighten the mount fasteners.
6   Rubber preservative may be applied to the mounts to slow deterioration.

Replacement

7   Disconnect the negative battery cable from the battery, then raise the vehicle and support it securely on jackstands (if not already done).
8   Raise the engine slightly with a jack or hoist. Install an engine support as described in the Warning above. Remove the fasteners and detach the mount from the frame bracket **(see illustrations)**.
9   Remove the mount-to-block bracket bolts/nuts and detach the mount.
10   Installation is the reverse of removal. Use thread locking compound on the threads and be sure to tighten everything securely.

22.8a   Engine mount details – exploded view (most 3.0 and 3.8 liter models)

1   *Mounting nut*   2   *Engine mount*

22.8b   Engine mount details – exploded view (later 3800 models)

Chapter 2 Part B
General engine overhaul procedures

Contents

2B

Specifications

General

Displacement
Engine VIN codes E or L (1987 and earlier) . . . . 181 cubic inches (3.0L)
Engine VIN code B and 3 . . . . 231 cubic inches (3.8L)
Engine VIN code C* . . . . 231 cubic inches (3.8L)
Engine VIN code L* (1992 through 1995) . . . . 231 cubic inches (3.8L)
Engine VIN code K* (1995 on) . . . . 231 cubic inches (3.8L)

Equipped with balance shaft

Cylinder compression pressure . . . . Lowest reading cylinder must be 70% of highest reading cylinder(100 psi minimum)

Oil pressure (minimum) . . . . 37 psi @ 2,400 rpm

Cylinder head

Warpage limit . . . . 0.0035 inch
Maximum allowable cut . . . . 0.010 in

Valves and related components

Minimum recommended valve margin . . . . 0.025 in
Intake valve
  Seat angle 45-degrees
  Stem diameter . . . . 0.3412 to 0.3401 in
  Stem-to-guide clearance . . . . 0.0015 to 0.0035 in
Exhaust valve
  Seat angle 45-degrees
  Stem diameter . . . . 0.3412 to 0.3405 in
  Stem-to-guide clearance . . . . 0.0015 to 0.0032 in
Valve spring installed height . . . . 1.727 in
Valve spring free length . . . . 1.981 inch

Cylinder bore

Diameter	3.800 in
Maximum taper/out-of-round	0.013 in

Crankshaft and connecting rods

Connecting rod journal	
Diameter	2.2487 to 2.2495 in
Bearing oil clearance	0.0005 to 0.0026 in
Maximum taper/out-of-round	0.0003 in
Connecting rod side clearance (end play)	0.003 to 0.015 in
Main bearing journal	
Diameter	2.4995 in
Bearing oil clearance	0.0003 to 0.0018 in
Maximum taper/out-of-round	0.003 in
Crankshaft end play (at thrust bearing)	0.003 to 0.011 in

Pistons and rings

Piston-to-bore clearance limits	
Top	0.001 to 0.002 in
Bottom	0.0015 to 0.0035 in
Piston ring end gap	
Compression rings	0.010 to 0.020 in
Oil ring	0.015 to 0.055 in
Piston ring side clearance	
Compression rings	0.003 to 0.005 in
Oil ring	0.0035 in

Camshaft

Camshaft lobe lift	
Intake	0.250 in
Exhaust	0.255 in
Bearing journal diameter (all)	1.785 to 1.786 in
Bearing oil clearance	
No. 1 journal	0.0005 to 0.0025 in
All others	0.0005 to 0.0035 in

Torque specifications*

	Ft-lbs (unless otherwise indicated)
Main bearing cap bolts	
1985 through 1987	100
1988 through 1990	90
1991 on	
Step one	26
Step two	Turn an additional 50-degrees
Main bearing side bolts (VIN K)	
Step one	11
Step two	Turn an additional 45-degrees
Connecting rod nuts or bolts	
1985 through 1991	43
1992 on	
Step one	20
Step two	Turn an additional 50-degrees
Balance shaft gear bolt	
Step one	14
Step two	Rotate an additional 35-degrees
Balance shaft retainer bolts	26

Note: Refer to Part A for additional torque specifications.

---

1   General information

Note: *On models equipped with the Delco Loc II audio system, be sure the lockout feature is turned off before performing any procedure which requires disconnecting the battery.*

Included in this portion of Chapter 2 are the general overhaul procedures for the cylinder heads and internal engine components.

The information ranges from advice concerning preparation for an overhaul and the purchase of replacement parts to detailed, step-by-step procedures covering removal and installation of internal engine components and the inspection of parts.

The following Sections have been written based on the assumption the engine has been removed from the vehicle. For information concerning in-vehicle engine repair, as well as removal and installation of the external components necessary for the overhaul, see Part A of this Chapter and Section 7 of this Part.

The Specifications included in this Part are only those necessary for the inspection and overhaul procedures which follow. Refer to Part A for additional Specifications.

2.4a   The oil pressure sending unit is located on top of the oil filter housing (arrow) – remove the sending unit . . .

2.4b   . . . and install a gauge to check the engine oil pressure

2   Engine overhaul – general information

Refer to illustrations 2.4a and 2.4b

It's not always easy to determine when, or if, an engine should be completely overhauled, as a number of factors must be considered.

High mileage isn't necessarily an indication an overhaul is needed, while low mileage doesn't preclude the need for an overhaul. Frequency of servicing is probably the most important consideration. An engine that's had regular and frequent oil and filter changes, as well as other required maintenance, will most likely give many thousands of miles of reliable service. Conversely, a neglected engine may require an overhaul very early in its life.

Excessive oil consumption is an indication that piston rings, valve seals and/or valve guides are in need of attention. Make sure oil leaks aren't responsible before deciding the rings and/or guides are bad. Perform a cylinder compression check to determine the extent of the work required (see Section 3).

Remove the oil pressure sending unit and check the oil pressure with a gauge installed in its place **(see illustrations)**. Compare the results to this Chapter's Specifications. As a general rule, engines should have ten psi oil pressure for every 1,000 rpm's. If the pressure is extremely low, the bearings and/or oil pump are probably worn out.

Loss of power, rough running, knocking or metallic engine noises, excessive valve train noise and high fuel consumption rates may also point to the need for an overhaul, especially if they're all present at the same time. If a complete tune-up doesn't remedy the situation, major mechanical work is the only solution.

An engine overhaul involves restoring the internal parts to the specifications of a new engine. During an overhaul, the piston rings are replaced and the cylinder walls are reconditioned (rebored and/or honed). If a rebore is done by an automotive machine shop, new oversize pistons will also be installed. The main bearings, connecting rod bearings and camshaft bearings are generally replaced with new ones and, if necessary, the crankshaft may be reground to restore the journals. Generally, the valves are serviced as well, since they're usually in less-than-perfect condition at this point. While the engine is being overhauled, other components, such as the starter and alternator, can be rebuilt as well. The end result should be a like new engine that will give many trouble free miles. **Note:** *Critical cooling system components such as the hoses, drivebelts, thermostat and water pump MUST be replaced with new parts when an engine is overhauled. The radiator should be checked carefully to ensure it isn't clogged or leaking (see Chapter 3). Also, we don't recommend overhauling the oil pump – always install a new one when an engine is rebuilt.*

Before beginning the engine overhaul, read through the entire procedure to familiarize yourself with the scope and requirements of the job. Overhauling an engine isn't particularly difficult, if you follow all of the instructions carefully, have the necessary tools and equipment and pay close attention to all specifications; however, it can be time consuming. Plan on the vehicle being tied up for a minimum of two weeks, especially if parts must be taken to an automotive machine shop for repair or reconditioning. Check on availability of parts and make sure any necessary special tools and equipment are obtained in advance. Most work can be done with typical hand tools, although a number of precision measuring tools are required for inspecting parts to determine if they must be replaced. Often an automotive machine shop will handle the inspection of parts and offer advice concerning reconditioning and replacement. **Note:** *Always wait until the engine has been completely disassembled and all components, especially the engine block, have been inspected before deciding what service and repair operations must be performed by an automotive machine shop. Since the block's condition will be the major factor to consider when determining whether to overhaul the original engine or buy a rebuilt one, never purchase parts or have machine work done on other components until the block has been thoroughly inspected. As a general rule, time is the primary cost of an overhaul, so it doesn't pay to install worn or substandard parts.*

As a final note, to ensure maximum life and minimum trouble from a rebuilt engine, everything must be assembled with care in a spotlessly clean environment.

3   Cylinder compression check

Refer to illustration 3.6

1   A compression check will tell you what mechanical condition the upper end (pistons, rings, valves, head gaskets) of the engine is in. Specifically, it can tell you if the compression is down due to leakage caused by worn piston rings, defective valves and seats or a blown head gasket. **Note:** *The engine must be at normal operating temperature and the battery must be fully charged for this check.*

2   Begin by cleaning the area around the spark plugs before you remove them. Compressed air should be used, if available, otherwise a small brush or even a bicycle tire pump will work. The idea is to prevent dirt from getting into the cylinders as the compression check is being done.

3   Remove all of the spark plugs from the engine (see Chapter 1).

4   Block the throttle wide open.

5   Disable the fuel and ignition systems by removing the ECM fuse (see Chapter 6).

3.6   A compression gauge with a threaded fitting for the spark plug hole is preferred over the type that requires hand pressure to maintain the seal

6   Install the compression gauge in the number one spark plug hole **(see illustration)**.

7   Crank the engine over at least seven compression strokes and watch the gauge. The compression should build up quickly in a healthy engine. Low compression on the first stroke, followed by gradually increasing pressure on successive strokes, indicates worn piston rings. A low compression reading on the first stroke, which doesn't build up during successive strokes, indicates leaking valves or a blown head gasket (a cracked head could also be the cause). Deposits on the undersides of the valve heads can also cause low compression. Record the highest gauge reading obtained.

8   Repeat the procedure for the remaining cylinders and compare the results to this Chapter's Specifications.

9   If the readings are below normal, add some engine oil (about three squirts from a plunger-type oil can) to each cylinder, through the spark plug hole, and repeat the test.

10   If the compression increases after the oil is added, the piston rings are definitely worn. If the compression doesn't increase significantly, the leakage is occurring at the valves or head gasket. Leakage past the valves may be caused by burned valve seats and/or faces or warped, cracked or bent valves.

11   If two adjacent cylinders have equally low compression, there's a strong possibility the head gasket between them is blown. The appearance of coolant in the combustion chambers or the crankcase would verify this condition.

12   If one cylinder is about 20 percent lower than the others, and the engine has a slightly rough idle, a worn exhaust lobe on the camshaft could be the cause.

13   If the compression is unusually high, the combustion chambers are probably coated with carbon deposits. If that's the case, the cylinder heads should be removed and decarbonized.

14   If compression is way down or varies greatly between cylinders, it would be a good idea to have a leak-down test performed by an automotive repair shop. This test will pinpoint exactly where the leakage is occurring and how severe it is.

15   Install the ECM fuse and drive the vehicle to restore the block learn memory.

---

4   Engine removal – methods and precautions

If you've decided the engine must be removed for overhaul or major repair work, several preliminary steps should be taken.

Locating a suitable place to work is extremely important. Adequate work space, along with storage space for the vehicle, will be needed. If a shop or garage isn't available, at the very least a flat, level, clean work surface made of concrete or asphalt is required.

Cleaning the engine compartment and engine before beginning the removal procedure will help keep tools clean and organized.

An engine hoist or A-frame will also be necessary. Make sure the equipment is rated in excess of the combined weight of the engine and transaxle. Safety is of primary importance, considering the potential hazards involved in lifting the engine out of the vehicle.

If the engine is being removed by a novice, a helper should be available. Advice and aid from someone more experienced would also be helpful. There are many instances when one person cannot simultaneously perform all of the operations required when lifting the engine out of the vehicle.

Plan the operation ahead of time. Arrange for or obtain all of the tools and equipment you'll need prior to beginning the job. Some of the equipment necessary to perform engine removal and installation safely and with relative ease are (in addition to an engine hoist) a heavy duty floor jack, complete sets of wrenches and sockets as described in the front of this manual, wooden blocks and plenty of rags and cleaning solvent for mopping up spilled oil, coolant and gasoline. If the hoist must be rented, be sure to arrange for it in advance and perform all of the operations possible without it beforehand. This will save you money and time.

Plan for the vehicle to be out of use for quite a while. A machine shop will be required to perform some of the work which the do-it-yourselfer can't accomplish without special equipment. These shops often have a busy schedule, so it would be a good idea to consult them before removing the engine in order to accurately estimate the amount of time required to rebuild or repair components that may need work.

Always be extremely careful when removing and installing the engine. Serious injury can result from careless actions. Plan ahead, take your time and a job of this nature, although major, can be accomplished successfully.

---

5   Engine – removal and installation

Refer to illustrations 5.4, 5.11, 5.12, 5.15, 5.19, 5.24a and 5.24b

Note: *Read through the following steps carefully and familiarize yourself with the procedure before beginning work.*

Warning: *Gasoline is extremely flammable, so take extra precautions when disconnecting any part of the fuel system. Don't smoke or allow open flames or bare light bulbs in or near the work area and don't work in a garage where a natural gas appliance (such as a clothes dryer or water heater) is installed. If you spill gasoline on your skin, rinse it off immediately. Have a fire extinguisher rated for gasoline fires handy and know how to use it! Also, the air conditioning system is under high pressure – have a dealer service department or service station discharge the system before disconnecting any of the hoses or fittings.*

Removal

1   Refer to Chapter 4 and relieve the fuel system pressure, then disconnect the negative cable from the battery.

2   Cover the fenders and cowl and remove the hood (see Chapter 11). Special pads are available to protect the fenders, but an old bedspread or blanket will also work.

3   Remove the air cleaner assembly and mass airflow sensor (see Chapter 4).

4   Remove the plastic firewall cover. Label the vacuum lines, emissions system hoses, wiring connectors, ground straps and fuel lines to ensure correct reinstallation, then detach them. Pieces of masking tape with numbers or letters written on them work well **(see illustration)**. If there's any possibility of confusion, make a sketch of the engine compartment and clearly label the lines, hoses and wires.

5   Raise the vehicle and support it securely on jackstands. Drain the cooling system (see Chapter 1).

6   Label and detach all coolant hoses from the engine.

7   Remove the windshield washer reservoir, cooling fan(s) and radiator (see Chapter 3).

5.4   One way to ensure proper reattachment of wires and hoses is to fasten numbered pieces of masking tape to both sides of the connection as shown here

5.11   Unbolt the power steering pump and move it aside, then use wire or rope to hold it in place

5.12   Unbolt the compressor and set it aside without disconnecting the hoses

5.15   Remove the engine shock absorber through bolt (arrow)

8   Remove the drivebelt (see Chapter 1).
9   Disconnect the fuel lines running from the engine to the chassis (see Chapter 4). Plug or cap all open fittings/lines.
10   Disconnect the throttle linkage (and TV linkage/speed control cable, if equipped) from the engine (see Chapters 4 and 7).
11   Unbolt the power steering pump and set it aside (see Chapter 10). Leave the lines/hoses attached and make sure the pump is kept in an upright position in the engine compartment **(see illustration)**. **Note:** *On some models, you may have to detach the pump.*
12   Unbolt the air conditioning compressor (see Chapter 3) and set it aside; do not disconnect the hoses **(see illustration)**.
13   Drain the engine oil and remove the filter (see Chapter 1).
14   Remove the starter and the alternator (see Chapter 5).
15   Disconnect the engine shock absorber **(see illustration)**.
16   Disconnect the exhaust system from the engine (see Chapter 4).
17   Support the transaxle with a jack. Position a block of wood on the jack head to prevent damage to the transaxle.
18   Attach an engine sling or a length of chain to the lifting brackets on the engine.
19   Roll the hoist into position and connect the sling to it **(see illustration)**. Take up the slack in the sling or chain, but don't lift the engine. **Warning:** *DO NOT place any part of your body under the engine when it's supported only by a hoist or other lifting device.*

5.19   Attach the chain or hoist cable to the engine brackets (arrows)

2B

5.24a   Raise the engine enough to clear the mounts, then separate it from the transaxle

20   Refer to Chapter 7 and remove the torque converter-to-driveplate fasteners.
21   Remove the transaxle-to-engine block bolts. Refer to Chapter 7.
22   Remove the engine mount-to-chassis bolts/nuts.
23   Recheck to be sure nothing is still connecting the engine to the vehicle. Disconnect anything still remaining.
24   Raise the engine slightly to disengage the mounts. Carefully separate the engine from the transaxle. Be sure the torque converter stays in place (clamp a pair of vise-grips to the housing to keep the converter from sliding out). Slowly raise the engine out of the vehicle **(see illustrations)**. Check carefully to make sure nothing is hanging up as the hoist is raised.
25   Remove the driveplate and mount the engine on an engine stand.

Installation

26   Check the engine and transaxle mounts. If they're worn or damaged, replace them.
27   **Caution:** *DO NOT use the transaxle-to-engine bolts to force the transaxle and engine together.* Take great care when installing the torque converter, following the procedure outlined in Chapter 7.
28   Carefully lower the engine into the engine compartment – make sure the mounts line up. Reinstall the remaining components in the reverse order of removal. Double-check to make sure everything is hooked up right.
29   Add coolant, oil, power steering and transmission fluid as needed.
30   Run the engine and check for leaks and proper operation of all accessories, then install the hood and test drive the vehicle.

6   Engine rebuilding alternatives

The home mechanic is faced with a number of options when performing an engine overhaul. The decision to replace the engine block, piston/connecting rod assemblies and crankshaft depends on a number of factors, with the number one consideration being the condition of the block. Other considerations are cost, access to machine shop facilities, parts availability, time required to complete the project and the extent of prior mechanical experience.

Some of the rebuilding alternatives include:

Individual parts – If the inspection procedures reveal the engine block and most engine components are in reusable condition, purchasing individual parts may be the most economical alternative. The block, crankshaft and piston/connecting rod assemblies should all be inspected

5.24b   Lift the engine off the mounts and guide it carefully around any obstacles, as an assistant raises the hoist, until it clears the front of the vehicle

carefully. Even if the block shows little wear, the cylinder bores should be surface honed.

Short block – A short block consists of an engine block with a crankshaft and piston/connecting rod assemblies already installed. All new bearings are incorporated and all clearances will be correct. The existing camshaft, valve train components, cylinder heads and external parts can be bolted to the short block with little or no machine shop work necessary.

Long block – A long block consists of a short block plus an oil pump, oil pan, cylinder heads, rocker arm covers, camshaft and valve train components, timing sprockets and chain and timing chain cover. All components are installed with new bearings, seals and gaskets incorporated throughout. The installation of manifolds and external parts is all that's necessary.

Give careful thought to which alternative is best for you and discuss the situation with local automotive machine shops, auto parts dealers and experienced rebuilders before ordering or purchasing replacement parts.

7   Engine overhaul – disassembly sequence

Refer to illustrations 7.3a, 7.3b, 7.3c and 7.5

1   It's much easier to disassemble and work on the engine if it's mounted on a portable engine stand. A stand can often be rented quite cheaply from an equipment rental yard. Before it's mounted on a stand, the flywheel/driveplate should be removed from the engine.
2   If a stand isn't available, it's possible to disassemble the engine with it blocked up on the floor. Be extra careful not to tip or drop the engine when working without a stand.

3   If you're going to obtain a rebuilt engine, all external components **(see illustrations)** must come off first, to be transferred to the replacement engine, just as they will if you're doing a complete engine overhaul yourself. These include:

Alternator and brackets
Emissions control components
Ignition coil/module assembly, spark plug wires and spark plugs
Thermostat and housing cover
Water pump
EFI components
Intake/exhaust manifolds
Oil filter
Engine mounts
Driveplate
Engine rear plate (if equipped)

Note: *When removing the external components from the engine, pay close attention to details that may be helpful or important during installation. Note the installed position of gaskets, seals, spacers, pins, brackets, washers, bolts and other small items.*

4   If you're obtaining a short block, which consists of the engine block, crankshaft, pistons and connecting rods all assembled, then the cylinder heads, oil pan and oil pump will have to be removed as well. See *Engine rebuilding alternatives* for additional information regarding the different possibilities to be considered.

5   If you're planning a complete overhaul, the engine must be disassembled and the internal components **(see illustration)** removed in the following general order:

Rocker arm covers
Intake and exhaust manifolds
Rocker arms and pushrods
Valve lifters
Cylinder heads
Timing chain cover and oil pump
Timing chain and sprockets
Camshaft
Balance shaft (3800 engine only)
Oil pan
Piston/connecting rod assemblies
Crankshaft and main bearings

7.3a   Engine – drivebelt end (typical)

7.3b   Engine – radiator side (typical)

7.3c   Engine – firewall side (typical)

7.5 Typical engine components – exploded view

1   Engine block
2   Manifold seal
3   Intake manifold gasket
4   Intake manifold
5   Gasket
6   Rocker arm cover
7   Acorn nut, washer and rubber seal
8   Pedestal, rocker arm and retainer
9   Cylinder head
10 Pushrod
11 Lifter
12 Head gasket
13 Driveplate
14 Piston and connecting rod
15 Rod bearing inserts
16 Rod bearing cap
17 Rod bolt
18 Crankshaft
19 Rear crankshaft oil seal
20 Main bearing insert

21 Main bearing cap
22 Main bearing cap bolt
23 Oil pick-up
24 Oil pan and gasket
25 Oil pan tensioner spring
26 Oil pump assembly
27 Front cover
28 Front cover oil seal
29 Vibration damper
30 Timing chain
31 Oil filter adapter
32 Cam sprocket
33 Timing chain tensioner
34 Camshaft
35 Cam bearings
36 Cam button and spring
37 Crankshaft sprocket
38 Key
39 Thrust bearing (main)

2B

6   Before beginning the disassembly and overhaul procedures, make sure the following items are available. Also, refer to Engine overhaul – reassembly sequence for a list of tools and materials needed for engine reassembly.

Common hand tools
Small cardboard boxes or plastic bags for storing parts
Gasket scraper
Ridge reamer
Vibration damper puller
Micrometers
Telescoping gauges
Dial indicator set
Valve spring compressor
Cylinder surfacing hone
Piston ring groove cleaning tool
Electric drill motor
Tap and die set
Wire brushes
Oil gallery brushes
Cleaning solvent

8   Cylinder head – disassembly

Refer to illustrations 8.2, 8.3 and 8.4

Note: New and rebuilt cylinder heads are commonly available for most engines at dealerships and auto parts stores. Due to the fact that some specialized tools are necessary for the disassembly and inspection procedures, and replacement parts aren't always readily available, it may be more practical and economical for the home mechanic to purchase replacement heads rather than taking the time to disassemble, inspect and recondition the originals.

1   Cylinder head disassembly involves removal of the intake and exhaust valves and related components. Remove the rocker arm bolts, pivots and rocker arms from the cylinder heads. Label the parts or store them separately so they can be reinstalled in their original locations.

2   Before the valves are removed, arrange to label and store them, along with their related components, so they can be kept separate and re-installed in their original locations (**see illustration**).
3   Compress the springs on the first valve with a spring compressor and remove the keepers (**see illustration**). Carefully release the valve spring compressor and remove the retainer, the spring and the spring seat (if used).
4   Pull the valve out of the head, then remove the oil seal from the guide. If the valve binds in the guide (won't pull through), push it back into the head and deburr the area around the keeper groove with a fine file or whetstone (**see illustration**).
5   Repeat the procedure for the remaining valves. Remember to keep all the parts for each valve together so they can be reinstalled in the same locations.

8.2   Have several plastic bags ready (one for each valve) before you start disassembling the head – label each bag and put the entire contents of each valve assembly in one bag as shown

8.3   Use a valve spring compressor to compress the springs, then remove the keepers from the valve stem with a magnet or small needle-nose pliers

8.4   If you can't pull the valve through the guide, deburr the edge of the stem end and the area around the top of the keeper groove with a file or whetstone

9.12   Check the cylinder head gasket surface for warpage by trying to slip a feeler gauge under the straightedge (see this Chapter's Specifications for the maximum warpage allowed and use a feeler gauge of that thickness)

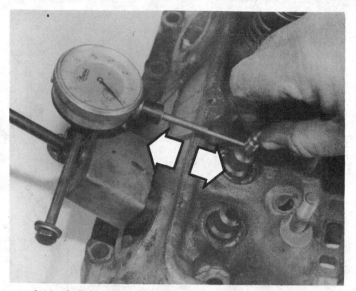

9.14   A dial indicator can be used to determine the valve stem-to-guide clearance (move the valve stem as indicated by the arrows)

6   Once the valves and related components have been removed and stored in an organized manner, the head should be thoroughly cleaned and inspected. If a complete engine overhaul is being done, finish the engine disassembly procedures before beginning the cylinder head cleaning and inspection process.

9   Cylinder head – cleaning and inspection

1   Thorough cleaning of the cylinder heads and related valve train components, followed by a detailed inspection, will enable you to decide how much valve service work must be done during the engine overhaul. **Note:** *If the engine was severely overheated, the cylinder head is probably warped (see Step 12).*

Cleaning

2   Scrape all traces of old gasket material and sealant off the head gasket, intake manifold and exhaust manifold mating surfaces. Be very careful not to gouge the cylinder head. Special gasket removal solvents that soften gaskets and make removal much easier are available at auto parts stores.
3   Remove all built up scale from the coolant passages.
4   Run a stiff wire brush through the various holes to remove deposits that may have formed in them.
5   Run an appropriate size tap into each of the threaded holes to remove corrosion and thread sealant that may be present. If compressed air is available, use it to clear the holes of debris produced by this operation. **Warning:** *Wear eye protection when using compressed air!*
6   Clean the rocker arm pivot stud threads with a wire brush.
7   Clean the cylinder head with solvent and dry it thoroughly. Compressed air will speed the drying process and ensure that all holes and recessed areas are clean. **Note:** *Decarbonizing chemicals are available and may prove very useful when cleaning cylinder heads and valve train components. They're very caustic and should be used with caution. Be sure to follow the instructions on the container.*
8   Clean the rocker arms, pivots, bolts and pushrods with solvent and dry them thoroughly (don't mix them up during the cleaning process). Compressed air will speed the drying process and can be used to clean out the oil passages.

9   Clean all the valve springs, spring seats, rotators, keepers and retainers with solvent and dry them thoroughly. Do the components from one valve at a time to avoid mixing up the parts.
10   Scrape off any heavy deposits that may have formed on the valves, then use a motorized wire brush to remove deposits from the valve heads and stems. Again, make sure the valves don't get mixed up.

Inspection

Refer to illustrations 9.12, 9.14, 9.15, 9.16, 9.17 and 9.18

Note: *Be sure to perform all of the following inspection procedures before concluding machine shop work is required. Make a list of the items that need attention.*

Cylinder head

11   Inspect the head very carefully for cracks, evidence of coolant leakage and other damage. If cracks are found, check with an automotive machine shop concerning repair. If repair isn't possible, a new cylinder head should be obtained.
12   Using a straightedge and feeler gauge, check the head gasket mating surface for warpage **(see illustration)**. If the warpage exceeds the limit in this Chapter's Specifications, it can be resurfaced at an automotive machine shop. **Note:** *If the heads are resurfaced, the intake manifold flanges will also require machining.*
13   Examine the valve seats in each of the combustion chambers. If they're pitted, cracked or burned, the head will require valve service that's beyond the scope of the home mechanic.
14   Check the valve stem-to-guide clearance by measuring the lateral movement of the valve stem with a dial indicator attached securely to the head **(see illustration)**. The valve must be in the guide and approximately 1/16-inch off the seat. The total valve stem movement indicated by the gauge needle must be divided by two to obtain the actual clearance. After this is done, if there's still some doubt regarding the condition of the valve guides, they should be checked by an automotive machine shop (the cost should be minimal).

Valves

15   Carefully inspect each valve face for uneven wear, deformation, cracks, pits and burned areas. Check the valve stem for scuffing and galling and the neck for cracks. Rotate the valve and check for any obvious indication that it's bent. Look for pits and excessive wear on the end of the

2B

9.15   Check for valve wear at the points shown here

1 Valve tip	4 Stem (most worn area)
2 Keeper groove	5 Valve face
3 Stem (least worn area)	6 Margin

9.16   The margin width on each valve must be as specified (if no margin exists, the valve cannot be reused)

stem. The presence of any of these conditions (see illustration) indicates the need for valve service by an automotive machine shop.

16   Measure the margin width on each valve (see illustration). Any valve with a margin narrower than specified in this Chapter will have to be replaced with a new one.

Valve components

17   Check each valve spring for wear (on the ends) and pits. Measure the free length and compare it to this Chapter's Specifications (see illustration). Any springs that are shorter than specified have sagged and shouldn't be reused. The tension of all springs should be checked with a special fixture before deciding they're suitable for use in a rebuilt engine (take the springs to an automotive machine shop for this check).

18   Stand each spring on a flat surface and check it for squareness (see illustration). If any of the springs are distorted or sagged, replace all of them with new parts.

19   Check the spring retainers and keepers for obvious wear and cracks. Any questionable parts should be replaced with new ones, as extensive damage will occur if they fail during engine operation.

Rocker arm components

20   Check the rocker arm faces (the areas that contact the pushrod ends and valve stems) for pits, wear, galling, score marks and rough spots. Check the rocker arm pivot contact areas and pivots as well. Look for cracks in each rocker arm and bolt.

21   Inspect the pushrod ends for scuffing and excessive wear. Roll each pushrod on a flat surface, like a piece of plate glass, to determine if it's bent.

9.17   Measure the free length of each valve spring with a dial or vernier caliper

22   Check the rocker arm bolt holes in the cylinder heads for damaged threads.

23   Any damaged or excessively worn parts must be replaced with new ones.

All components

24   If the inspection process indicates the valve components are in generally poor condition and worn beyond the limits specified, which is usually the case in an engine that's being overhauled, reassemble the valves in the cylinder head and refer to Section 10 for valve servicing recommendations.

9.18 Check each valve spring for squareness

11.4 Make sure the new valve stem seals are seated against the tops of the valve guides

| 1 | Valve seal seated in tool | 3 | Seal |
| 2 | Deburr the end of the valve stem before installing the seal | 4 | Valve seal installation tool |

10 Valves – servicing

1   Because of the complex nature of the job and the special tools and equipment needed, servicing of the valves, the valve seats and the valve guides, commonly known as a valve job, should be done by a professional.

2   The home mechanic can remove and disassemble the head, do the initial cleaning and inspection, then reassemble and deliver it to a dealer service department or an automotive machine shop for the actual service work. Doing the inspection will enable you to see what condition the head and valvetrain components are in and will ensure that you know what work and new parts are required when dealing with an automotive machine shop.

3   The dealer service department, or automotive machine shop, will remove the valves and springs, recondition or replace the valves and valve seats, recondition the valve guides, check and replace the valve springs, rotators, spring retainers and keepers (as necessary), replace the valve seals with new ones, reassemble the valve components and make sure the installed spring height is correct. The cylinder head gasket surface will also be resurfaced if it's warped.

4   After the valve job has been performed by a professional, the head will be in like new condition. When the head is returned, be sure to clean it again before installation on the engine to remove any metal particles and abrasive grit that may still be present from the valve service or head resurfacing operations. Use compressed air, if available, to blow out all the oil holes and passages.

11 Cylinder head – reassembly

Refer to illustrations 11.4 and 11.6

1   Regardless of whether or not the head was sent to an automotive repair shop for valve servicing, make sure it's clean before beginning reassembly.

2   If the head was sent out for valve servicing, the valves and related components will already be in place. Begin the reassembly procedure with Step 8.

3   Install the spring seats before the valve seals.

4   Install new seals on each of the valve guides. **Note:** *3.0 and 3.8 liter engines have seals only on the intake valves.* Using a hammer and a deep

11.6 Apply a small dab of grease to each keeper as shown here before installation – it'll hold them in place on the valve stem as the spring is released

socket or seal installation tool, gently tap each seal into place until it's completely seated on the guide **(see illustration)**. Don't twist or cock the seals during installation or they won't seal properly on the valve stems.

5   Beginning at one end of the head, lubricate and install the first valve. Apply moly-base grease or clean engine oil to the valve stem.

6   Position the valve springs (and shims, if used) over the valves. Compress the springs with a valve spring compressor and carefully install the keepers in the groove, then slowly release the compressor and make sure the keepers seat properly. Apply a small dab of grease to each keeper to hold it in place if necessary **(see illustration)**.

7   Repeat the procedure for the remaining valves. Be sure to return the components to their original locations – don't mix them up!

8   Check the installed valve spring height with a ruler graduated in 1/32-inch increments or a dial caliper. If the head was sent out for service work, the installed height should be correct (but don't automatically assume it is). The measurement is taken from the top of each spring seat, rotator or top shim to the bottom of the retainer. If the height is greater than specified in this Chapter, shims can be added under the springs to correct

2B

12.3   When checking the camshaft lobe lift, the dial indicator plunger must be positioned directly above and in-line with the pushrod

12.9   To verify camshaft lobe lift, measure the major (A) and minor (B) diameters of each lobe with a micrometer or vernier caliper – subtract each minor diameter from the major diameter to arrive at the lobe lift

it. **Caution:** *Do not, under any circumstances, shim the springs to the point where the installed height is less than specified.*

9   Apply moly-base grease to the rocker arm faces and the pivots, then install the rocker arms and pivots on the cylinder heads. Tighten the bolts finger-tight.

---

12   Camshaft, balance shaft and bearings – removal and inspection

---

Note: *Since there isn't enough room to remove the camshaft with the engine in the vehicle, the engine must be out of the vehicle and mounted on a stand for this procedure.*

Camshaft lobe lift check

With cylinder head installed
Refer to illustration 12.3

1   In order to determine the extent of cam lobe wear, the lobe lift should be checked prior to camshaft removal. Refer to Part A and remove the rocker arm covers.

2   Position the number one piston at TDC on the compression stroke (see Part A).

3   Beginning with the number one cylinder valves, mount a dial indicator on the engine and position the plunger against the top surface of the first rocker arm. The plunger should be directly above and in line with the pushrod **(see illustration)**.

4   Zero the dial indicator, then very slowly turn the crankshaft in the normal direction of rotation (clockwise) until the indicator needle stops and begins to move in the opposite direction. The point at which it stops indicates maximum cam lobe lift.

5   Record this figure for future reference, then reposition the piston at TDC on the compression stroke.

6   Move the dial indicator to the remaining number one cylinder rocker arm and repeat the check. Be sure to record the results for each valve.

7   Repeat the check for the remaining valves. Since each piston must be at TDC on the compression stroke for this procedure, work from cylinder-to-cylinder following the firing order sequence.

8   After the check is complete, compare the results to this Chapter's Specifications. If camshaft lobe lift is less than specified, cam lobe wear has occurred and a new camshaft should be installed.

With cylinder head removed
Refer to illustration 12.9

9   If the cylinder heads have already been removed, an alternate method of lobe measurement can be used. Remove the camshaft as described below. Using a micrometer, measure the lobe at its highest point. Then measure the base circle perpendicular (90-degrees) to the lobe **(see illustration)**. Do this for each lobe and record the results.

10   Subtract the base circle measurement from the lobe height. The difference is the lobe lift. See Step 8 above.

Removal
Refer to illustrations 12.12 and 12.13

11   Refer to the appropriate Sections in Part A and remove the timing chain and sprockets, lifters and pushrods.

12   Remove the camshaft thrust plate-to-block bolts. Thread long bolts into the camshaft sprocket bolt holes to use as a handle when removing the camshaft from the block **(see illustration)**. **Note:** *The balance shaft (3800 engine only) requires special tools for removal and installation. If the bearings are bad, have the shaft assembly replaced by an automotive machine shop (see step 19).*

12.12   Thread long bolts into the sprocket bolt holes to use as a handle when removing and installing the camshaft

12.13 Support the camshaft near the block to avoid damaging the bearings

12.15 The camshaft bearing journal diameters are checked to pinpoint excessive wear and out-of-round conditions

13 Carefully pull the camshaft out. Support the cam near the block so the lobes don't nick or gouge the bearings as it's withdrawn **(see illustration)**.

Inspection

Refer to illustration 12.15

14 After the camshaft has been removed from the engine, cleaned with solvent and dried, inspect the bearing journals for uneven wear, pitting and evidence of seizure. If the journals are damaged, the bearing inserts in the block are probably damaged as well. Both the camshaft and bearings will have to be replaced.

15 Measure the bearing journals with a micrometer **(see illustration)** to determine if they're excessively worn or out-of-round.

16 Check the camshaft lobes for heat discoloration, score marks, chipped areas, pitting and uneven wear. If the lobes are in good condition and if the lobe lift measurements are as specified, the camshaft can be reused.

17 Check the bearings in the block for wear and damage. Look for galling, pitting and discolored areas.

18 The inside diameter of each bearing can be determined with a small hole gauge and outside micrometer or an inside micrometer. Subtract the camshaft bearing journal diameter(s) from the corresponding bearing inside diameter(s) to obtain the bearing oil clearance. If it's excessive, new bearings will be required regardless of the condition of the originals.

19 Balance shaft and camshaft bearing replacement requires special tools and expertise that place it outside the scope of the home mechanic. Take the block to an automotive machine shop to ensure the job is done correctly.

20 Balance shaft gear installation and timing is covered in Section 24.

13 Pistons and connecting rods – removal

Refer to illustrations 13.1, 13.3, 13.4 and 13.6
Note: *Prior to removing the piston/connecting rod assemblies, remove the cylinder heads, the oil pan and the oil pump by referring to the appropriate Sections in Part A of Chapter 2.*

1 Use your fingernail to feel if a ridge has formed at the upper limit of ring travel (about 1/4-inch down from the top of each cylinder). If carbon deposits or cylinder wear have produced ridges, they must be completely removed with a special tool **(see illustration)**. Follow the manufacturer's instructions provided with the tool. Failure to remove the ridges before attempting to remove the piston/connecting rod assemblies may result in piston breakage.

2 After the cylinder ridges have been removed, turn the engine upside-down so the crankshaft is facing up.

3 Before the connecting rods are removed, check the endplay with feeler gauges. Slide them between the first connecting rod and the crankshaft throw until the play is removed **(see illustration)**. The endplay is equal to the thickness of the feeler gauge(s). If the endplay exceeds the service limit, new connecting rods will be required. If new rods (or a new crankshaft) are installed, the endplay may fall under the minimum specified in this Chapter (if it does, the rods will have to be machined to restore it – consult an automotive machine shop for advice if necessary). Repeat the procedure for the remaining connecting rods.

4 Check the connecting rods and caps for identification marks. If they aren't plainly marked, use a small center punch **(see illustration)** to make the appropriate number of indentations on each rod and cap (1, 2, 3, etc., depending on the cylinder they're associated with).

5 Loosen each of the connecting rod cap nuts 1/2-turn at a time until they can be removed by hand. Remove the number one connecting rod cap and bearing insert. Don't drop the bearing insert out of the cap.

2B

13.1 A ridge reamer is required to remove the ridge from the top of each cylinder – do this before removing the pistons!

13.3　Check the connecting rod endplay with a feeler gauge as shown

13.4　Mark the caps with a center punch

13.6　To prevent damage to the crankshaft journals and cylinder walls, slip sections of rubber or plastic hose over the rod bolts before removing the pistons

6　Slip a short length of plastic or rubber hose over each connecting rod cap bolt to protect the crankshaft journal and cylinder wall as the piston is removed **(see illustration)**.

7　Remove the bearing insert and push the connecting rod/piston assembly out through the top of the engine. Use a wooden or plastic hammer handle to push on the upper bearing surface in the connecting rod. If resistance is felt, double-check to make sure all of the ridge was removed from the cylinder.

8　Repeat the procedure for the remaining cylinders.

9　After removal, reassemble the connecting rod caps and bearing inserts in their respective connecting rods and install the cap nuts finger tight. Leaving the old bearing inserts in place until reassembly will help prevent the connecting rod bearing surfaces from being accidentally nicked or gouged.

10　Don't separate the pistons from the connecting rods (see Section 18 for additional information).

14　Crankshaft – removal

Refer to illustrations 14.1, 14.3, 14.4a, 14.4b and 14.4c

Note: *The crankshaft can be removed only after the engine has been removed from the vehicle. It's assumed the driveplate, vibration damper, timing chain, oil pan, oil pump and piston/connecting rod assemblies have already been removed.*

1　Before the crankshaft is removed, check the endplay. Mount a dial indicator with the stem in line with the crankshaft and just touching one of the crank throws **(see illustration)**.

2　Push the crankshaft all the way to the rear and zero the dial indicator. Next, pry the crankshaft to the front as far as possible and check the reading on the dial indicator. The distance it moves is the endplay. If it's greater than specified in this Chapter, check the crankshaft thrust surfaces for wear. If no wear is evident, new main bearings should correct the endplay.

3　If a dial indicator isn't available, feeler gauges can be used. Gently pry or push the crankshaft all the way to the front of the engine. Slip feeler gauges between the crankshaft and the front face of the thrust main bearing to determine the clearance **(see illustration)**.

4　On VIN K engines, loosen, then remove, the side bolts securing the main bearing caps to the sides of the cylinder block.

5　Check the main bearing caps to see if they're marked to indicate their locations. They should be numbered consecutively from the front of the engine to the rear. If they aren't, mark them with number stamping dies or a center punch **(see illustrations)**. Main bearing caps generally have a cast-in arrow, which points to the front of the engine **(see illustration)**. Loosen the main bearing cap bolts 1/4-turn at a time each, until they can be removed by hand. Note if any stud bolts are used and make sure they're returned to their original locations when the crankshaft is reinstalled.

6　Gently tap the caps with a soft-face hammer, then separate them from the engine block. If necessary, use the bolts as levers to remove the caps. Try not to drop the bearing inserts if they come out with the caps.

7　Carefully lift the crankshaft out of the engine. It may be a good idea to have an assistant available, since the crankshaft is quite heavy. With the bearing inserts in place in the engine block and main bearing caps, return the caps to their respective locations on the engine block and tighten the bolts finger tight.

14.1   Check crankshaft endplay with a dial indicator . . .

14.3   . . . or slip feeler gauges between the crankshaft and main bearing (number two) thrust surfaces – the endplay is equal to the feeler gauge thickness

14.5a   Use a center punch or number stamping dies to mark the main bearing caps to ensure installation in their original locations on the block – make the punch marks near one of the bolt heads

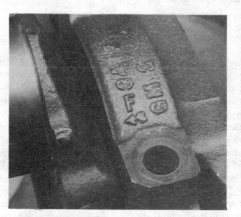

14.5b   Mark the caps in order from the front of the engine to the rear (one mark for the front cap, two for the second one and so on)

14.5c   The arrow on the main bearing cap indicates the front of the engine

15.4   Remove the core plugs with a puller – if they're driven into the block, they may be impossible to retrieve

15   Engine block – cleaning

Refer to illustrations 15.4, 15.8 and 15.10

1   Remove the main bearing caps and separate the bearing inserts from the caps and the engine block. Tag the bearings, indicating which cylinder they were removed from and whether they were in the cap or the block, then set them aside.

2   Using a gasket scraper, remove all traces of gasket material from the engine block. Be very careful not to nick or gouge the gasket sealing surfaces.

3   Remove all of the covers and threaded oil gallery plugs from the block. The plugs are usually very tight – they may have to be drilled out and the holes retapped. Use new plugs when the engine is reassembled.

4   Drill a small hole in the center of each core plug and pull them out with an auto body type dent puller **(see illustration)**. **Caution:** *The core plugs (also known as freeze or soft plugs) may be difficult or impossible to retrieve if they're driven into the block coolant passages.*

**15.8   Clean and restore all threaded holes in the block –
especially the main bearing cap and head bolt holes – with a tap
(be sure to remove debris from the holes when you're done)**

**15.10   A large socket on an extension can be used to drive the
new core plugs into the bores**

5   If the engine is extremely dirty, it should be taken to an automotive machine shop to be steam cleaned or hot tanked.

6   After the block is returned, clean all oil holes and oil galleries one more time. Brushes specifically designed for this purpose are available at most auto parts stores. Flush the passages with warm water until the water runs clear, dry the block thoroughly and wipe all machined surfaces with a light, rust preventive oil. If you have access to compressed air, use it to speed the drying process and blow out all the oil holes and galleries. **Warning:** *Wear eye protection when using compressed air!*

7   If the block isn't extremely dirty or sludged up, you can do an adequate cleaning job with hot soapy water and a stiff brush. Take plenty of time and do a thorough job. Regardless of the cleaning method used, be sure to clean all oil holes and galleries very thoroughly, dry the block completely and coat all machined surfaces with light oil.

8   The threaded holes in the block must be clean to ensure accurate torque readings during reassembly. Run the proper size tap into each of the holes to remove rust, corrosion, thread sealant or sludge and restore damaged threads **(see illustration)**. If possible, use compressed air to clear the holes of debris produced by this operation. Now is a good time to clean the threads on the head bolts and the main bearing cap bolts as well.

9   Reinstall the main bearing caps and tighten the bolts finger tight.

10   After coating the sealing surfaces of the new core plugs with Permatex no. 2 sealant, install them in the engine block **(see illustration)**. Make sure they're driven in straight and seated properly or leakage could result. Special tools are available for this purpose, but a large socket, with an outside diameter that will just slip into the core plug, a 1/2-inch drive extension and a hammer will work just as well.

11   Apply non-hardening sealant (such as Permatex no. 2 or Teflon pipe sealant) to the new oil gallery plugs and thread them into the holes in the block. Make sure they're tightened securely.

12   If the engine isn't going to be reassembled right away, cover it with a large plastic trash bag to keep it clean.

16   Engine block – inspection

Refer to illustrations 16.4a, 16.4b and 16.4c

Note: *The manufacturer recommends checking the block deck and trans-*

axle mounting bolt hole bosses for warpage and the main bearing bore concentricity and alignment. Since special measuring tools are needed, the checks should be done by an automotive machine shop.

1   Before the block is inspected, it should be cleaned as described in Section 15.

2   Visually check the block for cracks, rust and corrosion. Look for stripped threads in the threaded holes. It's also a good idea to have the block checked for hidden cracks by an automotive machine shop that has the special equipment to do this type of work. If defects are found, have the block repaired, if possible, or replaced.

3   Check the cylinder bores for scuffing and scoring.

4   Measure the diameter of each cylinder at the top (just under the ridge area), center and bottom of the cylinder bore, parallel to the crankshaft axis **(see illustrations)**. **Note:** *These measurements should not be made*

**16.4a   Measure the diameter of each cylinder just under the wear
ridge (A), at the center (B) and at the bottom (C)**

16.4b   The ability to "feel" when the telescoping gauge is at the correct point will be developed over time, so work slowly and repeat the check until you're satisfied the bore measurement is accurate

16.4c   The gauge is then measured with a micrometer to determine the bore size

with the bare block mounted on an engine stand – the cylinders will be distorted and the measurements will be inaccurate.

5   Next, measure each cylinder's diameter at the same three locations across the crankshaft axis. Compare the results to this Chapter's Specifications.

6   If the required precision measuring tools aren't available, the piston-to-cylinder clearances can be obtained, though not quite as accurately, using feeler gauge stock. Feeler gauge stock comes in 12-inch lengths and various thicknesses and is generally available at auto parts stores.

7   To check the clearance, select a feeler gauge and slip it into the cylinder along with the matching piston. The piston must be positioned exactly as it normally would be. The feeler gauge must be between the piston and cylinder on one of the thrust faces (90-degrees to the piston pin bore).

8   The piston should slip through the cylinder (with the feeler gauge in place) with moderate pressure.

9   If it falls through or slides through easily, the clearance is excessive and a new piston will be required. If the piston binds at the lower end of the cylinder and is loose toward the top, the cylinder is tapered. If tight spots are encountered as the piston/feeler gauge is rotated in the cylinder, the cylinder is out-of-round.

10   Repeat the procedure for the remaining pistons and cylinders.

11   If the cylinder walls are badly scuffed or scored, or if they're out-of-round or tapered beyond the limits given in this Chapter's Specifications, have the engine block rebored and honed at an automotive machine shop. If a rebore is done, oversize pistons and rings will be required.

12   If the cylinders are in reasonably good condition and not worn to the outside of the limits, and if the piston-to-cylinder clearances can be maintained properly, they don't have to be rebored. Honing is all that's necessary (see Section 17).

2B

17.3a   If this is the first time you've ever honed cylinders, you'll get better results with a "bottle brush" hone than you will with a traditional spring-loaded hone

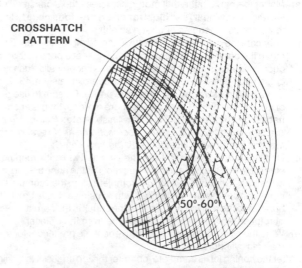

17.3b   The cylinder hone should leave a smooth, crosshatch pattern with the lines intersecting at approximately a 45-degree angle

18.4a　The piston ring grooves can be cleaned with a special tool, as shown here, . . .

18.4b　. . . or a piece of broken piston ring

17　Cylinder honing

Refer to illustrations 17.3a and 17.3b

1　Prior to engine reassembly, the cylinder bores must be honed so the new piston rings will seat correctly and provide the best possible combustion chamber seal. **Note:** If *you don't have the tools or don't want to tackle the honing operation, most automotive machine shops will do it for a reasonable fee.*

2　Before honing the cylinders, install the main bearing caps and tighten the bolts to the specified torque.

3　Two types of cylinder hones are commonly available – the flex hone or "bottle brush" type and the more traditional surfacing hone with spring-loaded stones. Both will do the job, but for the less experienced mechanic the "bottle brush" hone will probably be easier to use. You'll also need some honing oil (kerosene will work if honing oil isn't available), rags and an electric drill motor. Proceed as follows:

    a)　Mount the hone in the drill motor, compress the stones and slip it into the first cylinder **(see illustration on previous page)**. Be sure to wear safety goggles or a face shield!

    b)　Lubricate the cylinder with plenty of honing oil, turn on the drill and move the hone up-and-down in the cylinder at a pace that will produce a fine crosshatch pattern on the cylinder walls. Ideally, the crosshatch lines should intersect at approximately a 45-degree angle **(see illustration on previous page)**. Be sure to use plenty of lubricant and don't take off any more material than is absolutely necessary to produce the desired finish. **Note:** *Piston ring manufacturers may specify a different crosshatch angle – read and follow any instructions included with the new rings.*

    c)　Don't withdraw the hone from the cylinder while it's running. Instead, shut off the drill and continue moving the hone up-and-down in the cylinder until it comes to a complete stop, then compress the stones and withdraw the hone. If you're using a "bottle brush" type hone, stop the drill motor, then turn the chuck in the normal direction of rotation while withdrawing the hone from the cylinder.

    d)　Wipe the oil out of the cylinder and repeat the procedure for the remaining cylinders.

4　After the honing job is complete, chamfer the top edges of the cylinder bores with a small file so the rings won't catch when the pistons are installed. Be very careful not to nick the cylinder walls with the end of the file.

5　The entire engine block must be washed again very thoroughly with warm, soapy water to remove all traces of the abrasive grit produced during the honing operation. **Note:** *The bores can be considered clean when*

a lint-free white cloth – dampened with clean engine oil – used to wipe them out doesn't pick up any more honing residue, which will show up as gray areas on the cloth. Be sure to run a brush through all oil holes and galleries and flush them with running water.

6　After rinsing, dry the block and apply a coat of light rust preventive oil to all machined surfaces. Wrap the block in a plastic trash bag to keep it clean and set it aside until reassembly.

18　Pistons and connecting rods – inspection

Refer to illustrations 18.4a, 18.4b, 18.10 and 18.11

1　Before the inspection process can be carried out, the piston/connecting rod assemblies must be cleaned and the original piston rings removed from the pistons. **Note:** *Always use new piston rings when the engine is reassembled.*

2　Using a piston ring installation tool, carefully remove the rings from the pistons. Be careful not to nick or gouge the pistons in the process.

3　Scrape all traces of carbon from the top of the piston. A hand held wire brush or a piece of fine emery cloth can be used once the majority of the deposits have been scraped away. Do not, under any circumstances, use a wire brush mounted in a drill motor to remove deposits from the pistons. The piston material is soft and may be eroded away by the wire brush.

4　Use a piston ring groove cleaning tool to remove carbon deposits from the ring grooves. If a tool isn't available, a piece broken off the old ring will do the job. Be very careful to remove only the carbon deposits – don't remove any metal and do not nick or scratch the sides of the ring grooves **(see illustrations)**.

5　Once the deposits have been removed, clean the piston/rod assemblies with solvent and dry them with compressed air (if available). **Warning:** *Wear eye protection.* Make sure the oil return holes in the back sides of the ring grooves are clear.

6　If the pistons and cylinder walls aren't damaged or worn excessively, and if the engine block isn't rebored, new pistons won't be necessary. Normal piston wear appears as even vertical wear on the piston thrust surfaces and slight looseness of the top ring in its groove. New piston rings, however, should always be used when an engine is rebuilt.

7　Carefully inspect each piston for cracks around the skirt, at the pin bosses and at the ring lands.

8　Look for scoring and scuffing on the thrust faces of the skirt, holes in the piston crown and burned areas at the edge of the crown. If the skirt is scored or scuffed, the engine may have been suffering from overheating

18.10 Check the ring side clearance with a feeler gauge at several points around the groove

18.11 Measure the piston diameter at a 90-degree angle to the piston pin at the specified point on the skirt (see the text)

and/or abnormal combustion, which caused excessively high operating temperatures. The cooling and lubrication systems should be checked thoroughly. A hole in the piston crown is an indication that abnormal combustion (preignition) was occurring. Burned areas at the edge of the piston crown are usually evidence of spark knock (detonation). If any of the above problems exist, the causes must be corrected or the damage will occur again. The causes may include intake air leaks, incorrect fuel/air mixture, low octane fuel, ignition timing and EGR system malfunctions.

9   Corrosion of the piston, in the form of small pits, indicates coolant is leaking into the combustion chamber and/or the crankcase. Again, the cause must be corrected or the problem may persist in the rebuilt engine.

10   Measure the piston ring side clearance by laying a new piston ring in each ring groove and slipping a feeler gauge in beside it **(see illustration)**. Check the clearance at three or four locations around each groove. Be sure to use the correct ring for each groove – they are different. If the side clearance is greater than specified in this Chapter, new pistons will have to be used.

11   Check the piston-to-bore clearance by measuring the bore (see Section 16) and the piston diameter. Make sure the pistons and bores are correctly matched. Measure the piston across the skirt, at a 90-degree angle to the piston pin **(see illustration)**. The measurement must be taken at a specific point, depending on the engine type, to be accurate.

   a) The piston diameter on 3800 engines (with balance shaft) is measured directly in line with the piston pin centerline.

   b) 3.0 and 3.8 liter engine pistons are measured 3/4-inch (19 mm) below the center of the piston pin.

12   Subtract the piston diameter from the bore diameter to obtain the clearance. If it's greater than specified, the block will have to be rebored and new pistons and rings installed.

13   Check the piston-to-rod clearance by twisting the piston and rod in opposite directions. Any noticeable play indicates excessive wear, which must be corrected. The piston/connecting rod assemblies should be taken to an automotive machine shop to have the pistons and rods resized and new pins installed.

14   If the pistons must be removed from the connecting rods for any reason, they should be taken to an automotive machine shop. While they are there have the connecting rods checked for bend and twist, since automotive machine shops have special equipment for this purpose. **Note:** *Unless new pistons and/or connecting rods must be installed, do not disassemble the pistons and connecting rods.*

15   Check the connecting rods for cracks and other damage. Temporarily remove the rod caps, lift out the old bearing inserts, wipe the rod and cap bearing surfaces clean and inspect them for nicks, gouges and scratches.

After checking the rods, replace the old bearings, slip the caps into place and tighten the nuts finger tight. **Note:** *If the engine is being rebuilt because of a connecting rod knock, be sure to install new rods.*

19 Crankshaft – inspection

Refer to illustrations 19.1, 19.2, 19.4, 19.6 and 19.8

1   Remove all burrs from the crankshaft oil holes with a stone, file or scraper **(see illustration)**.

2   Clean the crankshaft with solvent and dry it with compressed air (if available). **Warning:** *Wear eye protection when using compressed air.* Be sure to clean the oil holes with a stiff brush **(see illustration)** and flush them with solvent.

19.1 Chamfer the oil holes to remove sharp edges that might gouge or scratch the new bearings

2B

19.2   Clean the crankshaft oil passages with a wire or stiff plastic bristle brush and flush them out with solvent

19.4   Rubbing a penny lengthwise on each journal will give you a quick idea of its condition – if copper rubs off the penny and adheres to the crankshaft, the journals should be reground

3   Check the main and connecting rod bearing journals for uneven wear, scoring, pits and cracks.

4   Rub a penny across each journal several times **(see illustration)**. If a journal picks up copper from the penny, it's too rough and must be reground.

5   Check the rest of the crankshaft for cracks and other damage. It should be magnafluxed to reveal hidden cracks – an automotive machine shop will handle the procedure.

6   Using a micrometer, measure the diameter of the main and connecting rod journals and compare the results to this Chapter's Specifications **(see illustration)**. By measuring the diameter at a number of points around each journal's circumference, you'll be able to determine whether or not the journal is out-of-round. Take the measurement at each end of the

journal, near the crank throws, to determine if the journal is tapered.

7   If the crankshaft journals are damaged, tapered, out-of-round or worn beyond the limits given in the Specifications, have the crankshaft reground by an automotive machine shop. Be sure to use the correct size bearing inserts if the crankshaft is reconditioned.

8   Check the oil seal journals at each end of the crankshaft for wear and damage. If the seal has worn a groove in the journal, or if it's nicked or scratched **(see illustration)**, the new seal may leak when the engine is reassembled. In some cases, an automotive machine shop may be able to repair the journal by pressing on a thin sleeve. If repair isn't feasible, a new or different crankshaft should be installed.

9   Refer to Section 20 and examine the main and rod bearing inserts.

19.6   Measure the diameter of each crankshaft journal at several points to detect taper and out-of-round conditions

19.8   If the seals have worn grooves in the crankshaft journals, or if the seal journals are nicked or scratched, the new seal(s) will leak (typical crankshaft shown)

CRATERS OR POCKETS

FATIGUE FAILURE

BRIGHT (POLISHED) SECTIONS

IMPROPER SEATING

SCRATCHES

DIRT IMBEDDED INTO BEARING MATERIAL

SCRATCHED BY DIRT

OVERLAY WIPED OUT

LACK OF OIL

OVERLAY GONE FROM ENTIRE SURFACE

EXCESSIVE WEAR

RADIUS RIDE

TAPERED JOURNAL

20.1   Typical bearing failures

20   Main and connecting rod bearings – inspection

Refer to illustration 20.1

1   Even though the main and connecting rod bearings should be replaced with new ones during the engine overhaul, the old bearings should be retained for close examination, as they may reveal valuable information about the condition of the engine **(see illustration)**.

2   Bearing failure occurs because of lack of lubrication, the presence of dirt or other foreign particles, overloading the engine and corrosion. Regardless of the cause of bearing failure, it must be corrected before the engine is reassembled to prevent it from happening again.

3   When examining the bearings, remove them from the engine block, the main bearing caps, the connecting rods and the rod caps and lay them out on a clean surface in the same general position as their location in the engine. This will enable you to match any bearing problems with the corresponding crankshaft journal.

4   Dirt and other foreign particles get into the engine in a variety of ways. It may be left in the engine during assembly, or it may pass through filters or the PCV system. It may get into the oil, and from there into the bearings. Metal chips from machining operations and normal engine wear are often present. Abrasives are sometimes left in engine components after reconditioning, especially when parts aren't thoroughly cleaned using the proper cleaning methods. Whatever the source, these foreign objects often end up embedded in the soft bearing material and are easily recognized. Large particles won't embed in the bearing and will score or gouge the

bearing and journal. The best prevention for this cause of bearing failure is to clean all parts thoroughly and keep everything spotlessly clean during engine assembly. Frequent and regular engine oil and filter changes are also recommended.

5   Lack of lubrication (or lubrication breakdown) has a number of interrelated causes. Excessive heat (which thins the oil), overloading (which squeezes the oil from the bearing face) and oil leakage or throw off (from excessive bearing clearances, worn oil pump or high engine speeds) all contribute to lubrication breakdown. Blocked oil passages, which usually are the result of misaligned oil holes in a bearing shell, will also oil starve a bearing and destroy it. When lack of lubrication is the cause of bearing failure, the bearing material is wiped or extruded from the steel backing of the bearing. Temperatures may increase to the point where the steel backing turns blue from overheating.

6   Driving habits can have a definite effect on bearing life. Full throttle, low speed operation (lugging the engine) puts very high loads on bearings, which tends to squeeze out the oil film. These loads cause the bearings to flex, which produces fine cracks in the bearing face (fatigue failure). Eventually the bearing material will loosen in pieces and tear away from the steel backing. Short trip driving leads to corrosion of bearings because insufficient engine heat is produced to drive off the condensed water and corrosive gases. These products collect in the engine oil, forming acid and sludge. As the oil is carried to the engine bearings, the acid attacks and corrodes the bearing material.

7   Incorrect bearing installation during engine assembly will lead to bearing failure as well. Tight fitting bearings leave insufficient oil clearance and will result in oil starvation. Dirt or foreign particles trapped behind a bearing insert result in high spots on the bearing which lead to failure.

21   Engine overhaul – reassembly sequence

1   Before beginning engine reassembly, make sure you have all the necessary new parts, gaskets and seals as well as the following items on hand:

> Common hand tools
> Torque wrench (1/2-inch drive)
> Piston ring installation tool
> Piston ring compressor
> Vibration damper installation tool
> Short lengths of rubber or plastic hose to fit over
>   connecting rod bolts
> Plastigage
> Feeler gauges
> Fine-tooth file
> New engine oil
> Engine assembly lube or moly-base grease
> Gasket sealant
> Thread locking compound

2   In order to save time and avoid problems, engine reassembly must be done in the following general order:

> Crankshaft and main bearings
> Piston/connecting rod assemblies
> Balance shaft (3800 engine only)
> Camshaft
> Timing chain and sprockets
> Timing chain cover and oil pump
> Oil pan
> Cylinder heads
> Valve lifters
> Rocker arms and pushrods
> Intake and exhaust manifolds
> Rocker arm covers

2B

22.3   When checking the piston ring end gap, the ring must be square in the cylinder bore – this is done by pushing the ring down with the top of a piston

22.4   Once the ring is at the lower limit of travel and square in the cylinder, measure the end gap with a feeler gauge

22.5   If the end gap is too small, clamp a file in a vise and file the ring ends (from the outside in only) to enlarge the gap slightly

22   Piston rings – installation

Refer to illustrations 22.3, 22.4, 22.5, 22.9a, 22.9b and 22.12

1   Before installing the new piston rings, the ring end gaps must be checked. It's assumed the piston ring side clearance has been checked and verified correct (see Section 18).

2   Lay out the piston/connecting rod assemblies and the new ring sets so the ring sets will be matched with the same piston and cylinder during the end gap measurement and engine assembly.

3   Insert the top (number one) ring into the first cylinder and square it up with the cylinder walls by pushing it in with the top of the piston **(see illustration)**. The ring should be near the bottom of the cylinder, at the lower limit of ring travel.

4   To measure the end gap, slip feeler gauges between the ends of the ring until a gauge equal to the gap width is found **(see illustration)**. The feeler gauge should slide between the ring ends with a slight amount of drag. Compare the measurement to this Chapter's Specifications. If the gap is larger or smaller than specified, double-check to make sure you have the correct rings before proceeding.

5   If the gap is too small, it must be enlarged or the ring ends may come in contact with each other during engine operation, which can cause serious engine damage. The end gap can be increased by filing the ring ends very carefully with a fine file. Mount the file in a vise equipped with soft jaws, slip the ring over the file with the ends contacting the file teeth and slowly move the ring to remove material from the ends. When performing this operation, file only from the outside in **(see illustration)**.

6   Excess end gap isn't critical unless it's greater than 0.040-inch. Again, double-check to make sure you have the correct rings for the engine.

7   Repeat the procedure for each ring that will be installed in the first cylinder and for each ring in the remaining cylinders. Remember to keep rings, pistons and cylinders matched up.

8   Once the ring end gaps have been checked/corrected, the rings can be installed on the pistons.

9   The oil control ring (lowest one on the piston) is usually installed first. It's composed of three separate components. Slip the spacer/expander into the groove **(see illustration)**. If an anti-rotation tang is used, make sure it's inserted into the drilled hole in the ring groove. Next, install the lower side rail. Don't use a piston ring installation tool on the oil ring side rails, as they may be damaged. Instead, place one end of the side rail into the groove between the spacer/expander and the ring land, hold it firmly in place and slide a finger around the piston while pushing the rail into the groove **(see illustration)**. Next, install the upper side rail in the same manner.

22.9a   Install the three-piece oil control ring first, one part at a time, beginning with the spacer/expander, . . .

22.9b   . . . followed by the side rails – DO NOT use a piston ring installation tool to install the oil ring side rails

2B

10   After the three oil ring components have been installed, check to make sure both the upper and lower side rails can be turned smoothly in the ring groove.

11   The number two (middle) ring is installed next. It's usually stamped with a mark, which must face up, toward the top of the piston. **Note:** *Always follow the instructions printed on the ring package or box – different manufacturers may require different approaches. Don't mix up the top and middle rings, as they have different cross sections.*

12   Use a piston ring installation tool and make sure the identification mark is facing the top of the piston, then slip the ring into the middle groove on the piston **(see illustration)**. Don't expand the ring any more than necessary to slide it over the piston.

13   Install the number one (top) ring in the same manner. Make sure the mark is facing up. Be careful not to confuse the number one and number two rings.

14   Repeat the procedure for the remaining pistons and rings.

---

23   Crankshaft – installation and main bearing oil clearance check

Refer to illustrations 23.11 and 23.15

1   Crankshaft installation is the first step in engine reassembly. It's assumed at this point that the engine block and crankshaft have been cleaned, inspected and repaired or reconditioned.

2   Position the engine with the bottom facing up.

3   Remove the main bearing cap bolts and lift out the caps. Lay them out in the proper order to ensure correct installation.

4   If they're still in place, remove the original bearing inserts from the block and the main bearing caps. Wipe the bearing surfaces of the block and caps with a clean, lint-free cloth. They must be kept spotlessly clean.

Main bearing oil clearance check

Note: *Don't touch the faces of the new bearing inserts with your fingers. Oil and acids from your skin can etch the bearings.*

5   Clean the back sides of the new main bearing inserts and lay one in each main bearing saddle in the block. If one of the bearing inserts from

22.12   Install the compression rings with a ring expander – the mark (arrow) must face up

each set has a large groove in it, make sure the grooved insert is installed in the block. Lay the other bearing from each set in the corresponding main bearing cap. Make sure the tab on the bearing insert fits into the recess in the block or cap. **Caution:** *The oil holes in the block must line up with the oil holes in the bearing inserts. Do not hammer the bearing into place and don't nick or gouge the bearing faces. No lubrication should be used at this time.*

6   The flanged thrust bearing must be installed in the number two cap and saddle (counting from the front of the engine).

7   Clean the faces of the bearings in the block and the crankshaft main bearing journals with a clean, lint-free cloth.

23.11   Lay the Plastigage strips (arrow) on the main bearing journals, parallel to the crankshaft centerline

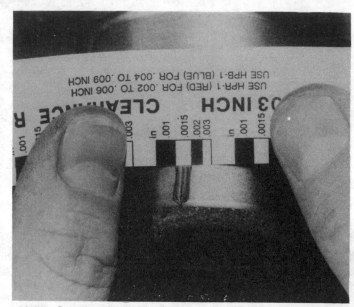

23.15   Compare the width of the crushed Plastigage to the scale on the envelope to determine the main bearing oil clearance (always take the measurement at the widest point of the Plastigage); be sure to use the correct scale – standard and metric ones are included

8   Check or clean the oil holes in the crankshaft, as any dirt here can go only one way – straight through the new bearings.

9   Once you're certain the crankshaft is clean, carefully lay it in position in the main bearings.

10   Before the crankshaft can be permanently installed, the main bearing oil clearance must be checked.

11   Cut several pieces of the appropriate size Plastigage (they should be slightly shorter than the width of the main bearings) and place one piece on each crankshaft main bearing journal, parallel with the journal axis **(see illustration)**.

12   Clean the faces of the bearings in the caps and install the caps in their original locations (don't mix them up) with the arrows pointing toward the front of the engine. Don't disturb the Plastigage.

13   Starting with the center main and working out toward the ends, tighten the main bearing cap bolts, in three steps, to the torque figure listed in this Chapter's Specifications. Don't rotate the crankshaft at any time during this operation.

14   Remove the bolts and carefully lift off the main bearing caps. Keep them in order. Don't disturb the Plastigage or rotate the crankshaft. If any of the main bearing caps are difficult to remove, tap them gently from side-to-side with a soft-face hammer to loosen them.

15   Compare the width of the crushed Plastigage on each journal to the scale printed on the Plastigage envelope to obtain the main bearing oil clearance **(see illustration)**. Check the Specifications to make sure it's correct.

16   If the clearance is not as specified, the bearing inserts may be the wrong size (which means different ones will be required). Before deciding different inserts are needed, make sure no dirt or oil was between the bearing inserts and the caps or block when the clearance was measured. If the Plastigage was wider at one end than the other, the journal may be tapered (refer to Section 20).

17   Carefully scrape all traces of the Plastigage material off the main bearing journals and/or the bearing faces. Use your fingernail or the edge of a credit card – don't nick or scratch the bearing faces.

Final crankshaft installation

18   Carefully lift the crankshaft out of the engine.

19   Clean the bearing faces in the block, then apply a thin, uniform layer of moly-base grease or engine assembly lube to each of the bearing sur-

faces. Be sure to coat the thrust faces as well as the journal face of the thrust bearing. Install the rear oil seal (1990 and earlier models only) (see Section 25).

20   Make sure the crankshaft journals are clean, then lay the crankshaft back in place in the block.

21   Clean the faces of the bearings in the caps, then apply lubricant to them.

22   Install the caps in their original locations with the arrows pointing toward the front of the engine.

23   Install the bolts.

24   Tighten all except the thrust bearing cap bolts to the specified torque (work from the center out and approach the final torque in three steps).

25   Tighten the thrust bearing cap bolts to 10-to-12 ft-lbs.

26   Tap the ends of the crankshaft forward and backward with a lead or brass hammer to line up the main bearing and crankshaft thrust surfaces.

27   Retighten all main bearing cap bolts to the torque specified in this Chapter, starting with the center main and working out toward the ends.

28   On VIN K engines, install the side bolts securing the main bearing caps to the sides of the cylinder block. Tighten to the torque listed in this Chapter's Specifications.

29   Rotate the crankshaft a number of times by hand to check for any obvious binding.

30   The final step is to check the crankshaft endplay with feeler gauges or a dial indicator as described in Section 14. The endplay should be correct if the crankshaft thrust faces aren't worn or damaged and new bearings have been installed.

---

24   Camshaft and balance shaft – installation

Refer to illustrations 24.1 and 24.6

Camshaft

1   Lubricate the camshaft bearing journals and cam lobes with moly-base grease or engine assembly lube **(see illustration)**.

2   Slide the camshaft into the engine. Support the cam near the block and be careful not to scrape or nick the bearings. Install the thrust plate and tighten the bolts to the torque listed in the Part A Specifications.

3   Refer to Part A for further instructions and complete the installation of the timing chain, sprockets and lifters.

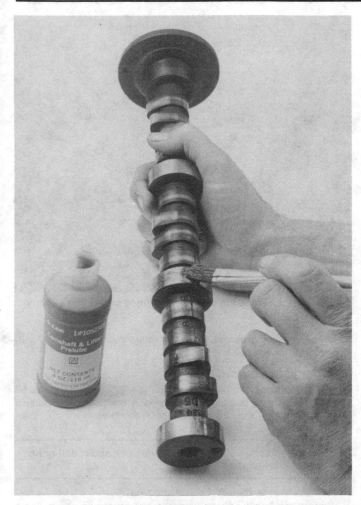

24.1   Be sure to prelube the camshaft bearing journals and lobes before installation

Balance shaft (3800 engine only)

4   If the balance shaft timing was disturbed during engine repair, turn the camshaft so that with the camshaft sprocket temporarily installed, the timing mark is straight down.

24.6   Align the marks on the gears as shown here (3800 engine only)

5   With the camshaft sprocket and the camshaft gear removed, turn the balance shaft so the timing mark on the gear points straight down.
6   Align the marks on the balance shaft gear and the camshaft gear **(see illustration)** by turning the balance shaft.
7   Install the timing chain and sprockets (see Part A).

---

25   Crankshaft rear oil seal – installation

2B

1985 through 1990 models

Refer to illustrations 25.1, 25.2, 25.3a, 25.3b, 25.4 and 25.7

Note: *The crankshaft rear oil seal must be in place prior to crankshaft installation.*

1   Lay one seal section on edge in the seal groove in the block and push it into place with your thumbs. Both ends of the seal should extend out of the block slightly **(see illustration)**.
2   Seat it in the groove by rolling a large socket or piece of bar stock along the entire length of the seal **(see illustration)**. As an alternative, roll the seal very carefully into place with a wooden hammer handle.

25.1   When correctly installed, the ends of the seal should extend out of the block slightly

25.2   Set the seal in the groove, but don't depress it below the bearing surface (the seal must contact the crankshaft journal)

25.3a   Trim the seal ends flush with the block, . . .

25.3b   . . . but leave the inner edge (arrow) protruding slightly

3   Once the seal is completely seated in the groove, trim off the excess on the ends with a single edge razor blade or razor knife **(see illustrations)**. The seal ends must be flush with the block-to-cap mating surfaces. Make sure the cut is clean so no seal fibers get caught between the block and cap.

4   Repeat the entire procedure to install the the other half of the seal in the bearing cap. Apply a thin film of assembly lube or moly-base grease to the edge of the seal where it contacts the crankshaft **(see illustration)**.

5   Soak the bearing cap side seals in kerosene or light oil prior to installation. They swell in the presence of oil and heat. The seals are slightly longer than the bearing cap grooves and must be cut to length.

6   Lightly coat the crankshaft journal with assembly lube or moly-base grease, then refer to Section 23 and install the crankshaft.

7   During final installation of the crankshaft (after the main bearing oil clearances have been checked with Plastigage), apply a thin, even coat of anerobic gasket sealant to the parting surfaces of the bearing cap or block **(see illustration)**. Don't get any sealant on the bearing or seal faces.

8   Install the cap, bearing and oil seal assembly and tighten the cap bolts to the torque listed in this Chapter's specifications.

9   After the cap is bolted in place, insert the side seals into the grooves

and make sure they're seated. As an alternative, you can inject RTV sealant into the grooves.

1991 and later models

10   These models use a one-piece, lip type seal. The crankshaft must be in place and the main bearing caps installed before the seal is installed. See Chapter 2, Part A for the replacement procedure.

---

26   Pistons and connecting rods – installation and rod bearing oil clearance check

Refer to illustrations 26.9, 26.11, 26.13 and 26.17

1   Before installing the piston/connecting rod assemblies, the cylinder walls must be perfectly clean, the top edge of each cylinder must be chamfered, and the crankshaft must be in place.

2   Remove the cap from the end of the number one connecting rod (check the marks made during removal). Remove the original bearing inserts and wipe the bearing surfaces of the connecting rod and cap with a clean, lint-free cloth. They must be kept spotlessly clean.

25.4   Lubricate the seal with assembly lube or moly-base grease

25.7   When applying sealant, be sure it gets into each corner and onto the vertical cap-to-block mating surfaces or oil leaks will result

1. NOTCH ON PISTON TOWARDS FRONT OF ENGINE
2. LEFT BANK: NO. 1, 3 & 5 TWO BOSSES ON ROD
                 TOWARDS REAR OF ENGINE (NOT
                 SHOWN)
   RIGHT BANK: NO. 2, 4 & 6 TWO BOSSES ON ROD
                 TOWARDS FRONT OF ENGINE (NOT
                 SHOWN)
3. LEFT BANK: CHAMFERED CORNERS ON ROD CAP
                 TOWARDS FRONT OF ENGINE
   RIGHT BANK: CHAMFERED CORNERS ON ROD CAP
                 TOWARDS REAR OF ENGINE

26.9   The notch or arrow on each piston must face the front (timing chain) end of the engine as the pistons are installed

26.11   Drive the piston gently into the cylinder bore with the end of a wooden or plastic hammer handle

Connecting rod bearing oil clearance check

Note: *Don't touch the faces of the new bearing inserts with your fingers. Oil and acids from your skin can etch the bearings.*

3   Clean the back side of the new upper bearing insert, then lay it in place in the connecting rod. Make sure the tab on the bearing fits into the recess in the rod. Don't hammer the bearing insert into place and be very careful not to nick or gouge the bearing face. Don't lubricate the bearing at this time.

4   Clean the back side of the other bearing insert and install it in the rod cap. Again, make sure the tab on the bearing fits into the recess in the cap, and don't apply any lubricant. It's critically important that the mating surfaces of the bearing and connecting rod are perfectly clean and oil free when they're assembled.

5   Position the piston ring gaps at 120-degree intervals around the piston.

6   Slip a section of plastic or rubber hose over each connecting rod cap bolt.

7   Lubricate the piston and rings with clean engine oil and attach a piston ring compressor to the piston. Leave the skirt protruding about 1/4-inch to guide the piston into the cylinder. The rings must be compressed until they're flush with the piston.

8   Rotate the crankshaft until the number one connecting rod journal is at BDC (bottom dead center) and apply a coat of engine oil to the cylinder walls.

9   With the mark or notch on top of the piston **(see illustration)** facing the front of the engine, gently insert the piston/connecting rod assembly into the number one cylinder bore and rest the bottom edge of the ring compressor on the engine block.

10   Tap the top edge of the ring compressor to make sure it's contacting the block around its entire circumference.

11   Gently tap on the top of the piston with the end of a wooden or plastic hammer handle **(see illustration)** while guiding the end of the connecting rod into place on the crankshaft journal. The piston rings may try to pop out of the ring compressor just before entering the cylinder bore, so keep some downward pressure on the ring compressor. Work slowly, and if any resistance is felt as the piston enters the cylinder, stop immediately. Find out what's hanging up and fix it before proceeding. Do not, for any reason, force the piston into the cylinder – you might break a ring and/or the piston.

12   Once the piston/connecting rod assembly is installed, the connecting rod bearing oil clearance must be checked before the rod cap is permanently bolted in place.

13   Cut a piece of the appropriate size Plastigage slightly shorter than the width of the connecting rod bearing and lay it in place on the number one connecting rod journal, parallel with the journal axis **(see illustration)**.

14   Clean the connecting rod cap bearing face, remove the protective hoses from the connecting rod bolts and install the rod cap. Make sure the mating mark on the cap is on the same side as the mark on the connecting rod.

15   Install the nuts and tighten them to the torque listed in this Chapter's Specifications. Work up to it in three steps. **Note:** *Use a thin-wall socket to avoid erroneous torque readings that can result if the socket is wedged between the rod cap and nut. If the socket tends to wedge itself between the nut and the cap, lift up on it slightly until it no longer contacts the cap. Do not rotate the crankshaft at any time during this operation.*

16   Remove the nuts and detach the rod cap, being very careful not to disturb the Plastigage.

26.13   Lay the Plastigage strips on each rod bearing journal, parallel to the crankshaft centerline

26.17   Measure the width of the crushed Plastigage with the scale on the envelope to determine the rod bearing oil clearance (be sure to use the correct scale – standard and metric ones are included)

17   Compare the width of the crushed Plastigage to the scale printed on the Plastigage envelope to obtain the oil clearance **(see illustration)**. Compare it to this Chapter's Specifications to make sure the clearance is correct.

18   If the clearance is not as specified, the bearing inserts may be the wrong size (which means different ones will be required). Before deciding different inserts are needed, make sure no dirt or oil was between the bearing inserts and the connecting rod or cap when the clearance was measured. Also, recheck the journal diameter. If the Plastigage was wider at one end than the other, the journal may be tapered (refer to Section 19).

Final connecting rod installation

19   Carefully scrape all traces of the Plastigage material off the rod journal and/or bearing face. Be very careful not to scratch the bearing – use your fingernail or the edge of a credit card.

20   Make sure the bearing faces are perfectly clean, then apply a uniform layer of clean moly-base grease or engine assembly lube to both of them. You'll have to push the piston into the cylinder to expose the face of the bearing insert in the connecting rod – be sure to slip the protective hoses over the rod bolts first.

21   Slide the connecting rod back into place on the journal, remove the protective hoses from the rod cap bolts, install the rod cap and tighten the nuts to the torque specified in this Chapter. Again, work up to the torque in three steps.

22   Repeat the entire procedure for the remaining pistons/connecting rods.

23   The important points to remember are . . .
   a) Keep the back sides of the bearing inserts and the insides of the connecting rods and caps perfectly clean when assembling them.
   b) Make sure you have the correct piston/rod assembly for each cylinder.
   c) The arrow or mark on the piston must face the front (timing chain end) of the engine.
   d) Lubricate the cylinder walls with clean oil.
   e) Lubricate the bearing faces when installing the rod caps after the oil clearance has been checked.

24   After all the piston/connecting rod assemblies have been properly installed, rotate the crankshaft a number of times by hand to check for any obvious binding.

25   As a final step, the connecting rod endplay must be checked. Refer to Section 13 for this procedure.

26   Compare the measured endplay to this Chapter's Specifications to make sure it's correct. If it was correct before disassembly and the original crankshaft and rods were reinstalled, it should still be right. If new rods or a new crankshaft were installed, the endplay may be inadequate. If so, the rods will have to be removed and taken to an automotive machine shop for resizing.

27   Initial start-up and break-in after overhaul

Warning: *Have a fire extinguisher handy when starting the engine for the first time.*

1   Once the engine has been installed in the vehicle, double-check the oil and coolant levels.

2   With the spark plugs out of the engine and the ECM fuse removed, crank the engine until oil pressure registers on the gauge or the light goes out.

3   Install the spark plugs, hook up the plug wires and install the ECM fuse.

4   Start the engine. It may take a few moments for the fuel system to build up pressure, but the engine should start without a great deal of effort. **Note:** *If the engine keeps backfiring, recheck the valve timing and spark plug wires.*

5   After the engine starts, it should be allowed to warm up to normal operating temperature. While the engine is warming up, make a thorough check for fuel, oil and coolant leaks.

6   Shut the engine off and recheck the engine oil and coolant levels.

7   Drive the vehicle to an area with minimum traffic, accelerate at full throttle from 30 to 50 mph, then allow the vehicle to slow to 30 mph with the throttle closed. Repeat the procedure 10 or 12 times. This will load the piston rings and cause them to seat properly against the cylinder walls. Check again for oil and coolant leaks.

8   Drive the vehicle gently for the first 500 miles (no sustained high speeds) and keep a constant check on the oil level. It's not unusual for an engine to use oil during the break-in period.

9   At approximately 500 to 600 miles, change the oil and filter.

10   For the next few hundred miles, drive the vehicle normally. Don't pamper it or abuse it.

11   After 2000 miles, change the oil and filter again and consider the engine broken in.

Chapter 3   Cooling, heating and air conditioning systems

Contents

Specifications

General

Cooling system capacity .... See Chapter 1
Radiator cap pressure rating .... See Chapter 1
Thermostat rating .... 195 degrees F
Drivebelt tension .... See Chapter 1

Torque specifications   **Ft-lbs**

Thermostat cover bolts 20
Water pump mounting bolts
    Long bolts .... 22 to 29
    Short bolts .... 7 to 8
Water pump pulley bolts .... 9 to 11

1   General information

Note: *On models equipped with the Delco Loc II audio system, be sure the lockout feature is turned off before performing any procedure which requires disconnecting the battery.*

Engine cooling system

All vehicles covered by this manual employ a pressurized engine cooling system with thermostatically controlled coolant circulation. An impeller type water pump mounted on the engine block pumps coolant through the engine and radiator. The coolant flows around each cylinder and back to the radiator. Cast-in coolant passages direct coolant around the intake and exhaust ports, near the spark plug areas and the exhaust valve guides.

A wax pellet type thermostat is located in a housing connected to the upper radiator hose. During warm up the closed thermostat prevents coolant from circulating through the radiator. As the engine nears normal operating temperature, the thermostat opens and allows hot coolant to travel through the radiator, where it's cooled before returning to the engine.

The cooling system is sealed by a pressure-type radiator cap, which raises the boiling point of the coolant and increases the cooling efficiency of the radiator. If the system pressure exceeds the cap pressure relief value, the excess pressure in the system forces the spring-loaded valve inside the cap off its seat and allows the coolant to escape through a hose into a coolant reservoir. When the system cools, the excess coolant is automatically drawn from the reservoir back into the radiator.

The coolant reservoir does double duty as both the point at which fresh coolant is added to the cooling system to maintain the proper level and as a holding tank for expelled coolant.

This type of cooling system is known as a closed design because coolant that escapes past the pressure cap is saved and reused.

Heating system

The heating system consists of a blower fan and heater core located in the heater box, the hoses connecting the heater core to the engine cooling system and the heater/air conditioning control head on the dashboard. Hot engine coolant is circulated through the heater core. When the heater mode is activated, a trap door opens to expose the heater box to the passenger compartment. A fan switch on the control head activates the blower motor, which forces air through the core, heating the air.

Air conditioning system

The air conditioning system consists of a condenser mounted in front of the radiator, an evaporator mounted adjacent to the heater core, a compressor mounted on the engine, a filter-drier (accumulator), which contains a high pressure relief valve, and the hoses and lines connecting all of the above components.

A blower fan forces the warmer air of the passenger compartment through the evaporator core (sort of a radiator-in-reverse), transferring the heat from the air to the refrigerant. The liquid refrigerant boils off into low pressure vapor, taking the heat with it when it leaves the evaporator.

2   Antifreeze – general information

Warning: *Don't allow antifreeze to come in contact with your skin or painted surfaces of the vehicle. Rinse off spills immediately with plenty of water. Never leave antifreeze lying around in an open container or in a puddle on the driveway or the garage floor. Children and animals are attracted by its sweet smell. Antifreeze is toxic, so use common sense when disposing of it. Some communities maintain toxic material disposal sites and/or offer regular pick-up of hazardous materials. Antifreeze is also combustible, so don't store or use it near open flames.*

The cooling system should be filled with a water/ethylene glycol based antifreeze solution, which will prevent freezing down to at least -20-degrees F, or lower if local climate requires it. It also provides protection against corrosion and increases the coolant boiling point.

The cooling system should be drained, flushed and refilled at the specified intervals (see Chapter 1). Old or contaminated antifreeze solutions are likely to cause damage and encourage the formation of rust and scale in the system. Use distilled water with the antifreeze.

Before adding antifreeze, check all hose connections, because antifreeze tends to search out and leak through very minute openings. Engines don't normally consume coolant, so if the level goes down, find the cause and correct it.

The exact mixture of antifreeze-to-water which you should use depends on the relative weather conditions. The mixture should contain at least 50 percent antifreeze, but should never contain more than 70 percent antifreeze. Consult the mixture ratio chart on the antifreeze container before adding coolant. Hydrometers are available at most auto parts stores to test the coolant. Use antifreeze which meets the vehicle manufacturer's specifications.

3   Thermostat – check and replacement

Warning: *DO NOT remove the radiator cap, drain the coolant or replace the thermostat until the engine has cooled completely.*

Check

1   Before assuming the thermostat is to blame for a cooling system problem, check the coolant level, drivebelt tension (see Chapter 1) and temperature gauge (or light) operation.
2   If the engine seems to be taking a long time to warm up (based on heater output or temperature gauge operation), the thermostat is probably stuck open. Replace the thermostat with a new one.
3   If the engine runs hot, use your hand to check the temperature of the upper radiator hose. If the hose isn't hot, but the engine is, the thermostat is probably stuck closed, preventing the coolant inside the engine from escaping to the radiator. Replace the thermostat. **Caution:** *Don't drive the vehicle without a thermostat. The computer may stay in open loop and emissions and fuel economy will suffer.*
4   If the upper radiator hose is hot, it means the coolant is flowing and the thermostat is open. Consult the Troubleshooting Section at the front of this manual for cooling system diagnosis.

Replacement

Refer to illustrations 3.9a, 3.9b, 3.9c and 3.13

5   Disconnect the negative battery cable from the battery and drain the cooling system (see Chapter 1). If the coolant is relatively new or in good condition, save it and reuse it.
6   Follow the upper radiator hose to the engine to locate the thermostat housing.
7   Loosen the hose clamp, then detach the hose from the fitting. If the hose sticks, grasp it near the end with a pair of adjustable pliers and twist it to break the seal, then pull it off. If the hose is old or deteriorated, cut it off and install a new one. **Note:** *3.0 liter engines have two hoses – remove both of them.*
8   If the outer surface of the large fitting that mates with the hose is deteriorated (corroded, pitted, etc.) it may be damaged further by hose removal. If it is, the thermostat cover will have to be replaced.
9   Remove the bolts and detach the thermostat cover **(see illustrations).** If the cover is stuck, tap it with a soft-face hammer to jar it loose. Be prepared for some coolant to spill as the gasket seal is broken.
10   Note how it's installed (which end is facing up), then remove the thermostat.

**3.9a   3.0 liter engine thermostat components –
exploded view**

1	Thermostat	3	Thermostat cover
2	Gasket	4	Bolts

3.9b   3.8 liter engine thermostat components – exploded view

1	Thermostat cover	4	Clamp
2	O-ring	5	Bolt
3	Thermostat		

**3.9c   3800 engine thermostat components – exploded
view (typical)**

1	Thermostat cover	4	Thermostat
2	Cover-to-manifold O-ring	5	Bolt
3	Thermostat-to-cover gasket		
	(nubs face up)		

**3.13   Install the thermostat with the spring end toward
the engine**

15   Install the cover and bolts. Tighten them to the torque figure listed in this Chapter's Specifications.
16   The remaining steps are the reverse of removal.
17   Refill the cooling system (see Chapter 1).
18   Start the engine and allow it to reach normal operating temperature, then check for leaks and proper thermostat operation (as described in Steps 2 through 4).

---

4   Engine cooling fans – check and replacement

Check

Refer to illustration 4.1

1   To test the fan motor, unplug the electrical connector at the motor and use jumper wires to connect the fan directly to the battery **(see illustration)**. If the fan still doesn't work, replace the motor.

11   Remove all traces of old gasket material and sealant from the housing and cover with a gasket scraper. Clean the gasket mating surfaces with lacquer thinner or acetone.
12   On 3800 engines, replace the gasket on the thermostat with the nubs facing up.
13   Install the new thermostat in the housing. Make sure the correct end faces up – the spring end is normally directed into the engine **(see illustration)**.
14   On 3.0 liter engines, apply a thin, uniform layer of RTV sealant to both sides of the new gasket and position it on the housing. On 3.8 liter engines, install a new O-ring. On 3800 engines, install a new O-ring and gasket.

4.1   The motor may be tested by running fused jumper wires directly from the battery to the connector (arrow)

FAN RETAINING NUTS ARE LEFT HAND THREAD.

4.7   Engine cooling fan – exploded view

1	Fan	4	Resistor
2	Motor	5	Bracket
3	Shroud	6	Nut (left-hand thread)

4.6   Engine cooling fan mounting details – exploded view

1	Fan assembly	3	Clip nut
2	Bolt	4	Fan assembly (optional HD cooling)

2   If the motor tested OK, the fault lies in the coolant temperature switch, the relay or the wiring which connects the components. Carefully check all wiring and connections. If no obvious problems are found, further diagnosis should be done by a dealer service department or a repair shop.

Replacement

Refer to illustrations 4.6 and 4.7

3   Disconnect the negative battery cable from the battery.
4   Remove the fan guard and hose support.
5   Insert a small screwdriver into the connector to lift the lock tab and unplug the fan wire harness.
6   Unbolt the fan assembly **(see illustration)**, then carefully lift it out of the engine compartment.
7   To detach the fan from the motor, remove the motor shaft nut **(see illustration)**.

8   To remove the fan motor from the bracket, remove the mounting bolts/nuts.
9   Installation is the reverse of removal.

___

5   Radiator – removal and installation

Refer to illustrations 5.4a, 5.4b, 5.7 and 5.9
Warning: *Wait until the engine is completely cool before beginning this procedure.*
1   Disconnect the negative battery cable from the battery.
2   Drain the cooling system (see Chapter 1). If the coolant is relatively new or in good condition, save it and reuse it.
3   Remove the air cleaner intake duct.
4   Disconnect the transaxle cooler lines from the radiator **(see illustrations)**. Use a drip pan to catch spilled fluid.
5   Remove the engine cooling fan assemblies (see Section 4).
6   Loosen the hose clamps, then detach the radiator hoses from the fittings. If they're stuck, grasp each hose near the end with a pair of adjustable pliers and twist it to break the seal, then pull it off – be careful not to distort the radiator fittings! If the hoses are old or deteriorated, cut them off and install new ones.

5.4a The transaxle cooler lines (arrows) are located in the upper . . .

5.4b . . . and lower corners of the radiator (viewed from below)

5.7 The coolant reservoir hose (arrow) connects to the right side of the radiator

5.9 Radiator mounting details – exploded view

1 Upper radiator panel	3 Lower insulator
2 Upper insulator	4 Lower insulator (HD cooling)

7   Disconnect the reservoir hose from the radiator neck (see illustration).

8   Plug the lines and fittings.

9   Remove the upper radiator panel mounting bolts (see illustration).

10   Carefully lift out the radiator. Don't spill coolant on the vehicle or scratch the paint.

11   With the radiator removed, it can be inspected for leaks and damage. If it needs repair, have a radiator shop or dealer service department perform the work as special techniques are required.

12   Bugs and dirt can be removed from the radiator with compressed air and a soft brush. Don't bend the cooling fins as this is done.

13   Check the radiator mounts for deterioration and make sure there's nothing in them when the radiator is installed.

14   Installation is the reverse of the removal procedure.

15   After installation, fill the cooling system with the proper mixture of antifreeze and water. Refer to Chapter 1 if necessary.

16   Start the engine and check for leaks. Allow the engine to reach normal operating temperature, indicated by the upper radiator hose becoming hot. Recheck the coolant level and add more if required.

17   Check and add transmission fluid as needed.

---

6   Coolant reservoir – removal and installation

Refer to illustration 6.3

1   Remove the battery (see Chapter 5).

2   Disconnect the radiator overflow hose from the top of the radiator.

6.3   Remove the mounting bolt (arrow) to detach the coolant reservoir

3   Remove the mounting bolt **(see illustration)** and lift the coolant reservoir from the vehicle.
4   Installation is the reverse of removal.

7   Water pump – check

Refer to illustrations 7.4 and 7.5
1   A failure in the water pump can cause serious engine damage due to overheating.
2   There are three ways to check the operation of the water pump while it's installed on the engine. If the pump is defective, it should be replaced with a new or rebuilt unit.
3   With the engine running at normal operating temperature, squeeze the upper radiator hose. If the water pump is working properly, a pressure surge should be felt as the hose is released. **Warning:** *Keep your hands away from the fan blades!*

4   Water pumps are equipped with weep or vent holes. If a failure occurs in the pump seal, coolant will leak from the hole **(see illustration)**. In most cases you'll need a flashlight and mirror to find the hole on the under side of the water pump to check for leaks.
5   If the water pump shaft bearings fail there may be a howling sound coming from the drivebelt area while the engine is running. Shaft wear can be felt if the water pump pulley is rocked up-and-down **(see illustration)**. Don't mistake drivebelt slippage, which causes a squealing sound, for water pump bearing failure.

8   Water pump – removal and installation

Refer to illustrations 8.4, 8.5 and 8.8
Warning: *Wait until the engine is completely cool before beginning this procedure.*
1   Disconnect the negative battery cable from the battery.
2   Drain the cooling system (see Chapter 1). If the coolant is relatively new or in good condition, save it and reuse it.
3   Remove the windshield washer reservoir.
4   Loosen the water pump pulley mounting bolts **(see illustration)**. Remove the drivebelt (see Chapter 1) and then remove the water pump pulley.
5   Remove the bolts and detach the water pump from the engine **(see illustration)**. **Note:** *On some models it may be necessary to remove a long bolt through an access hole in the frame rail.*
6   Clean the fastener threads and any threaded holes in the engine to remove corrosion and sealant.
7   Compare the new pump to the old one to make sure they're identical.
8   Remove all traces of old gasket material from the engine with a gasket scraper **(see illustration).**
9   Clean the engine and water pump mating surfaces with lacquer thinner or acetone.
10   Apply a thin coat of RTV sealant to the *engine* side of the new gasket.
11   Apply a thin layer of RTV sealant to the gasket mating surface of the new pump, then carefully mate the gasket and the pump. Slip a couple of bolts through the pump mounting holes to hold the gasket in place.
12   Carefully attach the pump and gasket to the engine and start the bolts finger tight.
13   Tighten the bolts in 1/4-turn increments to the torque figure listed in this Chapter's Specifications. Don't overtighten them or the pump may be distorted.

7.4   If the pump is leaking, stains will form below the shaft (arrow) – pump removed for clarity

7.5   Rock the pulley back and forth to check for bearing play

14   Reinstall all parts removed for access to the pump. Tighten the pulley bolts to the torque listed in this Chapter's Specifications.
15   Refill the cooling system (see Chapter 1). Run the engine and check for leaks.

---

9   Coolant temperature sending unit – check and replacement

Refer to illustrations 9.1a and 9.1b
Warning: *Wait until the engine is completely cool before beginning this procedure.*

1   The coolant temperature indicator system is composed of a light or temperature gauge mounted in the instrument panel and a coolant temperature sending unit mounted on the engine (**see illustrations**). Most vehicles have more than one sending unit, but the one used for the indicator system has only one dark green wire.
2   If the light or gauge indicates the engine is overheating, check the coolant level in the system and then make sure the wiring between the light or gauge and the sending unit is secure and all fuses are intact.
3   When the ignition switch is turned on and the starter motor is turning, the indicator light (if equipped) should be on (overheated engine indication).
4   If the light isn't on, the bulb may be burned out, the ignition switch may be faulty or the circuit may be open. Test the circuit by grounding the wire to

8.4   Loosen the water pump pulley bolts with the drivebelt in place

8.5   Water pump mounting details – exploded view

1	Water pump	4	Short bolts
2	Timing chain cover	5	Long bolts
3	Gasket		

8.8   Remove all traces of old gasket material with a scraper

9.1a   On 3.0 and 3.8 liter engines, the coolant temperature sending unit is located at the drivebelt end of the intake manifold (arrow)

3

FRONT OF CAR

EXHAUST GAS RECIRCULATION (EGR) MODULE

IDLE AIR CONTROL VALVE

9.1b   On 3800 engines, the sending unit is located at the transaxle end of the engine

COOLANT TEMPERATURE SENDER

FUEL INJECTORS

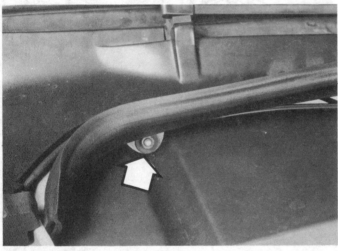

10.2a   This nut . . .

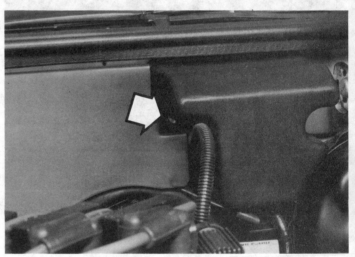

10.2b   . . . and this one secure the firewall cover

10.3   Detach the wiring harness clip and remove the mounting screws around the perimeter of the blower

1   Wiring harness clip   2   Blower mounting screws

the sending unit while the ignition is on (engine not running for safety). If the gauge now deflects full scale or the light comes on, replace the sending unit.

5   As soon as the engine starts, the light should go out and remain out unless the engine overheats. Failure of the light to go out may be due to a grounded wire between the light and the sending unit, a defective sending unit or a faulty ignition switch. Check the coolant to make sure it's the proper type. Plain water may have too low a boiling point to activate the sending unit.

6   If the sending unit must be replaced, simply unscrew it from the engine and install the replacement. Use a light coat of sealant on the threads. Make sure the engine is cool before removing the defective sending unit. There will be some coolant loss as the unit is removed, so be prepared to catch it. Check the level after the replacement has been installed.

---

10   Heater and air conditioner blower motor – removal and installation

Refer to illustrations 10.2a, 10.2b, 10.3, 10.4 and 10.6

1   Disconnect the cable from the negative battery terminal.

2   Working in the engine compartment, remove the plastic firewall cover (see illustrations).

3   Disconnect the wires from the blower motor (see illustration).

10.4   Blower motor components – exploded view

1   Blower motor
2   Fan
3   Nut
4   Housing
5   Blower motor resistor
6   Motor cooling tube

10.6   Remove the nut (arrow) and slip the fan off the motor shaft

11.5   The heater hoses connect to the heater core in the right (passenger's) side of the engine compartment at the firewall – remove the plastic firewall cover for access

1	Housing	4	Clamp
2	Heater outlet fitting	5	Heater inlet hose
3	Heater flow control valve	6	Heater outlet hose

4   Detach the blower motor cooling tube **(see illustration)**.

5   Remove the blower motor mounting bolts and separate the motor/fan assembly from the housing. **Note:** *On some models it may be necessary to remove the rear rocker arm cover for access (see Chapter 2A).*

6   Remove the retaining nut and slide the fan off the motor shaft **(see illustration)**.

7   Installation is the reverse of the removal procedure.

11   Heater core – removal and installation

Refer to illustrations 11.5 and 11.8

1   Disconnect the battery cables (negative cable first, then the positive one).

2   Raise the front of the vehicle and support it securely on jackstands. Apply the parking brake and block the rear wheels to keep the vehicle from rolling off the jackstands.

3   Drain the cooling system (see Chapter 1).

4   Remove the drain hose from the bottom of the heater case.

5   Working in the engine compartment, disconnect the heater hoses at the firewall **(see illustration)**.

6   Remove the right sound insulator and steering column trim cover.

7   Disassemble the dash as necessary for access (see Chapter 11). Remove the heater outlet duct and glove box.

11.8 Typical heater components – exploded view (your vehicle may differ slightly)

1   Heater and evaporator case cover
2   Heater and evaporator case cover seal
3   Heater core mounting clamp
4   Heater core with fitting
5   Heater core seal
6   Evaporator and blower modulator to dash gasket
7   Temperature valve cable mount bracket
8   Temperature valve control lever
9   Evaporator case drain grommet
10 Valve stop with baffle
11 Evaporator case seal
12 Heater core tube seal
13 Heater core mounting clamp
14 Heater and evaporator
15 Temperature valve
16 Evaporator water filter
17 Closed clip
18 Evaporator core
19 Evaporator seal
20 Blower case nut
21 Motor cooling tube
22 Blower motor terminal
23 Blower motor
24 Fan support washer
25 Blower fan
26 Blower fan nut
27 Blower case with fitting
28 Evaporator and blower support with cutoff
29 O-ring gasket
30 Not used
31 Fitting connector O-ring seal
32 Fitting connector O-ring seal
33 Fitting cap
34 Hex bolt
35 Air inlet management gasket
36 Air inlet management actuator
37 Air inlet valve with lever
38 Air inlet case
39 Front distribution duct bleed cover
40 Lower mode valve shaft with bracket and spring
41 Distribution front duct
42 Lower mode lever with seal, and valve
43 Upper mode valve with seal
44 Distribution right rear duct
45 Upper mode valve shaft with lever
46 Upper mode valve vacuum actuator
47 Upper mode valve link
48 Lower mode valve vacuum actuator
49 Push-on nut
50 Stamped nut
51 Linear baffle
52 Evaporator blower barrier with insulation
53 Evaporator core blower
54 Evaporator case drain seal
55 Slave valve vacuum actuator (four-season air conditioner only)
56 Slave valve (four-season air conditioner only)

12.2 Remove the trim panel screws (arrows) and detach the panel (typical)

12.3 Remove the screws on both sides of the heater and air conditioner control (arrows) (typical)

8   Remove the heater core cover **(see illustration)**. Pull straight back to avoid breaking the drain tube.
9   Remove the heater core clamps and remove the heater core.
10 Installation is the reverse of removal.

---

12 Heater and air conditioner control assembly – removal and installation

---

Refer to illustrations 12.2, 12.3, 12.4 and 12.5
1   Disconnect the negative battery cable from the battery.
2   Remove the trim panel from around the heater and air conditioner control **(see illustration)**.
3   Remove the two screws on each side of the heater and air conditioner control assembly **(see illustration)**.

3

12.4   Unplug the electrical and vacuum connectors from the back of the control panel – be sure to unplug the entire vacuum connector, not the individual hoses (typical manual control shown)

12.5   On manual systems, two mounting clips (arrows) attach the temperature control cable and cable housing to the heater and air conditioner control assembly (typical manual control shown)

4   Pull the control out of the dash far enough to label the various wires and/or vacuum hoses. **Note:** *Do not disconnect the individual vacuum lines – disconnect the vacuum connector (if equipped) as a unit* **(see illustration)**.
5   On manually controlled units, carefully pry the cable housing and cable retaining clips off with a small screwdriver **(see illustration)**.
6   Installation is the reverse of removal.

---

13   Air conditioning system – check and maintenance

Refer to illustration 13.11
Warning: *The air conditioning system is under high pressure. DO NOT loosen any hose or line fittings or remove any components until after the system has been discharged by a dealer service department or service station. Always wear eye protection when disconnecting air conditioning system fittings.*

Note 1: *The air conditioning system on 1994 and later models uses the non-ozone depleting refrigerant, referred to as R-134a. The R-134a refrigerant and its lubricating oil are not compatible with the R-12 system and under no circumstances should the two different types of refrigerant and lubricating oil be intermixed. If mixed, it could result in costly compressor failure due to improper lubrication.*

Note 2: *Because of recent Federal regulations proposed by the Environmental Protection Agency, R-12 refrigerant is no longer available to the do-it-yourselfer. If you are properly certified and can obtain R-12 refrigerant, refer to the* Haynes Automotive Heating and Air Conditioning Manual *for recharging instructions.*

Check
1   The following maintenance checks should be performed on a regular basis to ensure the air conditioner continues to operate at peak efficiency.
   a) Check the compressor drivebelt. If it's worn or deteriorated, replace it (see Chapter 1).
   b) Check the system hoses. Look for cracks, bubbles, hard spots and deterioration. Inspect the hoses and all fittings for oil bubbles and seepage. If there's any evidence of wear, damage or leaks, replace the hose(s).

   c) Inspect the condenser fins for leaves, bugs and other debris. Use a "fin comb" or compressed air to clean the condenser.
   d) Make sure the system has the correct refrigerant charge.
2   It's a good idea to operate the system for about 10 minutes at least once a month, particularly during the winter. Long term non-use can cause hardening, and subsequent failure, of the seals.
3   Because of the complexity of the air conditioning system and the special equipment necessary to service it, in-depth troubleshooting and repairs are not included in this manual (refer to the Haynes *Automotive Heating & Air Conditioning* manual). However, simple checks and component replacement procedures are provided in this Chapter.
4   The most common cause of poor cooling is simply a low system refrigerant charge. If a noticeable loss of cool air output occurs, one of the following quick checks may help you determine if the refrigerant level is low.
5   Warm the engine up to normal operating temperature.
6   Place the air conditioning temperature selector at the coldest setting and put the blower at the highest setting. Open the doors (to make sure the air conditioning system doesn't cycle off as soon as it cools the passenger compartment).
7   With the compressor engaged – the compressor clutch will make an audible click and the center of the clutch will rotate – feel the orifice tube located adjacent to the accumulator.
8   If a significant temperature drop is noticed, the refrigerant level is probably okay. Further inspection of the system is beyond the scope of the home mechanic and should be left to a professional.
9   If the inlet line has frost accumulation or feels cooler than the accumulator surface, the refrigerant charge is low and the system must be charged. Take the vehicle to a qualified shop.

---

14   Air conditioner accumulator – removal and installation

Refer to illustrations 14.4 and 14.6
Warning: *The air conditioning system is under high pressure. DO NOT loosen any hose or line fittings or remove any components until after the system has been discharged by a dealer service department or service station. Always wear eye protection when disconnecting air conditioning system fittings.*

14.4   The accumulator is located in the right rear corner of the engine compartment

| 1 | Refrigerant line fittings | 2 | Charging port |

14.6   Accumulator mounting details – exploded view

| 1 | Accumulator | 3 | Heater housing |
| 2 | Mounting bolt | 4 | Refrigerant line |

1   Have the system discharged (see **Warning** above).
2   Disconnect the negative battery cable from the battery.
3   Remove the plastic firewall cover.
4   Disconnect the refrigerant lines from the accumulator **(see illustra-tion)**. Use a back-up wrench to prevent twisting the tubing.
5   Plug the open fittings to prevent entry of dirt and moisture.
6   Loosen the mounting bracket bolt **(see illustration)** and remove the accumulator.
7   If a new accumulator is being installed, remove the Schrader valve and pour the existing oil out into a measuring cup, noting the amount. Add the correct type of fresh refrigerant oil to the new accumulator, equal to the amount removed from the old unit, plus the following amount:
   a) 1985 through 1993 models: plus one ounce of fresh 525 viscosity refrigerant oil.
   b) 1994 and later models: plus one ounce of polyalkaline glycol (PAG) refrigerant oil.
8   Installation is the reverse of removal.
9   Have the system evacuated, recharged and leak tested by the shop that discharged it.

15   Air conditioner compressor – removal and installation

Refer to illustrations 15.6 and 15.8
Warning: *The air conditioning system is under high pressure. DO NOT loosen any hose or line fittings or remove any components until after the system has been discharged by a dealer service department or service station. Always wear eye protection when disconnecting air conditioning system fittings.*

Note: *The accumulator (see Section 14) should be replaced whenever the compressor is replaced.*

1   Have the system discharged (see **Warning** above).
2   Disconnect the negative battery cable from the battery.
3   Set the parking brake and block the rear wheels. Raise the front of the vehicle and support it securely on jackstands.

4   Remove the right lower splash shield.
5   Refer to Chapter 1, and remove the drivebelt.
6   Disconnect the compressor clutch wiring **(see illustration)**.
7   Disconnect the refrigerant lines from the rear of the compressor. Plug the open fittings to prevent entry of dirt and moisture.
8   Unbolt the compressor from the mounting brackets and lift it out of the vehicle **(see illustration on following page)**.
9   If a new compressor is being installed, follow the directions with the compressor regarding the draining of excess oil prior to installation.
10   The clutch may have to be transferred from the original to the new compressor.
11   Installation is the reverse of removal. Replace all O-rings with new ones specifically made for A/C system use and lubricate them with refrig-erant oil.
12   Have the system evacuated, recharged and leak tested by the shop that discharged it.

3

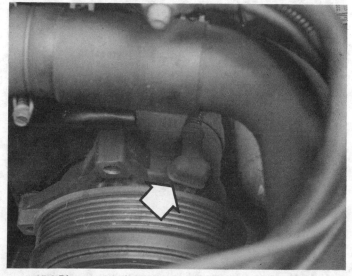

15.6 Disconnect the compressor clutch wiring (arrow)

15.8   Typical air conditioner compressor and related components – exploded view

1	Compressor
2	Brace
3	Bolt/stud
4	Bolt
5	Washer
6	Bolt
7	Positive battery cable
8	Nut

---

16   Air conditioner condenser – removal and installation

Refer to illustrations 16.4 and 16.6

Warning: *The air conditioning system is under high pressure. DO NOT loosen any hose or line fittings or remove any components until after the system has been discharged by a dealer service department or service station. Always wear eye protection when disconnecting air conditioning system fittings.*

Note: *The accumulator (see Section 14) should be replaced whenever the condenser is replaced.*

1   Have the system discharged (see **Warning** above).
2   Remove the battery (see Chapter 5).
3   Remove the cooling fans (see Section 4).
4   Disconnect the refrigerant lines from the condenser **(see illustration)**. Plug the lines to keep dirt and moisture out.
5   Remove the upper radiator panel from above the condenser.
6   Tilt the top of the radiator toward the engine and remove the condenser mounting bolts **(see illustration)**.
7   Remove the condenser from the vehicle.

16.4   Use a back-up wrench to loosen/tighten the refrigerant lines

16.6   Condenser mounting details – exploded view

1	Condenser	3	Bracket clamps
2	Insulators		

8   If the original condenser will be reinstalled, plug the line fittings to prevent oil from draining out.

9   If a new condenser is being installed, pour one ounce of refrigerant oil into it prior to installation.

10   Reinstall the components in the reverse order of removal. Be sure the rubber pads are in place under the condenser.

11   Have the system evacuated, recharged and leak tested by the shop that discharged it.

Chapter 4   Fuel and exhaust systems

Contents

Specifications

Fuel pressure – ignition on and engine off

1985 and 1986 (all)	37 to 43 psi
1987 on	
3.8 liter engine	43 to 40 psi
3800 engine	40 to 47 psi

Torque specifications

	Ft-lbs
PFI throttle body mounting nuts or bolts	10 to 15

---

1   General information

Note: *On models equipped with the Delco Loc II audio system, be sure the lockout feature is turned off before performing any procedure which requires disconnecting the battery.*

The fuel system consists of a fuel tank, an electric fuel pump, a fuel pump relay, an air cleaner assembly and a Port Fuel Injection (PFI) system. The PFI system is used on all V6 engines.

Port Fuel Injection (PFI) system

The PFI system utilizes six injectors: one for each cylinder. Each one has an electric solenoid that controls the amount of fuel injected. Fuel pressure at each injector is kept at a constant pressure by a pressure regulator, which returns excess fuel to the fuel tank. One injector is installed above each intake port. The throttle body serves only to control the amount of air passing into the system. Because each cylinder is equipped with an injector mounted immediately adjacent to the intake valve, much better control of the fuel/air mixture ratio is possible.

Fuel pump and lines

Fuel is circulated from the fuel tank to the fuel injection system, and back to the fuel tank, through a pair of metal lines running along the underside of the vehicle. An electric fuel pump is attached to the fuel sending unit inside the fuel tank. To reduce the likelihood of vapor lock, a vapor return system routes all vapors and hot fuel back to the fuel tank through a separate return line.

Exhaust system

The exhaust system includes an exhaust manifold fitted with an exhaust oxygen sensor, a catalytic converter, an exhaust pipe, and a tri-flow muffler.

The catalytic converter is an emission control device added to the exhaust system to reduce pollutants. A single-bed converter design is used in combination with a three-way (reduction) catalyst. Refer to Chapter 6 for more information regarding the catalytic converter.

2   Fuel pressure relief procedure

Note: *After the fuel pressure has been relieved, it's a good idea to use a shop towel around any fuel connection to absorb any residual fuel that may spray when servicing the fuel system.*

1   Before servicing any fuel system component, you must relieve the fuel pressure to minimize the risk of fire or personal injury.

2   Remove the cap from the gas tank – this will relieve any pressure built up in the tank.

3   On early models, remove the fuse marked FP (fuel Pump) from the fuse block. On later models, the fuel pump fuse is located in the relay center on the right hand side of instrument panel (see Chapter 12).

4   Crank the engine over. It will start and run until the fuel supply remaining in the fuel lines is used. When the engine stops, engage the starter again for another three seconds to assure that any remaining pressure is dissipated.

5   With the ignition turned to Off, replace the fuel pump fuse. Disconnect the negative battery cable terminal to avoid any accidental fuel discharge if an attempt is made to start the engine. Unless this procedure is followed before servicing fuel lines or connections, fuel spray (and possible injury) may occur.

6   Reconnect the negative battery cable.

3   Fuel pump/fuel pressure – testing

Warning: *Gasoline is extremely flammable, so extra precautions must be taken when working on any part of the fuel system. Don't smoke or allow open flames or bare light bulbs in or near the work area. Also, don't work in a garage where a natural gas-type appliance with a pilot light is present. Have a fire extinguisher rated for gasoline fires handy and know how to use it!*

Note: *In order to perform the fuel pressure test, you will have to obtain a fuel pressure gauge and adapter set for the fuel injection system being tested.*

Preliminary inspection

1   If the fuel system fails to deliver the proper amount of fuel, or any fuel at all, to the fuel injection system, inspect it as follows.

2   Always make certain that there is fuel in the tank.

3   With the engine running, inspect for leaks at the threaded fittings at both ends of the fuel line (see Chapter 1). Tighten any loose connections. Inspect all hoses for flattening or kinks which would restrict the flow of fuel.

Pressure check

Refer to illustration 3.5

4   Relieve the fuel system pressure (see Section 2).

5   Install a fuel pressure gauge at the Schrader valve on the fuel rail **(see illustration)**.

6   Turn the ignition switch on with the air conditioning off. The fuel pump should run for about two seconds. Note the reading on the pressure gauge. After the pump stops running the pressure should hold steady. It should be within the specified amount.

7   Start the engine and let it idle at normal operating temperature. The pressure should remain constant, although it might drop slightly from the previous reading. This is normal.

3.5   Install the fuel pressure gauge at the Schrader valve on the fuel rail

8   If the pressure reading was not within specification, disconnect the vacuum hose at the pressure regulator. Using a hand vacuum pump, apply 12-inches hg of vacuum to the pressure regulator. If the pressure is within specification, repair the vacuum source to the regulator. If the regulator does not hold vacuum, replace the regulator.

9   If the fuel pressure is not within specification, check the following:
   a) If the pressure is higher than specified, check for a faulty regulator or a pinched or clogged fuel return hose or pipe.
   b) If the pressure is lower than specified:
      1) Inspect the fuel filter – make sure it's not clogged.
      2) Look for a pinched or clogged fuel hose between the fuel tank and the fuel rail.
      3) Check the pressure regulator for a malfunction.
      4) Look for leaks in the fuel line.
      5) Look for a pinched, broken or disconnected regulator vacuum hose.
      6) Check for leaking injectors.

10   After the testing is done, relieve the fuel pressure (see Section 2) and remove the fuel pressure gauge.

11   If there are no problems with any of the above-listed components, check the fuel pump (see below).

Fuel pump check

Note: *See Chapter 6 for the test terminal location.*

Refer to illustration 3.15

12   If you suspect a problem with the fuel pump, verify the pump actually runs: Have an assistant turn the ignition switch to On – you should hear a brief whirring noise as the pump comes on and pressurizes the system. Have the assistant start the engine. This time you should hear a constant whirring sound from the pump (but it's more difficult to hear with the engine running).

13   If the pump does not come on (makes no sound), proceed to the next Step.

14   Check the fuel pump fuse located in the relay center or fuse panel (see chapter 12). If the fuse is good, see *Fuel pump relay check* (below). If the fuse is blown, replace the fuse and see if the pump works. If the pump still does not work, go to the next Step.

15   With the ignition off, apply 12 volts to the fuel pump test terminal **(see illustration)** and listen for the fuel pump running.

16   If the pump runs, then check the fuel pump relay. If the pump does not run, check for a open circuit between the relay and the fuel pump.

3.15   Apply battery voltage to the test lead (arrow) and listen for fuel pump operation – for location of the test lead, see Chapter 6 component location charts

Fuel pump relay check

Note: *See Chapter 6 for relay location.*
Refer to illustration 3.17

17   To test the fuel pump relay, start the engine and let it idle at normal operating temperature, then disconnect the fuel pump relay **(see illustration)**. If the engine does not continue to run, the oil pressure switch is faulty.

18   If the engine keeps on running, reconnect the relay and turn off the ignition. With a test light probe the fuel pump test terminal. If the light does not come on the fuel pump circuit is okay. If the test light comes on, the oil pressure switch is bad.

---

4   Fuel lines and fittings – repair and replacement

Refer to illustrations 4.12, 4.18 and 4.19

Warning: *Gasoline is extremely flammable, so extra precautions must be taken when working on any part of the fuel system. Don't smoke or allow open flames or bare light bulbs in or near the work area. Also, don't work in a garage where a natural gas-type appliance with a pilot light is present. Have a fire extinguisher rated for gasoline fires handy and know how to use it!*

1   Always relieve the fuel pressure before servicing fuel lines or fittings (Section 2).

2   The fuel feed and return lines extend from the in-tank fuel pump to the engine compartment. The lines are secured to the underbody with clip and screw assemblies. Both fuel feed lines must be occasionally inspected for leaks, kinks and dents.

3   If evidence of dirt is found in the system or fuel filter during disassembly, the line should be disconnected and blown out. Check the fuel strainer on the fuel gauge sending unit (see Section 7) for damage and deterioration.

Steel tubing

4   If replacement of a fuel line or emission line is called for, use welded steel tubing meeting GM specification 124-M or its equivalent.

5   Don't use copper or aluminum tubing to replace steel tubing. These materials cannot withstand normal vehicle vibration.

6   Because fuel lines used on fuel injected vehicles are under high pressure, they require special consideration.

7   Most fuel lines have threaded fittings with O-rings. Any time the fittings are loosened to service or replace components, make sure that:

    a) A back-up wrench is used while loosening and tightening the fittings.

3.17   Disconnect the relay with the engine running to check the fuel pump circuit – for location of the relay, see chapter 6 component location charts

    b) Check all O-rings for cuts, cracks and deterioration. Replace any that appear worn or damaged.

    c) If the lines are replaced, always use original equipment parts, or parts that meet the GM standards specified in this Section.

Flexible hose

8   When rubber hose is used to replace a metal line, use reinforced, fuel resistant hose (GM Specification 6163-M) with the word "Fluoroelastomer" imprinted on it. Hose(s) not clearly marked like this could fail prematurely and could fail to meet Federal emission standards. Hose inside diameter must match line outside diameter. Plastic hoses on later models should only be replaced with genuine factory parts.

9   Don't use flexible hose within four inches of any part of the exhaust system or within ten inches of the catalytic converter. Metal lines and flexible hoses must never be allowed to chafe against the frame. A minimum of 1/4-inch clearance must be maintained around a line or hose to prevent contact with the frame.

Removal and installation

10   The following procedure and accompanying illustrations are typical for vehicles covered by this manual.

11   Relieve the fuel pressure, if not already done (see Section 2).

12   Disconnect the fuel feed, return or vapor line at the fuel tank **(see illustration)**.

4.12   The fuel feed (A), fuel return (B) and vapor return (C) lines at the fuel tank

4.18 Typical fuel feed and return line threaded fittings in the left side of the engine compartment

4.19 Typical fuel feed and return line threaded fitting assembly on a 3.0 liter engine

1 O-rings
2 Fuel feed hose
3 Fuel return hose

13 Detach the bracket from the rear crossmember
14 Detach the bracket from the rear end of the left frame member, just in front of the left rear wheel.
15 Detach the three brackets from the left frame member.
16 Detach the bracket from the left front end of the left frame member, just behind the left front wheel.
17 Detach the bracket from the lower left rear corner of the engine compartment.
18 Detach the threaded fitting(s) that attach the metal lines to the engine compartment fuel hoses **(see illustration)**. Later models use quick-disconnect fittings, which are released by squeezing the plastic tabs and pulling the fitting apart.
19 Installation is the reverse of removal. Be sure to use new O-rings at the fittings **(see illustration)**.

Repair

20 In repairable areas, cut a piece of fuel hose four inches longer than the portion of the line removed. If more than a six inch length of line is removed, use a combination of steel line and hose so hose lengths won't be more than ten inches. Always follow the same routing as the original line.
21 Cut the ends of the line with a tube cutter. Using the first step of a double flaring tool, form a bead on the end of both line sections. If the line is too corroded to withstand bead operation without damage, the line should be replaced.
22 Use a screw type hose clamp. Slide the clamp onto the line and push the hose on. Tighten the clamps on each side of the repair.
23 Secure the lines properly to the frame to prevent chafing.

Quick-disconnect fittings
Refer to illustration 4.25

24 Twist the connector 1/4 turn in each direction to loosen any debris within the connector, then blow out the debris from the connector.
25 Squeeze the plastic tabs on the male end of the connector and pull it apart **(see illustration)**.
26 Wipe off the male end of the connector, then apply a drop of clean engine oil onto the fuel line male connector where it is inserted into the female connector.
27 Insert the female connector onto the male connector and push it on until the plastic tabs snap and lock into place.
28 Pull on the female end of the connector to make sure it is securely locked into place.

4.25 Insert the female quick-disconnect connector onto the male connector, push it on until the plastic tabs snap and lock into place, making sure it is securely locked

5 Fuel tank – removal and installation

Refer to illustrations 5.6 and 5.8
Warning: *Gasoline is extremely flammable, so extra precautions must be taken when working on any part of the fuel system. Don't smoke or allow open flames or bare light bulbs in or near the work area. Also, don't work in a garage where a natural gas-type appliance with a pilot light is present. Have a fire extinguisher rated for gasoline fires handy and know how to use it!*

1 Relieve the fuel pressure (see Section 2).
2 Detach the cable from the negative terminal of the battery.
3 If the tank is full or nearly full, either drain it into an approved gasoline container or drive the vehicle to use up the gas.
4 Raise the vehicle and place it securely on jackstands.
5 Loosen the exhaust heat shield at the rear, then remove the exhaust pipe hanger and lower the exhaust pipe down.

5.6   The vapor (A), return (B) and fuel feed (C) lines

6   Disconnect the fuel feed and return lines, the vapor return line and the filler neck and vent tubes **(see illustration)**.
7   Support the fuel tank with a floor jack.
8   Disconnect both fuel tank retaining straps **(see illustration)** then lower the tank enough to disconnect the wires and ground strap from the fuel pump/fuel gauge sending unit.
9   If there's any fuel left in the tank, siphon it out at the fuel filler neck.
10   Remove the tank from the vehicle.
11   Installation is the reverse of removal

---

6   Fuel tank cleaning and repair – general information

---

1   All repairs to the fuel tank or filler neck should be done by an experienced professional – the job is potentially dangerous! Even after cleaning and flushing of the fuel system, explosive fumes can remain and ignite during repair of the tank.
2   If the fuel tank is removed from the vehicle, it shouldn't be stored in an area where sparks or open flames could ignite the fumes coming out of it. Be especially careful inside a garage where a natural gas-type appliance is located, because the pilot light could cause an explosion.

---

7   Fuel pump – removal and installation

Refer to illustrations 7.5 and 7.8
Warning: *Gasoline is extremely flammable, so extra precautions must be taken when working on any part of the fuel system. Don't smoke or allow open flames or bare light bulbs in or near the work area. Also, don't work in a garage where a natural gas-type appliance with a pilot light is present. Have a fire extinguisher rated for gasoline fires handy and know how to use it!*

Removal

1   Relieve the fuel pressure (Section 2).
2   Remove the cable from the negative battery terminal.
3   Remove the fuel tank (Section 5).
4   The fuel pump/sending unit assembly is located inside the fuel tank. It's held in place by a cam lockring mechanism consisting of an inner ring with three locking cams and an outer ring with three retaining tangs.
5   To unlock the fuel pump/sending unit assembly, turn the inner lockring clockwise until the locking cams are free of the retaining tangs **(see illustration)**. **Note:** *If the rings are locked together too tightly to release by hand, tap them gently with a rubber or brass hammer.* **Warning:** *Do not use a steel hammer – a spark could cause an explosion!*
6   Pull the fuel pump/sending unit assembly out of the tank. **Caution:** *The fuel level float and sending unit are delicate. Don't bump them into the lockring during removal or the accuracy of the sending unit may be affected.*
7   Check the condition of the rubber gasket around the mouth of the lockring mechanism. If it's dried out, cracked or deteriorated, replace it.
8   Inspect the strainer on the lower end of the fuel pump **(see illustration)**. If it's dirty, remove it, clean it with solvent and blow it out with compressed air. If it's too dirty to be cleaned, replace it.

VIEW A   **VIEW B**

VIEW C

5.8   Typical fuel tank assembly components

1	*Fuel tank*	*5*	*Clamps*
2	*Exhaust pipe*	*6*	*Sending unit*
3	*Straps*	*7*	*Cam*
4	*Bolt*	*8*	*Gasket*

7.5   To remove the fuel gauge sending unit and fuel pump assembly (1), turn the inner lockring (3) clockwise and pull the pump and O-ring gasket (2) out of the tank – be extremely careful not to bang the float mechanism on the sides of the hole

9   If you have to separate the fuel pump and sending unit, pull the fuel pump assembly into the rubber connector and slide the pump away from the bottom support. Care should be taken to prevent damage to the rubber insulator and fuel strainer during removal. After the pump assembly is clear of the bottom support, pull the pump assembly out of the rubber connector.

Installation

10   Insert the fuel pump/sending unit assembly into the fuel tank.
11   Turn the inner lockring counterclockwise until the locking cams are fully engaged by the retaining tangs. **Note:** *If you've installed a new O-ring, it may be necessary to push down on the inner lockring until the locking cams slide under the retaining tangs.*
12   Install the fuel tank (Section 5).

---

8   Air filter housing assembly – removal and installation

1985 through 1991 models
Refer to illustrations 8.2 and 8.4
1   Detach the cable from the negative terminal of the battery.
2   Unplug the electrical connector and unclamp the air duct from the Mass Air Flow (MAF) sensor, and remove the MAF sensor from the vehicle **(see illustration).**

8.2   To remove the Mass Air Flow (MAF) sensor unplug the electrical connectors (A), then loosen the hose clamps (B) (1985 through 1991 models)

7.8   Exploded view of a typical fuel gauge sending unit and pump assembly

1	Sending unit	5	Sound insulator sleeve
2	Pulsator	6	Sound insulator
3	Bumper	7	Strainer
4	Fuel pump		

3   Remove the air filter element (see Chapter 1).
4   Remove the air filter housing bolts and nuts **(see illustration)**.
5   Installation is the reverse of removal.

8.4   To remove the air cleaner housing assembly, remove the nuts and bolts (arrows) and slide the assembly off the upper studs (1985 through 1991 models)

4

9.4   Typical PFI throttle body assembly

1   Throttle body/plenum gasket
2   Throttle body assembly
3   Idle stop screw plug
4   Idle stop screw
5   Idle stop screw spring
6   Throttle Position Sensor (TPS)
7   TPS attaching screw
8   TPS attaching screw retainer
9   TPS lever
10   Coolant cavity cover
11   Coolant cavity cover screw
12   Coolant cover/throttle body O-ring
13   Idle air/vacuum signal housing assembly
14   Idle air/vacuum signal assembly screw
15   Idle air/vacuum signal gasket
16   Idle Air Control (IAC) valve assembly
17   IAC valve assembly gasket

9.5   Typical PFI fuel rail assembly (VIN L shown)

A   Fuel rail
B   Fuel pressure regulator
C   Fuel injectors
D   Fuel injector harness electrical connector

1992 and later models

6   Detach the cable from the negative terminal of the battery.
7   On 1992 through 1997 models, remove the air filter element (see Chapter 1). Completely remove the rear cover.
8   On 1993 and later models, disconnect the electrical connector from the intake temperature sensor on the front cover or the air intake duct. On 1993 through 1995 models, remove the special nut on the inlet snorkel.
9   On 1993 through 1997 models, remove the air filter front cover bolts and special nut and remove the front cover. On 1995 and later models, remove the lower bolt.
10   On 1998 models, loosen the hose clamp and unhook the air intake duct from the throttle body. Remove the air filter cover screws and remove the complete housing.
11   Installation is the reverse of removal. On 1995 and later models, be sure to install the lower bolt.

9   Fuel injection system – general information

Refer to illustrations 9.4 and 9.5

Electronic fuel injection provides optimum fuel/air mixture ratios at all stages of combustion and offers immediate throttle response characteristics. It also enables the engine to run at the leanest possible fuel/air mixture ratio, reducing exhaust gas emissions.

These vehicles are fitted with a Port Fuel Injection (PFI) system. This system is controlled by an Electronic Control Module (ECM), which monitors engine performance and adjusts the air/fuel mixture accordingly.

An electric fuel pump located in the fuel tank with the fuel gauge sending unit pumps fuel to the fuel injection system through the fuel feed line and an in-line fuel filter. A pressure regulator keeps fuel available at a constant pressure. Fuel in excess of injector needs is returned to the fuel tank by a separate line.

11.2   There are two electrical connectors plugged into the throttle body – the IAC valve (A) and the TPS switch (B). The connector below the throttle body is for the knock sensor (C)

The throttle body **(see illustration)** has a throttle valve to control the amount of air delivered to the engine. The Throttle Position Sensor (TPS) and Idle Air Control (IAC) valves are located on the throttle body.

The fuel rail is mounted on the top of the engine. It distributes fuel to the individual injectors **(see illustration)**.

Fuel is delivered to the input end of the rail by the fuel lines goes through the rail and then to the pressure regulator. The regulator keeps the pressure to the injectors at a constant level.

The remaining fuel is returned to the fuel tank.

10   Fuel injection system – check

Warning: *Gasoline is extremely flammable, so extra precautions must be taken when working on any part of the fuel system. Don't smoke or allow open flames or bare light bulbs in or near the work area. Also, don't work in a garage where a natural gas-type appliance with a pilot light is present. Have a fire extinguisher rated for gasoline fires handy and know how to use it!*

Note: *The following procedure is based on the assumption that the fuel pump and fuel pressure are normal (see Section 3).*

1   Check the ground wire connections on the intake manifold for tightness. Check all wiring harness connectors that are related to the system. Loose connectors and poor grounds can cause many problems that resemble more serious malfunctions.

2   Check to see that the battery is fully charged, as the control unit and sensors depend on an accurate supply voltage in order to properly meter the fuel.

3   Check the air filter element – a dirty or partially blocked filter will severely impede performance and economy (see Chapter 1).

4   If a blown fuse is found, replace it and see if it blows again. If it does, search for a grounded wire in the harness to the fuel pump.

5   Check the air intake duct from the air mass sensor to the intake manifold for leaks, which will result in an excessively lean mixture. Also check the condition of all of the vacuum hoses connected to the intake manifold.

6   Remove the air intake duct from the throttle body and check for dirt, carbon or other residue build-up. If it's dirty, clean it with carburetor cleaner and a toothbrush.

7   With the engine running, place a screwdriver against each injector, one at a time, and listen through the handle for a clicking sound, indicating operation.

8   The remainder of the system checks should be left to a GM service department or other qualified repair shop, as there is a chance that the control unit may be damaged if not performed properly.

11.3   On early models, to remove the IAC valve from the throttle body, use a large adjustable wrench – if there is thread locking compound on the threads and you are going to install the same IAC, don't remove the thread compound

11   Port Fuel Injection (PFI) – component removal and installation

Warning: *Before servicing an injector, fuel rail or pressure regulator, always relieve the fuel pressure in the fuel system to minimize the risk of fire and injury. After servicing the system, always cycle the ignition on and off several times (wait 10 seconds between cycles) and check the system for leaks.*

Idle Air Control (IAC) valve

Refer to illustrations 11.2, 11.3 and 11.7

1   Detach the cable from the negative terminal of the battery.

2   Unplug the electrical connector from the IAC valve assembly **(see illustration)**.

3   On early models, unscrew the IAC valve assembly from the idle air/vacuum signal housing assembly **(see illustration)**. Remove the IAC valve assembly gasket and discard it. **Caution:** *Do not remove any thread locking compound from the threads.*

4   On later models, remove the two screws securing the IAC valve to the throttle body assembly. Remove the IAC valve assembly O-ring and discard it.

5   Clean the gasket mounting surface of the idle air/vacuum signal housing assembly to ensure a good seal. **Caution:** *The IAC valve assembly itself is an electrical component, and must not be soaked in any liquid cleaner or solvent, as damage may result.*

6   Before installing the IAC valve assembly, the position of the pintle must be checked. If the pintle is extended too far, damage to the assembly may occur.

7   Measure the distance from the gasket mounting surface of the IAC valve assembly to the tip of the pintle **(see illustration)**.

11.7   Before installing the IAC valve, make sure that dimension A is 1-1/8 inches

11.14   To detach the throttle body from the plenum/intake manifold assembly, remove these two nuts (arrows)

11.15   You can't see the two coolant hoses attached to the throttle body until you unbolt the throttle body from the plenum and turn it over

8   If the distance is greater than 1-1/8-inch, reduce it as follows:
    a) If the IAC valve assembly has a collar around its electrical connector end, use firm hand pressure on the pintle to retract it (a slight side-to-side motion may help).
    b) If the IAC valve assembly has no collar, compress the pintle retaining spring toward the body of the IAC valve and try to turn the pintle clockwise. If the pintle will turn, continue turning it until the 1-1/8-inch dimension is reached. Return the spring to its original position with the straight part of the spring end lined up with the flat surface under the pintle head. If the pintle will not turn, use firm hand pressure to retract it.
9   Installation is the reverse of removal. On early models be sure to use a new gasket and tighten the IAC valve securely. On later models, install a new O-ring and tighten the screws securely. **Note:** *No adjustment is made to the IAC valve assembly after reinstallation. IAC valve setting is controlled by the ECM when the vehicle is driven.*

Throttle Body

Refer to illustrations 11.14 and 11.15

10   Detach the cable from the negative terminal of the battery.
11   Remove the duct between the air cleaner housing and the throttle body (see Section 8).
12   Unplug the IAC, the TPS and the knock sensor electrical connectors **(see illustration 11.2)**. On 1995-on models, unplug the MAF sensor electrical connector.
13   Detach the throttle cable and, if equipped, the cruise control cables. Detach the cables from the bracket (see Section 12).
14   Remove the throttle body mounting nuts or bolts **(see illustration)** and separate the throttle body from the plenum/intake manifold assembly.
15   Turn the throttle body until its underside is exposed, loosen both hose clamps and detach the coolant hoses (models so equipped) **(see illustration)**.
16   Remove all old gasket material from the mating surfaces of the throttle body and the plenum.
17   Installation is the reverse of removal. Be sure to use a new gasket and tighten the throttle body mounting nuts or bolts to the specified torque.

Throttle position sensor (TPS)

Refer to illustrations 11.21, 11.22 and 11.23

18   Detach the cable from the negative terminal of the battery.
19   Unplug the connector from the TPS switch **(see illustration 11.2)**.
20   If the TPS switch on your vehicle is located on the side of the throttle body, proceed to the next Step. If the switch is attached to the underside of the throttle body (like the one shown in this book), remove the throttle body (see Steps 10 through 16), then proceed to the next Step.

21   If you intend to install the same TPS switch scribe or paint an alignment mark between the TPS and the throttle body **(see illustration)**. If you are installing a new switch, you will have to take your vehicle to a dealer service department or automotive repair shop to make the final adjustment. A digital voltmeter or scan tool is needed to make these adjustments.
22   Using a Phillips or Torx screwdriver or bit **(see illustration)**, remove the TPS switch.
23   Installation is the reverse of removal. Be sure to install the TPS switch onto the throttle body with the throttle valve in the closed position. Make sure that the TPS lever lines up with the TPS drive lever on the throttle shaft **(see illustration)**.
24   If you had to remove the throttle body to get at the TPS, install the throttle body at this time (see Steps 10 through 17).

Fuel pressure regulator

Refer to illustrations 11.27 and 11.28

Note: *The pressure regulator is factory adjusted and is not serviceable. Do not attempt to remove the regulator from the fuel rail unless you intend to replace it with a new unit.*

11.21   If you plan to install the same TPS switch, be sure to make an alignment mark between the plastic TPS switch body and the aluminum throttle body casting

11.22   On some models, you'll need a Torx bit or screwdriver to remove the TPS retaining screws

11.23   The TPS lever (A) must mate with the TPS drive lever (B) when you attach the TPS switch to the throttle body

Bolt mounted
25 Relieve the fuel pressure (see Section 2).
26 Detach the cable from the negative terminal of the battery.
27 Detach the vacuum line from the top of the pressure regulator **(see illustration)**.
28 Unscrew the fuel return line from the fuel pressure regulator. Be sure to use a back-up wrench **(see illustration)**.
29 Remove the pressure regulator bracket mounting bolts and remove the regulator.
30 Installation is the reverse of removal.

Snap-ring mounted
31 Relieve the fuel pressure (see Section 2).
32 Detach the cable from the negative terminal of the battery.
33 Detach the vacuum line from the side of the pressure regulator.
34 Clean all dirt from the top of the regulator next to the snap ring or circlip.
35 On models secured with a snap-ring or circlip, use a scribe or narrow screwdriver and pry out the snap ring. On some models, snap-ring pliers will be necessary to remove the snap-ring.

36 Wrap a shop cloth around the regulator, carefully twist the regulator and remove the regulator and O-rings.
37 Insert a clean shop cloth into the opening in the fuel rail to prevent the entry of foreign material.
38 Installation is the reverse of removal. Install new O-rings and apply a light coat of engine oil to them prior to installation.

Fuel rail assembly
Refer to illustrations 11.40a, 11.40b, 11.42, 11.43 and 11.45
Note: *There are three different configurations of fuel rails used among the various models and years. Although they visually appear different, removal and installation of the fuel rail assembly is similar for all models.*
Note: *If you are removing the fuel rail assembly to service or replace an injector, it is not necessary to remove the throttle body. Follow Steps 10 through 13, then continue with the Steps below. If, however, you intend to replace the fuel rail assembly itself, follow Steps 10 through 16, then proceed to the Steps below.*
39 Detach the vacuum hose from the pressure regulator **(see illustration 11.27).**

11.27   To remove the fuel pressure regulator from the fuel rail, detach the vacuum hose (A), unscrew the fuel return line threaded fitting (B) and remove the bracket mounting bolts (C) (bolt mounted)

11.28   Use a back-up wrench when disconnecting the fuel return line threaded fittings at the pressure regulator (bolt mounted)

11.40a   To detach the fuel injector wiring harness from the engine compartment wiring harness, slide the locking tab sideways with a small screwdriver, . . .

11.40b   . . . then release the locking tab on top of the plug and pull the two halves of the connector apart

40   Unplug the fuel rail wiring harness electrical connector **(see illustrations)**.

41   Unscrew the fuel return line from the fuel pressure regulator. Be sure to use a back-up wrench **(see illustration 11.28)**.

42   On hex fittings, use a back-up wrench and unscrew the fuel feed line threaded fittings. On quick-disconnect fittings, disconnect the fittings (see Section 4).

43   Remove the alternator support bracket nut, if equipped **(see illustration)**. Unscrew the alternator through bolt and remove the bracket.

44   Remove the four fuel rail assembly mounting bolts **(see illustration 11.35)**.

45   Using a gentle rocking motion, remove the fuel rail and fuel injector assembly **(see illustration)**.

46   Installation is the reverse of removal.

Fuel injectors

Refer to illustrations 11.49, 11.50, 11.51, 11.52 and 11.53

47   Relieve the fuel pressure (see Section 2).

11.42   Use a back-up wrench when detaching the fuel feed line from the fuel rail assembly (hex fitting only)

11.43   To detach the fuel rail assembly from the plenum, remove the nut (A) that attaches the alternator bracket to the right front fuel rail mounting bolt (if equipped), then remove the four fuel rail bolts (B)

11.45   Use a gentle side-to-side rocking motion while pulling straight up to release the injectors from their bores in the intake manifold

11.49   If you plan to remove more than one injector, it's a good idea to clearly label them to prevent mix-ups during reassembly

48   Detach the cable from the negative terminal of the battery.
49   If you intend to service/replace more than one injector on a cylinder bank, it's a good idea to label the injectors to prevent mix-ups of the electrical leads at reassembly **(see illustration)**.
50   To unplug the electrical connectors from the injectors you are going to service/replace, push in the connector wire retaining clip with your index finger **(see illustration)** and pull on the plug.
51   Pop off the fuel injector spring clip(s) with a small screwdriver **(see illustration)**.
52   Using a gentle side-to-side wiggling motion, pull the injector from the fuel rail **(see illustration)**. Use care when removing injectors to prevent damage to the electrical connector pins on the injector and the nozzle. Repeat the above Steps for each injector you wish to service or replace.
53   Even if you intend to reinstall the old injectors, be sure to remove the O-rings from both ends of each injector with a small screwdriver **(see illustration)** and install new ones. Coat the O-rings with a little engine oil and install them on the new injectors. If you are installing new injectors, they must also be fitted with new O-rings lubricated with a little engine oil.
54   Installation is the reverse of removal.

11.50   To unplug the electrical connectors from the injectors, push the wire retaining clip in and pull the connector straight up

11.51   To detach an injector from the fuel rail assembly, pop off the spring clip with a small screwdriver, . . .

11.52   . . . then pull on the injector while rocking it until the upper O-ring breaks loose from the fuel rail

11.53   If you plan to reuse the same injector, always remove the old O-rings with a small screwdriver and install new O-rings

12   Throttle cable – removal and installation

Refer to illustrations 12.3, 12.4, 12.5, 12.7a and 12.7b

1   Disconnect the cable from the negative terminal of the battery.
2   The throttle cable will be retained to the throttle linkage by either a retaining clip or a plastic cable retainer.
3   To remove the retaining clip, use a small screwdriver to pop the retaining clip off the post on the throttle lever arm and remove the cable end **(see illustration)**.
4   To remove the plastic cable retainer, push the cable end forward and lift up to detach the cable from the post on the throttle lever arm **(see illustration)**.
5   To detach the throttle cable and, if equipped, cruise control cables from the cable support bracket, use a pair of needle-nose pliers to squeeze the locking tabs on the top and bottom of the cable retainer **(see illustration)**, then pull the cable assembly through the bracket.
6   Carefully study the routing of the cable before proceeding.
7   Working inside the vehicle, pull the cable toward you and detach it from the accelerator pedal **(see illustrations)**.
8   Follow the cable with your hand until you locate the locking cable retainer on the passenger compartment side of the firewall. Again, with a pair of needle-nose pliers, squeeze the locking tabs of the retainer together and push the retainer through the firewall.

12.3   Use a small screwdriver to pop the clip off the post on the throttle arm

12.4   To remove the plastic cable retainer, push the cable end forward and lift up to detach the cable from the post

12.5   The throttle and cruise control cable retainers can be detached from the cable bracket by squeezing the locking tabs on the top and bottom of the retainer with a pair of needle-nose pliers

12.7a   The throttle cable at the pedal – once the cable is detached at the throttle body end, pull this end toward you and slide it out of the slot in the pedal

12.7b Exploded view showing the cable in the firewall area in greater detail

1	Accelerator pedal lever assembly	6	Retainer
2	Plate	7	Spring
3	Plate bolts	8	Support
4	Plate stud	9	Retainer
5	Accelerator pedal	10	Front of firewall

11 Cable assembly
12 Retainer must be securely seated past tapered end of the cable assembly as shown
13 Insulator

13.3 The exhaust pipe-to-exhaust manifold flange bolts – make sure you don't lose the springs when removing these bolts

13.4 To detach this rubber block type hanger from the exhaust pipe, remove the large bolt

13 Exhaust system – removal and installation

Refer to illustrations 13.3 and 13.4

Caution: *DO NOT attempt to work on any part of the exhaust system until the entire system has completely cooled. Be especially careful around the catalytic converter, where the highest temperatures are generated.*

1 Disconnect the cable from the negative terminal of the battery.
2 Raise the vehicle and support it securely on jackstands.
3 Disconnect the exhaust pipe from the exhaust manifold flange by removing the two bolts **(see illustration)**.

4 Remove the bolt from the rubber exhaust pipe hanger just in front of the fuel tank **(see illustration)**.
5 Remove the bolt and detach the hanger from the forward end of the muffler.
6 Remove the bolt and detach the hanger from the rear end of the muffler.
7 Remove the exhaust pipe, catalytic converter and muffler as an assembly. **Note:** *These components cannot be separated without a cutting torch. If you need to replace any of these parts, take the entire assembly to a dealer service department, service station or muffler shop for further service.*

Chapter 5 Engine electrical systems

Contents

---

1 Ignition system – general information

Warning: *Because of the very high voltage generated by the ignition system, extreme care should be taken whenever an operation involving ignition components is performed. This not only includes the distributor, coil(s), module and spark plug wires, but related items that are connected to the system as well.*

Note: *On models equipped with the Delco Loc II audio system, be sure the lockout feature is turned off before performing any procedure which requires disconnecting the battery.*

The 1985 models are equipped with a High Energy Ignition (HEI) system, consisting of an ignition switch, battery, coil, primary (low tension) and secondary (high tension) circuits, a distributor and spark plugs. The 1986 and later models are equipped with a distributorless ignition system (C3I).

High Energy Ignition (HEI) System

HEI equipped vehicles use a special HEI distributor with Electronic Spark Timing (EST). The HEI distributor combines all the ignition components into one unit with the ignition coil integrated into the distributor cap. All spark timing changes are controlled by the Electronic Control Module (ECM), which monitors data from various engine sensors, computes the desired spark timing and signals the distributor to change timing accordingly. No vacuum or mechanical advance is used.

Electronic Spark Control (ESC)

Some engines are equipped with Electronic Spark Control (ESC). This system uses a knock sensor and a ESC module in conjunction with the ECM to control spark timing. Thus allowing the engine to maintain maximum spark advance without spark knock. Driveability and fuel economy are improved with this system.

Computer controlled coil ignition (C3I) system

Note: *Since 1992, the ignition system is no longer referred to as the C3I system by GM. All ignition systems and components operate in the same manner. The only change is the Electronic Control Module (ECM) is now being referred to as the Ignition Control Module (ICM).*

This system, known as the computer controlled coil ignition (C3I) system, consists of the ECM, ignition module, ignition coils, a "Hall effect" cam, a crank sensor, a cam sensor and the connecting wires. On 3.0L V6 applications, the crank and cam sensor functions are combined into one dual sensor called a combination sensor, which is mounted at the vibration damper.

Two types of module/coil assemblies are commonly used. They can be distinguished by the configuration of their coil towers: Type I module/coil assemblies have evenly spaced towers, with three on either side; Type II's have all six towers (two per coil) placed on one side. The wiring harness and sensors, however, are interchangeable between either type.

The C3I system uses a "waste spark" method of spark distribution. Each cylinder is paired with its companion cylinder, i.e. 1-4, 5-2, 3-6. The spark occurs simultaneously in the cylinder coming up on compression and the cylinder coming up on exhaust.

The cylinder, on exhaust, requires very little of the available voltage to fire the spark plug. The remaining high voltage can then be used, as required, by the cylinder on compression.

The spark distribution is accomplished by a signal from the crank sensor, which is used by the ignition module to determine the proper time to trigger the next ignition coil. This signal is also processed by the C3I module into the reference signal used by the ECM.

The C3I system uses the electronic spark timing (EST) signal from the crankshaft to control spark timing.

Timing is controlled by the ECM using the following inputs:

Crankshaft position
Engine speed (rpm)
Engine temperature
Amount of air entering the intake (Mass air flow sensor)

---

2 Battery – removal and installation

Refer to illustration 2.3

Warning: *Hydrogen gas is produced by the battery, so keep open flames and lighted cigarettes away from it at all times. Always wear eye protection when working around a battery. Rinse off spilled electrolyte immediately with large amounts of water.*

1   The battery is located at the right or left front corner of the engine compartment.

Removal

2   Disconnect both cables from the battery terminals. **Caution:** *Always disconnect the negative cable first and hook it up last or the battery may be shorted by the tool being used to loosen the cable clamps.*

3   Remove the hold-down clamp **(see illustration)** from the battery carrier.

2.3 Typical battery installation

1	Bolt	3	Battery carrier
2	Hold-down clamp	4	Fender

4   Carefully lift the battery out of the carrier. **Warning:** *Always keep the battery in an upright position to reduce the possibility of electrolyte spills. If you spill electrolyte on yourself or the vehicle, rinse it off immediately with plenty of water.*

5   If you're installing a new battery, make sure you get one that's identical (same dimensions, amperage rating, cold cranking rating, etc.).

Installation

Note: *The battery carrier and hold-down clamp should be clean and free from corrosion before installing the battery. Make certain there are no parts in the carrier before installing the battery.*

6   Set the battery in position in the carrier. Don't tilt it.

7   Install the hold-down clamp and bolt. The bolt should be snug, but overtightening it may damage the battery case.

8   Install both battery cables – positive first, then negative. **Note:** *The battery terminals and cable ends should be cleaned if necessary (see Chapter 1).*

3   Battery – emergency jump starting

Refer to the *Booster battery (jump) starting* procedure at the front of this manual.

4   Battery cables – check and replacement

Refer to illustration 4.4

1   Periodically inspect the entire length of each battery cable for damage, cracked or burned insulation and corrosion. Poor battery cable connections can cause starting problems and decreased engine performance.

2   Check the cable-to-terminal connections at the ends of the cables for cracks, loose wire strands and corrosion. The presence of white, fluffy deposits under the insulation at the cable terminal connection is a sign the cable is corroded and should be replaced. Check the terminals for distortion, missing mounting bolts or nuts and corrosion.

3   When removing the cables, always disconnect the negative cable first and hook it up last or the battery may be shorted by the tool used to loosen the cable clamps. Even if only the positive cable is being replaced, be sure to disconnect the negative cable from the battery first (see Chapter 1 for additional information related to battery cable removal).

4   Disconnect the old cables from the battery, then trace each of them to their opposite ends and detach them from the starter solenoid and ground terminals. Note the routing of each cable to ensure correct installation **(see illustration)**.

5

4.4 Typical battery cable installation

1	Battery
2	Negative cable
3	Bolt
4	Nut
5	Positive cable

5.1   To use a spark plug tester, simply disconnect a spark plug wire, attach the wire to the tester, clip the tester to a convenient ground and operate the starter – if there's enough power to fire the plug, sparks will be viable between the electrode tip and the tester body

5.6   Use an ohmmeter to check the resistance of each plug wire – it should be less than 30,000 ohms

5   If you're replacing either or both cables, take the old ones with you when buying the new ones – the replacements must be identical. Cables have characteristics that make them easy to identify: Positive cables are normally red and larger in diameter. Ground cables are normally black and smaller in diameter.

6   Clean the threads of the solenoid or ground connection with a wire brush to remove rust and corrosion. Apply a light coat of petroleum jelly to the threads to prevent future corrosion.

7   Attach the cable to the solenoid or ground connection and tighten the mounting nut/bolt securely.

8   Before connecting a new cable to the battery, make sure it reaches the battery post without having to be stretched.

9   Connect the positive cable first, followed by the negative cable.

---

5   Ignition system – check

Refer to illustrations 5.1 and 5.6

Warning: *Because of the very high voltage generated by the ignition system, extreme care should be taken whenever an operation is performed involving ignition components. This not only includes the coil(s), control module and spark plug wires, but related items connected to the system as well, such as the plug connections, tachometer and any test equipment.*

1   If the engine turns over but wont start, disconnect a spark plug wire from any spark plug and attach a calibrated ignition tester (available at most auto parts stores) **(see illustration)**.

2   Crank the engine and watch for a well defined bright blue spark at the tester. If spark occurs, sufficient voltage is reaching the plug to fire it. However, the plugs may be fouled, so remove them and check as described in Chapter 1. Repeat the check with the spark tester at the remaining plug wires to verify that the wires, distributor cap and rotor (if equipped), or coil(s) are OK.

3   On HEI systems, if no spark or intermittent spark occurs, remove the distributor cap and check the cap and rotor as described in Chapter 1.

4   On all models, if no spark occurs, check the spark plug wires and the wire connections at the coil(s). Check for voltage to the coil. Make any necessary repairs, then repeat the test again.

---

6   HEI distributor (1985 models only) – removal and installation

Removal

1   Disconnect the cable from the negative battery terminal.

2   Disconnect the electrical connectors at the distributor cap coil terminals.

3   Remove the distributor cap (see Chapter 1).

4   Mark the distributor housing at the point where the rotor tip is aligned. Also mark the relationship of the distributor-to block alignment at the base of the distributor.

5   Remove the distributor hold-down bolt and clamp and lift the distributor straight up and out of the engine. **Caution:** *Do not turn the crankshaft while the distributor is removed from the engine. If the crankshaft is turned, the alignment marks you made previously will be meaningless and the engine and distributor will have to be re-timed.*

Installation

6   Clean the distributor-to-engine block mounting area and install a new gasket or O-ring.

7   If the crankshaft was not turned while the distributor was removed, insert it into the engine in exactly the same position in which it was removed. It will be necessary to start the rotor slightly off the mark when installing the distributor so that as the gears mesh it ends up properly aligned. Also, it may be necessary to slightly turn the oil pump drive shaft before the distributor is installed (this can be done with a long screwdriver) to enable the distributor shaft to properly engage the oil pump drive shaft when the distributor is seated.

8   If it was necessary to turn the crankshaft while the distributor was removed, position the engine with number one cylinder on TDC (see Chapter 1). Install the distributor with the rotor aligned to the point where the number one spark plug wire is located (temporarily install the distributor cap to determine the number one plug wire location and mark the housing). Again, its necessary to start the rotor slightly off the mark and adjust the oil pump drive shaft alignment as described in Step 6.

9   Once the distributor is installed, be sure it is properly seated against the block (no gap between the distributor housing flange and the block) and that the rotor is pointing exactly at your alignment mark. If not, remove the distributor and try again meshing the gears in a different position.

10   The remainder of installation is the reverse of removal. Check and adjust the timing as described in Chapter 1.

---

7   HEI coil and ignition module (1985 models only) – removal and installation

Coil

Refer to illustration 7.3

1   Remove the distributor cap (see Chapter 1).

2   Remove the screws and the coil cover on top of the distributor cap.

3   Remove the coil retaining screws. With a pair of long-nose pliers pull the electrical connectors out of the cap and lift the coil off the cap **(see illustration)**.

4   Installation is the reverse of removal. Install a new carbon button and gasket if the coil is being replaced.

7.3   To separate the coil from the distributor cap, clearly mark the wires, detach the coil ground wire and push the leads from the underside of the connectors

7.6   To detach the ignition module from the HEI distributor, remove the two mounting screws and unplug the connector from the B and C terminals

8.3   Unbolt and unplug the connector from the C3I ignition coil/module assembly

Ignition module

Refer to illustration 7.6

5   Remove the distributor cap and rotor (see Chapter 1).
6   Remove the ignition module screws, disconnect the electrical connectors and lift the module from the distributor housing **(see illustration)**.
7   Installation is the reverse of removal. Be sure to coat the base of the module with a thin layer of silicone grease before installation.

---

8   Distributorless ignition coil and module (1986 and later) – removal and installation

---

All models

Refer to illustration 8.3

1   Detach the cable from the negative terminal of the battery.
2   Clearly label, then disconnect, all six spark plug wires from the coil.
3   Unbolt and unplug the electrical connector at the module **(see illustration)**.

1986 and 1987 models

Refer to illustration 8.5

4   Detach the vacuum lines and the electrical connector from the EGR valve solenoid on the left end of the coil/module assembly (see Chapter 6 if necessary).
5   Remove the front bracket leg mounting nut from the stud on the intake manifold (next to the EGR valve) and the two rear bracket nuts from the studs protruding from the exhaust manifold side of the rear cylinder head **(see illustration)**. **Note:** *It's possible to remove the coil/module assembly from the support bracket by removing the three nuts from the under side of the bracket, but it's difficult to get a wrench on these nuts.*
6   Remove the coil/module and support bracket assembly.

8.5   Exploded view of the ignition coil/module assembly and support bracket (1986 and 1987 model shown)

8.9   After removing the screws that hold the coil and module assemblies together, label, then detach, the wire leads from the module

1988 and later models

7   Remove the mounting nuts from the bracket on the front of the valve cover and detach the assembly from the vehicle.

All models

Refer to illustration 8.9

8   Using a Torx screwdriver or bit, remove the coil-to-module screws and separate the coil and module assemblies.
9   Open the coil and module halves as shown **(see illustration)**. Label, then detach, the wires between the module and the coil assemblies from

5

the spade terminals on the underside of the coils.

10   Unbolt the module **(see illustration 8.5)** from the support bracket.

11   Installation is the reverse of removal. Be sure to attach the wires of the new module to the coil assembly spade terminals in exactly the same order in which they were removed.

9   Charging system – general information and precautions

Note: *On models equipped with the Delco Loc II audio system, be sure the lockout feature is turned off before performing any procedure which requires disconnecting the battery.*

The charging system consists of a belt-driven alternator with an integral voltage regulator and the battery. These components work together to supply electrical power for the ignition system, the lights and all accessories.

There are two types of alternators used. Earlier vehicles have the SI type and later models are equipped with the CS type. There are two types of CS alternators in use: The CS-130 and the CS-144. All types have a conventional pulley and fan.

To determine which type of alternator is installed on a vehicle, look at the fasteners employed to attach the two halves of the alternator housing. All CS models have rivets or special bolts instead of screws. CS alternators are rebuildable once the rivets are drilled out. However, we don't recommend this practice. For all intents and purposes, CS types should be considered non-serviceable and, if defective, exchanged as cores for new or rebuilt units.

The purpose of the voltage regulator is to limit the alternator's voltage to a preset value. This prevents power surges, circuit overloads, etc., during peak voltage output. On all models with which this manual is concerned, the voltage regulator is mounted inside the alternator housing.

The charging system doesn't ordinarily require periodic maintenance. However, the drivebelt, battery and wires and connections should be inspected at the intervals outlined in Chapter 1.

The dashboard warning light should come on when the ignition key is turned to Start, then go off immediately. If it stays on or comes on when the engine is running, a charging system problem has occurred (see Section 8).

Be very careful when making electrical circuit connections to a vehicle equipped with an alternator and note the following:

a) When reconnecting wires to the alternator from the battery, be sure to note the polarity.

b) Before using arc welding equipment to repair any part of the vehicle, disconnect the wires from the alternator and the battery terminals.

c) Never start the engine with a battery charger connected.

d) Always disconnect both battery leads before using a battery charger.

e) The alternator is turned by an engine drivebelt which could cause serious injury if your hands, hair or clothes become entangled in it with the engine running.

f) Because the alternator is connected directly to the battery, it could arc or cause a fire if overloaded or shorted out.

g) Wrap a plastic bag over the alternator and secure it with rubber bands before steam cleaning the engine.

10   Charging system – check

Refer to illustration 10.5

1   If a malfunction occurs in the charging circuit, don't automatically assume the alternator is causing the problem. First check the following items:

a) Check the drivebelt tension and condition (Chapter 1). Replace it if it's worn or deteriorated.

10.5   To full field the alternator, ground the tab located inside the test hole on the end frame (backside) of the alternator by inserting a screwdriver blade into the hole and touching the tab and the case at the same time

b) Make sure the alternator mounting and adjustment bolts are tight.

c) Inspect the alternator wiring harness and the connectors at the alternator. They must be in good condition and tight.

d) Check the fusible link (if equipped) located between the starter solenoid and alternator. If it's burned, determine the cause, repair the circuit and replace the link (the engine won't start and/or the accessories won't work if the fusible link blows). Sometimes a fusible link may look good, but still be bad. If in doubt, remove it and check it for continuity.

e) Start the engine and check the alternator for abnormal noises (a shrieking or squealing sound indicates a bad bearing).

f) Check the specific gravity of the battery electrolyte. If it's low, charge the battery (doesn't apply to maintenance free batteries).

g) Make sure the battery is fully charged (one bad cell in a battery can cause overcharging by the alternator).

h) Disconnect the battery cables (negative first, then positive). Inspect the battery posts and cable clamps for corrosion. Clean them thoroughly if necessary (see Chapter 1). Reconnect the cable to the positive terminal.

i) With the key off, connect a test light between the negative battery post and the disconnected negative cable clamp.

   1)   If the test light doesn't come on, reattach the clamp and proceed to the next Step.

   2)   If the test light comes on, there's a short (drain) in the electrical system of the vehicle. The short must be repaired before the charging system can be checked.

   3)   Disconnect the alternator wiring harness.
       (a) If the light goes out, the alternator is bad.
       (b) If the light stays on, pull each fuse until the light goes out (this will tell you which component is shorted).

2   Using a voltmeter, check the battery voltage with the engine off. If should be approximately 12-volts.

3   Start the engine and check the battery voltage again. It should now be approximately 14-to-15 volts.

4   Locate the test hole in the back of the alternator. **Note:** *If there is no test hole, the vehicle is equipped with a newer CS type alternator. Further*

11.2 Remove the alternator electrical connectors

12.3 Inside a typical SI alternator

A   Brush holder   D   Resistor (not all models)
B   Paper clip retaining brushes   E   Diode trio
C   Regulator   F   Rectifier bridge

11 Alternator – removal and installation

Refer to illustration 11.2
1   Detach the cable from the negative terminal of the battery.
2   Detach the electrical connectors from the alternator **(see illustration)**.
3   Loosen the alternator mounting bolts and detach the drivebelt (see Chapter 1).
4   Remove the bolts and separate the alternator from the engine.
5   If you're replacing the alternator, take the old one with you when purchasing the new one. Make sure the new/rebuilt unit is identical to the old alternator. Look at the terminals – they should be the same in number, size and location as the terminals on the old alternator. Finally, look at the identification numbers – they'll be stamped into the housing or printed on a tag attached to the housing. Make sure the numbers are the same on both alternators.
6   Many new/rebuilt alternators DO NOT have a pulley installed, so you may have to switch the pulley from the old one to the new/rebuilt one. When buying an alternator, find out the shop's policy regarding pulleys – some shops will perform this service free of charge.
7   Installation is the reverse of removal.
8   Check the charging voltage to verify proper operation of the alternator (see Section 8).

12.4 After removing the bolts holding the stator assembly to the end frame, remove the stator

testing of this type of alternator must be done by a service station, dealer service department or auto electric shop.
5   Ground the tab inside the hole by inserting a screwdriver blade into the hole and touching the tab and the case at the same time **(see illustration)**. **Caution:** *Don't run the engine with the tab grounded any longer than necessary to obtain a voltmeter reading. If the alternator is charging, it's running unregulated during the test. This condition may overload the electrical system and cause damage to the components.*
6   The reading on the voltmeter should be 15-volts or higher with the tab grounded in the test hole.
7   If the voltmeter indicates low battery voltage, the alternator is faulty and should be replaced with a new one (Section 11).
8   If the voltage reading is 15-volts or higher and a no charge condition exists, the regulator or field circuit is the problem. Remove the alternator (Section 9) and have it checked by a service station, dealer service department or auto electric shop.

12 Alternator brushes – replacement

Refer to illustrations 12.3, 12.4, 12.5, 12.6, 12.7, 12.9a and 12.9b
Note: *The following procedure applies only to SI type alternators. CS types have riveted housings or special bolts and cannot be disassembled.*
1   Remove the alternator from the vehicle (Section 11).
2   Scribe or paint marks on the front and rear frame housings of the alternator to facilitate reassembly.
3   Remove the four through-bolts holding the front and rear end frames together, then separate the drive end frame from the rectifier end frame **(see illustration)**.
4   Remove the bolts holding the stator to the rear end frame and separate the stator from the end frame **(see illustration)**.

5

12.5   Remove the nuts attaching the diode trio to the rectifier bridge and remove the trio

12.6   After removing the screws that attach the regulator, brush holder and the resistor (if equipped) to the end frame, remove the brush holder

12.7   Remove the brushes from the brush holder

12.9a   To hold the brushes in place during reassembly, insert a paper clip through the hole in the end frame nearest to the rotor shaft

5   Remove the nuts attaching the diode trio to the rectifier bridge and remove the trio **(see illustration)**.

6   Remove the screws attaching the resistor (not used on all models), brush holder and regulator to the end frame and remove the brush holder **(see illustration)**.

7   Remove the brushes from the brush holder **(see illustration)**.

8   Remove the springs from the brush holder.

9   Installation is the reverse of the removal procedure, noting the following: When installing the brushes in the brush holder, install the brush closest to the end frame first. Slip a paper clip through the rear of the end frame to hold both brushes in place while reassembly is completed **(see illustrations)**. The paper clip should not be removed until the front and rear end frames have been bolted together.

12.9b   With the paper clip in place, carefully lower the rectifier end frame over the drive end frame

13   Starting system – general information and precautions

Note: *On models equipped with the Delco Loc II audio system, be sure the lockout feature is turned off before performing any procedure which requires disconnecting the battery.*

15.3 There are three terminals on the end of the typical starter solenoid

A *Battery terminal*   C *Motor terminal (M)*
B *Switch terminal (S)*

The sole function of the starting system is to turn over the engine quickly enough to allow it to start.

The starting system consists of the battery, the starter motor, the starter solenoid and the wires connecting them. The solenoid is mounted directly on the starter motor. The solenoid/starter motor assembly is installed on the lower part of the engine, next to the transmission bellhousing.

When the ignition key is turned to the Start position, the starter solenoid is actuated through the starter control circuit. The starter solenoid then connects the battery to the starter. The battery supplies the electrical energy to the starter motor, which does the actual work of cranking the engine.

The starter on a vehicle equipped with an automatic transaxle can only be operated when the selector lever is in Park or Neutral.

Always observe the following precautions when working on the starting system:

a) Excessive cranking of the starter motor can overheat it and cause serious damage. Never operate the starter motor for more than 15 seconds at a time without pausing to allow it to cool for at least two minutes.

b) The starter is connected directly to the battery and could arc or cause a fire if mishandled, overloaded or shorted out.

c) Always detach the cable from the negative terminal of the battery before working on the starting system.

14 Starter motor – testing in vehicle

Note: *Before diagnosing starter problems, make sure the battery is fully charged.*

1   If the starter motor doesn't turn at all when the switch is operated, make sure the shift lever is in Neutral or Park.

2   Make sure the battery is charged and all cables, both at the battery and starter solenoid terminals, are clean and secure.

3   If the starter motor spins but the engine isn't cranking, the overrunning clutch in the starter motor is slipping and the starter motor must be replaced.

4   If, when the switch is actuated, the starter motor doesn't operate at all but the solenoid clicks, then the problem lies with either the battery, the main solenoid contacts or the starter motor itself (or the engine is seized).

5   If the solenoid plunger can't be heard when the switch is actuated, the battery is bad, the fusible link is burned (the circuit is open) or the solenoid itself is defective.

15.4 Exploded view of a typical starter motor
1 *Shim*   2 *Bolts*

6   To check the solenoid, connect a jumper lead between the battery (+) and the ignition switch wire terminal (the small terminal) on the solenoid. If the starter motor now operates, the solenoid is okay and the problem is in the ignition switch, neutral start switch or the wiring.

7   If the starter motor still doesn't operate, remove the starter/solenoid assembly for disassembly, testing and repair.

8   If the starter motor cranks the engine at an abnormally slow speed, first make sure the battery is charged and all terminal connections are clean and tight. If the engine is partially seized, or has the wrong viscosity oil in it, it'll crank slowly.

9   Run the engine until normal operating temperature is reached, then disable the ignition system by unplugging the module.

10 Connect a voltmeter positive lead to the positive battery post and connect the negative lead to the negative post.

11 Crank the engine and take the voltmeter readings as soon as a steady figure is indicated. DO NOT allow the starter motor to turn for more than 15 seconds at a time. A reading of 9-volts or more, with the starter motor turning at normal cranking speed, is normal. If the reading is 9-volts or more but the cranking speed is slow, the motor is faulty. If the reading is less than 9-volts and the cranking speed is slow, the solenoid contacts are probably burned, the starter motor is bad, the battery is discharged or there's a bad connection.

15 Starter motor – removal and installation

Refer to illustrations 15.3 and 15.4

Note: *On some vehicles, it may be necessary to remove the exhaust pipe(s) or frame crossmember to gain access to the starter motor. In extreme cases it may even be necessary to unbolt the mounts and raise the engine slightly to get the starter out.*

1   Detach the cable from the negative terminal of the battery.

2   Raise the front of the vehicle and support it securely on jackstands. Apply the parking brake and block the rear wheels to keep the vehicle from rolling off the jackstands.

3   Working under the vehicle, clearly label, then disconnect the wires from the terminals on the starter motor and solenoid **(see illustration)**.

4   Remove the mounting bolts and detach the starter. Note the locations of the spacer shims (if used) – they must be reinstalled in the same positions **(see illustration)**.

5   Installation is the reverse of removal.

5

16.5   To remove the solenoid housing from the starter motor, remove the screws and turn it clockwise

16   Starter solenoid – removal and installation

Refer to illustration 16.5

1   Disconnect the cable from the negative terminal of the battery.
2   Remove the starter motor (Section 15).
3   Disconnect the strap from the solenoid to the starter motor terminal.
4   Remove the screws that secure the solenoid to the starter motor.
5   Twist the solenoid in a clockwise direction to disengage the flange from the starter body **(see illustration)**.
6   Installation is the reverse of removal.

Chapter 6 Emissions control systems

Contents

1 General information

Refer to illustration 1.7

To prevent pollution of the atmosphere from incompletely burned and evaporating gases, and to maintain good driveability and fuel economy, a number of emission control devices are incorporated. They include the:

Fuel control system
Electronic Spark Timing (EST)
Electronic Spark Control (ESC) system
Exhaust Gas Recirculation (EGR) system
Evaporative Emission Control System (EECS)
Positive Crankcase Ventilation (PCV) system
Transaxle Converter Clutch (TCC)
Catalytic converter

All of these systems are linked, directly or indirectly, to the Computer Command Control (CCC or C3) system.

The Sections in this Chapter include general descriptions, checking procedures within the scope of the home mechanic and component replacement procedures (when possible) for each of the systems listed above.

Before assuming an emissions control system is malfunctioning, check the fuel and ignition systems carefully. The diagnosis of some emission control devices requires specialized tools, equipment and training. If checking and servicing become too difficult or if a procedure is beyond the scope of your skills, consult a dealer service department. Remember, the most frequent cause of emissions problems is simply a loose or broken vacuum hose or wire, so always check the hose and wiring connections first.

This doesn't mean, however, that emission control systems are particularly difficult to maintain and repair. You can quickly and easily perform many checks and do most (if not all) of the regular maintenance at home with common tune-up and hand tools. **Note:** *Because of a Federally mandated extended warranty which covers the emission control system components, check with your dealer about warranty coverage before working on any emissions-related systems. Once the warranty has expired, you may wish to perform some of the component checks and/or replacement procedures in this Chapter to save money.*

Pay close attention to any special precautions outlined in this Chapter. It should be noted that the illustrations of the various systems may not exactly match the system installed on your vehicle because of changes made by the manufacturer during production or from year-to-year.

A Vehicle Emissions Control Information label is located in the engine compartment **(see illustration)**. This label contains important emissions specifications and ignition timing procedures, as well as a vacuum hose schematic and emissions components identification guide. When servicing the engine or emissions systems, the VECI label in your particular vehicle should always be checked for up-to-date information.

6

1.7 Look for the VECI label in the engine compartment – this one's on the shock tower

2   Computer Command Control (CCC) system and trouble codes

General information

Refer to illustrations 2.1a, 2.1b, 2.1c, 2.1d, 2.1e and 2.1f

Note: *Since 1992, the Electronic Control Module (ECM) is now being referred to as the Powertrain Control Module (PCM).*

The Computer Command Control (CCC) system consists of an Electronic Control Module (ECM) and information sensors which monitor various engine functions and send data back to the ECM **(see illustrations)**.

The CCC system is analogous to the central nervous system in the human body. The sensors (nerve endings) constantly relay information to the ECM (brain), which processes the data and, if necessary, sends out a command to change the operating parameters of the engine (body).

Here's a specific example of how one portion of this system operates: An oxygen sensor, located in the exhaust manifold, constantly monitors the oxygen content of the exhaust gas. If the percentage of oxygen in the exhaust gas is incorrect, an electrical signal is sent to the ECM. The ECM takes this information, processes it and then sends a command to the fuel injection system, telling it to change the fuel/air mixture. This happens in a fraction of a second and it goes on continuously when the engine is running. The end result is a fuel/air mixture ratio which is constantly maintained at a predetermined ratio, regardless of driving conditions.

☐ COMPUTER HARNESS

C1   Electronic Control Module (ECM)
C2   ALCL diagnostic connector
C3   "CHECK ENG/SERV ENG SOON" light
C4   ECM power
C5   ECM harness ground
C6   Fuse panel
C8   Fuel pump test connector

┆┄┆ NOT ECM CONNECTED

N1   Crankcase vent valve (PCV)
N12 A/C pressure switch
N13 Coolant fan temp. override switch

☐ CONTROLLED DEVICES

1   Fuel injector
2   Idle air control motor
3   Fuel pump relay
3a   Fuel pump/oil press. relay(Digital IP only)
5   Trans. Converter Clutch connector
7   Electronic Spark Control module
8   Low speed engine fan relay
8a   High speed engine fan relay
12   Exh. Gas Recirc. vacuum solenoid
13   A/C compressor relay
15   Fuel vapor canister solenoid
◇   Exhaust Gas Recirculation valve

◯ INFORMATION SENSORS

B   Exhaust oxygen
C   Throttle position
D   Coolant temperature
F   Vehicle speed
Fa   Vehicle speed sensor buffer
J   ESC knock
K   Mass Air Flow
M   P/N switch

2.1a   Emission control component locations – Typical 1985 3.8L V6 engine

COMPUTER HARNESS

- **C1** Electronic Control Module (ECM)
- **C2** ALCL diagnostic connector
- **C3** "SERVICE ENGINE SOON" light
- **C5** ECM harness ground
- **C6** Fuse panel
- **C8** Fuel pump test connector

NOT ECM CONNECTED

- **N1** Crankcase vent valve (PCV)
- **N13** Coolant fan temp. override switch

CONTROLLED DEVICES

- **1** Fuel injector
- **2** Idle air control motor
- **3** Fuel pump relay
- **5** Trans. Conv. Clutch connector
- **6** Comp. Controlled Coil Ignition (C³I)
- **7** Electronic Spark Control module
- **8** Engine LO fan relay
- **9** Engine HI fan relay
- **12** Exh. Gas Recirc. vacuum solenoid
- **13** A/C compressor relay
- **15** Fuel vapor canister solenoid
- Exhaust Gas Recirculation valve

INFORMATION SENSORS

- **B** Exhaust oxygen
- **C** Throttle position
- **D** Coolant temperature
- **E** Vehicle speed sender
- **F** Vehicle speed buffer
- **H** Crankshaft position reference/RPM (C³I)
- **J** ESC knock
- **K** Mass Air Flow
- **S** P/S pressure switch
- **V** Manifold Air Temp.
- **M** P/N Switch

2.1b   Emission control component locations – Typical 1986 3.0L V6 engine

COMPUTER HARNESS

- C1 Electronic Control Module (ECM)
- C2 ALCL diagnostic connector
- C3 "SERVICE ENGINE SOON" light
- C5 ECM harness ground
- C6 Fuse panel
- C8 Fuel pump test connector

NOT ECM CONNECTED

- N1   Crankcase vent valve (PCV)
- N13 Coolant fan temp. override switch

CONTROLLED DEVICES

- 1 Fuel injector
- 2 Idle air control motor
- 3 Fuel pump relay
- 5 Trans. Conv. Clutch connector
- 6 Comp. Controlled Coil Ignition (C³I)
- 7 Electronic Spark Control module
- 8 Engine LO fan relay
- 9 Engine HI fan relay
- 12 Exh. Gas Recirc. vacuum solenoid
- 13 A/C compressor relay
- 15 Fuel vapor canister solenoid

◇ Exhaust Gas Recirculation valve

INFORMATION SENSORS

- B Exhaust oxygen
- C Throttle position
- D Coolant temperature
- E Vehicle speed sensor
- F Vehicle speed buffer
- G Camshaft Position (C³I))
- H Crankshaft Position (C³I))
- J ESC knock
- K Mass Air Flow
- S P/S pressure switch
- V Manifold Air Temp.

2.1c   Emission control component locations – Typical 1986 and 1987 3.8L V6 engines

2.1d   Emission control component locations – Typical 1988 3800 V6 engine

☐ COMPUTER HARNESS

C1 Electronic Control Module (ECM).
C2 ALDL diagnostic connector.
C3 "SERVICE ENGINE SOON" light.
C5 ECM harness ground.
C6 Fuse panel.
C8 Fuel pump test connector.
C9 Relay Center.

⬚ NOT ECM CONNECTED

N1 Crankcase vent valve (PCV).
N2 Blower Motor Relay.
N3 Isolated Battery Source.

☐ CONTROLLED DEVICES

1 Fuel Injector .
2 Idle Air Control (IAC).
3 A/C Compressor Relay.
5 Torque Conv. Clutch connector.
6 Comp. Controlled Coil Ignition (C^{3}I).
8 Coolant Fan Relay, LO speed.
9 Coolant Fan Relay, HI speed.
12 Digital EGR Assembly.
15 Fuel vapor canister solenoid.

◯ INFORMATION SENSORS

B Exhaust oxygen sensor (O_2).
C Throttle position sensor (TPS).
D Coolant temperature sensor (CTS).
E Vehicle speed sensor (VSS).
G Camshaft Position sensor (C^{3}I)).
H Crankshaft Position sensor (C^{3}I)).
J ESC knock sensor.
K Mass Air Flow sensor (MAF).
V Manifold Air Temp. sensor (MAT).

☐ COMPUTER HARNESS

C1   Electronic Control Module (ECM)
C2   ALDL Diagnostic Connector
C3   "SERVICE ENGINE SOON" Light
C5   ECM Harness Ground
C6   Fuse Panel
C8   Fuel Pump Test Connector
C9   Relay Center

NOT ECM CONNECTED

N1   Crankcase Vent Valve (PCV)
N13   Coolant Fan Temp. Override Switch

☐ CONTROLLED DEVICES

1   Fuel Injector
2   Idle Air Control Motor (IAC)
5   Trans. Conv. Clutch Connector (TCC)
6   Comp. Controlled Coil Ignition (C^3I)
7   Electronic Spark Control Module (ESC)
8   LO Coolant Fan Relay
9   HI Coolant Fan Relay
12   Exh. Gas Recirc. Vacuum Solenoid
13   A/C Compressor Relay
15   Fuel Vapor Canister Solenoid

◈   Exhaust Gas Recirculation Valve

◯ INFORMATION SENSORS

B   Exhaust Oxygen Sensor (O^2)
C   Throttle Position Sensor (TPS)
D   Coolant Temperature Sensor (CTS)
E   Vehicle Speed Sensor (VSS)
F   Vehicle Speed Buffer
G   Camshaft Position Sensor (C^3I))
H   Crankshaft Position Sensor (C^3I))
J   ESC Knock Sensor
K   Mass Air Flow Sensor
S   P/S Pressure Switch (PSPS)
V   Manifold Air Temp. Sensor (MAT)

2.1e   Emission control component locations – Typical 1988 3.8L V6 engine

COMPUTER HARNESS

C1 Electronic Control Module (ECM)
C2 ALDL diagnostic connector
C3 "SERVICE ENGINE SOON" light
C5 ECM harness ground
C6 Fuse panel.
C8 Fuel pump test connector
C9 Relay Center

NOT ECM CONNECTED

N1 Crankcase vent valve (PCV)
N2 Blower Motor Relay(C60 A/C only)
N3 Isolated Battery Source

CONTROLLED DEVICES

1 Fuel Injector
2 Idle Air Control (IAC)
3 A/C Compressor Relay
5 Torque Conv. Clutch connector
6 Comp. Controlled Coil Ignition (C^3I)
8 Coolant Fan Relay, LO speed
9 Coolant Fan Relay, HI speed
10 Heavy Duty Fan Relay (V08)
12 Digital EGR Assembly
15 Fuel vapor canister solenoid

INFORMATION SENSORS

B Exhaust oxygen sensor (O_2)
C Throttle position sensor (TPS)
D Coolant temperature sensor (CTS)
E Vehicle speed sensor (VSS)
G Camshaft Position sensor (C^3I)
H Crankshaft Position sensor (C^3I)
J ESC knock sensor.
K Mass Air Flow sensor (MAF)
V Manifold Air Temp. sensor (MAT)

6

2.1f   Emission control component locations – Typical 1989 through 1993 3800 V6 engines

1627-6-02.01g HAYNES

COMPUTER COMMAND CONTROL

C1   Powertrain Control Module (PCM)
C2   Diagnostic Link Connector (DLC)
C3   MIL ("SERVICE ENGINE SOON")
C4   Ignition control ground
C5   Fuse panel
C6   Fuel pump test connector
C7   I/P relay center
C8   8-way ignition jumper connector
C9   PCM harness ground

CONTROLLED DEVICES

1   Fuel injector
2   Idle air control (IAC)
3   A/C compressor relay
4   Transmission converter clutch connector
5   Ignition Control Module/coil assembly
6   Cooling fan relay, high speed
7   Cooling fan relay, low speed
8   EVAP purge control
9   Maxifuse relay center
         PCM/VATS fuse – 20 amp
         A/C fuse – 30 amp
         Cooling fan fuse – 40 amp
10   Linear exhaust recirculation valve
11   Cruise control servo

EMISSION COMPONENTS (NOT CONTROLLED)

N1   Crankcase vent
N2   Blower motor relay (C60 A/C only)
N3   Oil pressure sending unit

INFORMATION SENSORS

A   Heated Exhaust Oxygen Sensor (HO2S)
B   Throttle Position sensor (TPS)
C   Engine Coolant Temperature sensor (ECT)
D   Vehicle speed sensor (VSS)
E   Camshaft position sensor
F   Crankshaft position sensor
G   Front Knock sensor (KS)
H   Mass Air Flow sensor (MAF)
J   Intake Air Temperature sensor (IAT)
K   Transmission range switch
L   A/C head pressure switch
M   A/C high pressure cutoff switch
N   A/C pressure cycling switch
P   Rear knock sensor (KS)
R   Transmission Fluid Temperature sensor (TFT)
         (inside transaxle)

⚠ SIR SYSTEM COMPONENTS

add graphic box or circle in front of heading

2.1g Emission control component locations – typical 1994 and later 3800 V6 engines

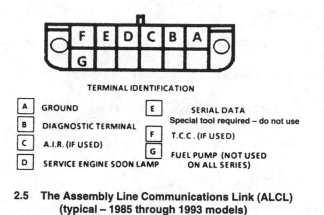

TERMINAL IDENTIFICATION

A	GROUND	E	SERIAL DATA Special tool required – do not use
B	DIAGNOSTIC TERMINAL	F	T.C.C. (IF USED)
C	A.I.R. (IF USED)	G	FUEL PUMP (NOT USED ON ALL SERIES)
D	SERVICE ENGINE SOON LAMP		

2.5 The Assembly Line Communications Link (ALCL) (typical – 1985 through 1993 models)

Trouble code retrieval and identification

Refer to illustration 2.5

Note: *On 1994 and later models, the Service Engine Soon light on the instrument panel no longer will flash the trouble code. The only way to retrieve the trouble codes is with the use of the GM special tool, Tech 1 Diagnostic Scan Tool (part no. TK-0/TK-0-A & 7000001). The proper use of this special tool is beyond the scope of the home mechanic and any problems that arise within the system should be entrusted to a dealer service department.*

One might think that a system which uses an on-board computer and electrical sensors would be difficult to diagnose. This is not necessarily the case. The CCC system has a built-in diagnostic feature which indicates a problem by flashing a Service Engine Soon light on the instrument panel. When this light comes on during normal vehicle operation, a fault in one of the information sensor circuits or the ECM itself has been detected. More importantly, the source of the malfunction is stored in the ECM's memory.

To retrieve this information from the ECM memory, you must use a short jumper wire to ground a diagnostic terminal. This terminal is part of a wiring connector known as the Assembly Line Communications Link (ALCL) **(see illustration)**. The ALCL is located underneath the dashboard, just below the instrument panel and to the left of the steering column. To use the ALCL, push one end of the jumper wire into the diagnostic terminal and the other end into the ground terminal.

When the diagnostic terminal is grounded with the ignition on and the engine stopped, the system will enter the Diagnostic Mode. In this mode the ECM will display a "Code 12" by flashing the service engine soon light, indicating the system is operating. A code 12 is simply one flash, followed by a brief pause, then two flashes in quick succession. This code will be flashed three times. If no other codes are stored, Code 12 will continue to flash until the diagnostic terminal ground is removed.

After flashing Code 12 three times, the ECM will display any stored trouble codes. Each code will be flashed three times, then Code 12 will be flashed again, indicating the display of stored trouble codes has been completed.

When the ECM sets a trouble code, the service engine soon light will come on and a trouble code will be stored in memory. If the problem is intermittent, the light will go out after 10-seconds, when the fault goes away. However, the trouble code will stay in the ECM memory until the battery voltage to the ECM is interrupted. Removing battery voltage for 30-seconds will clear all stored trouble codes. Trouble codes should always be cleared after repairs have been completed. **Caution:** *To prevent damage to the ECM, the ignition switch must be off when disconnecting power to the ECM.*

Following is a list of the typical trouble codes which may be encountered while diagnosing the Computer Command Control System. Also included are simplified troubleshooting procedures. If the problem persists after these checks have been made, more detailed service procedures will have to be done by a dealer service department.

Trouble code**	Circuit or system	Probable cause
Code 12 (1 flash, pause, 2 flashes) stored	Diagnostic	This code will flash whenever the diagnostic terminal is grounded with the ignition turned On and the engine not running. If additional trouble codes are in the ECM they will appear after this code has flashed three times.
Code 13 (1 flash, pause, 3 flashes)	Oxygen sensor circuit (open circuit)	Check the wiring and connectors from the oxygen sensor. Replace the oxygen sensor.*
Code 14 (1 flash, pause, 4 flashes)	Coolant sensor circuit (high temperature)	If the engine is experiencing overheating problems the problem must be rectified before continuing. Check all wiring and connectors associated with the coolant temperature sensor. Replace the coolant temperature sensor.*
Code 15 (1 flash, pause, 5 flashes)	Coolant sensor circuit (low temperature)	See above, then check the wiring connections at the ECM.
Code 16 (1 flash, pause, 6 flashes)	System voltage high	A code 16 will set if the voltage at the ECM is greater than 17.1 volts for 2 seconds. Check the charging system (see Chapter 5).
Code 21 (2 flashes, pause, 1 flash)	Throttle position sensor	Check for a sticking or misadjusted TPS plunger. Check all wiring and connections between the TPS and the ECM. Adjust or replace the TPS (see Chapter 4).*
Code 22 (2 flashes, pause, 2 flashes)	Throttle position sensor	Check the TPS adjustment (Chapter 4). Check the ECM connector. Replace the TPS (Chapter 4).*
Code 23 (2 flashes, pause, 3 flashes)	Manifold air temperature	Check the MAT sensor, wiring and connectors for an open sensor circuit. Replace the MAT sensor.*
Code 24 (2 flashes, pause, 4 flashes)	Vehicle speed sensor	A fault in this circuit should be indicated only when the vehicle is in motion. Disregard Code 24 if it is set when the drive wheels are not turning. Check the connections at the ECM. A dealer service department should perform further checks.

* Component replacement may not cure the problem in all cases. For this reason, you may want to seek professional advice before purchasing replacement parts.

** Trouble codes are flashed only on 1985 through 1993 models.

6

Trouble code**	Circuit or system	Probable cause
Code 25 (2 flashes, pause, 5 flashes)	Manifold air temperature	Check the voltage signal from the MAT sensor to the ECM. It should be above 4 volts.
Code 26 (2 flashes, pause, 6 flashes)	Quad driver circuit	Have the vehicle checked by a dealer service department.
Code 27 (2 flashes, pause, 7 flashes)	Gear switch diagnosis	Have vehicle checked by a dealer service department.
Code 28 (2 flashes, pause, 8 flashes)	Same as code 27	Same as code 27
Code 29 (2 flashes, pause, 9 flashes)	Same as code 27	Same as code 27
Code 31 (3 flashes, pause, 1 flash)	Park/neutral switch	Check for a faulty switch or connections.*
Code 32 (3 flashes, pause, 2 flashes)	EGR system	Check vacuum hoses and connections for leaks and restrictions. Replace the EGR solenoid or valve.*
Code 33 (3 flashes, pause, 3 flashes)	MAF sensor	Replace the MAF sensor.*
Code 34 (3 flashes, pause, 4 flashes)	MAF sensor	Check for loose or damaged air duct, misadjusted minimum idle speed and vacuum leaks. Inspect the MAF sensor and the electrical connections.
Code 38 (3 flashes, pause, 8 flashes)	Brake input circuit	Check brake light switch connections, adjustment or replace switch.*
Code 39 (3 flashes, pause, 9 flashes)	Torque converter clutch	Check for faulty connections or TCC solenoid.*
Code 41 (4 flashes, pause, 1 flash)	Cam sensor	Check for faulty connections or a faulty cam sensor.*
Code 42 (4 flashes, pause, 2 flashes)	Electronic Spark Timing	Check for faulty connections or a faulty ignition module.
Code 43 (4 flashes, pause, 3 flashes)	Electronic spark control	Check for a faulty knock sensor or MEM-CAL.*
Code 44 (4 flashes, pause, 4 flashes)	Lean exhaust	Check the ECM wiring connections. Check for vacuum leaks at the hoses and intake manifold gasket.*
Code 45 (4 flashes, pause, 5 flashes)	Rich exhaust	Check the evaporative charcoal canister and its components for the presence of fuel.
Code 46 (4 flashes, pause, 6 flashes)	Power steering pressure switch	Check for faulty connections or a faulty switch.*
Code 48 (4 flashes, pause, 8 flashes)	Misfire diagnosis	Check the ignition and fuel systems.
Code 51 (5 flashes, pause, 1 flash)	Prom or MEM–CAL	Make sure the MEM-CAL or PROM is properly installed in the ECM. Replace the MEM-CAL or PROM.*
Code 52 (5 flashes, pause, 2 flashes)	CAL–PAK	Check the CAL-PAK to insure proper installation. Replace the CAL-PAK.*
Code 55 (5 flashes, pause, 5 flashes)	ECM	Check for faulty connections. Replace ECM.*
Code 63 (6 flashes, pause, 3 flashes)	EGR flow check	Have vehicle checked by a dealer service department.
Code 64 (6 flashes, pause, 4 flashes)	Same as code 63	Same as code 63
Code 65 (6 flashes, pause, 5 flashes)	Same as code 63	Same as code 63

* Component replacement may not cure the problem in all cases. For this reason, you may want to seek professional advice before purchasing replacement parts.

** Trouble codes are flashed only on 1985 through 1993 models.

3.1   Make sure that the service numbers on the ECM and the PROM are the same – otherwise, depending on what you are replacing, you could end up with the wrong ECM or PROM

3.5   To remove the Electronic Control Module (ECM) from the vehicle, remove the mounting bolts and slide it out far enough to unplug the electrical connectors

3   Electronic Control Module (ECM)/Programmable Read Only Memory (PROM)/CALPAK/MEM-CAL/Powertrain Control Module

ECM replacement

Refer to illustrations 3.1 and 3.5

1   If you are replacing the ECM, check the service number on the new and old ECM to verify that they are the same **(see illustration)**.

2   The Electronic Control Module (ECM) is located under the right hand side of the instrument panel.

3   Disconnect the negative battery cable from the battery.

4   Remove the right sound insulator panel.

5   Remove the retaining bolts **(see illustration)** and carefully slide the ECM out far enough to unplug the electrical connector.

6   Unplug both electrical connectors from the ECM. **Caution:** *The ignition switch must be turned off when pulling out or plugging in the connectors to prevent damage to the ECM.*

7   Installation is the reverse of removal.

PROM

Refer to illustration 3.8

8   To allow one model of ECM to be used for many different vehicles, a device called a PROM (Programmable Read Only Memory) is used **(see illustration)**. The PROM is located inside the ECM and contains information on the vehicle's weight, engine, transaxle, axle ratio, etc. One ECM part number can be used by many GM vehicles but the PROM is very specific and must be used only in the vehicle for which it was designed. For this reason, it's essential to check the latest parts book and Service Bulle-

tin information for the correct part number when replacing a PROM. An ECM purchased at a dealer doesn't come with a PROM. The PROM from the old ECM must be carefully removed and installed in the new ECM.

CALPAK

9   A device known as a CALPAK **(see illustration 3.8)** is used to allow fuel delivery if other parts of the ECM are damaged. The CALPAK has an access door in the ECM and replacement is the same as described for the PROM.

MEM-CAL (1985 through 1993 models)

Refer to illustration 3.10

10   The MEM-CAL **(see illustration)** contains the functions of the PROM, CALPAK and ESC module used on later models. Like the PROM, it contains the calibrations needed for a specific vehicle as well as the back-up fuel control circuitry required if the rest of the ECM is damaged or defective.

3.8   Once the access cover is removed from the ECM (1), you can replace either the PROM (2), or the CALPAK (4) – be sure to use the proper tool – a PROM carrier (3)

3.10   A typical electronic control module (ECM)

1   ECM assembly   3   Access cover
2   MEM-CAL unit

6

3.13   Grasp the PROM carrier at the narrow ends with the PROM removal tool and gently rock the removal tool until the PROM is unplugged from the socket

3.14   Note how the notch in the PROM is matched up with the smaller notch in the carrier

3.15   Press only on the ends of the PROM carrier – pressure on the area in between could result in bent or broken pins or damage to the PROM

3.25   Gently squeeze each end of the blue locking tabs on the PROM unit, pull it upward out of the PCM socket and remove it

PROM/CALPAK replacement

1985 through 1993 models

Refer to illustrations 3.13, 3.14 and 3.15

11   If you are replacing the PROM, check to make sure that the service numbers match on both the old and new PROM.

12   Remove the PROM/CALPAK access cover.

13   Using a PROM removal tool (available at GM dealers), grasp the PROM carrier at the narrow ends **(see illustration)**. Gently rock the carrier from end-to-end while pulling up firmly. The PROM carrier and PROM should lift off the PROM socket easily. **Caution:** *The PROM carrier should only be removed with the special rocker-type PROM removal tool. Removal without this tool or with any other type of tool may damage the PROM or the PROM socket.*

14   Note the reference end of the PROM carrier **(see illustration)** before setting it aside.

15   Position the PROM carrier assembly squarely over the PROM socket with the small notched end of the carrier aligned with the small notch in the socket at the pin 1 end. Press on the PROM carrier until it seats firmly in the socket **(see illustration)**.

16   If the PROM is new, make sure the notch in the PROM is matched to the small notch in the carrier **(see illustration 3.14)**. **Caution:** *If the PROM is installed backwards and the ignition switch is turned on, the PROM will be destroyed.*

17   Attach the access cover to the ECM and tighten the two screws.

18   Install the ECM.

19   Start the engine and enter the diagnostic mode (see Section 2). If no trouble codes occur, the PROM is correctly installed.

20   If Trouble Code 51 occurs, or if the Service Engine Soon light comes on and remains on, the PROM isn't seated, is installed backwards, has bent pins or is defective.

21   If the PROM isn't seated, pressing firmly on both ends of the carrier should correct the problem.

22   If the pins have been bent, remove the PROM, straighten the pins and reinstall it. If the bent pins break or crack when you attempt to straighten them, discard the PROM and replace it with a new one.

1994 and 1995 models

Refer to illustration 3.25

23   If you are replacing the PROM, check to make sure the service numbers match on both the old and new PROM.

24   Remove the PROM access cover.

25   Using your thumb and index finger, gently squeeze each end of the blue locking tabs on the PROM unit and pull it upward out of the PCM socket **(see illustration)**.

26   Gently press the PROM into place until it is firmly seated in the PCM socket. **Caution:** *Press only on the each end of the blue locking tabs, NOT on the PROM unit.*

27   Install the PROM access cover.

MEM-CAL replacement (1985 through 1993 models)

Refer to illustrations 3.29 and 3.30

Note: *If you are replacing either the ECM or MEL-CAL, verify that the service numbers match between the new and old part.*

28   Remove the MEM-CAL access cover.

29   Using two fingers, push both retaining clips back away from the MEM-CAL **(see illustration)**. At the same time, grasp the MEM-CAL at both ends and lift it up out of the socket. Don't remove the MEM-CAL cover itself. **Caution:** *Use of unapproved removal or installation methods may damage the MEM-CAL or socket.*

30   To install the MEM-CAL, the small notches in the MEM-CAL must be aligned with the small notches in the MEM-CAL socket. Press on the ends of the MEM-CAL until the retaining clips snap into the ends of the MEM-CAL. Don't press on the middle of the MEM-CAL – press only on the ends **(see illustration)**.

3.29 Using two fingers, push the retaining clips (arrows) away from the MEM-CAL and simultaneously grasp it at both ends and lift it up, out of the socket

3.30 To install the MEM-CAL, press only on the ends (arrows) until the retaining clips snap into the ends of the MEM-CAL – make sure the notches in the MEM-CAL are aligned with the small notches in the socket

31   The remainder of the installation is the reverse of removal.
32   Once the new MEM-CAL is installed in the old ECM (or the old MEM-CAL is installed in the new ECM), check the installation to verify its been installed properly by doing the following test:

   a) Turn the ignition switch on.
   b) Enter the diagnostics mode at the ALCL (see Section 2).
   c) Allow Code 12 to flash four times to verify that no other codes are present. This indicates the MEM-CAL is installed properly and the ECM is functioning properly.

33   If trouble codes 41, 42, 43, 51 or 52 occur, or if the Service Engine soon light is on constantly but isn't flashing any codes, the MEM-CAL is either not completely seated or it's defective. If it's not seated, press firmly on the ends of the MEM-CAL. If it's necessary to remove the MEM-CAL, follow the above Steps again.

Powertrain control module replacement (1996 and later models)

Caution: *The ignition switch must be turned off when pulling out or plugging in the connectors to prevent damage to the PCM.*
Note 1: *If the PCM is going to be replaced, remove the knock sensor module and reinstall it on the new PCM.*
Note 2: *The power train control module performs basically the same function as the electronic control module. It is not equipped with a replaceable PROM unit.*
Note 3: *If you replace the PCM, the new unit **will not be programmed**. It must be programmed by the dealer for your specific year and model vehicle.*

34   If you are replacing the PCM, check the service number on the new and old PCM to verify that they are the same.
35   The PCM is located in the front left-hand corner of the engine compartment.
36   Turn the ignition switch to the OFF position.
37   Detach the cable from the negative terminal of the battery.
38   On 1997 and later Park Avenue models, remove the air filter top cover bolts and cover. Carefully pull the PCM unit up and out of the air filter case, then disconnect the electrical connectors.
39   On all other 1996 and later models, either unscrew the wing nuts and remove the top cover (1996 and 1997 models) or release the three hooks and remove the cover shield (1998 models). Carefully pull the PCM unit up and out of the mounting bracket, then disconnect the electrical connectors.
40   Installation is the reverse of removal.

4   Information sensors

Note: *See the component location illustrations in Section 2 for the location of the following information sensors.*

4.2 A typical engine coolant temperature sensor (1) harness connector (2) has a locking tab (3) that must be released to unplug the connector

4.3 To prevent coolant leakage, be sure to wrap the temperature sensor threads with Teflon tape before installation

Engine coolant temperature sensor

Refer to illustrations 4.2 and 4.3

1   The coolant sensor is a thermistor (a resistor which varies the value of its voltage output in accordance with temperature changes). A failure in the coolant sensor circuit should set either a Code 14 or a Code 15. These codes indicate a failure in the coolant temperature circuit, so the appropriate solution to the problem will be either repair of a wire or replacement of the sensor.
2   To remove the sensor, release the locking tab **(see illustration)**, unplug the electrical connector, then carefully unscrew the sensor. **Caution:** *Handle the coolant sensor with care. Damage to this sensor will affect the operation of the entire fuel injection system.*
3   Before installing the new sensor, wrap the threads with Teflon sealing tape to prevent leakage and thread corrosion **(see illustration)**.
4   Installation is the reverse of removal.

6

4.7   Removing a MAT sensor from the air cleaner housing (air cleaner housing removed from engine for clarity)

4.9   A typical Mass Air Flow (MAF) sensor installation (arrow)

4.12   The oxygen sensor is located in the exhaust manifold

Manifold Air Temperature (MAT) sensor

Refer to illustration 4.7

Note: *On later models, the Manifold Air Temperature (MAT) sensor is referred to as the Intake Air Temperature (IAT) sensor. The sensor is the same, only the name has changed.*

5   The Manifold Air Temperature (MAT) sensor is a thermistor (a resistor which changes the value of its voltage output as the temperature changes). The ECM uses the MAT sensor signal to delay EGR until the manifold air temperature reaches 40-degrees F.

6   A failure in the MAT sensor circuit should set either a Code 23 or a Code 25.

7   To remove a MAT sensor, unplug the electrical connector and remove the sensor with a wrench **(see illustration)**.

8   Installation is the reverse of removal.

Mass Air Flow (MAF) sensor

Refer to illustration 4.9

9   The Mass Air Flow (MAF) sensor, which is located in a housing between the air cleaner housing and the intake duct **(see illustration)** or on top of the throttle body, measures the amount of air entering the engine. The ECM uses this information to control fuel delivery. A large quantity of air indicates acceleration, while a small quantity indicates deceleration or idle.

10   To replace the MAF sensor, unplug the electrical connector, remove the clamps and carefully lift it from the vehicle.

11   Installation is the reverse of removal.

Oxygen sensor

Refer to illustration 4.12

Note: *On 1994 and later models, the Oxygen Sensor is now being referred to as the Heated Oxygen Sensor (HO2S). The sensor is the same, only the name has changed.*

12   The oxygen sensor is mounted in the exhaust system where it can monitor the oxygen content of the exhaust gas stream **(see illustration)**.

13   By monitoring the voltage output of the oxygen sensor, the ECM will know what fuel mixture command to give the injector.

14   An open in the oxygen sensor circuit should set a Code 13. A low voltage in the circuit should set a Code 44. A high voltage in the circuit should set a Code 45. Codes 44 and 45 may also be set as a result of fuel system problems.

15   See Section 5 for the oxygen sensor replacement procedure.

Throttle Position Sensor (TPS)

16   The Throttle Position Sensor (TPS) is located on the lower end of the throttle shaft.

4.20   The Park/Neutral switch (arrow) is located on the upper rear part of the automatic transaxle

17   By monitoring the output voltage from the TPS, the ECM can determine fuel delivery based on throttle valve angle (driver demand). A broken or loose TPS can cause intermittent bursts of fuel from the injector and an unstable idle because the ECM thinks the throttle is moving.

18   A problem in any of the TPS circuits will set either a Code 21 or 22. Once a trouble code is set, the ECM will use an artificial default value for the TPS and some vehicle performance will return.

19   If the TPS must be replaced, the complete procedure is contained in Chapter 4.

Park/Neutral switch

Refer to illustration 4.20

20   The Park/Neutral (P/N) switch, located on the rear upper part of the automatic transaxle **(see illustration)**, indicates to the ECM when the transaxle is in Park or Neutral. This information is used for Transaxle Converter Clutch (TCC), Exhaust Gas Recirculation (EGR) and Idle Air Control (IAC) valve operation. **Caution:** *The vehicle should not be driven with the Park/Neutral switch disconnected because idle quality will be adversely affected and a false Code 24 (failure in the Vehicle Speed Sensor circuit) may be set.*

21   For more information regarding the P/N switch, which is part of the Neutral/start and back-up light switch assembly, see Chapter 7.

A/C On signal

22   This signal tells the ECM the A/C selector switch is in the On position and the high side low pressure switch is closed. The ECM uses this information to turn on the A/C and adjust the idle speed when the air conditioning system is working. If this signal isn't available to the ECM, idle may be rough, especially when the A/C compressor cycles.

5.3   A typical electrical connector for an oxygen sensor pigtail lead – if you have trouble finding the connector, locate the sensor first, then trace the pigtail lead to the connector

6.2a   A typical crankshaft sensor (arrow) – adjustment should be left to a dealer service department

6.2b   A typical camshaft sensor, located near the water pump (arrow)

23   Diagnosis of the circuit between the A/C On signal and the ECM should be left to a dealer service department.

Vehicle Speed Sensor (VSS)

24   The Vehicle Speed Sensor (VSS) sends a pulsing voltage signal to the ECM, which the ECM converts to miles per hour. This sensor controls the operation of the TCC system.

Crankshaft Sensor/Camshaft Sensor

25   The crankshaft sensor sends a signal to the ECM to tell it both engine rpm and crankshaft position. The camshaft sensor sends a signal to the ECM to tell it when the number one piston is in it's power stroke. See electronic Spark Timing (Section 6) for further information.

5   Oxygen sensor – replacement

Refer to illustration 5.3

Note: *On 1994 and later models, the Oxygen Sensor is now being referred to as the Heated Oxygen Sensor (HO2S). The sensor is the same, only the name has changed.*

Note: *Because it's installed in the exhaust manifold or pipe, which contracts when cool, the oxygen sensor may be very difficult to loosen when the engine is cold. Rather than risk damage to the sensor (assuming you're planning to reuse it in another manifold or pipe), start and run the engine for a minute or two, then shut it off. Be careful not to burn yourself during the following procedure.*

1   Disconnect the cable from the negative terminal of the battery.
2   Raise the vehicle and support it securely on jackstands.
3   Carefully disconnect the electrical connector **(see illustration)**.
4   Note the position of the silicone boot, if equipped, and carefully unscrew the sensor from the exhaust manifold. **Caution:** *Excessive force may damage the threads.*
5   Anti-seize compound must be used on the threads of the sensor to facilitate future removal. The threads of a new sensor will already be coated with it, but if an old sensor is removed and reinstalled, recoat the threads.
6   Installation is the reverse of removal.

6   Electronic Spark Timing (EST)

Refer to illustrations 6.2a and 6.2b

1   To provide improved engine performance, fuel economy and control

of exhaust emissions, the Electronic Control Module (ECM) controls spark advance (ignition timing) with the Electronic Spark Timing (EST) system.
2   The ECM receives a reference pulse from the crankshaft sensor, which indicates both engine rpm and crankshaft position **(see illustration)**. The ECM also receives a reference pulse from the camshaft sensor **(see illustration)**, which indicates the position of the number one piston on the power stroke. The ECM then determines the proper spark advance for the engine operating conditions and sends an EST pulse to the ignition module. A fault in the EST system will usually set a trouble code 42.

7   Electronic Spark Control (ESC) system

Refer to illustration 7.3

General description

1   Irregular octane levels in modern gasoline can cause detonation in an engine. Detonation is sometimes referred to as "spark knock."
2   The Electronic Spark Control (ESC) system is designed to retard spark timing up to 20-degrees to reduce spark knock in the engine. This allows the engine to use maximum spark advance to improve driveability and fuel economy.
3   The ESC knock sensor, which is located on the upper left end of the block under the throttle body **(see illustration)**, sends a voltage signal of 8

7.3   The Electronic Spark Control (ESC) knock sensor (arrow) is located on top of the block, underneath the throttle body

8.5a   An exploded view of a typical digital EGR valve

8.5b   An exploded view of a typical linear EGR valve assembly

1   Nut
2   Linear EGR valve
3   Gasket
4   Valve adapter assembly

to 10-volts to the ECM when no spark knock is occurring and the ECM provides normal advance. When the knock sensor detects abnormal vibration (spark knock), the ESC module turns off the circuit to the ECM and the voltage at ECM terminal B7 drops to zero volts. The ECM then retards the timing until spark knock is eliminated.

4   Failure of the ESC knock sensor signal or loss of ground at the ESC module will cause the signal to the ECM to remain high. This condition will result in the ECM controlling the EST as if no spark knock is occurring. Therefore, no retard will occur and spark knock may become severe under heavy engine load conditions. At this point, the ECM will set a Code 43.

5   Loss of the ESC signal to the ECM will cause the ECM to constantly retard EST. This will result in sluggish performance and cause the ECM to set a Code 43.

Knock sensor replacement

6   Detach the cable from the negative terminal of the battery.
7   Disconnect the wiring harness connector from the ESC sensor.
8   Remove the ESC sensor from the block.
9   Installation is the reverse of the removal procedure.

---

8   Exhaust Gas Recirculation (EGR) system

General description

1   The Exhaust Gas Recirculation (EGR) system is used to lower NOx (oxides of nitrogen) emission levels caused by high combustion temperatures. It does this by decreasing combustion temperature. The main element of the system is the EGR valve, which feeds small amounts of exhaust gas back into the combustion chamber.

2   The EGR valve is usually open during warm engine operation and anytime the engine is running above idle speed. The amount of gas recirculated is controlled by variations in vacuum and exhaust back pressure.

3   There are two types of EGR valves: a conventional EGR valve and a digital EGR valve. The conventional EGR valve is controlled by manifold vacuum, through an EGR solenoid valve, which is controlled by the ECM. The digital EGR valve is electrically controlled directly by the ECM.

Digital EGR valve

Refer to illustrations 8.5a and 8.5b

Note: *On 1994 and later models, the Digital EGR valve is replaced with a Linear EGR valve. The new type of valve operates similarly to the older version except the exhaust flow is controlled through a single orifice instead of three as on the digital EGR valve. Both types of valves perform the same function within the exhaust gas recirculation system.*

4   The digital EGR valve feeds small amounts of exhaust gas back into the intake manifold, which then flows into the combustion chamber.

5   The digital EGR valve is designed to accurately supply exhaust gasses to the engine, independent of intake manifold vacuum. The valve controls EGR flow from the exhaust to the intake manifold through three orifices, which increment in size, to produce seven combinations. When a solenoid in the valve is energized, an armature, with an attached shaft and swivel pintle, is lifted, opening the orifice. The flow accuracy is dependent on metering orifice size only, which results in improved control **(see illustrations)**.

6   The digital EGR valve is opened by the ECM, grounding each solenoid circuit. This activates the the solenoid, raises the pintle, and allows exhaust gas flow into the intake manifold. The exhaust gas then moves with the air/fuel mixture into the combustion chamber.

Conventional EGR valve

7   This valve is controlled by a flexible diaphragm which is spring loaded to hold the valve closed. Ported vacuum applied to the top side of the diaphragm overcomes the spring pressure and opens the valve in the exhaust gas port.

8   The EGR vacuum control has a vacuum solenoid that uses pulse width modulation. This means the ECM turns the solenoid on and off many times a second and varies the amount of On time (the pulse width) to vary the amount of exhaust gas recirculated.

9   A diagnostic switch is part of the control and monitors vacuum to the EGR valve. This switch will trigger a Service Engine Soon light and set a Code 32 in the event of a vacuum circuit failure.

Checking

Conventional EGR valve

10   Disconnect the EGR solenoid vacuum harness. Rotate the harness and reinstall only the EGR valve side. Install a vacuum pump with a gauge on the manifold side of the EGR solenoid. Turn the ignition to On (engine stopped). Apply vacuum. Observe the EGR valve – it shouldn't move.

11   If the valve moves, disconnect the EGR solenoid electrical connector and repeat the test. If the valve still moves, replace the solenoid.

12   If the valve doesn't move, ground the diagnostic terminal and repeat the test. If the valve still doesn't move, replace the EGR valve.

13   If the valve moves, start the engine. Lift up on the EGR valve diaphragm and note the idle speed.

14   If there's no change in the idle, remove the EGR valve and check the passages for blockage. If the passages aren't plugged, replace the EGR valve.

15   Due to the complexity and the interrelationship with the ECM, any further checks should be left to a dealer service department.

8.18   Mounting details – conventional EGR valve

1	EGR valve	4	Nut
2	Gasket	5	Stud
3	Clamp	6	Intake manifold

Digital EGR valve

16   A special "scan" tool is needed to check this valve. Take the vehicle to a dealer service department.

Component replacement

EGR valve

Refer to illustration 8.18

17   Disconnect the vacuum hose or electrical connector from the EGR valve.

18   On 1985 through 1992 models, remove the nuts or bolts which secure the EGR valve and gasket to the intake manifold or throttle body adapter **(see illustration)**. On 1993 and later models, remove the nuts which secure the EGR valve and gasket to the EGR valve adapter attached to the cylinder block.

19   Separate the EGR valve from the engine.

20   In some cases, a conventional EGR valve and the passages in the intake manifold or adapter can be cleaned, and the old EGR valve can be returned to service (see below).

21   Using a scraper, remove all traces of old gasket material from the EGR valve (if it will be reused) and the manifold or adapter. Be careful not to gouge the delicate aluminum surfaces on the manifold or adapter.

22   Install the EGR valve, with a new gasket, on the intake manifold or adapter.

23   Installation is the reverse of removal.

EGR control solenoid (conventional systems only)

Refer to illustration 8.25

24   Disconnect the negative battery cable.

25   Unplug the solenoid electrical connector, then clearly label and remove the vacuum hoses **(see illustration)**.

26   Remove the mounting nut and the solenoid.

27   Installation is the reverse of removal.

EGR valve cleaning

Caution: *On digital and linear EGR valves, never wash the valve in solvents or degreaser – both agents will permanently damage the solenoids in the armature assembly. Sandblasting is also not recommended because it will affect the sealing ability of the swivel pintle seals.*

28   Sometimes, a conventional EGR valve can be returned to service after cleaning it and the EGR passages in the manifold or adapter.

29   Inspect the valve pintle(s) for deposits.

30   Depress the valve diaphragm and check for deposits around the valve seat area.

31   Use a wire brush to carefully clean deposits from the pintle.

32   Remove any deposits from the valve outlet with a screwdriver.

8.25   A typical EGR control solenoid assembly

33   If EGR passages in the intake manifold have an excessive build-up of deposits, the passages should be cleaned. Care should be taken to ensure that all loose particles are completely removed to prevent them from clogging the EGR valve or from being ingested into the engine. **Note:** *It's a good idea to place a rag in the passage opening to keep debris from entering while cleaning the manifold.*

9   Evaporative Emission Control System (EECS)

General description

Refer to illustration 9.2

1   This system is designed to trap and store fuel vapors that evaporate from the fuel tank, throttle body and intake manifold.

2   The Evaporative Emission Control System (EECS) consists of a charcoal-filled canister and the lines connecting the canister to the fuel tank, ported vacuum and intake manifold vacuum **(see illustration)**.

9.2   A typical charcoal canister

1	Purge tube	3	Solenoid valve
2	Vapor from fuel tank	4	Vapor from canister

9.10   **To replace the filter in the bottom of the canister, simply remove it and install another one**

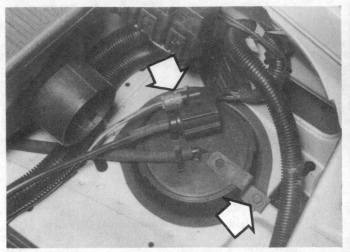

9.13   **A top view of the charcoal canister showing the solenoid electrical connector and the canister mounting bolt (arrows)**

3   Fuel vapors are transferred from the fuel tank, throttle body and intake manifold to a canister where they're stored when the engine isn't running. When the engine is running, the fuel vapors are purged from the canister by intake air flow and consumed in the normal combustion process.

4   On some engines, the ECM operates a solenoid valve (located on top of the canister) which controls vacuum to the purge valve in the charcoal canister. Under cold engine or idle conditions, the solenoid is turned on by the ECM, which closes the valve and blocks vacuum to the canister purge valve. The ECM turns off the solenoid valve and allows purge when the engine is warm.

Checking

Refer to illustration 9.10

5   Poor idle, stalling and poor driveability can be caused by an inoperative purge valve, a damaged canister, split or cracked hoses or hoses connected to the wrong tubes.

6   Evidence of fuel loss or fuel odor can be caused by liquid fuel leaking from fuel lines, a cracked or damaged canister, an inoperative purge valve or disconnected, misrouted, kinked, deteriorated or damaged vapor or control hoses.

7   Inspect each hose attached to the canister for kinks, leaks and cracks along its entire length. Repair or replace as necessary.

8   Inspect the canister. If it's cracked or damaged, replace it.

9   Look for fuel leaking from the bottom of the canister. If fuel is leaking, replace the canister and check the hoses and hose routing.

10   On models so equipped, check the filter at the bottom of the canister. If it's dirty, plugged or damaged, replace it **(see illustration)**.

11   Any further testing should be left to a dealer service department.

Charcoal canister replacement

Refer to illustration 9.13

12   Detach the cable from the negative terminal of the battery.

13   Unplug the solenoid electrical connector – if equipped **(see illustration)**.

14   Clearly label, then detach the vacuum hoses.

15   Remove the canister mounting bolt and lift it out of the vehicle.

16   Installation is the reverse of removal.

10   Positive Crankcase Ventilation (PCV) system

1   The Positive Crankcase Ventilation (PCV) system reduces hydrocarbon emissions by scavenging crankcase vapors. It does this by circulating fresh air from the air cleaner through the crankcase, where it mixes with blow-by gases and is then rerouted through a PCV valve to the intake manifold.

2   The main components of the PCV system are the PCV valve, a fresh air filtered inlet and the vacuum hoses connecting these two components with the engine and the EECS system.

3   To maintain idle quality, the PCV valve restricts the flow when the intake manifold vacuum is high. If abnormal operating conditions arise, the system is designed to allow excessive amounts of blow-by gases to flow back through the crankcase vent tube into the air cleaner to be consumed by normal combustion.

4   Checking and replacement of the PCV valve is covered in Chapter 1.

11   Transaxle Converter Clutch (TCC)

Refer to illustration 11.2

General description

1   The Transaxle Converter Clutch (TCC) uses a solenoid-operated valve in the automatic transaxle to mechanically couple the engine flywheel to the output shaft of the transmission through the torque converter. This reduces the slippage losses in the converter, reducing emissions because engine rpm at any given speed is reduced. It also increases fuel economy.

2   For the converter clutch to operate properly, two conditions must be met:

a) The engine must be warmed up before the clutch can apply. The engine coolant temperature sensor (see Section 4) tells the ECM when the engine is at normal operating temperature.

b) The vehicle must be traveling at the necessary minimum speed to raise the pressure to the level necessary to apply the valve. If the hydraulic pressure is correct, the ECM signals the solenoid to apply the converter clutch **(see illustration)**.

3   After the converter clutch applies, the ECM uses the information from the TPS to release the clutch when the vehicle is accelerating or decelerating at a certain rate.

4   Another switch used in the TCC circuit is a brake switch, which opens the power supply to the TCC solenoid when the brake is applied.

5   A Third gear switch is placed in series on the battery side of the TCC solenoid to prevent TCC application until the transmission is in Third gear.

Checking

6   If the converter clutch is applied at all times, the engine will stall immediately, just like a manual transaxle with the clutch applied.

7   If the converter clutch doesn't apply, fuel economy may be lower than expected. If the Vehicle Speed Sensor (VSS) (see Section 4) fails, the TCC will not apply.

8   A TCC-equipped transaxle has different operating characteristics than an automatic transaxle without TCC. If you detect a "chuggle" or "surge" condition, perform the following check.

11.2 A typical Transaxle Converter Clutch (TCC)

1	TCC solenoid	3	Check ball seat
2	Check ball		

9   Install a tachometer.

10   Drive the vehicle until normal operating temperature is reached, then maintain a 50 to 55 mph speed.

11   Lightly touch the brake pedal and check it for a slight bumpy sensation, indicating the TCC is releasing. A slight increase in rpm should also be noted.

12   Release the brake and check for reapplication of the converter clutch and a slight decrease in engine rpm.

13   If the TCC fails to perform satisfactorily during this test, take the vehicle to a dealer service department to have the TCC serviced.

12   Catalytic converter

General description

1   The catalytic converter is an emission control device added to the exhaust system to reduce pollutants from the exhaust gas stream. A single-bed converter design is used in combination with a three-way (reduction) catalyst. The catalytic coating on the three-way catalyst contains platinum and rhodium, which lowers the levels of oxides of nitrogen (NOx) as well as hydrocarbons (HC) and carbon monoxide (CO).

Checking

2   The test equipment for a catalytic converter is expensive and highly sophisticated. If you suspect the converter is malfunctioning, take it to a dealer service department or authorized emissions inspection facility for diagnosis and repair.

3   Whenever the vehicle is raised for servicing of underbody components, check the converter for leaks, corrosion and other damage. If damage is discovered, the converter should be replaced.

4   Because the converter is welded to the exhaust system, converter replacement requires removal of the exhaust pipe assembly (see Chapter 4). Take the vehicle, or the exhaust pipe system, to a dealer service department or a muffler shop.

5   Although catalytic converters don't break too often, they do become plugged. The easiest way to check for a restricted converter is to use a vacuum gauge to diagnose the effect of a blocked exhaust on intake vacuum.

   a) Open the throttle until the engine speed is about 2000 RPM.
   b) Release the throttle quickly.
   c) If there is no restriction, the gauge will quickly drop to not more than 2 in Hg or more above its normal reading.
   d) If the gauge does not show 5 in Hg or more above its normal reading, or seems to momentarily hover around its highest reading for a moment before it returns, the exhaust system, or the converter, is plugged (or an exhaust pipe is bent or dented or the core inside the muffler has shifted).

6

Chapter 7 Automatic transaxle

Contents

Specifications

Torque specifications

	Ft-lbs
TV cable bolt	6
Transaxle-to-engine block bolts	
4T60-E	55
4T65-E	83
Front left frame-to-body attachment bolt	74
Driveplate-to-converter bolts	46
Right rear transaxle mount	
Nuts	30
Bolts	40
Left rear transaxle mount-to-transaxle bolts	30
Right front transaxle mount-to-transaxle nuts	22
Left front transaxle mount	
Nuts	30
Bolts	40
Strut bracket-to-transaxle bolt(s)	
4T60-E	46
4T65-E	41

Underside view of the automatic transaxle

1	Transaxle pan	3	Left driveaxle	5	Front mount (obscured by
2	Right driveaxle	4	Rear mount		lower crossmember)

7

1   General information

Note: *On models equipped with the Delco Loc II audio system, be sure the lockout feature is turned off before performing any procedure which requires disconnecting the battery.*

Due to the complexity of the clutches and the hydraulic control system, and because of the special tools and expertise required to perform an automatic transaxle overhaul, it should not be undertaken by the home mechanic. Therefore, the procedures in this Chapter are limited to general diagnosis, routine maintenance, adjustment and transaxle removal and installation.

If the transaxle requires major repair work, it should be left to a dealer service department or an automotive or transmission repair shop. You can, however, remove and install the transaxle yourself and save the expense, even if the repair work is done by a transmission shop.

Replacement and adjustment procedures the home mechanic can perform include those involving the throttle valve (TV) cable (1985 through 1991 models) and the shift linkage. **Caution:** *Never tow a disabled vehicle with an automatic transaxle at speeds greater than 35 mph or distances over 50 miles.*

2   Diagnosis – general

1   Automatic transaxle malfunctions may be caused by a number of conditions, such as poor engine performance, improper adjustments, hydraulic malfunctions and mechanical problems.

2   The first check should be of the transaxle fluid level and condition. Refer to Chapter 1 for more information. Unless the fluid and filter have been recently changed, drain the fluid and replace the filter (also in Chapter 1).

3.2   To detach the TV cable from the throttle lever pin, grasp it firmly, move it forward and lift up

3.3   Use needle-nose pliers to compress the TV cable tangs, then push the housing back through the bracket

3.5   Remove the TV cable bolt (arrow) and pull up on the cable until it's out of the transmission

3.6   Hold the transaxle TV link and slide the cable link off the pin

3.9a   To adjust the TV cable, press down on the re-adjust tab, move the slider back against the fitting until it stops, release the re-adjust tab and rotate the throttle lever toward the wide open position until you hear an audible click

3.9b   TV cable adjuster details

3   Road test the vehicle and drive in all the various selective ranges, noting discrepancies in operation.

4   Verify that the engine isn't at fault. If the engine hasn't had a tune-up recently, refer to Chapter 1 and make sure all engine components are functioning properly.

5   On 1985 through 1991 models, check the adjustment of the throttle valve (TV) cable (Section 3).

6   Check the condition of all vacuum and electrical lines and fittings at the transaxle, or leading to it.

7   Check for proper adjustment of the shift control cable (Section 5).

8   If at this point a problem remains, there is one final check before the transaxle is removed for overhaul. The vehicle should be taken to a shop for a line pressure check.

---

3   Throttle valve (TV) cable (1985 through 1991 models) – replacement and adjustment

Note: *On 1992 and later models, the 4T60-E and 4T65-E electronic controlled transmission is not equipped with the Throttle Valve (TV) cable assembly. The 4T60 transmission functions that are controlled by the TV cable are controlled electronically in the 4T60-E and 4T65-E transmissions.*

Replacement

Refer to illustrations 3.2, 3.3, 3.5 and 3.6

1   Detach the cable from the negative battery terminal.

2   Disconnect the TV cable from the throttle lever by grasping the connector, pulling it forward to disconnect it and then lifting up and off the lever pin **(see illustration).**

3   Disconnect the TV cable housing from the bracket by compressing the tangs and pushing the housing back through the bracket **(see illustration).**

4   Disconnect any clips or straps retaining the cable to the transaxle.

5   Remove the bolt retaining the cable to the transaxle **(see illustration).**

6   Pull up on the cover until the end of the cable can be seen, then disconnect it from the transaxle TV link **(see illustration).** Remove the cable from the vehicle.

7   To install the cable, connect it to the transaxle TV link and install the bolt. Tighten the bolt to the specified torque and push the cover securely over the cable. Route the cable to the top of the engine, push the housing through the bracket until it clicks into place, place the connector over the throttle lever pin and pull back to lock it. Secure the cable with any retaining clips or straps.

Adjustment

Refer to illustrations 3.9a and 3.9b

8   The engine MUST NOT be running during this adjustment.

9   Depress the re-adjust tab and push the slider through the fitting (away from the throttle lever) as far as it will go **(see illustrations).**

10   Release the re-adjust tab.

11   Manually turn the throttle lever to the "wide open throttle" position until the re-adjust tab makes an audible click, then release the throttle lever. The cable is now adjusted. **Note:** *Don't use excessive force at the throttle lever to adjust the TV cable. If great effort is required to adjust the cable, disconnect the cable at the transaxle end and check for free operation. If it's still difficult, replace the cable. If it's now free, suspect a bent TV link in the transaxle or a problem with the throttle lever.*

12   Reattach the cable to the negative battery terminal.

---

4   Neutral start switch – replacement and adjustment

Replacement

Refer to illustrations 4.2, 4.4 and 4.5

1   Disconnect the negative cable from the battery.

2   Remove the cruise control servo assembly **(see illustration).**

3   Shift the transaxle into Neutral.

4   Disconnect the shift linkage **(see illustration).**

5   Trace the wire harness from the neutral start switch to the connector **(see illustration)** and unplug it.

6   Remove the bolts **(see illustration 4.9)** and detach the switch.

4.2   You'll need to remove the cruise control servo assembly to get at the neutral start switch: detach the vacuum hoses, remove the bracket nuts (arrows) and hang the cruise control servo assembly out of the way with a piece of wire

7

4.4   Detach the cable from the neutral start switch by prying it off with a screwdriver

4.5   Unplug the electrical connector from the neutral start switch

4.9 Neutral start switch installation details

1   Bolts
2   Switch
3   Transaxle shifter shaft
4   Adjustment hole
5   3/32-inch drill bit used
    for adjustment

5.2a Single-post type floor shift control cable assembly

1	Shift cable	9	Grommet retainer
2	Retainer	10	Nut
3	Nut	11	Bolt*
4	Nut	12	Grommet
5	Transaxle lever	13	Stud
6	Transaxle bracket		
7	Nut	***Note:** Tighten bolt (11)	
8	Screws	after nut (10)	

5.2b Dual-post type floor shift control cable assembly

1	Control assembly	6	Bolt
2	Mounting bracket	7	Washers
3	Screw	8	Nut
4	Nut	9	Park lock cable
5	Nut	10	Shift cable

7   To install the switch, line up the flats on the shift shaft with the flats in the switch and lower the switch onto the shaft.

8   Install the bolts. If the switch is new and the shaft hasn't been moved, tighten the bolts. If the switch requires adjustment, leave the bolts loose and follow the adjustment procedure below. The remainder of installation is the reverse of removal.

Adjustment

Refer to illustration 4.9

9   Insert a 3/32-inch drill bit into the switch gauge hole **(see illustration)**.

10   Rotate the switch until the drill bit can be felt dropping into the switch, indicating that it's now in the Neutral position. Tighten the switch bolts.

11   Install the cruise control assembly.

12   Connect the negative battery cable and verify that the engine will start only in Neutral or Park.

---

5   Automatic transaxle shift cable – replacement and adjustment

1   Disconnect the negative cable from the battery.

Replacement

Floor shift

Refer to illustrations 5.2a, 5.2b, 5.4a, 5.4b and 5.6

2   Working in the engine compartment, disconnect the shift cable from the transaxle lever **(see illustrations)**.

3   Remove the console between the seats (see Chapter 11).

4   Disconnect the shift cable from the shift lever and bracket **(see illustrations)**.

5   Remove the right and left side sound insulators from the under dash portion of the console, then pull back the carpet for access to the cable (see Chapter 11).

6   Working in the engine compartment, detach the cable from the transaxle bracket **(see illustration)**.

7   Trace the cable up to the firewall grommet. Remove the screws from the grommet retainer, detach the grommet and retainer from the firewall and pull the cable assembly through the firewall.

8   Installation is the reverse of removal. After installation, adjust the cable as described below.

Column shift

Refer to illustration 5.11

9   Working in the engine compartment, disconnect the cable from the transaxle lever and bracket **(see illustrations 5.2a and 5.6)**.

10   Working in the passenger compartment, remove the left sound insulator located under the dash (see Chapter 12).

11   Disconnect the cable bracket on the steering column and detach the cable from the column shift lever **(see illustration)**.

12   Dislodge the grommet in the firewall and withdraw the cable from the vehicle.

13   Installation is the reverse of removal. After installation, adjust the cable as described below.

5.4a   To disconnect the cable at the shift control assembly, pull off the clip with needle-nose pliers . . .

5.4b   . . . and pry the cable off the lever pin with a screwdriver (single-post type floor shift shown, dual-post type similar

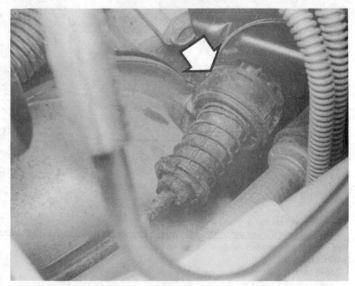

5.6   To detach the shift cable from the transaxle bracket, grasp the housing (arrow) firmly, cock it to one side and pull – though you can't see them in this photo, there's a tang on each side of the housing – the two tangs locate the housing in a square hole in the bracket, so when you rock the housing to one side, one of the tangs comes free (bracket design identical for column shift models)

7

1 CABLE
ASSEMBLY.

A SNAP CABLE
SECURELY ON
PIN AS SHOWN.

B CABLE IS NOT
TO BE KINKED OR
DAMAGED DURING
ASSEMBLY
OPERATION.

5.11   To detach the shift cable from the column shift control assembly, pop it loose with a small screwdriver – when installing the new cable, snap it securely onto the lever pin and make sure you don't kink it

VIEW A

6.4   Typical park/lock cable details

1	Park/lock cable	3	Pin
2	Strap	4	Locking button

Adjustment

14   Place the shift lever and the transaxle lever in Neutral, then push the locking tab on the shift cable to automatically adjust the cable (**see illustration 5.2a or 5.2b**).

15   Reconnect the negative battery cable.

---

6   Automatic transaxle park/lock cable – removal and installation (floor shift models only)

Refer to illustration 6.4
Note: *Column shift models don't have a park/lock cable.*

Removal

1   Disconnect the negative cable from the battery.
2   Remove the console (Chapter 11).
3   Place the shift lever in Park and the ignition switch in the Run position.
4   Insert a screwdriver blade into the slot in the ignition switch inhibitor, depress the cable latch and detach the cable (**see illustration**). **Note:** *If the vehicle has a dual-post type shift control assembly, refer to illustration 5.2b.*
5   Push the cable connector lock button (located at the shift control base) to the up position and detach the cable from the park lock lever pin. Depress the two cable connector latches and remove the cable from the shift control base.
6   Remove the cable clips.

7.3   Dislodge the metal-type differential seal by working around the outer edge with a chisel and hammer

7.6   Tap the new seal into place with a large socket and hammer – use a socket with a diameter slightly smaller than the outside diameter of the seal itself

Installation

7   Make sure the cable lock button is in the up position and the shift lever is in Park. Snap the cable connector into the shift control base.

8   With the ignition key in the Run position (this is very important), snap the cable into the inhibitor housing. Do *not* attempt to insert the cable with the key in any other position.

9   Turn the ignition key to the Lock position.

10   Snap the end of the cable onto the shifter park/lock pin.

11   Push the nose of the cable connector forward to remove the slack.

12   With no load on the connector nose, snap down the cable connector lock button.

13   Check the operation of the park/lock cable as follows.
   a) With the shift lever in Park and the key in Lock, make sure the shift lever cannot be moved to another position and the key can be removed.
   b) With the key in Run and the shift lever in Neutral, make sure the key cannot be turned to Lock.

14   If it operates as described above, the park/lock cable system is properly adjusted.

15   If the park/lock system doesn't operate as described, return the cable connector lock to the up position and repeat the adjustment procedure. Push the cable connector down and recheck the operation.

7   Transaxle differential seals – replacement

Refer to illustrations 7.3 and 7.6

1   Raise the vehicle and support it securely on jackstands.

2   Remove the driveaxle(s) (see Chapter 8).

3   Use a hammer and chisel to pry up the outer lip of the seal to dislodge it so it can be pried out of the housing **(see illustration)**.

4   Compare the new seal to the old one to make sure they're the same.

5   Coat the lips of the new seal with transmission fluid.

6   Place the new seal in position and tap it into the bore with a hammer and a large socket or a piece of pipe that's the same diameter as the outside edge of the seal **(see illustration)**.

7   Reinstall the various components in the reverse order of removal.

8   Automatic transaxle – removal and installation

Refer to illustrations 8.4, 8.6, 8.7, 8.8, 8.9, 8.10, 8.14, 8.15, 8.16, 8.18, 8.19, 8.20a, 8.20b, 8.21, 8.22, 8.23a, 8.23b, 8.23c, 8.23d, 8.24a, 8.24b, 8.25, 8.26, 8.27, 8.28 and 8.29

Removal

1   Detach the cable from the negative battery terminal.

2   Unplug the connector at the Mass Air Flow (MAF) sensor, loosen the hose clamps at the air intake duct and remove the duct and the MAF sensor as an assembly (see Chapter 4).

3   On 1985 through 1991 models, detach the TV cable from the throttle body linkage and the transaxle (see Section 3).

4   If the vehicle has cruise control, detach the cruise control cable from the throttle body, detach the vacuum hoses at the servo, remove the servo mounting bracket bolts **(see illustration 4.2)**, unplug the servo electrical connector **(see illustration)** and remove the servo assembly.

5   Detach the shift control linkage from the mounting bracket on the transaxle and the lever at the manual shaft (see Section 5).

6   Unplug the wiring connectors at the neutral start switch **(see illustration 4.5)** and the torque converter clutch **(see illustration)**.

7   Unplug the vacuum hose at the vacuum modulator **(see illustration)**.

8   Remove the dipstick tube bracket bolt **(see illustration)** and remove the dipstick tube assembly. Plug the hole to prevent leakage.

9   Remove the upper transaxle-to-engine bolts **(see illustration)**.

8.4   After you've detached the cruise control cable from the throttle body, detached the vacuum hoses from the cruise control servo and removed the servo mounting bracket bolts, unplug the electrical connector and remove the servo assembly

7

8.6   Unplug the wiring connector from the torque
converter clutch

8.7   Unplug the vacuum hose at the vacuum modulator

8.8   Remove the dipstick tube bracket bolt and detach the
dipstick tube assembly

8.9   Remove the upper transaxle-to-engine bolts (arrows)

8.10   Attach an engine support fixture or hoist – be sure to load
the support fixture by raising the engine slightly to relieve tension
on the frame and mounts

8.14   Unplug the vehicle speed sensor connector (arrow)

8.15   Unscrew and detach the oil cooler lines (arrows) from the transaxle

8.16   Detach this wire harness clip from the lower crossmember

8.18   Remove the left front transaxle mount (arrows)

8.19   Remove the right front engine mount-to-frame nuts (arrows)

8.20a   Remove the left rear transaxle mount-to-transaxle bolts (arrows) . . .

10   Attach an engine support fixture or hoist (see illustration). Be sure to "load" the support fixture by raising the engine slightly to relieve tension on the frame and mounts.
11   Loosen the wheel lug nuts.
12   Raise the vehicle and place it securely on jackstands.
13   Remove both the front wheels.
14   Unplug the vehicle speed sensor (see illustration).
15   Detach the oil cooler lines from the transaxle and plug them (see illustration).
16   Detach the wire harness clip from the lower crossmember (see illustration).
17   Remove both driveaxles (see Chapter 8).
18   Remove the left front transaxle mount (see illustration).
19   Remove the right front engine mount-to-frame nuts (see illustration).
20   Remove the left rear transaxle mount-to-transaxle bolts (see illustration). Then remove the left rear transaxle mount-to-frame nuts (see illustration) and remove the mount.
21   Remove the right rear transaxle mount (see illustration).

7

8.20b . . . then remove the left rear transaxle mount-to-frame
nuts (arrows)

8.21   Remove the right rear transaxle mount (arrows)

8.22   Place a transaxle stand or floorjack in position under the
transaxle pan – if you're using a floorjack, be sure to put a board
between the jack and the transaxle to protect the pan

8.23a   Remove the two right front engine subframe bolts . . .

8.23b . . . then remove the four left rear subframe bolts – the
lower left bolt is on the wheel well side . . .

8.23c . . . the lower right bolt is on the engine
compartment side . . .

8.23d . . . and the two upper bolts, which can also be accessed through the wheel well, are on top of the corner of the subframe assembly (one of them is also a bushing clamp bolt for the stabilizer bar)

8.24a   Remove the cover (arrow) . . .

8.24b . . . then remove the front left frame-to-body bolt

8.25   Remove the subframe assembly – this assembly is fairly heavy, so you may want assistance

8.26   Remove the torque converter access cover

8.27   Mark the converter-to-driveplate relationship

7

8.28   Remove the driveplate-to-converter bolts – wedge a large screwdriver or prybar between the bellhousing and the driveplate teeth to prevent the crankshaft from turning

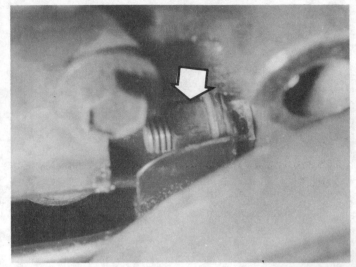

8.29   Remove the lower transaxle-to-engine stud nut (arrow) – a bolt (not visible in this photo) is located between the transaxle case and the engine block and is installed in the opposite direction

22   Place a transaxle stand, or a floorjack, in position under the transaxle **(see illustration)**. If you're using a floorjack, be sure to place a wooden board between the jack and the transaxle to protect the transaxle pan.

23   Remove the engine subframe bolts **(see illustrations)**. There are three bolts at the right front of the subframe and four bolts at the left rear (one of the four rear bolts is also a stabilizer bar clamp attaching bolts).

24   Remove the front left frame-to-body attaching bolt **(see illustrations)**.

25   Remove the subframe assembly **(see illustration)**.

26   Remove the torque converter access cover **(see illustration)**.

27   Mark the converter-to-driveplate relationship to ensure proper reassembly **(see illustration)**.

28   Remove the driveplate-to-converter bolts **(see illustration)**.

29   Remove the two lower transaxle-to-engine fasteners **(see illustration)**. **Note:** *One of them is located between the transaxle case and the engine block and is installed in the opposite direction from the other fasteners.*

30   Make a final check that all wiring, cables, etc. which could interfere with transaxle removal are disconnected or moved out of the way.

31   To separate the transaxle from the engine, pry the bellhousing away very carefully with a large screwdriver or pry bar. Secure the torque converter to the transaxle so it won't fall out of the bellhousing during removal.

32   Carefully lower the transaxle assembly from the vehicle. Make sure you don't damage the driveaxle shaft seals or any hoses, lines or wiring, during removal.

Installation

33   Inspect the driveplate for missing weights, cracks, corrosion and damaged or broken starter gear teeth. Refer to Chapter 2 if the driveplate must be replaced.

34   If the engine rear main oil seal is leaking, refer to Chapter 2 for the replacement procedure.

35   Inspect all hoses, cables and wires that connect to the transaxle for damage and repair or replace them as necessary.

36   Whenever the transaxle is removed for overhaul or replacement of the torque converter, pump or case, make sure you flush the transaxle oil cooler lines with General Motors J-35944, or its equivalent prior to installation.

37   Make sure the torque converter hub is fully engaged in the oil pump.

38   Place the transaxle on a transaxle stand or a floorjack and raise it into position.

39   Install the lower transaxle-to-engine bolts and tighten them to the specified torque.

40   Install the rear transaxle mount bolts and tighten them securely.

41   Install the subframe assembly. **Note:** *When installing the subframe assembly, be sure to align the studs for the front engine and transaxle mounts.*

42   Install the front transaxle mount and front engine mount bolts.

43   Install the torque converter bolts.

44   Install the torque converter access cover.

45   Attach the oil cooler lines to the transaxle and tighten them securely.

46   Attach the vehicle speed sensor connector.

47   Install the driveaxles (see Chapter 8).

48   Attach the balljoint to the steering knuckle (see Chapter 10).

49   Attach the stabilizer bar link bolt to the control arm (see Chapter 10).

50   Attach the outer tie-rods to the steering knuckles (see Chapter 10).

51   Install the wheels and hand tighten the lug nuts.

52   Lower the vehicle and tighten the lug nuts to the torque specified in Chapter 1.

53   Install the upper transaxle-to-engine bolts and tighten securely.

54   Remove the engine support fixture.

55   Install the dipstick tube assembly.

56   On 1985 through 1991 models, attach the TV cable to the transaxle (see Section 3).

57   Attach the shift cable to the shift lever (see Section 5).

58   Attach the starter safety switch and torque converter clutch electrical connectors.

59   Attach the vacuum modulator hose.

60   Install the cruise control servo assembly.

61   Install the air intake duct (see Chapter 4).

62   Attach the cable to the negative battery terminal.

63   Start the engine and check for leaks.

Chapter 8 Driveaxles

Contents

Specifications

Driveaxles

Collapsed CV joint boot dimension
Tri-pot	5-1/16-in
Double offset	5-7/32-in

Torque specifications   Ft-lbs

Hub nut
1985 through 1990	180
1991	192
1992 on	107
Wheel lug nuts	See Chapter 1

---

1   General information

Refer to illustrations 1.1a, 1.1b and 1.1c

Note: *On models equipped with the Delco Loc II audio system, be sure the lockout feature is turned off before performing any procedure which requires disconnecting the battery.*

Power is transmitted from the transaxle to the front wheels by two driveaxles, which consist of splined solid axles with constant velocity (CV) joints at each end. There are two types of inner CV joints used. On certain models a double-offset design using ball bearings with an inner and outer race is used to allow angular movement. The other CV joint used is a tri-pot design, with a spider bearing assembly and tri-pot housing to allow angular movement **(see illustrations)**. To determine which CV joint is used on your vehicle, look at the housing while it's still installed on the vehicle and compare it to the accompanying illustrations, noting that the tri-pot housing will have three major indentations in it and a very thin retaining clamp holding the boot in position **(see illustration)**. All outer CV joints are the double-offset type.

1.1a   Driveaxle and CV joint component layout (double offset design)

1   Deflector ring
2   Outer bearing race
3   Bearing cage
4   Inner bearing race
5   Ball bearings
6   Race retaining ring
7   Boot retaining clamp
8   Outer driveaxle boot
9   Boot retaining clamp
10 Driveaxle
11 Inner driveaxle boot
12 Ball bearing retaining ring
13 Inner race
14 Bearing cage
15 Outer race
16 Retaining ring

(LH AUTO ONLY)
(EQUAL LENGTH, RH MAN ONLY)

**1.1b   Driveaxle and CV joint component layout
(tri-pot design inner joint)**

1	Outer CV joint outer race	13	Tri-pot joint balls
2	CV joint cage	14	Tri-pot housing (left)
3	CV joint inner race	15	Driveaxle (right)
4	Shaft retaining ring	16	Spacer
5	Ball bearings	17	Race retaining ring
6	Splines	18	Boot clamp
7	Boot	19	Needle bearing retainer
8	Boot clamp	20	Needle retainer ring
9	Driveaxle (left)	21	Joint retaining ring
10	Tri-pot joint boot	22	Tri-pot housing (right)
11	Tri-pot spider	23	Damper and shaft assembly
12	Needle bearings	24	Deflector ring
		25	Tri-pot bushing

The CV joints are protected by rubber boots, which are retained by clamps so the joints are protected from water and dirt. The boots should be inspected periodically (see Chapter 1). The inner boots have very small breather holes which may leak a small amount of lubricant under some circumstances, such as when the joint is compressed during removal. Damaged CV joint boots must be replaced immediately or the joints can be damaged. Boot replacement involves removing the driveaxles (Section 10). It's a good idea to disassemble, clean, inspect and repack the CV joint whenever replacing a CV joint boot to make sure the joint isn't contaminated with moisture or dirt, which would cause premature failure of the CV joint.

The most common symptom of worn or damaged CV joints, besides lubricant leaks, are a clicking noise in turns, a clunk when accelerating from a coasting condition or vibration at highway speeds.

2   Driveaxles – removal and installation

Refer to illustrations 2.2, 2.5a, 2.5b, 2.6 and 2.8

Removal

1   Remove the wheel cover and loosen the hub nut. Loosen the wheel lug nuts, raise the front of the vehicle and support it securely on jackstands. Apply the parking brake and block the rear wheels to keep the vehicle from rolling off the jackstands. Remove the front wheel.
2   Remove the driveaxle hub nut. To prevent the hub from turning, insert a screwdriver through the caliper and into a rotor cooling vane, then remove the nut **(see illustration)**.
3   Remove the brake caliper and disc and support the caliper out of the way with a piece of wire (see Chapter 9).
4   Remove the control arm-to-steering knuckle balljoint stud nut and separate the lower arm from the steering knuckle (see Chapter 10 if necessary).
5   Push the driveaxle out of the hub with a puller, then support the outer end of the driveaxle with a piece of wire to prevent damage to the inner CV joint **(see illustrations)**.

1.1c   Two types of inner CV joint housings – note the indents on the tri-pot housing

2.2   A pry bar will hold the hub stationary while loosening the hub nut

2.5a   A two-jaw puller works well for pushing the stub axle out of the hub

2.5b   Support the driveaxle with a piece of wire after it's been freed from the hub – don't let it hang unsupported or the CV joint could be damaged

2.6   Use a large pry bar positioned as shown to "pop" the inner CV joint out of the transaxle – it may be necessary to tap the pry bar with a hammer if the driveaxle is stuck

2.8   A large punch or screwdriver, positioned in the groove on the CV joint housing, can be used to seat the joint in the transaxle

3.4   Snap-ring pliers should be used to remove both the inner and outer retaining rings

6   Carefully pry the inner end of the driveaxle out of the transaxle, using a large pry bar positioned between the transaxle housing and the CV joint housing **(see illustration)**.

7   Support the CV joints and carefully remove the driveaxle from the vehicle.

Installation

8   Lubricate the differential seal with multi-purpose grease, raise the driveaxle into position while supporting the CV joints and insert the splined end of the inner CV joint into the differential side gear. Seat the shaft in the side gear by positioning the end of a screwdriver in the groove in the CV joint and tapping it into position with a hammer **(see illustration)**.

9   Apply a light coat of multi-purpose grease to the outer CV joint splines, pull out on the strut/steering knuckle assembly and install the stub axle in the hub.

10   Insert the control arm balljoint stud into the steering knuckle and tighten the nut. Be sure to use a new cotter pin (refer to Chapter 10).

11   Install the brake disc and caliper (see Chapter 9 if necessary).

12   Install the hub nut. Lock the disc so it can't turn, using a screwdriver or punch inserted through the caliper into a disc cooling vane, and tighten the hub nut to the initial specified torque.

13   Grasp the inner CV joint housing (not the driveaxle) and pull out to make sure the axle has seated securely in the transaxle.

14   Install the wheel and lower the vehicle.

15   Tighten the hub nut to the final specified torque and install the wheel cover.

---

3   **Driveaxle boot replacement and constant velocity (CV) joint overhaul**

Note: *If the CV joints exhibit wear indicating the need for an overhaul (usually due to torn boots), explore all options before beginning the job. Complete rebuilt driveaxles are available on an exchange basis, which eliminates a lot of time and work. Whatever is decided, check on the cost and availability of parts before disassembling the vehicle.*

1   Remove the driveaxle (see Section 2).

2   Place the driveaxle in a vise lined with rags to avoid damage to the shaft.

Inner CV joint

Tri-pot design

Refer to illustrations 3.4, 3.5, 3.9, 3.11, 3.12 and 3.15

3   Cut off the boot seal retaining clamps and slide the boot towards the center of the driveaxle. Mark the tri-pot housing and driveaxle so they can be reinstalled in the same relative positions, then slide the housing off the spider assembly.

4   Remove the spider assembly from the axle by first removing the inner retaining ring and sliding the spider assembly back to expose the front retaining ring. Remove the front retaining ring and slide the joint off the driveaxle **(see illustration)**.

5   Use tape or a cloth wrapped around the spider bearing assembly to retain the bearings during removal and installation **(see illustration)**.

6   Remove the spider assembly from the axle.

7   Slide the boot off the axle.

8   On 1985 through 1992 and 1997 and later models, clean all of the old grease out of the housing and spider assembly. Carefully disassemble each section of the spider assembly, one at a time, and clean the needle bearings with solvent. Inspect the rollers, spider cross, bearings and housing for scoring, pitting and other signs of abnormal wear. Apply a coat of CV joint grease to the inner bearing surfaces to hold the needle bearings in place when reassembling the spider assembly.

3.5   Boot installation layout for a tri-pot inner CV joint – note the tape around the spider assembly to prevent it from coming apart on 1985 through 1992 models

8

1627-8-03.09 HAYNES

3.9 Install the bearing blocks onto the flats on the tri-pot, rotate them 90-degrees in either direction and lock them in place (1993 through 1996 models)

3.11   Before installing the CV joint boot, wrap the axle splines with tape to prevent damage to the boot

3.12   When installing the spider assembly on the driveaxle, make sure the recess in the counterbore (arrow) is facing the end of the driveaxle

9   On 1993 through 1996 models, clean all of the old grease out of the housing and spider assembly. Rotate each bearing block 90-degrees in either direction and remove the bearing blocks from the tri-pot spider, then clean the bearing in solvent. Inspect the tri-pot spider, bearings and housing for scoring, pitting and other signs of abnormal wear. Apply a light coat of CV joint grease to the tri-pot inner bearing post, align the flats on the opening in the bearing block with the flats on the tri-pot, install the bearing blocks and rotate them 90-degrees in either direction to lock them in place **(see illustration)**.

10   Pack the housing with half of the grease furnished with the new boot and place the remainder in the boot.

11   Wrap the driveaxle splines with tape to avoid damaging the boot, then slide the boot onto the axle **(see illustration)**.

12   Install the spider bearing with the recess in the counterbore facing the end of the driveaxle **(see illustration)**.

13   On 1985 through 1992 models and 1997 and later, install the tri-pot housing onto the end of the axle. Remove the tape from the tri-pot spider as the housing is being installed onto the tri-pot spider.

14   On 1993 models, insert a small piece of sheet metal or heavy cardboard (cut to fit) between the boot and the bearing blocks to maintain bearing block alignment during installation of the tri-pot housing onto the spider assembly **(see illustration)**. Install the tri-pot housing onto the end of the axle. Remove the piece of metal or cardboard from the tri-pot spider as the housing is being installed.

15   Seat the boot in the housing and axle seal grooves, then adjust the collapsed dimension of the joint **(see illustration)**. Install the retaining clamps, then install the driveaxle as described in Section 2.

1627-8-03.14 HAYNES

3.14 To maintain bearing block alignment during installation of the housing onto the spider assembly, insert a small piece of sheet metal or heavy cardboard (cut to fit) between the boot and the bearing blocks (1993 through 1996 models)

3.15   The collapsed dimension of all inner CV joints must be adjusted before the large boot clamp is tightened

1   Boot
2   Clamp
3   Axleshaft
4   Adjust the collapsed length of the joint, from the small end of the boot to the groove in the outer race, to 5-1/16 inches on 1985 through 1992 models or 4.9 inches on 1993 and later models

3.16a   After the driveaxle has been removed from the joint assembly, remove the ball retaining ring and slide the inner race and cage out of the outer race

3.16b   The inner race must be assembled as shown, as the cage is not symmetrical – when installing the inner race and cage in the outer race, the large diameter side of the cage goes in first

Double offset design

Refer to illustrations 3.16a and 3.16b

16   Refer to the procedure outlined in Steps 17 through 35, but note that the cage and inner race assembly is retained in the outer race by a ball retaining ring, which is removed after the driveaxle is withdrawn from the CV joint **(see illustration)**. Also, the inner race and cage must be marked in relation to each other, as the cage is not symmetrical **(see illustration)**. Refer to Step 13 when adjusting the CV joint collapsed dimension.

Outer CV joint

Refer to illustrations 3.17, 3.19, 3.22, 3.23, 3.24, 3.25, 3.26a, 3.26b, 3.29, 3.30 and 3.34

17   Tap lightly around the outer circumference of the seal retainer with a hammer and punch to dislodge and remove it. Be very careful not to deform the retainer, or it won't seal properly **(see illustration)**.
18   Cut off the band retaining the boot to the shaft.
19   Remove the snap-ring and slide the joint assembly off **(see illustration)**.
20   Slide the old boot off the driveaxle.
21   Place marks on the inner race and cage so they both can be installed facing out when reassembling the joint.
22   Press down on the inner race far enough to allow a ball bearing to be removed. If it's difficult to tilt, tap the inner race with a brass punch and hammer **(see illustration)**.

3.17   Carefully tap around the circumference of the retaining ring to remove it from the housing

23   Pry the balls out of the cage, one at a time, with a blunt screwdriver or wooden tool **(see illustration)**.
24   With all of the balls removed from the cage and the cage/inner race assembly tilted 90-degrees, align the cage windows with the outer race

3.19   Use snap-ring pliers to remove the inner retaining ring

3.22   Gently tap the inner race with a brass punch to tilt it enough to allow ball bearing removal

3.23   Using a dull screwdriver, carefully pry the balls out of the cage

8

3.24   Tilt the inner race and cage 90-degrees, then align the windows in the cage (A) with the lands (B) and rotate the inner race up and out of the outer race

3.25   Align the inner race lands (A) with the cage windows (B) and rotate the inner race out of the cage

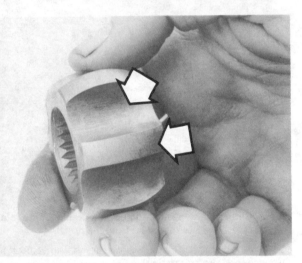

3.26a   Check the inner race lands and grooves for pitting and score marks

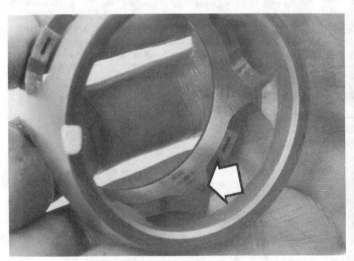

3.26b   Check the cage for cracks, pitting and score marks – shiny spots are normal and don't affect operation

3.29   Align the cage windows and the inner and outer race grooves, then tilt the cage and inner race to insert the balls

3.30   Apply grease through the splined hole, then insert a wooden dowel (approximately 15/16-inch diameter) through the splined hole and push down – the dowel will force the grease into the joint

3.34 Carefully tap around the circumference of the retaining ring to install it on the housing

lands and remove the assembly from the outer race **(see illustration)**.

25 Remove the inner race from the cage by turning the inner race 90-degrees in the cage, aligning the inner lands with the cage windows and rotating the inner race out of the cage **(see illustration)**.

26 Clean the components with solvent to remove all traces of grease. Inspect the cage and races for pitting, score marks, cracks and other signs of wear and damage. Shiny, polished spots are normal and won't adversely affect CV joint operation **(see illustrations)**.

27 Install the inner race in the cage by reversing the technique described in Step 22.

28 Install the inner race and cage assembly in the outer race by reversing the procedure in Step 21. The marks that were previously applied to the inner race and cage must both be visible after the assembly is installed in the outer race.

29 Press the balls into the cage windows **(see illustration)**.

30 Pack the CV joint assembly with lubricant through the inner splined hole. Force the grease into the bearing by inserting a wooden dowel through the splined hole and pushing it to the bottom of the joint. Repeat this procedure until the bearing is completely packed **(see illustration)**.

31 Install the boot on the driveaxle as described in Step 10. Apply a liberal amount of grease to the inside of the axle boot.

32 Position the CV joint assembly on the driveaxle, aligning the splines. Using a soft-face hammer, drive the CV joint onto the driveaxle until the retaining ring is seated in the groove.

33 Seat the inner end of the boot in the seal groove and install the retaining clamp.

34 Install the seal retainer securely by tapping evenly around the outer circumference with a hammer and punch **(see illustration)**.

35 Install the driveaxle as described in Section 2.

8

Chapter 9   Brakes

Contents

Specifications

General

Brake fluid type .... See Chapter 1

Disc brakes

Brake pad lining minimum thickness .... See Chapter 1
Disc thickness*
  1985 through 1991
    Standard .... 1.043 in
    Minimum thickness after resurfacing .... 0.972 in
    Discard thickness* .... 0.957 in
  1992 on
    Standard .... 1.276 in
    Minimum thickness after resurfacing .... 1.224 in
    Discard thickness* .... 1.209 in
Disc runout
  1985 through 1993 .... 0.004 in
  1994 and later .... 0.002 in
Disc thickness variation limit .... 0.0005 in
Caliper-to-bracket stop clearance .... 0.005 to 0.012 in
*Refer to marks cast into the disc (they supersede information printed here)

Drum brakes

Brake shoe lining minimum thickness .... See Chapter 1
Drum diameter
  Standard .... 8.860 in
  Service limit
    1985 through 1993 .... 8.880 in
    1994 and later .... 8.920 in
  Discard diameter* .... 8.909 in
Drum out-of-round limit .... 0.006 in
*Refer to marks cast into the disc (they supersede information printed here)

Torque Specifications

	Ft-lbs
Caliper mounting bolts	38
Brake hose-to-caliper bolt	33
Master cylinder-to-booster nuts	22
Proportioner valve caps	20
Booster-to-pedal bracket nuts	15
Wheel lug nuts	See Chapter 1

1 General information

Note: *On models equipped with the Delco Loc II audio system, be sure the lockout feature is turned off before performing any procedure which requires disconnecting the battery.*

All vehicles covered by this manual are equipped with hydraulically operated front and rear brake systems. The front brakes are disc type, and the rear brakes are drum type. Two types of rear brakes are used – anchor plate (duo servo) and leading/trailing.

All brakes are self-adjusting. The front disc brakes automatically compensate for pad wear, while the rear drum brakes incorporate an adjustment mechanism which is activated as the brakes are applied when the vehicle is driven in reverse.

The hydraulic system consists of separate front and rear circuits. The master cylinder has separate reservoirs for the two circuits; in the event of a leak or failure in one hydraulic circuit, the other circuit will remain operative. A visual warning of circuit failure, air in the system, or other pressure differential conditions in the brake system is given by a warning light activated by a failure warning switch in the master cylinder.

The parking brake mechanically operates the rear brakes only. It's activated by a pull-handle in the center console between the front seats.

The power brake booster, located in the engine compartment on the firewall, uses engine manifold vacuum and atmospheric pressure to provide assistance to the hydraulically operated brakes.

After completing any operation involving the disassembly of any part of the brake system, always test drive the vehicle to check for proper braking performance before resuming normal driving. Test the brakes while driving on a clean, dry, flat surface. Conditions other than these can lead to inaccurate test results. Test the brakes at various speeds with both light and heavy pedal pressure. The vehicle should stop evenly without pulling to one side or the other. Avoid locking the brakes because this slides the tires and diminishes braking efficiency and control.

Tires, vehicle load and front end alignment are factors which also affect braking performance.

2 Disc brake pads – replacement

Refer to illustrations 2.5 and 2.6a through 2.6k

Warning: *Disc brake pads must be replaced on both front wheels at the same time – never replace the pads on only one wheel. Also, the dust created by the brake system contains asbestos, which is harmful to your health. Never blow it out with compressed air and don't inhale any of it. An approved filtering mask should be worn when working on the brakes. Do not, under any circumstances, use petroleum-based solvents to clean brake parts. Use brake system cleaner or denatured alcohol only.*

Note: *When servicing the disc brakes, use only high-quality, nationally-recognized, brand name parts.*

1   Remove the cover from the brake fluid reservoir, siphon off about two-thirds of the fluid into a container and discard it.
2   Loosen the wheel lug nuts, raise the front of the vehicle and support it securely on jackstands. Apply the parking brake and block the rear wheels to keep the vehicle from rolling off the jackstands.

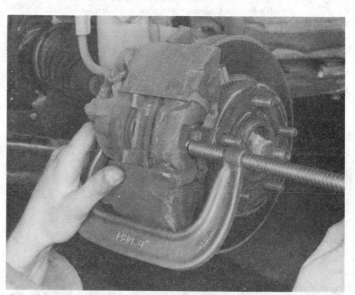

2.5   A large C-clamp can be used to compress the piston into the caliper for removal

2.6a   On most models, a Torx bit must be used to remove the two caliper mounting bolts (arrows)

2.6b   Remove the inner pad by snapping it out of the piston in the direction shown (arrow)

2.6c   To remove the outer pad, pry off the retaining clip on the back of the pad with a screwdriver

9

2.6d   Inspect the caliper bolts and bushings (A) for damage and the contact surfaces (B) for corrosion

3   Remove the front wheel, then reinstall two lug nuts (flat side toward the rotor) to hold the rotor in place. Work on one brake assembly at a time, using the assembled brake for reference if necessary.

4   Inspect the rotor carefully as outlined in Section 4. If machining is necessary, follow the information in that Section to remove the rotor, at which time the pads can be removed from the calipers as well.

5   Push the piston back into the bore. If necessary, a C-clamp can be used, but a pry bar will usually do the job **(see illustration)**. As the piston is depressed to the bottom of the caliper bore, the fluid in the master cylinder will rise. Make sure it doesn't overflow. If necessary, siphon off more of the fluid as directed in Step 1.

6   Follow the accompanying illustrations, beginning with 2.6a, for the actual pad replacement procedure. Be sure to stay in order and read the caption under each photograph.

7   When reinstalling the caliper, be sure to tighten the mounting bolts to the torque listed in this Chapter's Specifications. After the job has been completed, firmly depress the brake pedal a few times to bring the pads into contact with the rotor.

2.6e   Carefully peel back the edge of the piston boot and check for corrosion and leaking fluid

2.6f   Snap the inner pad retainer spring into the new pad in the direction shown (arrow)

2.6g   Lubricate the lower steering knuckle contact surface with a small amount of white lithium-base grease

2.6h   Apply a light coat of white lithium-base grease to the upper steering knuckle-to-caliper contact surface

3   Disc brake caliper – removal, overhaul and installation

Refer to illustrations 3.9, 3.10, 3.11, 3.12, 3.15, 3.16, 3.17, 3.18, 3.20 and 3.23

Warning: *Dust created by the brake system contains asbestos, which is harmful to your health. Never blow it out with compressed air and don't inhale any of it. An approved filtering mask should be worn when working on the brakes. Do not, under any circumstances, use petroleum-based solvents to clean brake parts. Use brake system cleaner or denatured alcohol only.*

Note: *If an overhaul is indicated (usually because of fluid leakage) explore all options before beginning the job. New and factory rebuilt calipers are available on an exchange basis, which makes this job quite easy. If you decide to rebuild the calipers, make sure rebuild kits are available before proceeding.*

Removal

1   Remove the cover from the brake fluid reservoir, siphon off two-thirds of the fluid into a container and discard it.
2   Loosen the wheel lug nuts, raise the front of the vehicle and support it securely on jackstands. Apply the parking brake and block the rear wheels to keep the vehicle from rolling off the jackstands. Remove the front wheels.
3   Reinstall two lug nuts on each rotor, flat side against the rotor, to hold them in place.
4   Bottom the piston in the caliper bore. This is accomplished by pushing on the caliper, although it may be necessary to carefully use a flat pry bar or a large C-clamp.
5   Remove the brake hose inlet fitting bolt and disconnect the fitting. Have a rag handy to catch spilled fluid and wrap a plastic bag tightly around the end of the hose to prevent fluid loss and contamination.

6   Using a no. 50 Torx bit, remove the two mounting bolts and detach the caliper from the vehicle (refer to Section 2 if necessary).

Overhaul

7   Refer to Section 2 and remove the brake pads from the caliper.

8   Clean the exterior of the caliper with brake cleaner or denatured alcohol. **Warning:** *DO NOT use gasoline, kerosene or petroleum-based cleaning solvents.* Place the caliper on a clean workbench.
9   Position a wood block or several shop rags in the caliper as a cushion, then use compressed air to remove the piston from the bore (**see illustration**). Use only enough air pressure to ease the piston out. If it's blown out, even with the cushion in place, it may be damaged. **Warning:** *Never place your fingers in front of the piston in an attempt to catch or protect it when applying compressed air – serious injury could result.*
10   Carefully pry the dust boot out of the caliper bore (**see illustration**).
11   Using a wood or plastic tool, remove the piston seal from the groove in the caliper bore (**see illustration**). Metal tools may damage the bore.

3.9   With the caliper padded to catch the piston, use compressed air to force the piston out of the bore – DO NOT position your hands or fingers between the piston and caliper!

3.10   Carefully pry the dust boot out of the housing, taking care not to scratch the bore surface

3.11   To avoid damage to the caliper bore or seal groove, remove the seal with a plastic or wooden tool (a pencil will do the job)

9

3.12   Exploded view of the disc brake caliper components

1	Mounting bolt boots	6	Inner brake pad
2	Mounting bolt and	7	Boot
	sleeve assemblies	8	Piston
3	Bushings	9	Piston seal
4	Outer brake pad	10	Bleeder valve
5	Wear indicator	11	Caliper housing

3.15   Position the seal in the caliper bore – make sure it isn't twisted

12   Remove the caliper bleeder valve, then remove and discard the sleeves and bushings from the caliper ears. Discard all rubber parts **(see illustration)**.

13   Clean the remaining parts with brake cleaner or denatured alcohol, then blow them dry with compressed air.

14   Carefully examine the piston for scratches, nicks, burrs and loss of plating. If surface defects are noted, a new piston will be needed. Check the caliper bore in a similar way. Light polishing with crocus cloth is permissible to remove light corrosion and stains. Discard the mounting bolts if they're corroded or damaged.

15   When reassembling the caliper, lubricate the piston bore and seal with clean brake fluid. Position the seal in the caliper bore groove **(see illustration)**.

16   Lubricate the piston with clean brake fluid, then install a new boot in the piston groove with the fold toward the open end of the piston **(see illustration)**.

17   Insert the piston squarely into the caliper bore, then apply force to bottom the piston in the bore **(see illustration)**.

18   Position the dust boot in the caliper counterbore, then use a punch to drive it into position **(see illustration)**. Make sure the boot is evenly installed below the caliper face.

19   Install the bleeder valve.

20   Install new bushings in the mounting bolt holes and fill the area between the bushings with silicone grease (supplied with the rebuild kit) **(see illustration)**. Push the sleeves into the mounting bolt holes.

Installation

21   Inspect the mounting bolts for corrosion. Use new ones if the originals are pitted.

22   Place the caliper in position over the rotor and mounting bracket, install the bolts and tighten them to the torque figure listed in this Chapter's Specifications.

23   Check to make sure the clearance between the caliper and the bracket stops is between 0.005 and 0.012-inch **(see illustration)**.

24   Install the brake hose-to-caliper bolt, using new copper washers, then tighten the bolt to the torque listed in this Chapter's Specifications. Bleed the brakes (Section 9).

3.16   Install the new dust boot in the piston groove with the folds toward the open end of the piston

3.17   Push the piston squarely into the caliper bore

3.18   Use a seal driver to seat the boot in the caliper housing counterbore – if a seal driver isn't available, carefully tap around the outer edge of the boot with a punch until it's seated

3.20   Pack the area between the mounting bolt sleeve bushings with silicone grease

1	Mounting bolt	3	Bushing
2	Sleeve	4	Caliper housing

3.23   Measure the clearance between the caliper and bracket stops at the points indicated

25   Install the wheels and lower the vehicle.

26   After the job has been completed, firmly depress the brake pedal a few times to bring the pads into contact with the rotor.

4   Brake rotor (disc) – inspection, removal and installation

Refer to illustrations 4.2, 4.3, 4.4a, 4.4b, 4.5a and 4.5b

Inspection

1   Loosen the wheel lug nuts, raise the front of the vehicle and support it securely on jackstands. Apply the parking brake and block the rear wheels to keep the vehicle from rolling off the jackstands. Remove the wheel and install two lug nuts to hold the rotor in place.

2   Remove the brake caliper as outlined in Section 3. You don't have to disconnect the brake hose. After removing the caliper bolts, suspend the caliper out of the way with a piece of wire – DO NOT let it hang by the hose **(see illustration)**.

3   Visually inspect the rotor surface for score marks and other damage. Light scratches and shallow grooves are normal and may not be detrimental to brake operation, but deep score marks – over 0.015-inch (0.38 mm) deep – require rotor removal and refinishing by an automotive machine

4.2   Suspend the caliper with a piece of wire whenever it's necessary to reposition it – DO NOT let it hang by the brake hose!

9

4.3   The brake pads on this vehicle were obviously neglected as they wore down completely and cut deep grooves into the rotor – wear this severe will require replacement of the rotor

4.4a   Check for runout with a dial indicator – mount it with the indicator needle about 1/2-inch from the outer edge

4.4b   If you don't have the rotors machined, at the very least be sure to break the glaze on the rotor surface with emery cloth

4.5a   The minimum wear (or discard) thickness (arrow) is cast into the inside of the rotor

4.5b   Measure the thickness of the rotor at several points with a micrometer

shop. Be sure to check both sides of the rotor **(see illustration)**. If pulsating has been felt during application of the brakes, suspect excessive rotor runout.

4   To check rotor runout, mount a dial indicator with the stem resting at a point about 1/2-inch from the outer edge of the rotor **(see illustration)**. Set the indicator to zero and turn the rotor. The indicator reading should not exceed the specified allowable runout limit. If it does, the rotor should be refinished by an automotive machine shop. **Note:** *The rotors should be resurfaced, regardless of the dial indicator reading, to impart a smooth finish and ensure perfectly flat brake pad surfaces (which will eliminate pedal pulsations. At the very least, if you don't have the rotors resurfaced, remove the glaze with medium-grit emery cloth using a swirling motion* **(see illustration)**.

5   Never machine the rotor to a thickness less than the specified minimum allowable refinish thickness. The minimum wear (or discard) thickness is cast into the inside of the rotor **(see illustration)**. This shouldn't be confused with the minimum refinish thickness. The rotor thickness can be checked with a micrometer **(see illustration)**.

Removal

6   Remove the two lug nuts that were put on to hold the rotor in place and remove the rotor from the hub.

Installation

7   Place the rotor in position over the threaded studs.

8   Install the caliper and brake pad assembly over the rotor and position it on the steering knuckle (refer to Section 3 for the caliper installation procedure, if necessary). Tighten the caliper bolts to the torque listed in this Chapter's Specifications.

9   Install the wheel, then lower the vehicle to the ground. Depress the brake pedal a few times to bring the brake pads into contact with the rotor. Bleeding of the system won't be necessary unless the brake hose was disconnected from the caliper. Check the operation of the brakes carefully before driving the vehicle in traffic.

---

5   Rear brake shoes – inspection and replacement

Warning: *Drum brake shoes must be replaced on both rear wheels at the same time – never replace the shoes on only one wheel. Also, the dust created by the brake system contains asbestos, which is harmful to your health. Never blow it out with compressed air and don't inhale any of it. An approved filtering mask should be worn when working on the brakes. Do not, under any circumstances, use petroleum-based solvents to clean brake parts. Use brake cleaner or denatured alcohol only!*

Caution: *Whenever the brake shoes are replaced, the return and hold-down springs should also be replaced. Due to the continuous heating/cooling cycle the springs are subjected to, they lose tension over a period of time and may allow the shoes to drag on the drum and wear at a much*

5.4a If the brake drum won't come off, it may be necessary to remove the plug with a hammer and chisel, then turn the adjuster screw to move the brake shoes away from the drum

5.4b Before removing anything, clean the brake assembly with brake system cleaner or denatured alcohol – DO NOT use compressed air to blow the dust out of the brake assembly!

5.4c Anchor plate (duo-servo) type drum brake components – exploded view

1	Return spring	15	Pivot nut
2	Return spring	16	Adjusting screw
3	Hold-down spring	17	Retaining ring
4	Lever pivot	18	Pin
5	Hold-down pin	19	Parking brake lever
6	Actuator link	20	Bleeder valve
7	Actuator lever	21	Cylinder retainer
8	Lever return spring	22	Boot
9	Parking brake strut	23	Piston
10	Strut spring	24	Seal
11	Primary shoe	25	Spring assembly
12	Secondary shoe	26	Wheel cylinder
13	Adjusting screw spring	27	Backing plate
14	Socket		

faster rate than normal. When replacing the rear brake shoes, use only high-quality, nationally-recognized brand name parts.

1   Loosen the wheel lug nuts, raise the rear of the vehicle and support it securely on jackstands. Block the front wheels to keep the vehicle from rolling off the jackstands.

2   Release the parking brake.

3   Remove the wheel. **Note:** *All four rear shoes must be replaced at the same time, but to avoid mixing up parts, work on only one brake assembly at a time.*

Anchor plate (duo-servo) type

Refer to illustrations 5.4a through 5.4z

4   Remove the brake drum. Refer to the accompanying photographs and perform the brake shoe inspection and, if necessary, the replacement procedure. Start with illustration 5.4a and be sure to read each caption. **Note:** *If the brake drum is stuck, make sure the parking brake is completely released, then apply some penetrating oil to the hub-to-brake drum joint. Allow the oil to soak in, then try to pull the drum off. If the drum still won't come off, the brake shoes will have to be retracted. This is done by remov-*

9

5.4d   Remove the return springs with a brake spring tool

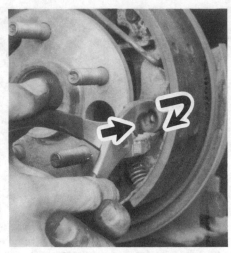

5.4e   Remove the hold-down springs and pins by pushing in with pliers and turning them (arrows)

5.4f   Lift up on the actuator lever and remove the actuating link from the anchor pin pivot along with the actuator lever and return spring (arrows)

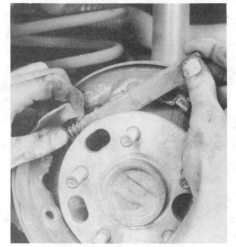

5.4g   Spread the shoes apart at the top and remove the parking brake strut

5.4h   With the shoe assembly spread to clear the hub flange, lift it away from the backing plate

5.4i   Disconnect the parking brake lever from the cable and remove the shoe assembly

5.4j   Remove the adjusting screw (A) and spring (B) from the shoe assembly – be sure to note how they're positioned

5.4k   Remove the parking brake lever by prying off the C-clip

5.4l   Install the parking brake lever on the new brake shoe and press the C-clip into place with needle-nose pliers

5.4m Lubricate the contact surfaces of the backing plate with high-temperature brake grease

5.4n Lubricate the adjuster screw with white lithium-base grease prior to installation

5.4o Connect the parking brake lever to the cable

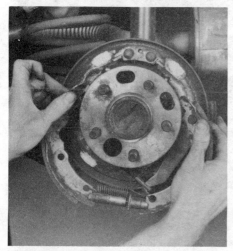

5.4p Spread the brake assembly apart sufficiently to clear the hub flange and raise it into position

5.4q Install the parking brake strut and spring

5.4r Make sure the parking brake strut is positioned in the shoes properly (arrows)

5.4s Install the primary brake shoe hold-down pin and spring

5.4t Attach the actuator link and lever to the secondary brake shoe

5.4u Install the actuator lever return spring

9

5.4v   Install the secondary brake shoe hold-down pin and spring

5.4w   Install the return springs

5.4x   Center the brake shoe assembly so the drum will
slide over it

5.4y   Turn the adjusting screw so the drum fits snugly over
the shoes

5.4z   Remove the glaze from the drum with emery cloth – use a
swirling motion

*ing the plug from the brake drum with a hammer and chisel (see illustra-
tion 5.4a). With the plug removed, pull the lever off the adjusting star
wheel with one small screwdriver while turning the star wheel with another*

*small screwdriver, moving the shoes away from the drum. The drum
should now come off.*

Leading/trailing type

Refer to illustrations 5.5a, 5.5b and 5.6a through 5.6af

5   Remove the brake drum. Refer to the accompanying photographs
and perform the brake shoe inspection and, if necessary, the replacement
procedure. If you're working on an early model equipped with coil return
springs, follow illustrations 5.5a, 5.5b and 5.6a through 5.6z **(see illustrations)**. If you're working on a later model equipped with the single horse-
shoe shaped return spring, begin with illustration 5.6aa **(see
illustrations)**. Be sure to stay in order and read the caption under each
illustration. If it's difficult to remove, back off the parking brake cable, remove the access hole plug from the backing plate **(see illustration)**, insert a screwdriver through the hole and press in to push the parking brake
lever off its stop **(see illustration)**. This will allow the brake shoes to retract slightly. Insert a punch through the hole at the bottom of the splash
shield and tap gently on the punch to loosen the drum. Use a rubber mallet
to tap gently on the outer rim of the drum and/or around the inner drum
diameter by the spindle. Avoid using excessive force.

6   Clean the brake assembly with brake system cleaner or denatured
alcohol – DO NOT use compressed air to blow the dust out of the brake
assembly. Refer to the accompanying photographs for the actual shoe replacement procedure. Start with illustration 5.6a and be sure to read each
caption.

5.5a Leading/trailing type rear drum brake components – exploded view

1	Actuator spring	15	Retaining ring
2	Upper return spring	16	Pin
3	Spring connecting link	17	Spring washer
4	Adjuster actuator	18	Parking brake lever
5	Spring washer	19	Screw and lock washer
6	Lower return spring	20	Boot
7	Hold-down spring assembly	21	Piston
8	Hold-down pin	22	Seal
9	Adjuster brake shoe	23	Spring assembly
10	Brake shoe	24	Bleeder valve
11	Adjuster socket	25	Wheel cylinder
12	Spring clip	26	Bleeder valve cap
13	Adjuster nut	27	Backing plate assembly
14	Adjuster screw	28	Access hole plug
		29	Adjuster pin

5.5b If you have trouble removing the drum, remove the access hole plug (arrow), insert a screwdriver through the hole and press in to push the parking brake lever off its stop – this will allow the brake shoes to retract slightly

9

5.6a   Unhook the upper return spring with a pair of pliers . . .

5.6b   . . . and remove it (to ensure proper reassembly, be sure to note the relationship of the spring to the front shoe and the parking brake lever)

5.6c   To remove the front shoe hold-down spring, grasp the spring retainer firmly with a pair of pliers and twist it until the slot in the retainer is aligned with the flat on the end of the hold-down pin, then pull the retainer and spring off (don't lose the hold-down pin, which is installed through the back side of the backing plate)

5.6d   To remove the front shoe, pull it down . . .

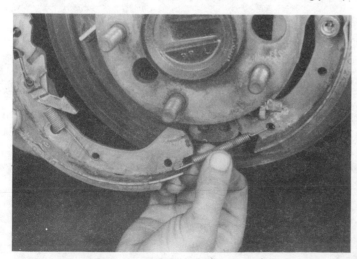

5.6e   . . . and detach the lower spring

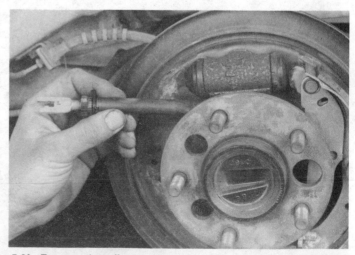

5.6f   Remove the adjuster assembly (be sure to note the relationship between the adjuster socket and the parking brake lever)

5.6g Remove the rear shoe hold-down spring the same way you removed the front one, then pull down the rear shoe and parking brake lever assembly

5.6h To separate the rear shoe from the parking brake lever, remove the C-clip and spring washer, then press out the lever pin – unless you're replacing the parking brake cable, it's not necessary to disconnect the cable and lever

5.6i Place the front shoe assembly on a workbench and note the relationship of the actuator spring, the spring connecting link and the adjuster actuator . . .

5.6j . . . then remove the actuator spring, . . .

5.6k . . . the spring connecting link . . .

5.6l . . . and the adjuster actuator - transfer these parts to the new front shoe (see illustration 5.62)

9

5.6m   Lubricate the raised contact surfaces of the backing plate with white lithium base grease

5.6n   Install the parking brake lever on the new rear brake shoe, push the lever pin into place, install the spring washer and pop the C-clip into place with a pair of pliers (make sure the concave side of the spring washer faces toward the parking brake lever)

5.6o   Clean the adjuster screw with brake cleaner or denatured alcohol, check the threads for smooth rotation over their full length, then lubricate the adjuster threads, the inside surface of the socket and the socket face with white lithium base grease

5.6p   Reattach the parking brake cable, if you disconnected it, place the rear brake shoe in position . . .

5.6q   . . . and install the hold-down spring: install the spring and retainer over the hold-down pin, compress the spring, twist the retainer until its slot is at a right angle to the flat tip of the hold-down pin and release tension on the spring

5.6r   Attach the lower return spring to the brake shoes as shown – make sure the spring runs behind the anchor plate, not in front of it (see illustration 5.5a)

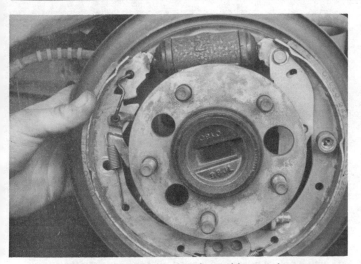

5.6s   Place the front brake shoe in position as shown . . .

5.6t   . . . and install the hold-down spring

LUBRICATE WITH THIN
COATING OF 5450032
LUBRICANT (OR EQUIVALENT)

5.6u   Details of the adjusting
       screw assembly

1   Adjuster brake shoe
2   Brake shoe
3   Adjuster socket
4   Spring clip
5   Adjuster nut
6   Adjuster screw
7   Parking brake lever
8   Adjusting screw assembly

Note: *Refer to this illustration to
ensure proper lubrication of
the adjusting screw assembly*

5.6v   Install the adjuster assembly – make sure the parking brake
lever is seated properly against the adjuster socket (see
illustration 5.5a) . . .

5.6w   . . . and the adjuster actuator is properly seated against the
adjuster screw (see view CC of illustration 5.6z)

9

5.6x Install the upper return spring – be sure the rear end of the spring (the angled hook end) is installed through the parking brake lever and the rear shoe (see view AA of illustration 5.6z) . . .

5.6y . . . then grasp the forward end (the long straight section) with a pair of pliers and hook it over the crook in the spring connecting link (see illustration 5.6z)

5.6z Details of the leading/trailing rear brake assembly (with special views)

1   Actuator spring
2   Upper return spring
3   Spring connecting link
4   Adjuster actuator
5   Adjuster shoe
6   Shoe
7   Spring clip
8   Adjuster nut
9   Adjuster screw
10 Parking brake lever
11 Backing plate
12 Lever stop

VIEW BB

VIEW AA

VIEW CC

Note: *The adjuster shoe faces the front of the vehicle on the left brake assembly (shown here) and the rear of the vehicle on the right brake assembly*

5.6aa   Drum brake components – single return spring

1	Actuator spring	5	Adjusting screw
2	Trailing shoe	6	Actuator lever
3	Return spring	7	Wheel cylinder
4	Leading shoe	8	Backing plate

5.6ab   Use a pair of needle-nose pliers to remove the actuator spring

5.6ac   Wedge a flat-bladed screwdriver under the return spring and pry it out of the leading brake shoe, then remove the shoe, adjusting screw and actuator lever

5.6ad   Lift the retractor spring from the trailing brake shoe and swing the shoe out of the hub area to gain access to the parking brake cable

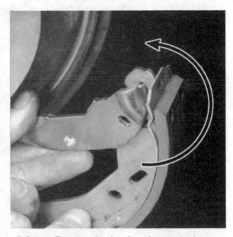

5.6ae   Rotate the brake shoe to release the parking brake lever from the shoe

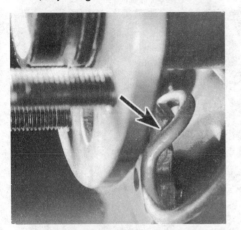

5.6af   Use a screwdriver to pry the return spring over the alignment peg (arrow)

5.6ag   Lubricate the contact surfaces of the backing plate with high-temperature grease

5.6ah   Lubricate the adjuster screw with high-temperature grease prior to installation – to install new shoes on these models, reverse the removal steps, then center the brake shoe assembly so the drum will slide over it and adjust the star wheel so the shoes will barely drag on the drum

5.7   The drum has a maximum permissible diameter cast into it (arrow) which is a wear dimension, not a refinish dimension

Both types

Refer to illustration 5.7

7   Before reinstalling the drum, check it for cracks, score marks, deep scratches and hard spots, which will appear as blue discolored areas. If the hard spots can't be removed with fine emery cloth or if any of the other conditions listed above exist, the drum must be taken to an automotive machine shop to have it turned. **Note:** *The drums should be resurfaced, regardless of the surface appearance, to impart a smooth finish and ensure a perfectly round drum (which will eliminate brake pedal pulsations related to out-of-round drums).* At the very least, if you don't have the drums resurfaced, remove the glaze from the surface with medium-grit emery cloth using a swirling motion. If the drum won't "clean up" before the maximum service limit is reached in the machining operation, install a new one. The maximum wear diameter is cast into each brake drum **(see illustration)**. This shouldn't be confused with the service limit (the dimension that requires the drum to be thrown away).

8   Install the brake drum on the axle flange.

9   Mount the wheel, install the lug nuts, then lower the vehicle.

10   If the vehicle is equipped with anchor plate type brakes, make a number of forward and reverse stops to adjust the brakes until satisfactory pedal feel is obtained. If it's equipped with leading/trailing type brakes, apply and release the brake pedal 30 to 35 times using normal pedal force. Pause about one second between pedal applications. After adjustment, make sure that both wheels turn freely.

9

6.4   A flare nut wrench should be used to disconnect the brake line (arrow)

6.5   To remove the wheel cylinder, remove these two bolts (arrows) (strut removed for clarity)

6.7   Wheel cylinder components – exploded view

1 Bleeder valve	4 Seal
2 Boot	5 Spring assembly
3 Piston	6 Wheel cylinder body

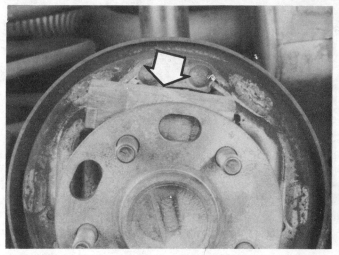

6.13   A wood block (arrow) should be used to hold the wheel cylinder in position

---

6   Rear wheel cylinder – removal, overhaul and installation

Refer to illustrations 6.4, 6.5, 6.7 and 6.13

Note: *If an overhaul is indicated (usually because of fluid leakage or sticking brakes) explore all options before beginning the job. New wheel cylinders are available, which makes this job quite easy. If you do rebuild the wheel cylinder, make sure rebuild kits are available before proceeding.*

Removal

1   Raise the rear of the vehicle and support it securely on jackstands. Block the front wheels to keep the vehicle from rolling off the jackstands.
2   Remove the brake shoe assembly (Section 5).
3   Carefully clean the area around the wheel cylinder on both sides of the backing plate.
4   Unscrew the brake line fitting **(see illustration)**, but don't pull the line away from the wheel cylinder.
5   Remove the wheel cylinder retaining bolts **(see illustration)**.
6   Remove the wheel cylinder from the brake backing plate and place it on a clean workbench. Immediately plug the brake line to prevent fluid loss and contamination.

Overhaul

7   Remove the bleeder valve, seals, pistons, boots and spring assembly from the wheel cylinder body **(see illustration)**.
8   Clean the wheel cylinder with brake fluid, denatured alcohol or brake system cleaner. **Warning:** *Do not, under any circumstances, use petroleum-based solvents to clean brake parts.*
9   Use compressed air to dry the wheel cylinder and blow out the passages.
10   Check the bore for corrosion and score marks. Crocus cloth may be used to remove light corrosion and stains, but the cylinder must be replaced with a new one if the defects can't be removed easily, or if the bore is scored.
11   Lubricate the new seals with brake fluid.
12   Assemble the brake cylinder components, making sure the boots are properly seated.

Installation

13   Place the wheel cylinder in position **(see illustration)**.
14   Connect the brake lines loosely.
15   Install the wheel cylinder bolts and tighten them securely.
16   Tighten the brake line fittings.
17   Install the brake shoes (see Section 5).
18   Bleed the brakes (see Section 9).

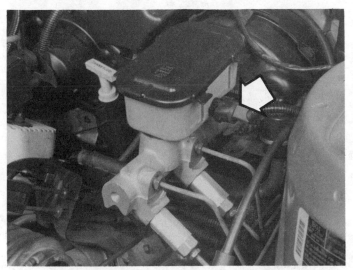

7.2 Unplug the fluid level sensor connector (arrow) and unscrew the brake line fittings (arrows)

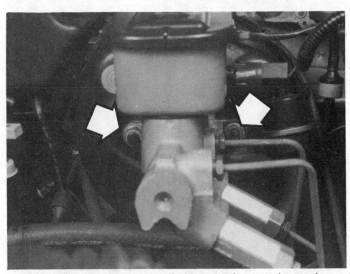

7.6 Remove the master cylinder mounting nuts (arrows)

---

7   Master cylinder – removal, overhaul and installation

Refer to illustrations 7.2, 7.6, 7.9, 7.11, 7.12, 7.16, 7.18, 7.19a, 7.19b, 7.19c, 7.19d, 7.19e, 7.19f and 7.20
Note: *Before deciding to overhaul the master cylinder, check on the availability and cost of a new or factory-rebuilt unit and the availability of a rebuild kit.*

Removal

1   Detach the cable from the negative battery terminal.
2   Unplug the fluid level sensor switch connector **(see illustration)**.
3   Place rags under the line fittings and prepare caps or plastic bags to cover the ends of the lines once they're disconnected. **Caution:** *Brake fluid will damage paint. Cover all painted parts and be careful not to spill fluid during this procedure.*
4   Loosen the fittings at the ends of the brake lines where they enter the master cylinder. To prevent rounding off the flats on the fittings, use a flare-nut wrench, which wraps around the hex.
5   Pull the brake lines away from the master cylinder and plug the ends to prevent contamination.
6   Remove the two mounting nuts **(see illustration)** and detach the master cylinder from the vehicle.
7   Remove the reservoir cover and reservoir diaphragm, then discard any remaining fluid in the reservoir.
8   Mount the master cylinder in a vise. Be sure to line the vise jaws with blocks of wood to prevent damage to the cylinder body.
9   Pull straight up on the reservoir assembly and separate it from the master cylinder body **(see illustration)**. Remove and discard the two O-rings.
10   Remove the proportioner valves and the O-rings. Set each proportioner valve assembly aside.
11   Remove the primary piston lock ring by depressing the piston and prying the ring out with a screwdriver **(see illustration)**.
12   Remove the primary piston assembly from the bore **(see illustration)**.
13   Remove the secondary piston assembly from the bore. It may be necessary to remove the master cylinder from the vise and invert it, carefully tapping it against a block of wood to expel the piston.

Overhaul

14   Clean the master cylinder body, the primary and secondary piston assemblies, the proportioner valve assemblies and the reservoir in dena-

tured alcohol and dry them off with unlubricated compressed air or a clean (lint-free) shop rag. **Warning:** *DO NOT, under any circumstances, use petroleum-based solvents to clean brake parts.*
15   Inspect the master cylinder piston bore for corrosion and score marks. If any corrosion or damage in the bore is evident, replace the master cylinder body – don't use abrasives to try to clean it up.
16   Remove the old seals from the secondary piston assembly and install the new seals with the cup lips facing out **(see illustration)**.
17   Attach the spring retainer to the secondary piston assembly.
18   Lubricate the cylinder bore with clean brake fluid and install the spring and secondary piston assembly **(see illustration)**.
19   Disassemble the primary piston assembly, noting the locations of the parts, then lubricate the new seals with clean brake fluid and install them on the piston **(see illustrations)**.
20   Install the primary piston assembly in the cylinder bore **(see illustration)**, depress it and install the lock ring.
21   Inspect the proportioner valves for corrosion and score marks. Replace them if necessary.
22   Lubricate the new O-rings and proportioner valve seals with the silicone grease supplied with the rebuild kit. Also lubricate the stem of the proportioner valve pistons.
23   Install the new seals on the proportioner valve pistons with the seal lips facing toward the cap assembly.
24   Install the proportioner valve pistons and seals in the master cylinder body.
25   Install the springs in the master cylinder body.
26   Install the new O-rings in their respective grooves in the proportioner valve cap assemblies.
27   Install the proportioner valve caps in the master cylinder and tighten them to the specified torque.
28   Inspect the reservoir for cracks and distortion. If any damage is evident, replace it.
29   Lubricate the new reservoir O-rings with clean brake fluid and press them into their respective grooves in the master cylinder body. Make sure they're properly seated.
30   Lubricate the reservoir fittings with clean brake fluid and install the reservoir on the master cylinder body by pressing it straight down.
31   Inspect the reservoir diaphragm and cover for cracks and deformation. Replace any damaged parts with new ones and attach the diaphragm to the cover. **Note:** *Whenever the master cylinder is removed, the complete hydraulic system must be bled. The time required to bleed the system can be reduced if the master cylinder is filled with fluid and bench bled (refer to Steps 32 through 35) before it's installed on the vehicle.*

9

7.9 Exploded view of the master cylinder components

1	Fluid level sensor	10	Lock ring
2	Proportioner valve	11	Primary piston assembly
3	O-ring	12	Secondary seal
4	Proportioner valve	13	Spring retainer
5	O-ring	14	Primary seal
6	Reservoir cover	15	Secondary piston
7	Diaphragm	16	Spring
8	Reservoir	17	Cylinder body
9	Grommet		

QUICK TAKE-UP
VALVE (NOT
SERVICEABLE)

7.11 Press down on the piston and remove the primary piston lock ring

7.12 Remove the primary piston assembly

7.16   The secondary piston seals must be installed with the lips facing out as shown

7.18   Install the secondary piston assembly

7.19a   The primary piston seal must be installed with the lip facing away from the piston

7.19b   Install the seal guard over the seal

7.19c   Place the primary piston spring in position

7.19d   Insert the spring retainer into the spring

9

7.19e Insert the spring retaining bolt through the retainer and spring and thread it into the piston

7.19f Install the O-ring on the piston

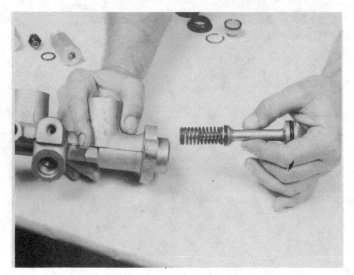

7.20   Insert the primary piston assembly into the body

8.2   Using a back-up wrench on the flexible hose side of the fitting (A), loosen the tube nut (B) with a flare nut wrench and remove the U-clip (C) from the hose fitting

32   Insert threaded plugs of the correct size into the brake line outlet holes and fill the reservoirs with brake fluid. The master cylinder should be supported so brake fluid won't spill during the bench bleeding procedure.

33   Loosen one plug at a time and push the piston assembly into the bore to force air from the master cylinder. To prevent air from being drawn back in, the appropriate plug must be replaced before allowing the piston to return to its original position.

34   Stroke the piston three or four times for each outlet to ensure that all air has been expelled.

35   Since high pressure isn't involved in the bench bleeding procedure, there is an alternative to the removal and replacement of the plugs with each stroke of the piston assembly. Before pushing in on the piston assembly, remove one of the plugs completely. Before releasing the piston, however, instead of replacing the plug, simply put your finger tightly over the hole to keep air from being drawn back into the master cylinder. Wait several seconds for the brake fluid to be drawn from the reservoir into the piston bore, then repeat the procedure. When you push down on the piston it'll force your finger off the hole, allowing the air inside to be expelled. When only brake fluid is being ejected from the hole, replace the plug and go on to the other port.

36   Refill the master cylinder reservoirs and install the diaphragm and cover assembly. **Note:** *The reservoirs should only be filled to the top of the reservoir divider to prevent overflowing when the cover is installed.*

Installation

37   Carefully install the master cylinder by reversing the removal steps, then bleed the brakes at each wheel (see Section 9).

---

8   Brake hoses and lines – inspection and replacement

Refer to illustrations 8.2 and 8.11

1   About every six months, raise the vehicle and support it securely on jackstands, then check the flexible hoses that connect the steel brake lines to the front and rear brake assemblies. Look for cracks, chafing of the outer cover, leaks, blisters and other damage. The hoses are important and vulnerable parts of the brake system and the inspection should be thorough. A light and mirror will be helpful to see into restricted areas. If a hose exhibits any of the above conditions, replace it with a new one.

Front brake hose

2   Using a back-up wrench, disconnect the brake line from the hose fitting, being careful not to bend the frame bracket or brake line (**see illustration**).

3   Use pliers to remove the U-clip from the female fitting at the bracket, then remove the hose from the bracket.

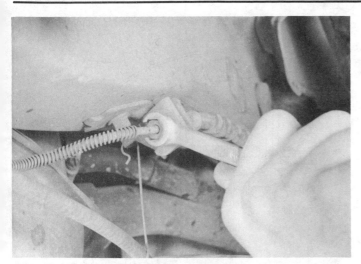

8.11 To loosen the rear brake hose/line fitting, simply loosen the nut and pull the clip off the bracket

9.8 When bleeding the brakes, a hose is connected to the bleeder valve at the caliper (or wheel cylinder) and then submerged in brake fluid – air will be seen as bubbles in the container or in the tube (all air must be expelled before continuing to the next wheel)

4   At the caliper end of the hose, remove the bolt from the fitting block, then remove the hose and the copper gaskets on either side of the fitting block.

5   When installing the hose, always use new copper gaskets on either side of the fitting block and lubricate all bolt threads with clean brake fluid before installation.

6   With the fitting flange engaged with the caliper locating ledge, attach the hose to the caliper.

7   Without twisting the hose, install the female fitting in the hose bracket. It'll fit the bracket in only one position.

8   Install the U-clip retaining the female fitting to the frame bracket.

9   Using a back-up wrench, attach the brake line to the hose fitting.

10   When the brake hose installation is complete, there shouldn't be any kinks in the hose. Make sure the hose doesn't contact any part of the suspension. Check it by turning the wheels to the extreme left and right positions. If the hose makes contact, remove the hose and correct the installation as necessary.

Rear brake hose

11   Using a back-up wrench, if necessary, disconnect the hose at both ends, being careful not to bend the bracket or steel lines (**see illustration**).

12   Remove the two U-clips with pliers and separate the female fittings from the brackets.

13   Unbolt the hose retaining clip and remove the hose.

14   Without twisting the hose, install the female ends in the frame brackets. It'll fit the bracket in only one position.

15   Install the U-clips retaining the female end to the bracket.

16   Using a back-up wrench, attach the steel line fittings to the female fittings. Again, be careful not to bend the bracket or steel line.

17   Make sure the hose installation didn't loosen the frame bracket. Tighten the bracket if necessary.

18   Fill the master cylinder reservoir and bleed the system (refer to Section 9).

Metal brake lines

19   When replacing brake lines, be sure to buy the correct replacement parts. Don't use copper or any other tubing for brake lines.

20   Prefabricated brake lines, with the ends already flared and fittings installed, are available at auto parts stores and dealer service departments. The lines are also bent to the proper shapes if necessary.

21   If prefabricated lines aren't available, obtain the recommended steel tubing and fittings to match the line to be replaced. Determine the correct length by measuring the old brake line (a piece of string can usually be used for this) and cut the new tubing to length, allowing about 1/2-inch extra for flaring the ends.

22   Install the fittings on the cut tubing and flare the ends of the line with an ISO flaring tool.

23   If necessary, carefully bend the line to the proper shape. A tube bender is recommended for this. **Caution:** *Don't crimp or damage the line.*

24   When installing the new line, make sure it's securely supported in the brackets with plenty of clearance between moving or hot components.

25   After installation, check the master cylinder fluid level and add fluid as necessary. Bleed the brake system as outlined in the next Section and test the brakes carefully before driving the vehicle in traffic.

9   Brake system bleeding

Refer to illustration 9.8

Warning: *Wear eye protection when bleeding the brake system. If you get fluid in your eyes, rinse them immediately with water and seek medical attention.*

Note: *Bleeding the brakes is necessary to remove air that manages to find its way into the system when its been opened during removal and installation of a hose, line, caliper or master cylinder.*

1   It'll probably be necessary to bleed the system at all four brakes if air has entered the system due to low fluid level, or if the brake lines have been disconnected at the master cylinder.

2   If a brake line was disconnected at only one wheel, then only that caliper or wheel cylinder must be bled.

3   If a brake line is disconnected at a fitting located between the master cylinder and any of the brakes, that part of the system served by the disconnected line must be bled.

4   Remove any residual vacuum from the power brake booster by applying the brake several times with the engine off.

5   Remove the master cylinder reservoir cover and fill the reservoir with brake fluid. Reinstall the cover. **Note:** *Check the fluid level often during the bleeding procedure and add fluid as necessary to prevent the level from falling low enough to allow air bubbles into the master cylinder.*

6   Have an assistant on hand, as well as a supply of new brake fluid, an empty, clear plastic container, a length of 3/16-inch plastic, rubber or vinyl tubing to fit over the bleeder valve and a wrench to open and close the bleeder valve.

7   Beginning at the right rear wheel, loosen the bleeder valve slightly, then tighten it to a point where it's snug but can still be loosened quickly and easily.

8   Place one end of the tubing over the bleeder valve and submerge the other end in brake fluid in the container (**see illustration**).

9

10.5 With a pair of locking pliers clamped to the end of the threaded rod to hold it still, turn the adjusting nut until the right rear wheel can just barely be turned backwards but not forward

9   Have your assistant pump the brakes slowly a few times to get pressure in the system, then hold the pedal down firmly.
10   While the pedal is held down, open the bleeder valve just enough to allow fluid to flow out of the valve. Watch for air bubbles to exit the submerged end of the tube. When the fluid slows after a couple of seconds, close the valve and have your assistant release the pedal.
11   Repeat Steps 9 and 10 until no more air is seen leaving the tube, then tighten the bleeder valve and proceed to the left rear wheel, the right front wheel and the left front wheel, in that order, and perform the same procedure. Be sure to check the fluid in the master cylinder reservoir frequently.
12   Never use old brake fluid. It contains moisture which will deteriorate the brake system components.
13   Refill the master cylinder with fluid at the end of the operation.
14   Check the operation of the brakes. The pedal should feel firm when depressed. If necessary, repeat the entire procedure. **Warning:** *Don't operate the vehicle if you're in doubt about the effectiveness of the brake system.*

---

10   Parking brake – adjustment

Vehicles with anchor plate (duo-servo) type rear brakes

Refer to illustration 10.5
1   Adjust the brakes (see Step 10 in Section 5).
2   Apply the parking brake lever exactly three ratchet clicks.
3   Raise the vehicle and support it securely on jackstands.
4   Before adjusting the parking brake, make sure the equalizer nut groove is lubricated with multi-purpose grease.
5   Tighten the adjusting nut **(see illustration)** until the right rear wheel can barely be turned backwards with two hands, but locks when turned forward.
6   Release the parking brake lever and check to make sure the rear wheels turn freely in both directions.
7   Lower the vehicle.

Vehicles with leading/trailing type rear brakes

Refer to illustration 10.14
8   Adjust the brakes (see Step 10 in Section 5).
9   Apply and release the parking brake six times to ten ratchet clicks.

10.14   Parking brake adjustment details (leading/trailing type rear brakes)

1	*Brake shoe*	*3 Drill bit*
2	*Parking brake lever*	

10   Check the parking brake pedal assembly for full release by turning the ignition to On and noting whether the Brake warning light is off. If it's on even though the brake appears to be released, operate the pedal release lever and pull down on the front parking brake cable to remove slack from the assembly. Check both rear wheels to make sure they still turn freely.
11   Apply the parking brake to four clicks.
12   Raise the vehicle and place it securely on jackstands.
13   Remove the access hole plug.
14   Adjust the parking brake cable until you can insert a 1/8-inch drill bit – but not a 1/4-inch bit – through the access hole into the space between the shoe web and the parking brake **(see illustration)**. **Note:** *The drill bit must be perpendicular (at a right angle) to the backing plate.*
15   Release the parking brake and verify that both wheels rotate freely.
16   Replace the access hole plug.
17   Lower the vehicle.

---

11   Parking brake cables – removal and installation

1   Detach the cable from the negative battery terminal.
2   If you're going to remove or replace a rear cable, loosen the wheel lug nuts.
3   Raise the vehicle and place it securely on jackstands.

Front cable

Refer to illustrations 11.4, 11.5, 11.6 and 11.7
4   Locate the equalizer assembly along the left side of the underbody **(see illustration)**.
5   Loosen the equalizer assembly **(see illustration)** and detach the front cable.
6   Remove the nut from the front cable **(see illustration)**.

Unknown

11.4   Details of the parking brake cable assembly

1	Right rear cable	4	Bolt	7	Intermediate cable
2	Underbody	5	Left rear cable	8	Equalizer assembly
3	Guide	6	Front cable	9	Nut

11.5   To disconnect the front or intermediate cable from the equalizer assembly, simply loosen the threaded adjuster until the cables are slack

11.6   Before the front cable will slide through the floor, you'll have to unscrew this nut from the underbody

9

11.7   Details of the parking brake cable lever assembly

1	Lever assembly	5	Front cable assembly
2	Nut	6	Dashboard
3	Bolt	7	Nut
4	Handle	8	Stud

11.10   To detach the intermediate cable from this mounting bracket, pinch the tabs on the cable housing with a pair of pliers

11.11a   To detach the intermediate cable from the underbody, detach this guide . . .

11.11b   . . . and detach this cable clip

7   Working inside the vehicle, detach the cable housing and cable from the parking brake lever assembly **(see illustration)**.

8   Installation is the reverse of removal.

Intermediate cable

Refer to illustrations 11.10, 11.11a, 11.11b, 11.12a and 11.12b

9   Disconnect the intermediate cable from the forward equalizer assembly **(see illustration 11.5)**.

10   Detach the intermediate cable housing from the bracket **(see illustration)**.

11   Detach the intermediate cable guide and clip from the underbody **(see illustrations)**.

12   Disconnect the intermediate and right rear cables **(see illustration)**, then disconnect the intermediate cable from the left rear cable **(see illustration)**.

13   Installation is the reverse of removal.

Left rear cable

Refer to illustrations 11.18 and 11.19

14   Back off the equalizer nut until cable tension is eliminated **(see illustration 11.5)**.

15   Remove the left rear wheel.

16   Remove the left brake drum (see Section 5).

17   Remove the left rear brake shoe and the parking brake lever as an assembly and detach the cable from the lever (see Section 5).

18   Detach the cable fitting from the backing plate **(see illustration)**.

19   Detach the cable bracket **(see illustration)**.

20   Disconnect the intermediate and right rear cables, then disconnect the left rear cable from the intermediate cable **(see illustrations 11.12a and 11.12b)**.

21   Installation is the reverse of removal.

11.12a   Disconnect the intermediate and right rear cables . . .

11.12b   . . . then disconnect the intermediate cable from the left rear cable

11.18   To detach the cable from the rear drum brake assembly, pinch the tabs on the housing with a pair of pliers and slide it through the hole in the brake backing plate

11.19   To remove the left rear cable from the underbody, detach this cable clip

Right rear cable

Refer to illustration 11.27

22   Back off the equalizer nut until cable tension is eliminated **(see illustration 11.5).**

23   Remove the right rear wheel.

24   Remove the right brake drum (see Section 5).

25   Remove the right front brake shoe and the parking brake lever as an assembly and detach the cable from the lever (see Section 5).

26   Detach the cable fitting from the backing plate **(see illustration 11.18).**

27   Detach the right rear cable housing from the underbody **(see illustration).**

28   Disconnect the intermediate and right rear cables, then disconnect the left rear cable from the intermediate cable **(see illustrations 11.12a and 11.12b).**

29   Installation is the reverse of removal.

All cables

30   Be sure to adjust the parking brake cable after installation (see Section 10).

11.27   To remove the right rear cable from the underbody, pinch the tabs on this housing (not visible in this photo, they're on the other side of the housing bracket) with a pair of pliers and slide the housing and cable out of the bracket

9

12.6   Remove the retaining clip and slide the power brake pushrod (A) off the brake pedal pin, then remove the booster-to-firewall nuts (B)

13.3   The brake light switch (arrow) is located to the right of the steering column at the end of the mounting bracket

12   Power brake booster – inspection, removal and installation

Refer to illustration 12.6

Note: *On 1994 and later models, the power brake booster cannot be disassembled for service. If defective, it must be replaced.*

1   The power brake booster unit requires no special maintenance apart from periodic inspection of the vacuum hose and the case. Early models have an in-line filter which should be inspected periodically and replaced if clogged or damaged.

2   Dismantling of the power unit requires special tools and is not ordinarily done by the home mechanic. If a problem develops, install a new or factory rebuilt unit.

3   Remove the nuts attaching the master cylinder to the booster (see Section 7) and carefully pull the master cylinder forward until it clears the mounting studs. Be careful to avoid bending or kinking the brake lines.

4   Disconnect the vacuum hose where it attaches to the power brake booster.

5   From the passenger compartment, disconnect the power brake pushrod from the top of the brake pedal.

6   Also from this location, remove the nuts attaching the booster to the firewall **(see illustration)**.

7   Carefully lift the booster unit away from the firewall and out of the engine compartment.

8   To install the booster, place it in position and tighten the mounting nuts. Reconnect the brake pedal.

9   Install the master cylinder and vacuum hose.

10   Carefully test the operation of the brakes before driving the vehicle in traffic.

13   Brake light switch – removal, installation and adjustment

Refer to illustration 13.3

Removal

1   The brake light switch is located on a bracket at the top of the brake pedal. The switch activates the brake lights at the rear of the vehicle when the pedal is depressed.

2   Remove the under dash cover and disconnect the wiring to the courtesy light in the panel.

3   Locate the switch at the top of the brake pedal **(see illustration)**. If the vehicle is equipped with cruise control, there will be another switch very similar in appearance. The brake light switch is the one towards the end of the bracket.

4   Disconnect the negative battery cable from the battery.

5   On 1985 through 1995 models, detach the wiring connectors at the brake switch. Depress the brake pedal and pull the switch out of the clip. The switch appears to be threaded, but it's designed to be pushed into and out of the clip, not turned.

6   On 1996 and later models, twist the switch clockwise to unlock and pull it out of the retainer. Detach the wiring connectors at the brake switch.

Installation and adjustment (1985 through 1995 models)

7   With the brake pedal depressed, push the new switch into the clip. Note that audible clicks will be heard as this is done.

8   Pull the brake pedal all the way to the rear, against the pedal stop until the clicking sounds can no longer be heard. This action will automatically move the switch the proper amount and no further adjustment will be required. **Caution:** *Don't apply excessive force during this adjustment procedure, as power booster damage may result.*

9   Connect the wiring at the switch and the battery. Make sure the brake lights are functioning properly.

Installation (1996 and later models)

Note: *When installing the brake light switch, ensure the brake pedal is fully up (at rest). The switch will be damaged, or misadjusted, if the brake pedal position is not as specified. Do not apply any side load to the switch during installation.*

Note: *This type of brake switch is self-adjusting and requires no adjustment after it is installed correctly in the fully locked position.*

10   Connect the wiring connectors to the brake switch.

11   Slide the switch into the retainer and press the switch in until the plunger is fully depressed into the switch barrel. Twist the switch counterclockwise approximately 60 degrees until it reaches its stop. When installed correctly, the electrical connector will be at the 3 o'clock position.

12   Connect the battery negative cable, then make sure the brake lights are functioning properly.

14   Anti-lock Brake System (ABS) and Traction Control System (TCS) – general information

This system is available as an option. It is designed to reduce lost traction during heavy braking or on slippery surfaces. The system is similar to the non-ABS system except for the Electronic Brake Control Module (EBCM) and related wiring, speed sensors and the hydraulic pump which replaces the master cylinder and power brake booster.

Anti-lock braking occurs only when a wheel is about to lock up (lose traction). Input signals from the wheel speed sensors to the computer are used to determine when a wheel is about to lose traction during braking. Hydraulic pressure will be reduced for the wheel about to lose traction.

Some models are also equipped with a Traction Control System (TCS). This system uses the ABS speed sensors to monitor the speed of the drive wheels. If the computer senses one of the drive wheels spinning significantly faster than the other, the computer, through the ABS system, will apply brake pressure to the more rapidly spinning wheel. This allow torque to be transferred to the wheel with the most traction.

Due to the special tools required and the extremely involved diagnostic procedures, all diagnosis and service to either of these systems must be performed by a dealer service department or other qualified repair shop.

Chapter 10
Suspension and steering systems

Contents

Specifications

Torque specifications

Ft-lbs (unless otherwise indicated)

Front suspension

Balljoint mounting nuts 50
Balljoint-to-steering knuckle nut .... 88 in-lbs (plus an additional 2/3-turn)
Brake line bracket bolt 13
Control arm
    Front mounting nut 140
    Rear mounting nut 90
Hub retaining bolts 70
Stabilizer bar bushing 13
Stabilizer bar mounting bracket bolts 37
Steering knuckle-to-strut assembly bolts
    1985 through 1990 144
    1991 180
    1992 on 140
Strut assembly upper mounting nuts 18
Tie–rod end nut 35

Rear suspension

Adjustment link-to-knuckle nut 33
Adjustment link-to-control arm nut 63
Balljoint stud nuts 22
Control arm pivot nuts 85
Control arm pivot bolts 125

10

Rear suspension (continued)

Hub and bearing assembly bolts   52
Stabilizer bar bushing assembly nut   37
Stabilizer bar bushing pinch bolt   37
Stabilizer bar link nut   13
Stabilizer bar mounting bracket bolt   13
Strut-to-knuckle nuts   144
Strut tower mounting nuts   18

Steering

Steering gear shaft pinch bolt   35
Outer tie–rod jam nut   30
Steering wheel nut   30
Tie-rod end castellated nut   35
Steering gear mounting bolts   68

Wheel lug nuts . . . .   See Chapter 1

---

1   General information

Refer to illustrations 1.1, 1.2a and 1.2b

Warning: *Whenever any of the suspension or steering fasteners are loosened or removed, they must be inspected and, if necessary, replaced with new ones of the same part number or of original equipment quality and design. Torque specifications must be followed for proper reassembly and component retention. Never attempt to heat or straighten any suspension or steering components. Instead, replace any bent or damaged part with a new one.* .

Note: *On models equipped with the Delco Loc II audio system, be sure the lockout feature is turned off before performing any procedure which requires disconnecting the battery.*

The front suspension is a combination strut and spring design. The steering knuckles are located by lower control arms which are mounted to longitudinally positioned, removable frame members. The lower end of the steering knuckle pivots on a balljoint riveted to the control arm. The balljoint is fastened to the steering knuckle with a castellated nut. The control arms are connected by a stabilizer bar, which reduces body lean during cornering **(see illustration)**.

The rear suspension is fully independent with each suspension knuckle supported by a lower control arm, coil spring and strut. A stabilizer bar minimizes body roll. Each control arm is equipped with a suspension adjustment link to provide for toe adjustment and to minimize alignment variation with suspension movement. The rear control arm is attached to the suspension knuckle through a balljoint to reduce friction.

1.1   Front suspension components

1	Control arm	3	Outer tie–rod
2	Stabilizer bar	4	Balljoint

1.2a   Rear suspension components

| 1 | Stabilizer bar | 2 | Control arm | 3 | Suspension adjustment links |

1.2b   Details of the rear suspension assembly

1   Strut
2   Stabilizer bar
3   Coil spring
4   Suspension adjustment link
5   Control arm

10

The power rack-and-pinion steering system is located behind the engine/transaxle assembly on the firewall and actuates the tie–rods which transmit steering inputs to the steering knuckles. The steering column is connected to the steering gear through an insulated coupler. The steering column is designed to collapse in the event of an accident.

Note: *These vehicles have a combination of standard and metric fasteners on the various suspension and steering components, so it would be a good idea to have both types of tools available when beginning work.*

2   Front stabilizer bar and bushings – removal and installation

Refer to illustrations 2.2, 2.3, 2.10 and 2.11

Removal

1   Loosen the lug nuts on both front wheels, raise the front of the vehicle and support it securely on jackstands. Apply the parking brake and block the rear wheels to keep the vehicle from rolling off the jackstands. Remove the front wheels.

2   Remove the stabilizer bar-to-control arm bolts. Note how the link bushings, spacers and washers are arranged **(see illustration)**.

3   Remove the stabilizer bar bushing clamp bolts **(see illustration)**.

4   Detach the tie–rods from the steering knuckles (see Section 16).

5   Detach the exhaust pipe from the vehicle (see Chapter 4).

6   Turn the right strut to the right.

7   Slide the bar over the right steering knuckle, then pull down until the bar clears the frame.

8   Inspect the bushings for wear and damage and replace them if necessary.

Installation

9   Guide the bar through the wheel well, over the suspension supports and into position.

10   Loosely install the bushings and clamps **(see illustration)**.

11   Center the bar in the vehicle and install the stabilizer bar-to-control arm bolts, spacers, bushings and washers **(see illustration)**. Tighten all of the fasteners to the torque figures listed in this Chapter's Specifications at this time.

12   Install the wheels and lower the vehicle. Tighten the lug nuts to the torque specified in Chapter 1.

2.2   The stabilizer bar link has washers, rubber bushings and spacers to connect the stabilizer bar to the control arm

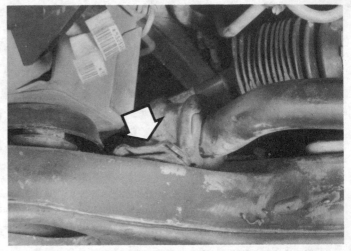

2.3   Remove the two bolts from each stabilizer bar bushing clamp (arrow)

2.10   Stabilizer bar clamp and bushing assembly

1	Stabilizer bar	3	Bushing	5	Welded nuts
2	Clamp	4	Bolt	6	Frame

2.11   Stabilizer bar link bolt and bushing assembly

1	Stabilizer bar	3	Bushings	5	Link bolt
2	Control arm	4	Washers	6	Nut

3.3a   Check for movement between the balljoint and steering knuckle (arrow) when prying up

3.3b   With the pry bar positioned between the steering knuckle boss and the balljoint, pry down and check for play in the balljoint – if there's any play, replace the balljoint

3.11   Replacement balljoint installation details (typical) – be sure to tighten the bolts to the torque specified on the instruction sheet

1	Replacement balljoint	5	Nut
2	Bolt	6	Castellated nut
3	Steering knuckle	7	Cotter pin
4	Control arm		

---

3   Balljoint – check and replacement

Refer to illustrations 3.3a, 3.3b and 3.11

Check

1   Raise the front of the vehicle and support it securely on jackstands. Apply the parking brake and block the rear wheels to keep the vehicle from rolling off the jackstands.

2   Visually inspect the rubber seal for damage, deterioration and leaking grease. If any of these conditions are noticed, the balljoint should be replaced.

3   Place a large pry bar under the balljoint and attempt to push the balljoint up. Next, position the pry bar between the steering knuckle and control arm and pry down (**see illustrations**). If any movement is seen or felt during either of these checks, a worn out balljoint is indicated.

4   Have an assistant grasp the tire at the top and bottom and move the top of the tire in-and-out. Touch the balljoint stud castellated nut. If any looseness is felt, suspect a worn out balljoint stud or a widened hole in the steering knuckle boss. If the latter problem exists, the steering knuckle should be replaced as well as the balljoint.

5   Separate the control arm from the steering knuckle (Section 4). Using your fingers (don't use pliers), try to twist the stud in the socket. If the stud turns, replace the balljoint.

Replacement

6   Loosen the wheel lug nuts, raise the front of the vehicle and support it securely on jackstands. Apply the parking brake and block the rear wheels to keep the vehicle from rolling off the jackstands. Remove the wheel.

7   Separate the control arm from the steering knuckle (Section 4). Temporarily insert the balljoint stud back into the steering knuckle (loosely). This will ease balljoint removal after Step 9 has been performed, as well as hold the assembly stationary while drilling out the rivets.

8   Using a 1/8-inch drill bit, drill a pilot hole into the center of each balljoint-to-control arm rivet. Be careful not to damage the CV joint boot in the process.

9   Using a 1/2-inch drill bit, drill the head off each rivet. Work slowly and carefully to avoid deforming the holes in the control arm.

10   Loosen (but don't remove) the stabilizer bar-to-control arm nut. Pull the control arm and balljoint down to remove the balljoint stud from the steering knuckle, then dislodge the balljoint from the control arm.

11   Position the new balljoint on the control arm and install the bolts (supplied in the balljoint kit) from the top of the control arm (**see illustration**). Tighten the bolts to the torque specified in the new balljoint instruction sheet.

12   Insert the balljoint into the steering knuckle, install the castellated nut, tighten it to the torque listed in this Chapter's Specifications and install a new cotter pin. It may be necessary to tighten the nut some to align the cotter pin hole with an opening in the nut, which is acceptable. Never loosen the castellated nut to allow cotter pin insertion.

13   Tighten the stabilizer bar-to-control arm nut to the torque listed in this Chapter's Specifications.

14   Install the wheel, lower the vehicle and tighten the lug nuts to the specified torque. It's a good idea to take the vehicle to a dealer service department or service station to have the front end alignment checked and, if necessary, adjusted.

10

4.3   Remove the cotter pin and castellated nut (arrow) from the balljoint stud

4.4   Pry the balljoint out of the steering knuckle – if it's stubborn and won't come out, strike the steering knuckle boss on both sides (arrow) simultaneously with two hammers, then try again

4.5a   Remove the control arm pivot bolts

4.5b   Control arm and subframe assembly

1	Control arm	5	Subframe bushing nut
2	Subframe	6	Control arm bushing nut
3	Subframe bushing	7	Washer
4	Control arm bushing		

4   Control arm – removal and installation

Refer to illustrations 4.3, 4.4, 4.5a and 4.5b

Removal

1   Loosen the wheel lug nuts, raise the front of the vehicle and support it securely on jackstands. Apply the parking brake and block the rear wheels to keep the vehicle from rolling off the jackstands. Remove the wheel.

2   If only one control arm is being removed, disconnect only that end of the stabilizer bar. If both control arms are being removed, disconnect both ends (see Section 2 if necessary).

3   Remove the balljoint stud-to-steering knuckle castellated nut and cotter pin **(see illustration)**.

4   Using a large pry bar positioned between the control arm and steering knuckle, "pop" the balljoint out of the knuckle **(see illustration)**. **Caution:** *When removing the balljoint from the knuckle, be careful not to overextend the inner CV joint or it may be damaged.*

5   Remove the two control arm pivot bolts and detach the control arm **(see illustrations)**.

6   The control arm bushings are replaceable, but special tools and expertise are necessary to do the job. Carefully inspect the bushings for

hardening, excessive wear and cracks. If they appear to be worn or deteriorated, take the control arm to a dealer service department or repair shop.

Installation

7   Position the control arm in the suspension support and install the pivot bolts. Do not tighten them completely at this time.

8   Insert the balljoint stud into the steering knuckle boss, install the castellated nut and tighten it to the torque listed in this Chapter's Specifications. If necessary, tighten the nut a little more if the cotter pin hole doesn't line up with an opening on the nut. Install a new cotter pin.

9   Install the stabilizer bar-to-control arm bolt, spacer, bushings and washers and tighten the nut to the torque listed in this Chapter's Specifications.

10   Install the wheel and lower the vehicle. Tighten the lug nuts to the specified torque.

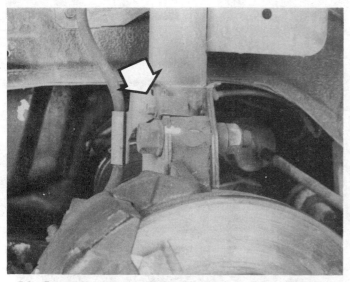

5.2 Detach the front brake line bracket (arrow) from the strut

5.4a Mark the strut-to-steering knuckle relationship and draw a line around the nuts with paint or a scribe

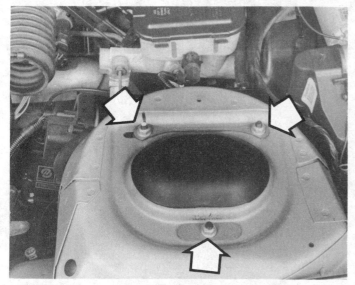

5.4b Before you remove the three strut-to-shock tower nuts (arrows), be sure to mark their relationship to the body

5.6 Remove the strut-to-knuckle nuts and bolts – the bolts are splined and must be driven out with a brass, lead or plastic hammer

11 With the weight of the vehicle on the suspension, tighten the control arm pivot bolts to the torque listed in this Chapter's Specifications. **Caution:** *If the bolts aren't tightened with the weight of the vehicle on the suspension, control arm bushing damage may occur.*

12 Drive the vehicle to a dealer service department or an alignment shop to have the front wheel alignment checked and, if necessary, adjusted.

5 Front strut and spring assembly – removal, inspection and installation

Removal

Refer to illustrations 5.2, 5.4a, 5.4b, 5.6 and 5.7

1 Loosen the wheel lug nuts, raise the front of the vehicle and support it securely on jackstands. Apply the parking brake and block the rear wheels to keep the vehicle from rolling off the jackstands. Remove the wheel.

2 Remove the brake line bracket from the strut **(see illustration)**.

3 If the vehicle is equipped with anti-lock brakes, disconnect the front sensors. If the vehicle is equipped with the computer command ride (CCR), disconnect the CCR electrical connector from the front strut.

4 Using white paint or a scribe, mark the strut-to-steering knuckle relationship and make a line around the strut-to-steering knuckle nuts **(see illustration)**. Also mark the relationship of the upper strut mounting studs to the body **(see illustration)**.

5 Separate the tie-rod end from the steering arm as described in Section 16.

6 Remove the strut-to-knuckle nuts **(see illustration)** and knock the bolts out with a brass, lead or plastic hammer.

10

5.7   Push in on the strut while pulling out on the top of the brake rotor to separate the knuckle and strut

7   Separate the strut from the steering knuckle **(see illustration)**. Be careful not to overextend the inner CV joint or stretch the brake hose.
8   Have an assistant support the strut assembly. Remove the three strut-to-shock tower nuts. Remove the assembly out through the fender well.

Inspection

9   Check the strut body for leaking fluid, dents, cracks and other obvious damage which would warrant repair or replacement.
10   Check the coil spring for chips and cracks in the spring coating (this will cause premature spring failure due to corrosion). Inspect the spring seat for hardening, cracks and general deterioration.
11   If wear or damage is evident, proceed to Section 6 for the strut disassembly procedure.

Installation

Refer to illustration 5.12

12   Install the strut **(see illustration)**. Once the three studs protrude from the shock tower, install the nuts so the strut won't fall back through. This may require an assistant, since the strut is quite heavy and awkward. Be sure to align the marks you made on disassembly.
13   Slide the steering knuckle into the strut flange and insert the two bolts. They should be positioned with the flats situated horizontally. Install the nuts, align the marks and tighten the nuts to the torque listed in this Chapter's Specifications.
14   Install the tie-rod end to the steering knuckle and tighten the castellated nut to the specified torque. Install a new cotter pin. If the cotter pin won't pass through, tighten the nut a little more, but just enough to align the hole in the stud with a castellation on the nut (don't loosen the nut).
15   Install the wheel, lower the vehicle and tighten the lug nuts to the torque listed in the Chapter 1 Specifications.
16   Tighten the three upper mounting nuts to the specified torque.

---

6   Strut cartridge – replacement

Refer to illustrations 6.4, 6.5a, 6.5b, 6.6, 6.7, 6.11, 6.12, 6.14, 6.15a, 6.15b and 6.15c
1   If the struts exhibit the telltale signs of wear (leaking fluid, loss of dampening capability) explore all options before beginning any work. The

5.12   Strut assembly details

1   Strut assembly
2   Strut-to-body nuts
3   Brake line bracket bolt
4   Strut-to-steering knuckle nuts

---

strut cartridges can be replaced. However, rebuilt strut assemblies (some complete with springs) are available on an exchange basis which eliminates much time and work. Whichever route you choose to take, check on the cost and availability of parts before disassembling anything. **Warning:** *Disassembling a strut is a dangerous job. Be very careful and follow the instructions to the letter or serious injury may result. Use only a high quality spring compressor and carefully follow the manufacturer's instructions furnished with the tool. After removing the coil spring from the strut assembly, set it aside in a safe, isolated area (a steel cabinet is preferred).*
2   Remove the strut and spring assembly following the procedure described in Section 5. Mount the strut assembly in a vise. Cushion the vise jaws with rags or blocks of wood.
3   Following the tool manufacturer's instructions, install the spring compressor (which can be obtained at most auto parts stores or equipment yards on a daily rental basis) on the spring and compress it sufficiently to relieve all pressure from the spring seat. This can be verified by wiggling the spring seat.

6.4   After the spring has been compressed, remove the damper shaft nut

6.5a   Remove the bearing cap . . .

6.5b   . . . and the upper spring seat and insulator from the damper shaft

6.6   Remove the compressed spring assembly – be EXTREMELY CAREFUL when handling the spring!

6.7   Using a tubing cutter, cut the end cap off the strut body at the groove (arrow)

STRUT RESERVOIR TUBE

STRUT CARTRIDGE

3 GROOVES ON CARTRIDGE MUST LINE UP WITH 3 PADS IN BASE OF RESERVOIR TUBE.

6.11   Turn the cartridge until it seats in the depressions at the bottom of the tube

NUT

CARTRIDGE

6.12   Install the cartridge retaining nut – be careful not to cross-thread it

A

B

6.14   Extend the damper shaft (A) and hold it in place with a clothes pin (B)

10

6.15a   Strut assembly details

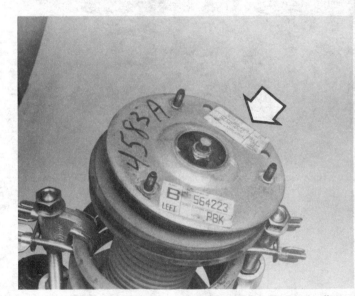

6.15b   Install the upper spring seat with the flat (arrow) facing the steering knuckle flange

4   Loosen the damper shaft nut while using a socket wrench on the shaft hex to prevent it from turning (see illustration).
5   Lift the bearing cap, upper spring seat and upper insulator off the damper shaft (see illustrations). Inspect the bearing in the spring seat for smooth operation and replace it if necessary.
6   Carefully remove the compressed spring assembly (see illustration) and set it in a safe place, such as inside a steel cabinet. Warning: *Don't position your head near the end of the spring!*
7   Locate the groove cut in the strut reservoir tube, 3/4-inch from the top of the tube (see illustration). Using a tubing cutter, cut around the groove until the reservoir tube is severed. Lift out the piston rod assembly with the cylinder and end cap. Discard these items.
8   Remove the strut reservoir tube from the vise and pour the damper fluid into an approved oil container.
9   Place the strut back in the vise and lightly file around the inner edge of the opening to eliminate any burrs that may have resulted from the cutting operation. Be careful not to damage the internal threads in the strut body.
10   Thread the cartridge retaining nut into the reservoir tube, as straight as possible, to establish a clean path in the existing threads. Remove the nut.
11   Insert the replacement strut cartridge into the reservoir tube and turn it until you feel the pads on the bottom of the cartridge seat in the depressions at the bottom of the reservoir tube (see illustration).
12   Slide the nut over the cartridge and thread it into the tube (see illustration), tightening it to the torque specified in the kit instructions.
13   Stroke the damper shaft up-and-down a few times to verify proper operation.
14   Extend the damper shaft all the way and hold it in place with a clothes pin at the bottom of the rod (see illustration).
15   Assemble the strut beginning with the lower spring insulator and spring, then the upper spring insulator, spring seat and bearing cap. Position the spring seat and bearing cap with the flats facing the steering knuckle flange (see illustrations).
16   Install the damper shaft nut and tighten it securely. Remove the clothes pin from the damper shaft.
17   Install the strut and spring assembly as outlined in Section 5.

6.15c   The bearing cap must also be positioned with the flat (arrow) facing the knuckle flange

7   Front hub and wheel bearing assembly – removal and installation

Refer to illustrations 7.6, 7.7, 7.8, 7.9 and 7.10
Note: *The front hub and wheel bearing assembly is sealed-for-life and must be replaced as a unit.*

1   Loosen the wheel lug nuts, raise the front of the vehicle and support it securely on jackstands. Don't place the jackstands under the control arms. Apply the parking brake and block the rear wheels to keep the vehicle from rolling off the jackstands. Remove the wheel.

7.6 A no. 55 Torx bit is required to remove the hub bolts – DO NOT use an Allen wrench or the bolts will be damaged

7.7 Pull the hub and bearing assembly and the rotor shield out of the steering knuckle

7.8 Pry the seal out of the knuckle with a screwdriver

7.9 Using a large socket, drive the new seal into place

2   Disconnect the stabilizer bar from the control arm (see Section 2 if necessary).

3   Remove the balljoint-to-steering knuckle nut and separate the control arm from the knuckle (see Section 4).

4   Remove the caliper from the steering knuckle and hang it out of the way with a piece of wire (see Chapter 9).

5   Pull the rotor off the hub and remove the driveaxle (see Chapter 8 if necessary).

6   Using a no. 55 Torx bit, remove the three hub retaining bolts through the opening in the flange **(see illustration)**.

7   Wiggle the hub and bearing assembly back-and-forth and pull it out of the steering knuckle, along with the rotor shield **(see illustration)**.

8   If the hub and bearing assembly is being replaced with a new one, it's a good idea to replace the dust seal in the back of the steering knuckle. Pry it out of the knuckle with a screwdriver **(see illustration)**.

9   Drive the new dust seal into the knuckle with a large socket or a seal driver and a hammer **(see illustration)**. Try not to cock the seal in the bore.

10   Install a new O-ring around the rear of the bearing and push it up against the bearing flange **(see illustration)**.

11   Clean the mating surfaces on the steering knuckle, bearing flange and knuckle bore. Lubricate the outside diameter of the bearing and the seal lips with high-temperature grease and insert the hub and bearing into the steering knuckle. Position the rotor shield and install the three bolts, tightening them to the torque listed in this Chapter's Specifications.

12   Install the driveaxle (see Chapter 8).

13   Attach the control arm to the steering knuckle (see Section 4).

14   Reconnect the stabilizer bar to the control arm (see Section 2).

15   Install the brake rotor and caliper (see Chapter 9).

16   Install the hub nut and tighten it securely. Prevent the axle from turning by inserting a screwdriver through the caliper and into a rotor cooling vane (see Chapter 8 if necessary).

17   Install the wheel, lower the vehicle and tighten the lug nuts to the specified torque.

18   Tighten the hub nut to the torque specified in Chapter 8.

10

3   Remove the caliper and suspend it out of the way with a piece of wire. Lift the rotor off the hub.

4   Mark the position of the two strut-to-knuckle nuts and remove them **(see illustration 5.4a)**. Don't drive out the bolts at this time.

5   Separate the control arm balljoint from the steering knuckle (see Section 4 if necessary).

6   Attach a puller to the hub flange and push the driveaxle out of the hub (see Chapter 8). Hang the driveaxle with a piece of wire to prevent damage to the inner CV joint.

7   Support the knuckle and drive out the two strut-to-knuckle bolts with a soft-face hammer. Remove the steering knuckle assembly from the strut.

Installation

8   Position the knuckle in the strut and insert the two splined bolts, with the flats on the bolt heads in the horizontal position. Tap the bolts into place and install the nuts, but don't tighten them at this time.

9   Install the driveaxle in the hub.

10   Connect the control arm to the steering knuckle and tighten the castellated nut to the torque listed in this Chapter's Specifications. Install a new cotter pin.

11   Align the strut-to-knuckle nuts with the previously applied marks and tighten them to the specified torque.

12   Install the brake rotor and caliper.

13   Tighten the hub nut securely.

14   Install the wheel, lower the vehicle and tighten the lug nuts to the specified torque.

15   Tighten the hub nut to the torque specified in Chapter 8.

7.10   Hub and bearing installation details

1	Hub and bearing assembly	5	Hub nut
2	Steering knuckle	6	Seal
3	Rotor shield	7	Hub and bearing retaining bolt
4	Washer	8	O-ring

---

8   Steering knuckle and hub – removal and installation

Removal

1   Loosen the wheel lug nuts, raise the front of the vehicle and support it securely on jackstands. Apply the parking brake and block the rear wheels to keep the vehicle from rolling off the jackstands. Remove the wheel.

2   Remove the hub nut. Insert a screwdriver through the caliper and into a rotor cooling vane to prevent the driveaxle from turning.

---

9   Rear stabilizer bar – removal and installation

Refer to illustrations 9.5, 9.6, 9.7 and 9.8

1   Detach the cable from the negative battery terminal.

2   Loosen the rear wheel lug nuts.

3   Raise the rear of the vehicle and place it securely on jackstands. Block the front wheels.

4   Remove the rear wheels.

5   Detach the stabilizer bar link bolt assemblies from the knuckle brackets **(see illustration)**.

6   If you're replacing the stabilizer bar and/or the lower bushing from the hanger clamp only, remove the pinch bolt from each hanger clamp **(see illustration)**, bend the end of the clamp open and remove the stabilizer bar and bushings.

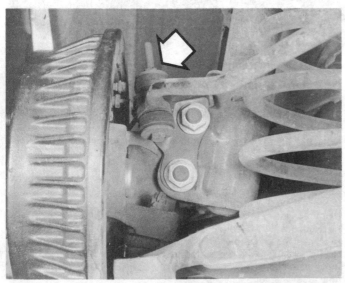

9.5   To detach the rear stabilizer bar link bolt assembly from the knuckle, simply remove the nut on the upper end (arrow) and tap the link bolt out – don't lose any of the bushings or washers

9.6   If you're replacing the rear stabilizer bar and/or lower bushing, remove this bolt on each hanger clamp, bend the clamp open and remove the bar

9.7 If you're going to reinstall the same stabilizer bar or replace both bushings, simply remove the upper hanger clamp bolt and leave the clamp attached to the bar during removal

7   If you plan to reinstall the same bar or replace both bushings, simply remove the upper bolt from the hanger clamp **(see illustration)** and leave the hanger attached to the stabilizer bar.

8   Installation is the reverse of removal **(see illustration)**. Tighten the fasteners to the torques listed in this Chapter's Specifications.

---

10   Rear strut – removal and installation

Refer to illustrations 10.3, 10.9, 10.10 and 10.12

1   Detach the cable from the negative battery terminal.
2   Remove the rear speaker assembly (see Chapter 12).
3   Remove the trunk side cover **(see illustration)**.
4   Loosen the rear wheel lug nuts.
5   Raise the rear of the vehicle and place it securely on jackstands. Block the front wheels.
6   Remove the rear wheels.
7   If the vehicle is equipped with electronic level control (ELC), remove the ELC air tube from the strut air tube fitting. If the vehicle is equipped with the computer command ride (CCR), disconnect the CCR electrical connector from the front strut.
8   Support the control arm at the balljoint with a jackstand or floorjack **(see illustration 11.9).**
9   Remove the strut tower mounting nuts from inside the trunk **(see illustration).**

9.8 Details of the rear stabilizer bar assembly

1	Bolt	7	Bolt
2	Washer	8	Stabilizer bar
3	Bushings	9	Bolts
4	Stabilizer bar bracket	10	Nut
5	Nut	11	Bracket
6	Hanger clamp		

10.3   Remove the trunk side cover . . .

10.9   . . . then remove the strut tower mounting nuts (arrows)

10

10.10   Remove the nuts and pull out the bolts (arrows) from the knuckle – don't lose the washers

11.9   Support the control arm at the balljoint with a floor jack or a jackstand – place a chain through the spring and the control arm to prevent the chain from flying off when the control arm is lowered

10   Remove the nuts, bolts and washers from the knuckle **(see illustration)**.
11   Remove the strut.
12   Installation is the reverse of removal **(see illustration)**. Tighten the fasteners to the torques listed in this Chapter's Specifications.

11   Rear springs and insulators – removal and installation

Refer to illustrations 11.9 and 11.13

1   Detach the cable from the negative battery terminal.
2   Loosen the rear wheel lug nuts.
3   Raise the rear of the vehicle and place it securely on jackstands. Make sure the jackstands aren't under the control arms. Block the front wheels.
4   Remove the rear wheels.
5   Detach the parking brake cable retaining clip from the left control arm.

10.12   Details of the rear strut assembly

1	Strut	5	Washers
2	Stabilizer bar bracket	6	Bolts
3	Knuckle	7	Nuts
4	Nuts		

6   If the vehicle is equipped with electronic level control (ELC), detach the ELC height sensor link from the right control arm.
7   Detach the rear stabilizer bar (see Section 9).
8   Detach the suspension adjustment link (see Section 13).
9   Place a floor jack under the spring pocket of the control arm **(see illustration)**. Raise the jack just enough to remove tension from the control arm.
10   Place a chain around the spring and through the control arm as a safety measure.
11   Remove the strut-to-knuckle bolts and detach the strut from the knuckle (see Section 10).
12   Slowly lower the jack to relieve tension on the control arm. When all compression is removed from the spring, remove the safety chain, spring and insulators.
13   Installation is the reverse of removal **(see illustration)**. Tighten the fasteners to the torques listed in this Chapter's Specifications.

12   Rear hub and wheel bearing assembly – removal and installation

Refer to illustration 12.6
Note: *The rear hub and bearing assembly is sealed for life and must be replaced as a unit.*

11.13   Details of the rear coil spring assembly

1	Control arm	4	Bolts
2	Coil spring	5	Nuts
3	Insulators		

1   Detach the cable from the negative battery terminal.
2   Loosen the rear wheel lug nuts.
3   Raise the rear of the vehicle and place it securely on jackstands. Block the front wheels.
4   Remove the rear wheel.
5   Remove the brake drum (see Chapter 9).
6   To remove the hub and bearing assembly, you'll need to rotate the stud flange to align one of it holes with each of the four mounting flange Torx bolts **(see illustration)**. When the last bolt is removed, support the backing plate assembly, remove the hub and bearing assembly and rein-

12.6   To remove the rear hub and wheel bearing assembly, rotate the stud flange until one of its holes is aligned with each of the four flange mounting Torx bolts (the brake shoe assembly is shown removed for clarity)

stall two of the bolts finger tight. This will prevent the brake line from being strained under the weight of the backing plate.
7   Installation is the reverse of removal. Be sure tighten the bolts to the specified torque.

13   Rear suspension adjustment link – removal and installation

Refer to illustrations 13.5, 13.7 and 13.9

1   Detach the cable from the negative battery terminal.
2   Loosen the rear wheel lug nuts.
3   Raise the vehicle and place it securely on jackstands.
4   Remove the wheel.
5   Remove the cotter pin and nut **(see illustration)**.
6   Separate the outer suspension adjustment link from the knuckle with a puller **(see illustration 16.2b)**.
7   To detach the inner end of the link from the control arm, remove the retaining nut, washer and spacer **(see illustration)**.

13.5   Remove the cotter pin and nut (arrow) from the suspension adjustment link stud

13.7   To detach the inner end of the suspension adjustment link from the control arm, remove this nut (arrow) – don't lose the washer and spacer

10

14.9   Remove the rear control arm pivot bolts (arrow)

13.9   Details of the suspension adjustment link assembly

1	Control arm	6	Nut
2	Knuckle	7	Washer
3	Cotter pin	8	Spacer
4	Nut	9	Boot (left side only)
5	Suspension adjustment link	10	Nut

8   Remove the suspension adjustment link from the control arm.
9   Installation is the reverse of removal **(see illustration)**. Tighten the fasteners to the specified torques and use a new cotter pin.

14   Rear control arm – removal and installation

Refer to illustrations 14.9 and 14.11
Note: *Replacement of the bushings in the rear control arms requires a number of special tools. Balljoint replacement is difficult if special tools are not available. If a bushing or balljoint must be replaced, take the control arm to a dealer service department.*

1   Detach the cable from the negative battery terminal.
2   Loosen the rear wheel lug nuts.
3   Raise the rear of the vehicle and place it securely on jackstands. Block the front wheels.
4   Remove the electronic level control (ELC) height sensor link, if equipped, from the right control arm.
5   Remove the parking brake cable retaining clip from the left control arm.
6   Remove the suspension adjustment link from the control arm (see Section 13).
7   Remove the coil spring (see Section 11).
8   To separate the knuckle from the balljoint stud, refer to Section 4 (the procedure for splitting the rear knuckle and ball stud is identical to the procedure for splitting a front knuckle and stud).
9   Remove the control arm pivot bolts **(see illustration)**.
10   Remove the control arm from the vehicle.
11   Installation is the reverse of removal **(see illustration)**. Tighten the fasteners to the torques listed in this Chapter's Specifications.

15   Steering system – general information

Warning: *Whenever any of the steering fasteners are removed, they must be inspected and, if necessary, replaced with new ones of the same part*

14.11   Exploded view of the rear control arm assembly

1	Control arm	5	Front pivot bolt
2	Knuckle	6	Cotter pin
3	Rear pivot bolt	7	Castellated nut
4	Pivot bolt nuts		

number or of original equipment quality and design. Torque specifications must be followed for proper reassembly and component retention. Never attempt to heat or straighten any suspension or steering components. Instead, replace any bent or damaged part with a new one.

All vehicles covered by this manual have power rack-and-pinion steering systems. The components making up the system are the steering wheel, steering column, rack and pinion assembly, tie-rods and tie-rod ends. The power steering system has a belt-driven pump to provide hydraulic pressure.

In the power steering system, the motion of turning the steering wheel is transferred through the column to the pinion shaft in the rack-and-pinion assembly. Teeth on the pinion shaft are meshed with teeth on the rack, so when the shaft is turned, the rack is moved left or right in the housing. A rotary control valve in the rack-and-pinion unit directs hydraulic fluid under pressure from the power steering pump to either side of the integral rack piston, which is connected to the rack, thereby reducing manual steering force. Depending on which side of the piston this hydraulic pressure is

16.2a   Remove the cotter pin and castellated nut from the tie–rod end stud . . .

16.2b   . . . then separate the tie-rod end from the steering knuckle arm with a two-jaw puller – DO NOT pound on the stud!

16.3   Using white paint, mark the relationship of the tie-rod end and the threaded adjuster

applied to, the rack will be forced either left or right, which moves the tie-rods, etc. If the power steering system loses hydraulic pressure it will still function manually, though with increased effort.

The steering column is a collapsible, energy-absorbing type, designed to compress in the event of a front end collision to minimize injury to the driver. The column also houses the ignition switch lock, key warning buzzer, turn signal controls, headlight dimmer control and windshield wiper controls. The ignition and steering wheel can both be locked while the vehicle is parked.

Due to the column's collapsible design, it's important that only the specified screws, bolts and nuts be used as designated and that they're tightened to the specified torque. Other precautions particular to this design are noted in appropriate Sections.

In addition to the standard steering column, optional tilt and key release versions are also offered. The tilt model can be set in five different positions, while with the key release model the ignition key is locked in the column until a lever is depressed to extract it.

Because disassembly of the steering column is more often performed to repair a switch or other electrical part than to correct a problem in the steering, the upper steering column disassembly and reassembly procedure is included in Chapter 12.

---

16   Tie-rod ends – removal and installation

Refer to illustrations 16.2a, 16.2b and 16.3

Removal

1   Loosen the wheel lug nuts, raise the front of the vehicle and support it securely on jackstands. Apply the parking brake and block the rear wheels to keep the vehicle from rolling off the jackstands. Remove the wheel.
2   Remove the cotter pin and castellated nut from the tie-rod, then disconnect the tie-rod from the steering knuckle arm with a puller **(see illustrations)**.
3   Mark the relationship of the tie-rod end to the threaded adjuster **(see illustration)**. This will ensure the toe-in setting is restored when reassembled.
4   Unscrew the tie-rod end from the tie-rod.

Installation

5   Thread the tie-rod end onto the tie-rod to the marked position and connect the tie-rod end to the steering arm. Install the castellated nut and tighten it to the torque listed in this Chapter's Specifications. Install a new cotter pin.
6   Install the wheel. Lower the vehicle and tighten the lug nuts to the specified torque.
7   Have the front end steering geometry checked by a dealer service department or an alignment shop.

---

17   Steering gear – removal and installation

Refer to illustrations 17.5, 17.11, 17.12a, 17.12b, 17.15a and 17.15b

1   Detach the cable from the negative battery terminal.
2   Loosen the wheel lug nuts.
3   Raise the vehicle and place it securely on jackstands.
4   Remove the wheels.

10

17.5   Remove the pinch bolt from the end of the steering column and unplug the compressor cutout switch wire (arrows)

17.11   Remove the two subframe-to-body mounting bolts (arrows) at each rear corner of the subframe

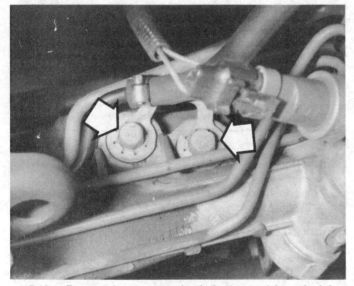

17.12a   Remove the two mounting bolts (arrows) from the left end of the rack and pinion assembly

17.12b   Remove the two bolts from each of the clamps (arrows) on the right end of the rack and pinion assembly

5   Remove the pinch bolt at the steering gear (**see illustration**).

6   Unplug the compressor cutout switch wire.

7   Detach the power steering line fittings from the steering gear.

8   Detach the tie–rod ends from the steering knuckle (see Section 16).

9   Support the engine/transaxle assembly with a floorjack. Put a block of wood between the jack and the pan to prevent damage.

10   Loosen – but do not remove – the two front subframe mounting bolts (see Section 8, Chapter 7).

11   Remove the four rear subframe-to-body bolts (**see illustration**).

12   Remove the two mounting bolts from the left side of the steering gear assembly and the four bolts from the two clamps on the right (**see illustrations**).

13   Lower the sub-frame about three inches.

14   Slide the steering gear assembly out the left wheel well to remove it.

15   Installation is the reverse of removal (**see illustrations**). Tighten the fasteners to the torques listed in this Chapter and Chapter 7.

18   Steering gear boots – replacement

1   Remove the steering gear from the vehicle (see Section 17).

2   Detach the tie-rod ends from the steering gear (see Section 16).

3   Cut off both boot clamps and discard them.

4   Slide the old boots off (they can be pulled off the ends of the vent cross tube).

5   Before installing the new boots, wrap the threads and serrations on the ends of the steering rods with a layer of tape so the small ends of the new boots aren't damaged.

6   Slide the new boots on.

7   Loosely install the clamps.

8   Push the boots onto both ends of the vent tube.

9   Tighten the clamps.

10   Install the tie-rods (see Section 16).

11   Install the steering gear assembly.

17.15a   Details of the power steering hoses

1	Inlet hose	7	Washer
2	Outlet hose	8	Fitting
3	Outlet pipe	9	Idle speed power steering
4	Screw		pressure switch
5	Retainer	10	Heat shield
6	Clamps		

17.15b   Exploded view of the steering gear assembly

1	Bolt	6	Washer
2	Steering gear	7	Steering knuckle
3	Frame	8	Use RTV sealer
4	Nut		around these inserts
5	Retainer		

19   Power steering pump – removal and installation

Refer to illustrations 19.3, 19.4 and 19.6

Removal
1   Disconnect the cable from the negative battery terminal.

2   Remove the pump drivebelt (see Chapter 1).
3   Remove the pump mounting bolts and detach the pump from the engine **(see illustration)**.
4   Detach the return line from the pump **(see illustration)**, and drain the fluid in the line.
5   Disconnect the pressure line from the pump **(see illustration 19.4)**.

19.3   Remove the power steering pump mounting bolts (one is shown with a socket on it and the other one is indicated by an arrow)

19.4   Detach the power steering pump return line (1), drain the contents into a container, then disconnect the pressure line (2)

10

19.6   Exploded view of the power steering pump assembly

1	*Power steering pump*	*3*	*Pulley*
2	*Bolts*	*4*	*Bolt*

Installation

6   Installation is the reverse of removal **(see illustration)**.

7   Fill the reservoir with the recommended fluid and bleed the system, following the procedure described in the next Section.

20   Power steering system – bleeding

1   Following any operation in which the power steering fluid lines have been disconnected, the power steering system must be bled to remove air and obtain proper steering performance.

2   With the front wheels turned all the way to the left, check the power steering fluid level and, if low, add fluid until it reaches the Cold mark on the dipstick.

3   Start the engine and allow it to run at fast idle. Recheck the fluid level and add more if necessary to reach the Cold mark on the dipstick.

4   Bled the system by turning the wheels from side-to-side, without hitting the stops. This will work the air out of the system. Don't allow the reservoir to run out of fluid.

5   When the air is worked out of the system, return the wheels to the straight ahead position and leave the engine running for several minutes before shutting it off. Recheck the fluid level.

6   Road test the vehicle to be sure the steering system is functioning normally with no noise.

7   Recheck the fluid level to be sure it's up to the Hot mark on the dipstick while the engine is at normal operating temperature. Add fluid if necessary.

21   Steering wheel – removal and installation

Refer to illustrations 21.2, 21.3, 21.4 and 21.5

Warning: *If the vehicle is equipped with an air bag DO NOT attempt to remove the steering wheel. Have the procedure performed by a dealer service department or other qualified shop.*

1   Disconnect the cable from the negative battery terminal.

2   Remove the two bolts retaining the horn pad from the backside of the steering wheel. Pull the horn pad off the steering wheel and detach the horn wire **(see illustration)**.

3   Remove the safety clip from the steering shaft **(see illustration)**.

4   Remove the steering wheel retaining nut, then mark the relationship of the steering shaft and hub to simplify installation and ensure steering wheel alignment **(see illustration)**.

5   Use a puller to disconnect the steering wheel from the shaft **(see illustration)**.

6   To install the wheel, align the mark on the steering wheel hub with the mark made on the shaft during removal and slip the wheel onto the shaft. Install the hub nut and tighten it to the torque listed in this Chapter's Specifications. Install the safety clip.

7   Install the horn contact and press the horn pad into place on the steering wheel. Install the horn pad retaining bolts.

8   Connect the negative battery cable.

21.2   To remove the horn pad, remove the two screws on the backside of the steering wheel spokes (not visible in this photo), pull off the pad and detach the horn wire

21.3   Pop off the safety clip from the steering shaft with a small screwdriver

21.4   Apply alignment marks to the steering wheel hub and shaft

21.5   Use a steering wheel puller to separate the steering wheel from the shaft – DO NOT attempt to remove the wheel with a hammer!

22   Wheel studs – replacement

Refer to illustrations 22.3 and 22.4
Note: *This procedure applies to both the front and rear wheel studs.*
1   Remove the hub and wheel bearing assembly (see Section 7 or 12).
2   Install a lug nut part way onto the stud being replaced.
3   Push the stud out of the hub flange with GM tool no. J-6627-A or equivalent **(see illustration)**.
4   Insert the new stud into the hub flange from the back side and install four flat washers and a lug nut on the stud **(see illustration)**.
5   Tighten the lug nut until the stud is seated in the flange.
6   Reinstall the hub and wheel bearing assembly.

23   Wheels and tires – general information

Refer to illustration 23.1
　All vehicles covered by this manual are equipped with metric-size fiberglass or steel belted radial tires **(see illustration)**. The use of other size or type tires may affect the ride and handling of the vehicle. Don't mix different types of tires, such as radials and bias belted, on the same vehicle, since handling may be seriously affected. Tires should be replaced in pairs on the same axle, but if only one tire is being replaced, be sure it's the same size, structure and tread design as the other.
　Because tire pressure affects handling and wear, the tire pressures should be checked at least once a month or before any extended trips (see Chapter 1).

22.3   Use GM tool no. J-6627-A or equivalent to push the stud out of the flange

1	Hub	3	Tool
2	Lug nut on stud		

22.4   Install four washers and a lug nut on the stud, then tighten the nut to draw the stud into place

1	Hub and wheel bearing assembly	2	Washers installed on stud
		3	Lug nut

10

METRIC TIRE SIZES
P 185 / 80 R 13

TIRE TYPE
P – PASSENGER
T – TEMPORARY
C – COMMERCIAL

SECTION WIDTH
(MILLIMETERS)
185
195
205
ETC

ASPECT RATIO
(SECTION HEIGHT)
(SECTION WIDTH)
70
75
80

RIM DIAMETER
(INCHES)
13
14
15

CONSTRUCTION TYPE
R – RADIAL
B – BIAS — BELTED
D – DIAGONAL (BIAS)

SECTION
WIDTH

SECTION
HEIGHT

23.1   Metric tire size code

Wheels must be replaced if they're bent, dented, leak air, have elongated bolt holes, are heavily rusted, out of vertical symmetry or if the lug nuts won't stay tight. Wheel repairs by welding or peening aren't recommended.

Tire and wheel balance is important to the overall handling, braking and performance of the vehicle. Unbalanced wheels can adversely affect handling and ride characteristics as well as tire life. Whenever a tire is installed on a wheel, the tire and wheel should be balanced by a shop with the proper equipment.

24   Wheel alignment – general information

Refer to illustration 24.1

Wheel alignment refers to the adjustments made to the wheels so they're in proper angular relationship to the suspension and the ground. Wheels that are out of proper alignment not only affect steering control, but also increase tire wear. The only adjustment normally required is the toe-in adjustment **(see illustration)**. Camber adjustments are also possible, but only after the strut has been modified.

Getting the proper wheel alignment is a very exacting process, one in which complicated and expensive machines are necessary to perform the job properly. Because of this, you should have a technician with the proper equipment perform these tasks. We will, however, attempt to give you a basic idea of what's involved with front end alignment so you can better understand the process and deal intelligently with the shop that does the work.

Toe-in is the turning in of the wheels. The purpose of a toe specification is to ensure parallel rolling of the wheels. In a vehicle with zero toe-in, the distance between the front edges of the wheels will be the same as the distance between the rear edges of the wheels. The actual amount of toe-in is normally only a fraction of an inch. On the front wheels, toe-in adjustment is controlled by the tie-rod end position on the inner tie-rod; on the rear wheels, toe-in is controlled by the tie-rod end position on the suspension adjustment link. Incorrect toe-in will cause the tires to wear improperly by making them scrub against the road surface.

24.1   A wheel alignment normally consists of a toe-in adjustment only; however, camber adjustment is possible after strut modification

Camber is the tilting of the wheels from the vertical when viewed from the front or rear of the vehicle. When the wheels tilt out at the top, the camber is said to be positive (+). When the wheels tilt in at the top the camber is negative (-). The amount of tilt is measured in degrees from the vertical and this measurement is called the camber angle. This angle affects the amount of tire tread which contacts the road and compensates for changes in the suspension geometry when the vehicle is cornering or travelling over an undulating surface. Camber is adjusted by altering the position of the upper strut mounting studs in relation to the body.

Caster is the tilting of the top of the front steering axis from the vertical. A tilt toward the rear is positive caster and a tilt toward the front is negative caster. Caster is not adjustable on these vehicles.

10

Chapter 11   Body

Contents

1   General information

Note: *On models equipped with the Delco Loc II audio system, be sure the lockout feature is turned off before performing any procedure which requires disconnecting the battery.*

These models are two or four-door sedans. The vehicle is a "unibody" type, which means the body is designed to provide vehicle rigidity so a separate frame isn't necessary.

Body maintenance is an important part of the retention of the vehicle's market value. It's far less costly to handle small problems before they grow into larger ones.

Major body components which are particularly vulnerable in accidents are removable. These include the hood, front fenders, grille, doors, trunk lid and tail light assembly. It's often cheaper and less time consuming to replace an entire panel than it is to attempt a restoration of the old one. However, this must be decided on a case-by-case basis.

2   Maintenance – body

1   The condition of the body is very important, because the value of the vehicle is dependent on it. It's much more difficult to repair a neglected or damaged body than it is to repair mechanical components. The hidden areas of the body, such as the fender wells and the engine compartment, are equally important, although they obviously don't require as frequent attention as the rest of the body.

2   Once a year, or every 12,000 miles, it's a good idea to have the underside of the body steam cleaned. All traces of dirt and oil will be removed and the underside can then be inspected carefully for rust, damaged brake lines, frayed electrical wiring, damaged cables and other problems. The front suspension components should be greased after completion of this job.

3   At the same time, clean the engine and the engine compartment with a water soluble degreaser.

4   The fender wells should be given particular attention, as undercoating can peel away and stones and dirt thrown up by the tires can cause the paint to chip and flake, allowing rust to set in. If rust is found, clean down to the bare metal and apply an anti-rust paint.

5   The body should be washed as needed. Wet the vehicle thoroughly to soften the dirt, then wash it down with a soft sponge and plenty of clean soapy water. If the surplus dirt isn't washed off very carefully, it will in time wear down the paint.

6   Spots of tar or asphalt coating thrown up from the road should be removed with a cloth soaked in solvent.

7   Once every six months, wax the body thoroughly. If a chrome cleaner is used to remove rust from any of the vehicle's plated parts, remember that the cleaner also removes part of the chrome, so use it sparingly.

3   Maintenance – upholstery and carpets

1   Every three months remove the carpets or mats and clean the interior of the vehicle (more frequently if necessary). Vacuum the upholstery and carpets to remove loose dirt and dust.

2   If the upholstery is soiled, apply upholstery cleaner with a damp sponge and wipe it off with a clean, dry cloth.

4   Vinyl trim – maintenance

Vinyl trim should not be cleaned with detergents, caustic soaps or petroleum-based cleaners. Plain soap and water or a mild vinyl cleaner is best for stains. Test a small area for color fastness. Bubbles under the vinyl can be eliminated by piercing them with a pin and then working the air out.

5   Body repair – minor damage

See photo sequence

Repair of minor scratches

1   If the scratch is superficial and does not penetrate to the metal of the body, repair is very simple. Lightly rub the scratched area with a fine rubbing compound to remove loose paint and built up wax. Rinse the area with clean water.

2   Apply touch-up paint to the scratch, using a small brush. Continue to apply thin layers of paint until the surface of the paint in the scratch is level with the surrounding paint. Allow the new paint at least two weeks to harden, then blend it into the surrounding paint by rubbing with a very fine rubbing compound. Finally, apply a coat of wax to the scratch area.

3   If the scratch has penetrated the paint and exposed the metal of the body, causing the metal to rust, a different repair technique is required. Remove all loose rust from the bottom of the scratch with a pocket knife, then apply rust inhibiting paint to prevent the formation of rust in the future. Us-

ing a rubber or nylon applicator, coat the scratched area with glaze-type filler. If required, the filler can be mixed with thinner to provide a very thin paste, which is ideal for filling narrow scratches. Before the glaze filler in the scratch hardens, wrap a piece of smooth cotton cloth around the tip of a finger. Dip the cloth in thinner and then quickly wipe it along the surface of the scratch. This will ensure that the surface of the filler is slightly hollow. The scratch can now be painted over as described earlier in this section.

Repair of dents

4   When repairing dents, the first job is to pull the dent out until the affected area is as close as possible to its original shape. There is no point in trying to restore the original shape completely as the metal in the damaged area will have stretched on impact and cannot be restored to its original contours. It is better to bring the level of the dent up to a point which is about 1/8-inch below the level of the surrounding metal. In cases where the dent is very shallow, it is not worth trying to pull it out at all.

5   If the back side of the dent is accessible, it can be hammered out gently from behind using a soft-face hammer. While doing this, hold a block of wood firmly against the opposite side of the metal to absorb the hammer blows and prevent the metal from being stretched.

6   If the dent is in a section of the body which has double layers, or some other factor makes it inaccessible from behind, a different technique is required. Drill several small holes through the metal inside the damaged area, particularly in the deeper sections. Screw long, self tapping screws into the holes just enough for them to get a good grip in the metal. Now the dent can be pulled out by pulling on the protruding heads of the screws with locking pliers.

7   The next stage of repair is the removal of paint from the damaged area and from an inch or so of the surrounding metal. This is easily done with a wire brush or sanding disk in a drill motor, although it can be done just as effectively by hand with sandpaper. To complete the preparation for filling, score the surface of the bare metal with a screwdriver or the tang of a file or drill small holes in the affected area. This will provide a good grip for the filler material. To complete the repair, see the Section on filling and painting.

Repair of rust holes or gashes

8   Remove all paint from the affected area and from an inch or so of the surrounding metal using a sanding disk or wire brush mounted in a drill motor. If these are not available, a few sheets of sandpaper will do the job just as effectively.

9   With the paint removed, you will be able to determine the severity of the corrosion and decide whether to replace the whole panel, if possible, or repair the affected area. New body panels are not as expensive as most people think and it is often quicker to install a new panel than to repair large areas of rust.

10   Remove all trim pieces from the affected area except those which will act as a guide to the original shape of the damaged body, such as headlight shells, etc. Using metal snips or a hacksaw blade, remove all loose metal and any other metal that is badly affected by rust. Hammer the edges of the hole inward to create a slight depression for the filler material.

11   Wire brush the affected area to remove the powdery rust from the surface of the metal. If the back of the rusted area is accessible, treat it with rust-inhibiting paint.

12   Before filling is done, block the hole in some way. This can be done with sheet metal riveted or screwed into place, or by stuffing the hole with wire mesh.

13   Once the hole is blocked off, the affected area can be filled and painted. See the following sub-section on filling and painting.

Filling and painting

14   Many types of body fillers are available, but generally speaking, body repair kits which contain filler paste and a tube of resin hardener are best for this type of repair work. A wide, flexible plastic or nylon applicator will be necessary for imparting a smooth and contoured finish to the surface of the filler material. Mix up a small amount of filler on a clean piece of wood or cardboard (use the hardener springly). Follow the manufacturer's instructions on the package, otherwise the filler will set incorrectly.

11

15   Using the applicator, apply the filler paste to the prepared area. Draw the applicator across the surface of the filler to achieve the desired contour and to level the filler surface. As soon as a contour that approximates the original one is achieved, stop working the paste. If you continue, the paste will begin to stick to the applicator. Continue to add thin layers of paste at 20-minute intervals until the level of the filler is just above the surrounding metal.

16   Once the filler has hardened, the excess can be removed with a body file. From then on, progressively finer grades of sandpaper should be used, starting with a 180-grit paper and finishing with 600-grit wet-or-dry paper. Always wrap the sandpaper around a flat rubber or wooden block, otherwise the surface of the filler will not be completely flat. During the sanding of the filler surface, the wet-or-dry paper should be periodically rinsed in water. This will ensure that a very smooth finish is produced in the final stage.

17   At this point, the repair area should be surrounded by a ring of bare metal, which in turn should be encircled by the finely feathered edge of good paint. Rinse the repair area with clean water until all of the dust produced by the sanding operation is gone.

18   Spray the entire area with a light coat of primer. This will reveal any imperfections in the surface of the filler. Repair the imperfections with fresh filler paste or glaze filler and once more smooth the surface with sandpaper. Repeat this spray-and-repair procedure until you are satisfied that the surface of the filler and the feathered edge of the paint are perfect. Rinse the area with clean water and allow it to dry completely.

19   The repair area is now ready for painting. Spray painting must be carried out in a warm, dry, windless and dust free atmosphere. These conditions can be created if you have access to a large indoor work area, but if you are forced to work in the open, you will have to pick the day very carefully. If you are working indoors, dousing the floor in the work area with water will help settle the dust which would otherwise be in the air. If the repair area is confined to one body panel, mask off the surrounding panels. This will help minimize the effects of a slight mismatch in paint color. Trim pieces such as chrome strips, door handles, etc., will also need to be masked off or removed. Use masking tape and several thicknesses of newspaper for the masking operations.

20   Before spraying, shake the paint can thoroughly, then spray a test area until the spray painting technique is mastered. Cover the repair area with a thick coat of primer. The thickness should be built up using several thin layers of primer rather than one thick one. Using 600-grit wet-or-dry sandpaper, rub down the surface of the primer until it is very smooth. While doing this, the work area should be thoroughly rinsed with water and the wet-or-dry sandpaper periodically rinsed as well. Allow the primer to dry before spraying additional coats.

21   Spray on the top coat, again building up the thickness by using several thin layers of paint. Begin spraying in the center of the repair area and then, using a circular motion, work out until the whole repair area and about two inches of the surrounding original paint is covered. Remove all masking material 10 to 15 minutes after spraying on the final coat of paint. Allow the new paint at least two weeks to harden, then use a very fine rubbing compound to blend the edges of the new paint into the existing paint. Finally, apply a coat of wax.

6   Body repair – major damage

1   Major damage must be repaired by an auto body/frame repair shop with the necessary welding and hydraulic straightening equipment.

2   If the damage has been serious, it is vital that the structure be checked for proper alignment or the vehicle's handling characteristics may be adversely affected. Other problems, such as excessive tire wear and wear in the driveline and steering may occur.

3   Due to the fact that all of the major body components (hood, fenders, etc.) are separate and replaceable units, any seriously damaged components should be replaced rather than repaired. Sometimes these compo-

9.1   Pad the back corners of the hood with rags so the windshield won't be damaged if the hood accidentally swings to the rear

nents can be found in a wrecking yard that specializes in used vehicle components, often at considerable savings over the cost of new parts.

7   Maintenance – hinges and locks

Every 3000 miles or three months, the door, hood and trunk lid hinges should be lubricated with a few drops of oil. The door striker plates should also be given a thin coat of white lithium-base grease to reduce wear and ensure free movement.

8   Windshield and fixed glass – replacement

1   Replacement of the windshield and fixed glass requires the use of special fast-setting adhesive/caulk materials. These operations should be left to a dealer or a shop specializing in glass work.

2   Windshield-mounted rear view mirror support removal is also best left to experts, as the bond to the glass also requires special tools and adhesives.

9   Hood – removal and installation

Refer to illustrations 9.1 and 9.2

1   Use rags or pads to protect the windshield from the rear of the hood **(see illustration)**.

2   Scribe or draw alignment marks around the hinge bolts **(see illustration)**.

3   On models so equipped, detach the assist strut and unplug the hood lamp connector.

4   Remove the bolts and, with the help of an assistant, detach the hood from the vehicle.

5   Installation is the reverse of removal.

9.2   Use a scribe or a felt-tip pen to mark the hood bolt positions

10.1   Remove the two screws with a Phillips screwdriver

10.3   The hood latch cable retainer can be detached from
the bracket by squeezing the locking tab with a pair of
needle-nose pliers

10.4   Pry the clip back and lift the cable up to detach it (arrows)

10   Hood latch cable – replacement

Refer to illustrations 10.1, 10.3 and 10.4

1   In the passenger compartment, remove the latch handle retaining
screws and detach the handle **(see illustration)**.
2   Remove the radiator upper panel (see Chapter 3).
3   In the engine compartment, remove the cable retainer from the bracket **(see illustration)**.
4   Spread the clip with a screwdriver and detach the end of the cable
from the latch **(see illustration)**.
5   Connect a piece of string or thin wire of suitable length to the end of
the wire to the cable and pull the cable through into the passenger compartment.

6   Connect the string or wire to the new cable and pull it back into the
engine compartment.
7   Connect the cable and install the latch screws and trim panel.

11   Front fender liner – removal and installation

Refer to illustrations 11.2, 11.4 and 11.6

1   Raise the vehicle, support it securely on jackstands and remove the
front wheel.
2   The fender liner is held in place with special plastic retainers or
screws. To remove the plastic retainers, use wire cutters or a similar tool to
pry the heads of the retainers out of the retainer bodies to release

11

These photos illustrate a method of repairing simple dents. They are intended to supplement *Body repair - minor damage* in this Chapter and should not be used as the sole instructions for body repair on these vehicles.

1 If you can't access the backside of the body panel to hammer out the dent, pull it out with a slide-hammer-type dent puller. In the deepest portion of the dent or along the crease line, drill or punch hole(s) at least one inch apart . . .

2 . . . then screw the slide-hammer into the hole and operate it. Tap with a hammer near the edge of the dent to help 'pop' the metal back to its original shape. When you're finished, the dent area should be close to its original contour and about 1/8-inch below the surface of the surrounding metal

3 Using coarse-grit sandpaper, remove the paint down to the bare metal. Hand sanding works fine, but the disc sander shown here makes the job faster. Use finer (about 320-grit) sandpaper to feather-edge the paint at least one inch around the dent area

4 When the paint is removed, touch will probably be more helpful than sight for telling if the metal is straight. Hammer down the high spots or raise the low spots as necessary. Clean the repair area with wax/silicone remover

5 Following label instructions, mix up a batch of plastic filler and hardener. The ratio of filler to hardener is critical, and, if you mix it incorrectly, it will either not cure properly or cure too quickly (you won't have time to file and sand it into shape)

6 Working quickly so the filler doesn't harden, use a plastic applicator to press the body filler firmly into the metal, assuring it bonds completely. Work the filler until it matches the original contour and is slightly above the surrounding metal

7   Let the filler harden until you can just dent it with your fingernail. Use a body file or Surform tool (shown here) to rough-shape the filler

8   Use coarse-grit sandpaper and a sanding board or block to work the filler down until it's smooth and even. Work down to finer grits of sandpaper - always using a board or block - ending up with 360 or 400 grit

9   You shouldn't be able to feel any ridge at the transition from the filler to the bare metal or from the bare metal to the old paint. As soon as the repair is flat and uniform, remove the dust and mask off the adjacent panels or trim pieces

10   Apply several layers of primer to the area. Don't spray the primer on too heavy, so it sags or runs, and make sure each coat is dry before you spray on the next one. A professional-type spray gun is being used here, but aerosol spray primer is available inexpensively from auto parts stores

11   The primer will help reveal imperfections or scratches. Fill these with glazing compound. Follow the label instructions and sand it with 360 or 400-grit sandpaper until it's smooth. Repeat the glazing, sanding and respraying until the primer reveals a perfectly smooth surface

12   Finish sand the primer with very fine sandpaper (400 or 600-grit) to remove the primer overspray. Clean the area with water and allow it to dry. Use a tack rag to remove any dust, then apply the finish coat. Don't attempt to rub out or wax the repair area until the paint has dried completely (at least two weeks)

11.2   Pry the head out of the retainer body – do not cut the head off

11.4   Grasp the fender liner and pull it out of the fender

11.6   Push the head of the retainer into the body until it locks in place

13.3   The radiator grille is held in place by Torx head screws (arrows)

them **(see illustration)**. Pry the heads out, do not cut them off to remove them.

3   Once all of the retainers are released, remove them from the fender liner.

4   Detach the liner and remove it from the vehicle **(see illustration)**.

5   To install, place the liner in position and align the retainer holes.

6   Install the screws or retainers and push the heads in to securely lock them in place **(see illustration)**.

---

12   Front fender – removal and installation

Refer to illustration 12.4

1   Raise the front of the vehicle, support it securely on jackstands and remove the front wheel.

2   Remove the front fender liner (Section 11).

3   On some models, it may be necessary to remove the grille and head-light assembly (Section 13).

4   Remove the retaining bolts and detach the fender from the vehicle **(see illustration)**.

5   To install, place the fender in place and install the retaining bolts. Tighten the bolts securely.

6   The remainder of installation is the reverse of removal.

---

13   Radiator grille – removal and installation

Refer to illustration 13.3

1   Open the hood.

2   On some models, it will be necessary to remove the headlight trim panel.

3   Remove the grille retaining screws **(see illustration)**.

4   Rotate the top of the grille out and lift it from the vehicle.

5   Installation is the reverse of removal.

12.4   Typical fender mounting details

**14.1a   Typical front door trim panel
with passive seat belt system**

1	Escutcheon
2	Screws
3	Retainer
4	Screws
5	Lower arm rest trim panel
6	Screw
7	Handle
8	Reflector
9	Screws
10	Screw
11	Pull cup
12	Arm rest mounting panel
13	Screw
14	Screw
15	Reflector
16	Screw
17	Screw
18	Trim panel

11

---

14   Door trim panel – removal and installation

Refer to illustrations 14.1a, 14.1b, 14.4 and 14.7

1   Remove door glass regulator handle (if equipped) (Section 17), and the visible door panel screws from the door trim panel **(see illustrations)**.

2   On models with a passive seat belt system, remove the lower arm rest trim panel and the seat belt escutcheon and retainer.

3   Remove the reflector(s) from the rear end of the trim panel.

4   Remove the electrical switch panel and unplug the connectors **(see illustration on next page)**.

14.1b   Remove the door glass regulator handle with a special upholstery tool

14.4   To remove the switch panel, pry up gently, as shown

14.7   Pry around the door panel with an upholstery tool or a large screwdriver

5   Remove the screws from the arm rest.

6   Remove the door handle cover assembly by removing the screw(s).

7   Pry around the outer circumference of the door panel with a pry bar or large screwdriver to disengage the clips **(see illustration)**.

8   Grasp the door trim panel securely and lift up to disengage it from the door upper edge.

9   Carefully peel the water shield from the door for access to the inner door components. Take care not to tear the water shield as it must be reinstalled.

10   Installation is the reverse of removal.

---

15   Door lock assembly – removal and installation

Refer to illustration 15.2

1   With the window glass in the full up position, remove the door trim panel and water shield (Section 14).

15.2   Typical door lock, handle and lock cylinder

1	Handle assembly	5	Gasket
2	Retainer	6	Connecting rod
3	Lock cylinder assembly with switch	7	Connecting rod
		8	Screw
4	Lock cylinder assembly	9	Screw
		10	Lock assembly

2   Disconnect spring clips from the remote control connecting rods at the lock assembly **(see illustration)**.

3   Remove the lock assembly-to-door screws and lift the assembly from the door.

4   To install, place the assembly in position and install the retaining screws.

5   Connect the lock rods.

6   Install the water shield and door trim panel.

16.3 Typical front door glass details

1	Screws	5	Lower sash channel
2	Front run channel	6	Guide on regulator
3	Guide on front of glass	7	Rear run channel
4	Guide on rear of glass	8	Down stop

16.10 Typical rear door glass details

1	Regulator assembly	5	Rivet
2	Stationary vent	6	Sash screw
	glass assembly	7	Sash screw
3	Window assembly	8	Sash screw
4	Division channel	9	Screws

16   Door window glass – removal and installation

1   With the window glass in the full up position, remove the door trim panel and water shield (Section 14).

Front door

Refer to illustration 16.3

2   Remove the trim panel retainer and sealer strip.
3   Remove the rubber stop bumper, screws and front run channel **(see illustration)**.
4   Lower the glass halfway, slide the window regulator guide block off the sash channel and tilt the glass outboard of the door frame to remove it.
5   To install, insert the glass into the door and engage the regulator guide block to the sash channel. Engage the rear guide clip on the glass to the rear run channel weatherstrip.
6   Raise the glass to the half way up position and install the front run channel bolts finger tight.
7   Engage the front clip on the glass in the front run channel and tighten the bolts securely.
8   Install the rubber stop bumper.

9   The remainder of installation is the reverse of removal.

Rear door

Refer to illustration 16.10

10   Remove the sash screws while supporting the glass **(see illustration)**.
11   Disengage the glass and lower it to the bottom of the door.
12   Remove the vent glass assembly.
13   Lift the glass from the door.
14   To install, insert the glass into the door and connect the channel, making sure to engage the glass guide securely to the channel.
15   The remainder of installation is the reverse of removal.

17   Door glass regulator – removal and installation

Refer to illustrations 17.2a and 17.2b

Removal

1   On power window equipped models, disconnect the negative cable at the battery. Place the cable out of the way so it cannot accidentally come in

11

17.2b   A special tool can be used to disengage the spring clip

17.2a   Disengage the manual door glass regulator handle spring clip and withdraw the assembly from the door

contact with the negative terminal of the battery, as this would once again allow power into the electrical system of the vehicle.

2   On manual window glass regulator equipped models, remove the handle by pressing the bearing plate and door trim panel in and, with a piece of hooked wire, pulling off the spring clip **(see illustration)**. A special tool is available for this purpose **(see illustration)** but its use is not essential. With the clip removed, take off the handle and the bearing plate.

3   With the window glass in the full up position, remove the door trim panel and water shield (Section 14).

4   Secure the window glass in the up position with strong adhesive tape fastened to the glass and wrapped over the door frame.

5   Punch out the center pins of the rivets that secure the window regulator and drill the rivets out with a 1/4-inch drill bit.

6   On power window equipped models, unplug the electrical connector.

7   Remove the retaining rivets or bolts and move the regulator until it is disengaged from the sash channel. Lift the regulator from the door.

Installation

8   Place the regulator in position in the door and engage it in the sash channel.

9   Secure the regulator to the door using 3/16-inch rivets and a rivet tool.

10   Install the bolts and tighten them securely.

11   Plug in the electrical connector (if equipped).

12   Install the water shield, door trim panel and window regulator handle. Connect the negative battery cable.

18.5   Inside door handle mounting details

Chapter 11 Body

253

20.2 Door lock striker details

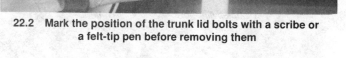

22.2 Mark the position of the trunk lid bolts with a scribe or a felt-tip pen before removing them

18 Door handles – removal and installation

1   With the window glass in the full up position, remove the door trim panel and water shield (Section 14).

Outside handle

2   Pry the remote rod out of the handle with a small screwdriver, remove the nuts and lift the handle off (see illustration 15.2).
3   Installation is the reverse of removal.

Inside handle

Refer to illustration 18.5

4   Disconnect the rod from the handle.
5   Punch out the center pins of the rivets that secure the window regulator and drill the rivets out with a 3/16-inch drill bit (see illustration).
6   Lift the handle from the door.
7   To install, place the handle in position and secure it to the door, using 3/16-inch rivets and a rivet tool.
8   The remainder of installation is the reverse of removal.

19 Door lock cylinder – removal and installation

1   With the window glass in the full up position, remove the door trim panel and water shield (Section 14).
2   Disconnect the rod from the lock cylinder.
3   Use a screwdriver to pry the retainer off and withdraw the lock cylinder from the door.
4   Installation is the reverse of removal.

20 Door lock striker – removal and installation

Refer to illustration 20.2

1   Mark the position of the striker bolt on the door pillar with a pencil.

2   It will be necessary to use a special tool to fit the star-shaped recess in the striker bolt head (tool J-23457 or BT-7107). Unscrew the bolt and remove it (see illustration).
3   To install, screw the lock striker bolt into the tapped cage plate in the door pillar and tighten it finger tight at the marked position. Tighten the bolt securely.

21 Door – removal and installation

1   Remove the door trim panel and water shield.
2   Unplug any wiring connectors.
3   Open the door all the way and support it on jacks or blocks covered with cloth or pads to prevent damage to the paint.
4   Scribe around the hinges to ensure correct realignment during installation.
5   Remove the bolts and nuts retaining the hinges to the door and with the help of an assistant lift the door away.
6   Install the door by reversing the removal procedure. Tighten the nuts and bolts securely.

22 Trunk lid – removal and installation

Refer to illustration 22.2

1   Open the trunk lid and unplug any electrical connectors and disconnect the solenoid (if equipped).
2   Scribe or mark around the heads of the retaining bolts to mark their locations for ease of reinstallation (see illustration).
3   With an assistant supporting the trunk lid, remove the bolts. Lift the trunk lid from the vehicle.
4   Installation is the reverse of removal.

23 Trunk lock cylinder – removal and installation

Refer to illustration 23.2

1   Open the trunk lid.

23.2 Typical trunk lock cylinder details

1	Lock cylinder	4	Retainer
2	Gasket	5	Rivet
3	Gasket		

2   Pry the retaining clip off and withdraw the lock cylinder from the vehicle. Some retaining clips will be secured with a rivet which must be drilled out with a 5/32-inch drill bit **(see illustration)**.

3   To install, place the lock cylinder in place and secure it with the retaining clip.

24   Trunk latch and striker – removal and installation

Refer to illustrations 24.2a, 24.2b and 24.3

1   Disconnect the negative cable from the battery. Place the cable out of the way so it cannot accidentally come in contact with the negative terminal of the battery, as this would once again allow power into the electrical system of the vehicle.

2   Remove the electronic solenoid (if equipped) and unbolt and remove the latch and (if equipped) the ajar switch **(see illustrations)**.

3   Remove the retaining nut and lift off the striker **(see illustration)**.

4   Installation is the reverse of removal.

25   Rear lens assembly – removal and installation

Refer to illustrations 25.3a and 25.3b

1   Disconnect the negative cable at the battery. Place the cable out of

24.2a Typical trunk latch and solenoid details

1	Latch
2	Bolt
3	Rivet
4	Bolt
5	Bolt
6	Connector
7	Solenoid

24.2b Typical trunk latch, solenoid and ajar switch details

1	Latch
2	Bolt
3	Rivets
4	Bolt
5	Bolt
6	Connector
7	Solenoid
8	Trunk lid ajar switch
9	Connector

24.3 Trunk latch striker details

1 *Striker*
2 *Nut*

the way so it cannot accidentally come in contact with the negative terminal of the battery, as this would once again allow power into the electrical system of the vehicle.

2   Open the trunk lid.

3   Unscrew the plastic wing nuts, pull the lens assembly out and lean it back **(see illustrations)**. Disconnect the bulb holders (Chapter 12) and lift the assembly from the vehicle.

4   Installation is the reverse of removal.

26   Console – removal and installation

Refer to illustration 26.4

1   Disconnect the negative cable at the battery. Place the cable out of the way so it cannot accidentally come in contact with the negative terminal of the battery, as this would once again allow power into the electrical system of the vehicle.

2   Remove the retaining clip from the shift handle and pull the handle or knob off the shift lever (see Chapter 7).

3   Remove the insert compartments.

4   Remove the console trim plates **(see illustration on next page)**.

5   Remove the mounting bolts and pull the console up.

6   Lift the console up for access and unplug the electrical connectors

7   Some or all of the retaining clips will probably come out during removal, so be sure to reinstall them prior to console installation.

8   Installation is the reverse of removal.

27   Seats – removal and installation

Front seat

1   Move the seat all the way forward.

2   Remove the seat track covers and pull the carpet away from the adjuster and retaining nuts.

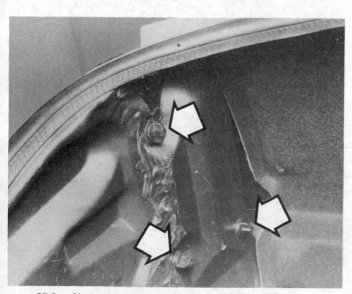

25.3a   **Unscrew the plastic retaining wing nuts and . . .**

25.3b   . . . **remove the lens assembly from the body of the vehicle**

11

26.4 Typical console details

1	Lower console	6	Compartment
2	Nut	7	Trim plate
3	Bracket	8	Shift pointer
4	Upper console	9	Storage tray
5	Bolt/screw		

28.3   Remove the mirror retaining nuts and bolt (arrows)

3   Remove the seat adjuster-to-floor panel retaining nuts.
4   Move the seat all the way to the rear.
5   Remove the front seat retaining nuts. On power seats, unplug the electrical connector. Lift the seat from the vehicle.
6   Installation is the reverse of removal.

Rear seat

7   Remove the seat cushion retaining bolts, detach the seat cushion and remove it from the vehicle .
8   Installation is the reverse of removal.

---

28   Outside mirror – removal and installation

Refer to illustration 28.3
1   Remove the door trim panel (Section 14).
2   On power mirrors, unplug the electrical connector.
3   Remove the two nuts and one bolt and lift off the mirror assembly **(see illustration)**.
4   Installation is the reverse of removal.

11

Chapter 12 Chassis electrical system

Contents

1 General information

Note: *On models equipped with the Delco Loc II audio system, be sure the lockout feature is turned off before performing any procedure which requires disconnecting the battery.*

The electrical system is a 12-volt, negative ground type. Power for the lights and all electrical accessories is supplied by a lead/acid-type battery which is charged by the alternator.

This Chapter covers repair and service procedures for the various electrical components not associated with the engine. Information on the battery, alternator, ignition system and starter motor can be found in Chapter 5.

It should be noted that when portions of the electrical system are serviced, the negative battery cable should be disconnected from the battery to prevent electrical shorts and/or fires.

2 Electrical troubleshooting – general information

A typical electrical circuit consists of an electrical component, any switches, relays, motors, fuses, fusible links or circuit breakers related to

that component and the wiring and connectors that link the component to both the battery and the chassis. To help you pinpoint an electrical circuit problem, wiring diagrams are included at the end of this book.

Before tackling any troublesome electrical circuit, first study the appropriate wiring diagrams to get a complete understanding of what makes up that individual circuit. Trouble spots, for instance, can often be narrowed down by noting if other components related to the circuit are operating properly. If several components or circuits fail at one time, chances are the problem is in a fuse or ground connection, because several circuits are often routed through the same fuse and ground connections.

Electrical problems usually stem from simple causes, such as loose or corroded connections, a blown fuse, a melted fusible link or a bad relay. Visually inspect the condition of all fuses, wires and connections in a problem circuit before troubleshooting it.

If testing instruments are going to be utilized, use the diagrams to plan ahead of time where you will make the necessary connections in order to accurately pinpoint the trouble spot.

The basic tools needed for electrical troubleshooting include a circuit tester or voltmeter (a 12-volt bulb with a set of test leads can also be used), a continuity tester, which includes a bulb, battery and set of test leads, and a jumper wire, preferably with a circuit breaker incorporated, which can be used to bypass electrical components. Before attempting to locate a problem with test instruments, use the wiring diagram(s) to decide where to make the connections.

Voltage checks

Voltage checks should be performed if a circuit is not functioning properly. Connect one lead of a circuit tester to either the negative battery terminal or a known good ground. Connect the other lead to a connector in the circuit being tested, preferably nearest to the battery or fuse. If the bulb of the tester lights, voltage is present, which means that the part of the circuit between the connector and the battery is problem free. Continue checking the rest of the circuit in the same fashion. When you reach a point at which no voltage is present, the problem lies between that point and the last test point with voltage. Most of the time the problem can be traced to a loose connection. **Note:** *Keep in mind that some circuits receive voltage only when the ignition key is in the Accessory or Run position.*

Finding a short

One method of finding shorts in a circuit is to remove the fuse and connect a test light or voltmeter in its place to the fuse terminals. There should be no voltage present in the circuit. Move the wiring harness from side-to-side while watching the test light.

If the bulb goes on, there is a short to ground somewhere in that area, probably where the insulation has rubbed through. The same test can be performed on each component in the circuit, even a switch.

Ground check

Perform a ground test to check whether a component is properly grounded. Disconnect the battery and connect one lead of a selfpowered test light, known as a continuity tester, to a known good ground. Connect the other lead to the wire or ground connection being tested. If the bulb goes on, the ground is good. If the bulb does not go on, the ground is not good.

Continuity check

A continuity check is done to determine if there are any breaks in a circuit – if it is passing electricity properly. With the circuit off (no power in the circuit), a self-powered continuity tester can be used to check the circuit. Connect the test leads to both ends of the circuit (or to the "power" end and a good ground), and if the test light comes on the circuit is passing current properly. If the light doesn't come on, there is a break somewhere in the circuit. The same procedure can be used to test a switch, by connecting the continuity tester to the switch terminals. With the switch turned On, the test light should come on.

Finding an open circuit

When diagnosing for possible open circuits, it is often difficult to locate them by sight because oxidation or terminal misalignment are hidden by the connectors. Merely wiggling a connector on a sensor or in the wiring harness may correct the open circuit condition. Remember this when an open circuit is indicated when troubleshooting a circuit. Intermittent problems may also be caused by oxidized or loose connections.

Electrical troubleshooting is simple if you keep in mind that all electrical circuits are basically electricity running from the battery, through the wires, switches, relays, fuses and fusible links to each electrical component (light bulb, motor, etc.) and to ground, from which it is passed back to the battery. Any electrical problem is an interruption in the flow of electricity to and from the battery.

For more information about electrical troubleshooting, refer to the *Haynes Automotive Electrical Manual.*

---

3   Fuses – general information

Refer to illustrations 3.1 and 3.3

The electrical circuits of the vehicle are protected by a combination of fuses, circuit breakers and fusible links. The fuse block is located under the instrument panel on the left side of the dashboard **(see illustration)**.

Each of the fuses is designed to protect a specific circuit, and the various circuits are identified on the fuse panel itself.

Miniaturized fuses are employed in the fuse block. These compact fuses, with blade terminal design, allow fingertip removal and replacement. If an electrical component fails, always check the fuse first. A blown fuse is easily identified through the clear plastic body. Visually inspect the element for evidence of damage **(see illustration)**. If a continuity check is called for, the blade terminal tips are exposed in the fuse body.

Be sure to replace blown fuses with the correct type. Fuses of different ratings are physically interchangeable, but only fuses of the proper rating should be used. Replacing a fuse with one of a higher or lower value than specified is not recommended. Each electrical circuit needs a specific amount of protection. The amperage value of each fuse is molded into the fuse body.

If the replacement fuse immediately fails, don't replace it again until the cause of the problem is isolated and corrected. In most cases, the cause will be a short circuit in the wiring caused by a broken or deteriorated wire.

3.1   The fuse box is located in the left side of the dashboard behind a small protective panel

3.3   To check for a blown fuse, pull it out and inspect it visually for an open (1), or, with the circuit activated, use a test light across the points shown (2)

12

FUSIBLE LINK BEFORE SHORT CIRCUIT

CONNECTOR COVERING

BROKEN CIRCUIT INSIDE INSULATION

CUT WIRE HERE

FUSIBLE LINK AFTER SHORT CIRCUIT

4.1   A typical fusible link before – and after – an overload has caused it to open the circuit

6.2   These relays (arrows) on the firewall are typical of the relays you'll find throughout this vehicle

4   Fusible links – general information

Refer to illustration 4.1

Some circuits are protected by fusible links **(see illustration)**. The links are used in circuits which are not ordinarily fused, such as the ignition circuit.

Although the fusible links appear to be a heavier gauge than the wire they are protecting, the appearance is due to the thick insulation. All fusible links are four wire gauges smaller than the wire they are designed to protect.

Fusible links cannot be repaired, but a new link of the same size wire can be put in its place. The procedure is as follows:

a) Disconnect the negative cable from the battery.
b) Disconnect the fusible link from the wiring harness.
c) Cut the damaged fusible link out of the wiring just behind the connector.
d) Strip the insulation back approximately 1/2-inch.
e) Position the connector on the new fusible link and crimp it into place.
f) Use rosin core solder at each end of the new link to obtain a good solder joint.
g) Use plenty of electrical tape around the soldered joint. No wires should be exposed.
h) Connect the battery ground cable. Test the circuit for proper operation.

5   Circuit breakers – general information

Circuit breakers protect components such as power windows, power door locks and headlights. Some circuit breakers are located in the fuse box.

On some models the circuit breaker resets itself automatically, so an electrical overload in a circuit breaker protected system will cause the circuit to fail momentarily, then come back on. If the circuit doesn't come back on, check it immediately. Once the condition is corrected, the circuit breaker will resume its normal function. Some circuit breakers must be reset manually.

6   Relays – general information

Refer to illustration 6.2

Several electrical accessories in the vehicle use relays to transmit the electrical signal to the component. If the relay is defective, that component will not operate properly.

The various relays are grouped together in several locations **(see illustration)**.

If a faulty relay is suspected, it can be removed and tested by a dealer service department or a repair shop. Defective relays must be replaced as a unit.

7   Flashers and relays – check and replacement

Note: *The turn signal and hazard flashers are located under the dash, near the steering column. Some relays are located in the same general area; others are in the engine compartment or under the right side of the dash. Right side relays are usually mounted either on the heater module or in a "relay center" located at the extreme right end of the dash. If you have trouble identifying a relay, refer to the Wiring Diagrams at the end of this Chapter and use the color(s) of the feed and ground wires to verify that you've located the one you want to check or replace.*

Relay check

Refer to illustrations 7.1a, 7.1b and 7.1c

1   Remove the left or right sound insulator **(see illustrations)**.
2   To verify that a relay is operating properly, locate the relay, activate the circuit – horn, blower motor, etc. – and listen for an audible click from the relay. If it doesn't click, check for an open in the circuit on the feed and ground sides of the relay and check for a short on the feed side. If the circuit itself is okay, the relay is bad. Replace it.

Replacement

3   Detach the cable from the negative battery terminal before replacing any of the following flashers or relays.

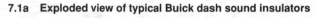

VIEW A

STUD
(PARKING BRAKE
CONTROL ASM)

STUD
(FRT OF DASH)

FRT

A

LEFT SOUND
INSULATOR

RIGHT SOUND
INSULATOR

AIR OUTLET
ASSEMBLY

7.1a Exploded view of typical Buick dash sound insulators

7.1b Exploded view of
typical Oldsmobile
dash sound insulators

FRT

FRT

12

7.1c Exploded view of typical Pontiac dash sound insulators

7.5a　A typical horn relay, located near the steering column

7.5b　A typical turn signal/hazard flasher unit, also located near the steering column

7.8　Exploded view of a typical junction block assembly and power antenna relay (arrow)

7.9　A typical relay center (not all relays used on all models)

1	Relay center	5	A/C select relay
2	Electronic level control relay	6	Rear window defogger relay
3	Horn relay	7	Bose radio relay
4	Fuel pump relay	8	Fuel pump and oil light relay

Driver's side (horn relay, turn signal/hazard, flasher, etc.)

Refer to illustrations 7.5a and 7.5b

4　Remove the screws, nuts and/or clips from the left sound insulator. Lower the insulator, detach the courtesy lights and remove the insulator.

5　Locate the horn relay or turn signal/hazard flasher **(see illustrations)**. Detach it from its mounting clip, pull it down, unplug the connector and remove the relay or flasher unit. **Note:** *Not all horn relays are mounted on this side – some are mounted under the right side instead. If you can't locate the horn relay on the left side, see below.*

6　Installation is the reverse of removal.

Passenger-side relays (junction block or relay center)

Refer to illustrations 7.8 and 7.9

7　Remove the right sound insulator.

8　On some models, relays are located immediately below a junction block located on the upper side of the right kick panel. Remove the single retaining screw and remove the relay **(see illustration)**.

9　On other models, relays are located on a relay center in the same general location **(see illustration)**. Simply pull out the bad relay and install a new unit.

10　Installation is the reverse of removal.

7.11 A typical array of relays mounted on the heater module programmer

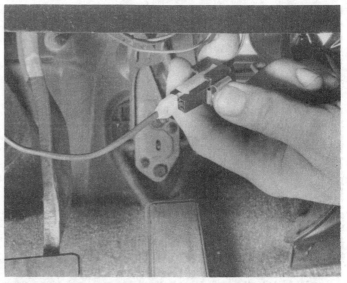

8.3 Before you pull off the multi-function switch lever, be sure to unplug the pigtail connector under the dash

8.5 To detach the multi-function switch lever, simply grasp it firmly and pull it straight off

Passenger-side relays (heater module)

Refer to illustration 7.11

11 On some models, the relays for the A/C blower motor, rear window defogger and A/C cut-out are located on the programmer for the heater module **(see illustration)**. **Note:** *On other models, these relays are located on the relay center (see Steps 7 through 10).*

12 The quickest way to get at these relays is through the glove compartment cavity in the dash. To remove the glove compartment on some models, you simply depress the side locking tabs and pull the glove compartment down and rearward. On others, you may have to remove some screws to get the glove box out.

13 Unclip the relay, unplug the connector and remove the relay.

14 Installation is the reverse of removal.

8 Multi-function/turn signal lever – replacement

Refer to illustrations 8.3 and 8.5

1 Detach the cable from the negative terminal of the battery.

2 The sound insulators under the instrument panel must be removed to gain access to the multi-function/turn signal lever pigtail connector.

3 Locate the multi-function lever electrical connector **(see illustration)** and unplug it.

4 Attach a suitable length of wire to the pigtail to pull the pigtail back through on installation.

5 Pull the lever straight out through the steering column **(see illustration)**.

6 Pull the pigtail lead up through the steering column. Detach the wire from the pigtail lead and attach it to the lead of the new lever.

7 Carefully thread the new connector and lead back through the steering column.

8 The remainder of installation is the reverse of removal.

9 Multi-function/turn signal switch assembly – replacement

Refer to illustrations 9.3a, 9.3b, 9.4a, 9.4b, 9.5, 9.6, 9.7, 9.8 and 9.10

Warning: *If the vehicle is equiped with an air bag DO NOT attempt to remove the steering wheel. Have it removed by a dealer service department or other qualified repair shop.*

1 Detach the cable from the negative terminal of the battery.

2 Remove the steering wheel (see Chapter 10).

3 Depress the shaft lock plate and cover, then remove the retaining clip **(see illustration)**. Remove the plate and cover **(see illustration)**.

4 Remove the cancelling cam and the spring **(see illustrations)**.

5 Remove the hazard flasher button **(see illustration)**.

6 Remove the switch lever screw **(see illustration)** and remove the lever.

7 Remove the three turn signal switch screws **(see illustration)**.

8 Remove the sound insulator and unplug the multi-function switch connector **(see illustration)**.

9 Pull the turn signal switch wire harness up through the steering column until there is sufficient slack to remove the turn signal switch.

10 Pull the turn signal switch out **(see illustration)**.

11 Installation is the reverse of removal.

12

9.3a   Depress the shaft lock plate and cover (you may need a special tool like the one shown), then remove the retaining clip from the steering shaft with a small screwdriver . . .

9.3b   . . . and remove the shaft lock and cover

9.4a   Remove the cancelling cam assembly . . .

9.4b   . . . and the spring

9.5   To detach the hazard flasher button from the steering column, simply remove the retaining screw in the middle of the button

9.6   Remove the multi-function/turn signal lever screw

9.7   Remove the multi-function/turn signal switch assembly mounting screws (arrows)

9.8   Unplug the multi-function switch connector under the dash

9.10   Pull the switch lead through the steering column and remove the switch assembly

10.2   Remove the key warning buzzer switch (if you can't get it out with your fingers, use a paper clip to pry it out)

10.3   Remove the lock retaining screw

10.4   Turn the ignition switch to the Run position and pull the lock out

12

11.2a   Exploded view of typical Buick dash trim panels

1 Defroster grille	5 Lower right trim plate	8 Retainers
2 Right accessory trim plate	6 Lower outer trim plate	9 Left accessory trim plate
3 Outer air outlet assembly	7 Lower left trim plate	10 Instrument panel trim pad
4 Center air outlet assemblies		

11.2b   Exploded view of a typical Oldsmobile center trim plate

10   Ignition switch/key lock cylinder – replacement

Refer to illustrations 10.2, 10.3 and 10.4
Warning: *If the vehicle is equiped with an air bag DO NOT attempt to remove the steering wheel. Have it removed by a dealer service department or other qualified repair shop.*

1   Remove the multi-function/turn signal switch assembly (see Section 9).
2   Remove the key warning buzzer switch **(see illustration)**. The easiest way to get the buzzer switch out is to use a paper clip to pry it out. **Note:** *Don't lose the small retainer clip that holds the buzzer switch in place. This clip must be installed in exactly the same position it is in in the accompanying illustration.*
3   Remove the lock retaining screw **(see illustration)**.
4   Turn the ignition switch to the Run position and pull it out **(see illustration)**.
5   Installation is the reverse of removal.

11   Headlight switch – replacement

Refer to illustrations 11.2a, 11.2b, 11.2c, 11.3a and 11.3b
1   Detach the cable from the negative terminal of the battery.
2   Remove the dash trim plate **(see illustrations)**.
3   Unscrew the headlight switch assembly **(see illustration)** and pull it out from the dash **(see illustration)**.
4   Installation is the reverse of removal.

12   Headlight – removal and installation

Refer to illustrations 12.2, 12.3, 12.4, 12.5a and 12.5b
1   Detach the cable from the negative terminal of the battery.
2   Remove the headlight bezel retaining screws **(see illustration)**. On some models you'll need to unplug the connector for the turn signal bulb.
3   Remove the headlight mounting screws **(see illustration)** and tilt the headlight assembly forward.

11.2c   Exploded view of a typical Pontiac center trim plate and defroster and speaker grilles

11.3a   After you've removed the dash trim plate, remove the headlight switch mounting screws (arrows) . . .

11.3b   . . . and simply pull the switch assembly straight out of the dash (the switch assemblies on the models covered by this manual are modular plug-in types – there are no wires or connectors)

12.2   Remove the headlight bezel retaining screws (arrows) (Oldsmobile shown, other models similar)

12.3   Remove the headlight retaining screws (arrows) (Oldsmobile shown, other models similar)

12

12.4　Unplug the electrical connector and remove the headlight (Oldsmobile shown, other models similar)

RETAINER

② TURN ¼-TURN COUNTER-CLOCKWISE: REMOVE BULB. **DO NOT TOUCH GLASS PART OF BULB!**

① DISCONNECT

12.5a　If the headlight assembly uses a removable quartz halogen bulb, follow this replacement sequence (Buick shown, other models similar)

① RAISE HOOD FRONT (ONLY)

② REMOVE TWO HAND SCREWS

③ TILT FORWARD AND LIFT OUT

④ DISCONNECT

⑥ REMOVE BULB **DO NOT TOUCH GLASS PART OF BULB!**

⑤ REMOVE

12.5b　Another type of removable quartz halogen bulb used on some models (Buick shown, other models similar)

13.1　Vertical and horizontal headlight adjustment screws (arrows)

4　Unplug the electrical connector (**see illustration**) and remove the headlight.
5　If the headlight has a removable bulb, remove the bulb holder assembly out of the headlight (**see illustrations**).
6　Installation is the reverse of removal.

13　Headlights – adjustment

Refer to illustration 13.1

Note: *The headlights must be aimed correctly. If adjusted incorrectly they could blind the driver of an oncoming vehicle and cause a serious accident or seriously reduce your ability to see the road. The headlights should be checked for proper aim every 12 months and any time a new headlight is installed or front end body work is performed. It should be emphasized that*

14.1   Exploded view of typical park and side marker lights (Buick shown, other models similar)

14.2a   To remove a typical dome light bulb, pry off the lens with a small screwdriver . . .

14.2b   . . . then pull the bulb straight out

6   Starting with the low beam adjustment, position the high intensity zone so it's two inches below the horizontal line and two inches to the right of the headlight vertical line. Adjustment is made by turning the top adjusting screw clockwise to raise the beam and counterclockwise to lower the beam. The adjusting screw on the side should be used in the same manner to move the beam left or right.

7   With the high beams on, the high intensity zone should be vertically centered with the exact center just below the horizontal line. **Note:** *It may not be possible to position the headlight aim exactly for both high and low beams. If a compromise must be made, keep in mind that the low beams are the most used and have the greatest effect on driver safety.*

8   Have the headlights adjusted by a dealer service department or service station at the earliest opportunity.

14   Bulb replacement

Refer to illustrations 14.1, 14.2a, 14.2b, 14.3a, 14.3b, 14.3c and 14.3d

1   The lenses of many lights are held in place by screws, which makes it a simple procedure to gain access to the bulbs **(see illustration)**.

2   On some lights, the lenses are held in place by tabs. Simply pop them off with your fingers or pry them off with a small screwdriver **(see illustrations)**.

3   Several types of bulbs are used **(see illustrations)**. Some are removed by pushing in and turning them counterclockwise; others can simply be pulled straight out of the socket.

4   To gain access to the instrument panel lights, the instrument cluster will have to be removed first (see Section 17).

the following procedure is only an interim step which will provide temporary adjustment until the headlights can be adjusted by a properly equipped shop.

1   Headlights have two spring loaded adjusting screws, one on the top controlling up-and-down movement and one on the side controlling left-and-right movement **(see illustration)**.

2   There are several methods of adjusting the headlights. The simplest method requires a blank wall 25-feet in front of the vehicle and a level floor.

3   Position masking tape vertically on the wall in reference to the vehicle centerline and the centerlines of both headlights.

4   Position a horizontal tape line in reference to the centerline of all the headlights. **Note:** *It may be easier to position the tape on the wall with the vehicle parked only a few inches away.*

5   Adjustment should be made with the vehicle sitting level, the gas tank half-full and no unusually heavy load in the vehicle.

15   Radio and speakers – removal and installation

1   Detach the cable from the negative terminal of the battery prior to performing any of the following procedures.

Radio

Refer to illustrations 15.2a, 15.2b, 15.4 and 15.5

2   Carefully pry off the trim plate **(see illustrations)**.

12

14.3a   Exploded view of a typical fog light assembly (Oldsmobile shown, others similar)

1	Nut	5	Bulb	9	Lens retainer screw
2	Electrical connector	6	Adjuster	10	Lens cover
3	Bracket	7	Lens	11	Bulb retainer
4	Housing	8	Lens retainer		

14.3b   To remove the holder for the rear brake/turn signal bulb from the tail light lens assembly, remove the lens retaining screw (arrow)

14.3c   Turn the holder counterclockwise and pull it out, then push down on the bulb, turn it counterclockwise and remove it from the holder (Oldsmobile shown, others similar)

14.3d   To replace an instrument cluster bulb, remove the instrument cluster (see Section 17), then twist the holder counterclockwise, pull it out of the cluster and pull the bulb straight out of the holder

IP CARRIER

RADIO

BRACKET

FRT

COVER (IF NO RADIO)

15.2a   Some radio installations have only a small trim piece around the radio (Buick unit shown, other models similar) . . .

15.2b ... while others cannot be removed until you take off a larger dash trim plate (exploded view of the center trim plates on an Oldsmobile dash, other models similar)

1	Dash	3	Applique	5	Left trim cover
2	Center trim cover	4	Right trim cover	6	Screws

15.4   Remove the radio assembly mounting screws (arrows)

15.5   Pull the radio out from the dash and unplug the antenna and all electrical connectors

3   Remove the knobs and heater control switches.
4   Remove the radio mounting screws **(see illustration)**.
5   Pull the radio out of the dash and unplug the antenna, speaker, power and ground connectors from the radio **(see illustration)**.
6   Installation is the reverse of removal.

Speakers

Dashboard speakers

7   Pry off the speaker cover.
8   Remove the speaker mounting screws.
9   Lift the speaker out of its enclosure, unplug the electrical connector and remove the speaker.
10   Installation is the reverse of removal.

Rear speakers

11   Open the trunk lid and locate the speakers – they're affixed to the underside of the package tray.
12   Remove the speaker enclosure retaining clips or screws and lower the enclosure to the trunk floor.
13   Remove the speaker mounting screws and remove the speaker from the enclosure.
14   Unplug the speaker electrical connector.
15   Installation is the reverse of removal.

16   Radio antenna – removal and installation

Refer to illustration 16.5a and 16.5b

1   Detach the cable from the negative battery terminal.

12

16.5a   Details of a typical fixed type antenna

1	Antenna	5	Antenna lead
2	Upper nut	6	Nuts
3	Bezel	7	Screws
4	Right fender	8	Right fender bracket

16.5b   Details of a typical power type antenna

1	Power antenna	4	Bezel
2	Nut	5	Nut
3	Screws	6	Right fender bracket

2   If the antenna is mounted in the fender, remove the screws and clips and pull out the inner fender liner. If the antenna is rear mounted, remove the right side trunk liner.

3   Remove the sound insulator from underneath the right side of the dash (see Section 7).

4   Unplug the antenna leads from the relay and radio (see Section 15). If the antenna is rear mounted, unplug it from the body harness.

5   Remove the antenna upper nut **(see illustrations)**.

6   Remove the antenna bracket screws.

7   Pull the antenna assembly up slightly to separate it, but don't remove it.

8   Wrap the lead with wire so it can be threaded back to it's proper location.

9   Remove the antenna assembly and the old grommet or bezel.

10   Install a new grommet or bezel.

11   Feed the new lead through the grommet or bezel and carefully thread it through with the wire.

12   The remainder of installation is the reverse of removal.

17   Instrument cluster – removal and installation

Note: *Vehicles covered by this manual are equipped with either a standard, gauge or digital instrument cluster. They may also have a trip calculator or driver information display center next to the cluster. Installation of all instrument clusters is basically the same.*

Refer to illustrations 17.3, 17.4, 17.5a, 17.5b and 17.6

1   Detach the cable from the negative battery terminal.

2   Remove all screws from the trim plate around the cluster.

3   If the gear indicator window is integral with the instrument cluster, remove the sound insulator under the dash and detach the gear indicator wire **(see illustration)**.

4   Move the gear selector lever to "1" (manual Low) and carefully remove the cluster trim plate **(see illustration)**.

17.3   Detach the gear indicator wire

17.4   Remove the cluster trim plate

17.5a A typical Buick instrument cluster assembly

17.5b A typical Pontiac instrument cluster assembly

5 Remove the mounting screws from the cluster **(see illustrations)**.
6 Pull the cluster out of the dash **(see illustration)**. **Note:** *If the cluster is on an older model, it may not have modular plug-in boards on back like newer units – so you'll have to unplug the connectors on back.*
7 Installation is the reverse of removal. Don't forget to attach the gear indicator wire.

18 Rear window defogger – check and repair

Refer to illustrations 18.5a, 18.5b and 18.11
1 This option consists of a rear window with a number of horizontal elements baked into the glass surface during the glass forming operation.
2 Small breaks in the element can be successfully repaired without re-

moving the rear window.
3 To test the grids for proper operation, start the engine and turn on the system.
4 Ground one lead of a test light and carefully touch the other lead to each element line.
5 The brilliance of the test light should increase as the lead is moved across the element **(see illustrations)**. If the test light glows brightly at both ends of the lines, check for a loose ground wire. All of the lines should be checked in at least two places.
6 To repair a break in a line, it is recommended that a repair kit specifically for this purpose be purchased from a GM dealer. Included in the repair kit will be a decal, a container of silver plastic and hardener, a mixing stick and instructions.
7 To repair a break, first turn off the system and allow it to de-energize for a few minutes.

17.6 Remove the instrument cluster (on newer units, the connectors are the plug-in type; on older models, you'll have to unplug the leads before you can detach the cluster from the dash)

18.5a The brilliance of a test light should vary in brightness when the rear window defogger is functioning normally

12

18.5b   When the grid is tested on the ground bus bar side of a break, the light will go out

18.11   To repair a broken grid, apply a strip of tape to either side of the grid, then apply the proper mixture of hardener and silver plastic with a small wooden stick or spatula

8   Lightly buff the element area with fine steel wool, then clean it thoroughly with alcohol.

9   Use the decal supplied in the repair kit or apply strips of electrician's tape above and below the area to be repaired. The space between the pieces of tape should be the same width as the existing lines. This can be checked from outside the vehicle. Press the tape tightly against the glass to prevent seepage.

10   Mix the hardener and silver plastic thoroughly.

11   Using the wood spatula, apply the silver plastic mixture between the pieces of tape, overlapping the undamaged area slightly on either end **(see illustration)**.

12   Carefully remove the decal or tape and apply a constant stream of hot air directly to the repaired area. A heat gun set at 500 to 700 degrees Fahrenheit is recommended. Hold the gun one inch from the glass for two minutes.

13   If the new element appears off color, tincture of iodine can be used to clean the repair and bring it back to the proper color. This mixture should not remain on the repair for more than 30 seconds.

14   Although the defogger is now fully operational, the repaired area should not be disturbed for at least 24 hours.

19   Windshield wiper motor/washer pump – removal and installation

Refer to illustrations 19.2, 19.5, 19.6, 19.7a, 19.7b, 19.8, 19.9, 19.13a and 19.13b

Note: *The windshield washer pump on 1987 and later models is located in the windshield washer reservoir. To replace the pump on 1987 and later models, first drain the reservoir then remove the reservoir, replace the pump and re-install the reservoir.*

1   Detach the cable from the negative terminal of the battery.

2   Unplug the electrical connectors from the motor and the pump **(see illustration)**.

3   Detach the windshield washer fluid hoses from the washer pump.

4   Disconnect the connector for the windshield washer fluid line at the wiper blade.

19.2   Unplug the electrical connectors from the windshield wiper motor and pump (arrows) and detach the windshield washer fluid hoses from the pump

19.5   Pry the windshield wiper arm retaining nut cap loose with a screwdriver

19.6 If you don't have a battery post puller or some other type of small puller, you can pry the windshield wiper arm off with a screwdriver, but be careful

5 Pry off the windshield wiper arm cap over the nut and remove the nut (see illustration).

6 Using a small battery post puller or similar tool, remove the left windshield wiper blade assembly. If you don't have a battery post puller, pry the blade off with a screwdriver (see illustration).

7 Some newer models don't use the same wiper arm installation. On these units the wiper is attached to the wiper motor shaft by a spring-loaded rotating clip (see illustration). To release the wiper arm, simply push in on the clip tang that protrudes from the underside of the arm assembly and lift straight up (see illustration).

8 Remove the vent grille (see illustration). Be careful when removing the vent grille fasteners – they break easily.

9 Remove the nut that fastens the transmission linkage arm to the motor shaft (see illustration) and detach the linkage from the motor.

10 Remove the motor mounting bolts and remove the motor (see illustration 19.9).

11 If you're replacing the motor, be sure to switch the washer pump to the new motor (see Step 13).

12 Installation is the reverse of removal.

19.7a This type of windshield wiper arm uses a special spring-loaded rotating clip to lock it onto the shaft

19.7b To release the clip from the wiper arm shaft, push in on the tang that protrudes from underneath the wiper arm and lift up at the same time

19.8 To get at the windshield wiper motor transmission (linkage), remove the rubber molding along the upper edge of the firewall, pry loose the fasteners (arrows) and remove the vent grille (left half of grille shown, right half similar)

19.9 Remove the nut that fastens the transmission linkage arm to the motor shaft (arrow) – to remove the windshield wiper motor/washer fluid pump assembly remove the three mounting bolts (arrows)

12

19.13a   To remove the windshield washer fluid pump from the motor, pop out this retaining clip with a small screwdriver . . .

19.13b   . . . and pull the pump out of the motor

13 If you're only replacing the windshield washer pump, remove the small locking clip **(see illustration)** and pull the pump from the bottom of the motor **(see illustration)**.

20   Horn – check and replacement

Refer to illustration 20.4
1   Detach the cable from the negative terminal of the battery.
2   Locate the horn. On some vehicles, it's located underneath the front of the vehicle, generally right behind the bumper. On others, it's mounted to the right inner fender well on the right side of the engine compartment.
3   If the horn is underneath, raise the vehicle and place it securely on jackstands and remove the protective panel from the underside of the front left corner of the bumper.
4   Remove the horn mounting bracket bolt **(see illustration)**, lower the horn, unplug the electrical connector and remove the horn.
5   Installation is the reverse of removal.

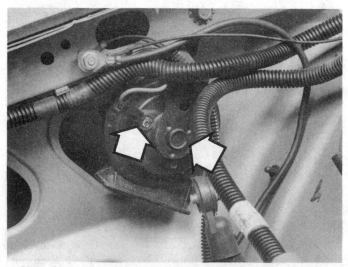

20.4   A typical horn installed in the engine compartment – to replace it, simply remove the mounting bracket bolt (arrow) and unplug the connector (arrow)

21   Cruise control system – description and check

The cruise control system maintains vehicle speed with a vacuum actuated servo motor located in the engine compartment, which is connected to the throttle linkage by a cable. The system consists of the servo motor, clutch switch, brake switch, control switches, a relay and associated vacuum hoses.
Because of the complexity of the cruise control system and the special tools and techniques required for diagnosis, repair should be left to a dealer service department or a repair shop. However, it is possible for the home mechanic to make simple checks of the wiring and vacuum connections for minor faults which can be easily repaired. These include:
a) Inspect the cruise control actuating switches for broken wires and loose connections.
b) Check the cruise control fuse.
c) The cruise control system is operated by vacuum so it's critical that all vacuum switches, hoses and connections are secure. Check the hoses in the engine compartment for tight connections, cracks and obvious vacuum leaks.

22   Power window system – description and check

The power window system operates the electric motors mounted in the doors which lower and raise the windows. The system consists of the control switches, the motors (regulators), glass mechanisms and associated wiring.
Because of the complexity of the power window system and the special tools and techniques required for diagnosis, repair should be left to a dealer service department or a repair shop. However, it is possible for the home mechanic to make simple checks of the wiring connections and motors for minor faults which can be easily repaired. These include:
a) Inspect the power window actuating switches for broken wires and loose connections.
b) Check the power window fuse/and or circuit breaker.
c) Remove the door panel(s) and check the power window motor wires to see if they're loose or damaged. Inspect the glass mechanisms for damage which could cause binding.

23   Power door lock system – description and check

The power door lock system operates the door lock actuators mounted in each door. The system consists of the switches, actuators and associated wiring. Since special tools and techniques are required to diagnose the system, it should be left to a dealer service department or a repair shop. However, it is possible for the home mechanic to make simple checks of the wiring connections and actuators for minor faults which can be easily repaired. These include:

a) Check the system fuse and/or circuit breaker.
b) Check the switch wires for damage and loose connections. Check the switches for continuity.
c) Remove the door panel(s) and check the actuator wiring connections to see if they're loose or damaged. Inspect the actuator rods (if equipped) to make sure they aren't bent or damaged. Inspect the actuator wiring for damaged or loose connections. The actuator

can be checked by applying battery power momentarily. A discernible click indicates that the solenoid is operating properly.

24   Wiring diagrams – general information

Since it isn't possible to include all wiring diagrams for every year covered by this manual, the following diagrams are those that are typical and most commonly needed.

Prior to troubleshooting any circuits, check the fuse and circuit breakers (if equipped) to make sure they're in good condition. Make sure the battery is properly charged and check the cable connections (Chapter 1).

When checking a circuit, make sure that all connectors are clean, with no broken or loose terminals. When unplugging a connector, do not pull on the wires. Pull only on the connector housings themselves.

Refer to the accompanying table for the wire color codes applicable to your vehicle.

Wiring diagram color codes

BLK. . . . . .Black		BLU . . . . .Blue
BRN. . . . . .Brown		PPL . . . . .Purple
CHK. . . . . .Check		TR . . . . .Tracer
CR . . . . .Cross		YEL . . . . .Yellow
GRN. . . . . .Green		//. . . . . .Parallel
NAT . . . . .Natural		WHT. . . . . .White
SGL . . . . .Single		STR . . . . .Stripe
ORN . . . . .Orange		PNK . . . . .Pink
GR . . . . .Gray		DK . . . . .Dark

12

Typical headlight circuit (Oldsmobile Ninety-eight Regency shown)

Typical fog light circuit

Typical front lighting (turn/hazard/park/front marker) circuit – Oldsmobile Delta Eighty-eight shown (1 of 3)

Typical front lighting (turn/hazard/park/front marker) circuit (2 of 3)

Typical front lighting (turn/hazard/park/front marker) circuit (3 of 3)

Typical rear lighting (turn/hazard/brake) circuit – Oldsmobile Ninety-eight Regency shown

Typical rear lighting (turn/hazard/brake) circuit (continued)

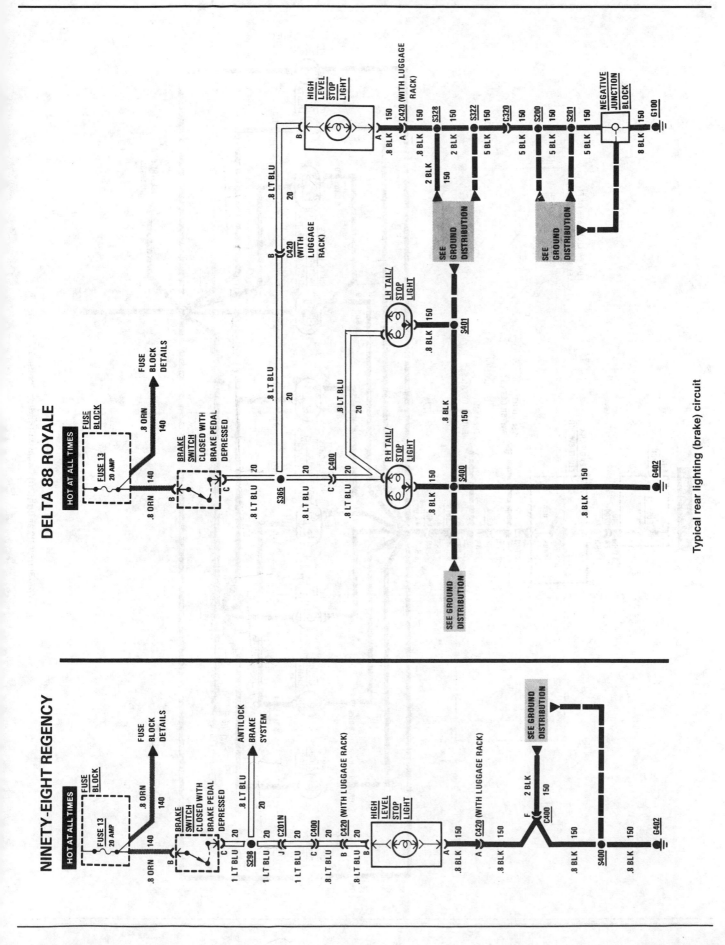

Typical rear lighting (brake) circuit

Typical rear lighting (tail/rear marker/license)

Typical rear lighting (backup, with indicators and gauge type cluster) circuit

Typical rear lighting (backup, with digital cluster) circuit

Typical cornering light circuit

Typical C3I ignition system circuit

Typical Electronic Spark Control (ESC) system circuit

Typical Exhaust Gas Recirculation (EGR) system circuit

Typical coolant fan wiring circuit (without A/C)

Typical coolant fan wiring circuit (with A/C)

Index